The Structure of Soci

Over the last three decades, social theory has become an increasingly important sub-discipline within sociology. Social theory has attempted to elucidate the philosophical basis of sociology by defining the nature of social reality. According to social theory, society consists of structure, objective institutions, on the one hand, and agency, individuals, on the other. *The Structure of Social Theory* lays out a new paradigm for sociology today. In place of structure and agency, it promotes human social relations, insisting that in every instance social reality consists of these relations.

The book begins by defining and criticising contemporary social theory. It analyses the work of Giddens, Bourdieu, Foucault, Bhaskar and Habermas to demonstrate that their commitment to structure and agency is unsustainable. The book then proceeds to recover a sociology which focuses on social relations by reference to the works of classical sociology; to Hegel, Marx, Weber and Durkheim. Finally, the book establishes a new 'hermeneutic' paradigm in which social relations are primary.

Drawing on the work of Gadamer, the book demonstrates that a sociology which focuses on social relations does not imply a return to idealism, nor a retreat into individualism, nor a rejection of critique. Rather, a hermeneutic sociology which prioritises human social relations is the only coherent paradigm which is available today. The author argues that sociologists studying the dramatic social transformations which are currently occurring should focus on social relations between humans; they should not attempt to understand contemporary changes in terms of structure and agency.

The Structure of Social Theory will be of essential value to those working in the fields of sociology and social theory.

Anthony King is a reader in sociology at the University of Exeter. In addition to his work on social theory, he has carried out extensive research on English and European football. His latest book on this topic, *The European Ritual*, was published in 2003. He is currently researching European defence policy and capability.

Routledge Studies in Social and Political Thought

1 Hayek and After
Hayekian liberalism as a research
programme
Jeremy Shearmur

2 Conflicts in Social Science
Edited by Anton van Harskamp

3 Political Thought of André Gorz
Adrian Little

**4 Corruption, Capitalism and
Democracy**
John Girling

**5 Freedom and Culture in Western
Society**
Hans Blokland

6 Freedom in Economics
New perspectives in
normative analysis
*Edited by Jean-Francois Laslier, Marc
Fleurbaey, Nicolas Gravel and Alain Trannoy*

7 Against Politics
On government, anarchy and order
Anthony de Jasay

8 Max Weber and Michel Foucault
Parallel life works
Arpad Szakolczai

**9 The Political Economy of Civil
Society and Human Rights**
G. B. Madison

**10 On Durkheim's Elementary
Forms of Religious Life**
*Edited by W. S. F. Pickering, W. Watts
Miller and N. J. Allen*

11 Classical Individualism
The supreme importance of each
human being
Tibor R. Machan

12 The Age of Reasons
Quixotism, sentimentalism and
political economy in eighteenth-
century Britain
Wendy Motooka

**13 Individualism in Modern
Thought**
From Adam Smith to Hayek
Lorenzo Infantino

**14 Property and Power in Social
Theory**
A study in intellectual rivalry
Dick Pels

**15 Wittgenstein and the Idea
of a Critical Social Theory**
A critique of Giddens, Habermas
and Bhaskar
Nigel Pleasants

16 Marxism and Human Nature
Sean Sayers

17 Studies in a Sociological Legacy
Edited by Greg Smith

18 Situating Hayek
Phenomenology and the
neo-liberal project
Mark J. Smith

19 The Reading of Theoretical Texts
Peter Ekegren

20 The Nature of Capital
Marx after Foucault
Richard Marsden

21 The Age of Chance
Gambling in Western culture
Gerda Reith

22 Reflexive Historical Sociology
Arpad Szakolczai

23 Durkheim and Representations
Edited by W. S. F. Pickering

**24 The Social and Political Thought
of Noam Chomsky**
Alison Edgley

**25 Hayek's Liberalism and Its
Origins**
His idea of spontaneous order and
the Scottish Enlightenment
Christina Petsoulas

**26 Metaphor and the Dynamics of
Knowledge**
Sabine Maasen and Peter Weingart

27 Living with Markets
Jeremy Shearmur

28 Durkheim's Suicide
A century of research and debate
*Edited by W. S. F. Pickering and Geoffrey
Walford*

29 Post-Marxism
An intellectual history
Stuart Sim

30 The Intellectual as Stranger
Studies in spokespersonship
Dick Pels

**31 Hermeneutic Dialogue and Social
Science**
A critique of Gadamer and Habermas
Austin Harrington

32 Methodological Individualism
Background, history and meaning
Lars Udehn

33 The Genesis of a Theory
K. C. O'Rourke

**34 The Politics of Atrocity
and Reconciliation**
From terror to trauma
Michael Humphrey

35 Marx and Wittgenstein
Knowledge, morality, politics
*Edited by Gavin Kitching and Nigel
Pleasants*

36 The Genesis of Modernity
Arpad Szakolczai

37 Ignorance and Liberty
Lorenzo Infantino

38 Deleuze, Marx and Politics
Nicholas Thoburn

39 The Structure of Social Theory
Anthony King

**40 Adorno, Habermas and the
Search for a Rational Society**
Deborah Cook

**41 Tocqueville's Political and
Moral Thought**
New liberalism
M. R. R. Ossewaarde

The Structure of
Social Theory

Anthony King

Routledge
Taylor & Francis Group

LONDON AND NEW YORK

First published 2004
by Routledge
2 Park Square, Milton Park, Abingdon, Oxfordshire O 14 4RN

Simultaneously published in the USA and Canada
by Routledge
711 Third Avenue, New York, NY 10017

Routledge is an imprint of the Taylor & Francis Group, an informa business

First issued in paperback 2012

© 2004 Anthony King

Typeset in Baskerville by Taylor & Francis Books Ltd

British Library Cataloguing in Publication Data
A catalogue record for this book is available from the British Library

Library of Congress Cataloging in Publication Data
King, Anthony, 1967
The structure of social theory / Anthony King.
   p. cm.
Includes bibliographical references and index.
1. Sociology History. 2. Sociology Philosophy. I. Title.
HM445.K56 2004
301'.09 dc22
                          2003023222

ISBN13 978-0-415-26334-4 hardback
ISBN13 978-0-415-65206-3 paperback

Contents

Acknowledgements   ix

PART I
Contemporary Social Theory   **1**

1 Structure and Agency   3

2 The Relevance of Parsons   20

3 Structure, Habitus, Discourse   39

4 The Reality of Realism   68

PART II
Classical Sociology   **87**

5 Hegel and the Concept of *Geist*   89

6 From Praxis to Historical Materialism   107

7 Status Groups and the Protestant Ethic   122

8 Society and Ritual   140

PART III
Towards a Hermeneutic Sociology   **163**

  9 Hermeneutics and Idealism   165

10 Hermeneutics and Individualism   192

11 Hermeneutics and Critique   209

12 Beyond Structure and Agency   227

    Notes   239
    Bibliography   247
    Index   261

Acknowledgements

Since his time as my undergraduate supervisor, Keith Hart has provided me with invaluable support and encouragement. This book is no exception and I am further indebted to him for his advice and comments on earlier drafts of the manuscript. Here at Exeter, I have benefited enormously from my conversations with Barry Barnes; his comments on Chapter 7 were especially welcome. Nigel Pleasants was typically supportive throughout and I am indebted to him. Liz Kingdom's commentary on the manuscript was very useful and is much appreciated. I am also grateful to Robert Witkin and Marta Trzebiatowska for their comments on the manuscript.

Part I

Contemporary Social Theory

1   Structure and Agency

Social Theory

Sociologists today have an underdeveloped sense of humour. For all their talk of reflexivity, they themselves conspicuously lack a sense of self-awareness. This is unfortunate since it ensures that sociologists are incapable of appreciating the irony of their predicament. From its origins in the early nineteenth century, sociology made a distinctive intellectual contribution. Sociology sought to examine the general nature of social reality and to analyse the specific characteristics of emergent modern society. Auguste Comte, who invented the term 'sociology', emphasised the importance of this discovery of social reality. For him, the expansion of knowledge to this new and hitherto under-examined realm of human existence promised intellectual benefits on a par with physics or the other natural sciences. Although Comte's method was untenably positivistic, his neologism 'sociology' remains a useful reminder of the original purpose of the discipline. Sociology seeks to demonstrate the decisive role which the social context plays in all human activity. In particular, sociology has illuminated the extraordinary potency of social relations between humans which are implicated in even the most apparently private individual acts. These all-pervading social relations cannot be reduced to psychological, biological or economic factors. Social relations constitute a fascinating reality which must be understood in its own terms. To use Durkheim's term, social relations are sacred; in their effervescent interaction, humans develop a powerful emotional attachment to each other which binds them together, inspiring them to particular forms of activity.

> It [collective life] brings about a state of effervescence which changes the conditions of psychic activity. Vital energies are over-excited, passions more active, sensations stronger; there are even some which are produced only at this moment. A man does not recognise himself; he feels himself transformed and consequently he transforms the environment which surrounds him.
>
> (Durkheim 1976: 422)

In the course of social interaction, humans mutually transform each other to produce a completely new level of reality. This social reality is the world which humans inhabit. As Durkheim recognised, although this social reality is binding and indeed sacred, it depends upon the mere fact that humans recognise their relations to each other. Yet, although always dependent upon human understanding, social relations endow humans with powers which would be inconceivable if they were alone. The sacredness with which social relations are invested is unique to the intercourse of humans. These social relations which inspire the humans engaged in them should also excite the analytic interest of the sociologist. Certainly, Durkheim's work, whatever its limitations, effuses a sense of wonder at human social interaction. Weber was similarly impressed by the potency of human social relations and he described sociology as 'a science concerning itself with the interpretive understanding of *social* action' (Weber 1978: 4, emphasis added). Weber clarified what he meant by social action: 'action is "social" insofar as its subjective meaning takes account of the behaviour of others and is thereby oriented in its course' (Weber 1978: 4). For Weber, human social action was distinctive because it was directed towards others. The mutual reaction of others was an intrinsic and dynamic element of human interaction. Moreover, these interactions were never independent of human consciousness. Humans had to come to a mutual understanding of what their interactions signified. They had to understand what their social relations involved and what they demanded of them. Human social relations were ultimately dependent on the shared meanings which the participants attached to their actions and relations. For Weber, these meanings transformed mere existence into something distinctively human: *life*. It was the task of the sociologists to analyse life in any historical period. Weber, like Durkheim, enthused about the infinite potential of human social relations: 'Life with its irrational reality and its store of possible meanings is inexhaustible' (Weber 1949: 111). Although Marx concentrated on the alienation and degradation of human life, he too recognised the unique character of human social relations. Indeed, his disgust with capitalism was primarily motivated by a belief that it represented a negation of human social existence. For Marx, human existence was fundamentally social.

> Therefore, even when the manifestation of his life does not take the form of a communal manifestation performed in the company of other men, it is still a manifestation and confirmation of social life. The individual and the species-life of man are not different.
>
> (Marx 1990: 91)

Even when they are alone, humans cannot be understood in individual terms. The very individual characteristics which they display are a product of their social existence: their relations to others. Humans could never be considered separately from the social relations in which they existed: 'for only to social man is nature available as a bond with other men, as the basis of his own existence for others and theirs for him, and as the vital element in human reality' (Marx 1990: 90). Humans could not be identified in some primordial natural state apart from their social relations. Their specific humanity – their species being – lay precisely in their social existence; in their mutual interrelations with each other. For Marx, human existence was, by nature, social. Human history could only be comprehended by recognising this fertile interdependence of humans on each other, making each what they were. Durkheim, Weber and Marx were all inspired by the power of human social relations and dedicated themselves to the analysis of the unique and sacred properties of this reality. In this way, they represent the distinctive intellectual contribution of sociology; they tried to explain human action in terms of the social relations in which it arose. As Durkheim declared: 'Thus sociology appears destined to open a new way to the science of man' (Durkheim 1976: 447). As Durkheim, Marx and Weber recognised, sociology will be significant as long as social relations between humans remain the primary focus of all research which is conducted in the name of this discipline.

Unfortunately, sociologists have increasingly forgotten what is distinctive about sociology. Today, sociologists seem incapable of recognising the special character of social reality. Sociology has become a misnomer for a discipline which is no longer interested in the social relations between humans. Instead, the dynamic power of social intercourse has been reduced to a deadening dualism. For sociologists now, society consists of two divisible elements; structure and agency. On the one hand, stand the cold institutions of the modern society and, on the other, the creative individual. This dualism is particularly prevalent in contemporary social theory, even though it has been involved in philosophical debates which have focused precisely on the nature of social reality. Social theory emerged as a distinctive subdiscipline within sociology in the 1970s to become particularly prominent in the 1980s and 1990s. It sought to elaborate specifically upon the ontological and epistemological basis of sociology often independently of empirical analysis. Ironically, its search for ontological and epistemological grounding led it in almost every case away from the reality of social life. Contemporary social theory seems determined to ignore the fecund interplay of human social life, in favour of abstraction. In the last two decades, realism, represented most prominently in Britain by Roy Bhaskar and Margaret Archer, has attained an increasingly central position in social theory. According to realism, society consists of a dual or stratified ontology in which the individual reproduces an already existing social structure. Thus, Archer insists that 'it is fully justifiable to refer to structures (being irreducible to individuals or groups) as pre-existing them both' (Archer 1995: 75). Bhaskar has similarly stated that 'there is an ontological hiatus between society and people' (Bhaskar 1979: 46).

> While society exists only in virtue of human agency, and human agency (or being) always presupposes (and expresses) some or other definite social form, they cannot be reduced or reconstructed from one another.
>
> (Bhaskar 1986: 124)

Bhaskar's transformational model of social activity and Archer's morphogenetic social theory propose a three-stage model of social reproduction in which pre-existing, independent and causally efficacious structure is reproduced or transformed by individual action. Anticipating realism, Peter Blau similarly argued for a dialectical social theory in which structure was reproduced and transformed by the individual in the course of social exchange: 'structural change, therefore, assumes a dialectical pattern' (Blau 1964: 338). Other social theorists, who have not always formally described themselves as realists, have similarly professed their support for this realist ontology of structure and agency:

> The thesis I present is that an adequate account must come to terms with the fact that 'society' and its constituent elements are preconstituted and objective structures which constrain interaction.
>
> (Layder 1981: 1)

Nicos Mouzelis has been even more forthright.

> The subject–object distinction is another one that it is impossible to eliminate without paying too high a price…As with the micro–macro distinction, the divide between objectivist and subjectivist sociologies should neither be ignored (as in post-structuralism), nor transcended in a decorative, rhetorical manner (*a la* Bourdieu, Giddens or Elias).
>
> (Mouzelis 1995: 156)

Similarly, Stones calls for a 'post-modernist realism whose acknowledgement of a rich, complex ontology is accompanied and matched by the adoption of a finely grained set of reflexive guidelines' (Stones 1996: 232). For Stones, social theorists must recognise that individuals are reflexive but that these individuals are themselves confronted by certain real structural conditions. They are ultimately reflexive about the objective conditions of their existence. He too has presumed a dualistic ontology of structure and agency.

Many other theorists are similarly committed to ontological dualism. In his encyclopaedic outline of sociology, Alexander has promoted a 'multi-dimensional' theory which takes account of the diverse aspects of society (Alexander 1983, 1984). Alexander calls his theory multi-dimensional because he advocates the consideration of social, cultural, political and economic factors. However, his criticisms of Weber, Marx, Durkheim and Parsons reveal that he too is ultimately committed to ontological dualism (Alexander 1984: 230, 241). He rejects sociologists when they promote an explanatory account which emphasises only the social interactions between humans. Alexander believes that to focus merely on human social relations is analytically flawed since society manifestly consists of objective subsystems which interact with each other independently of the individual and, indeed, which impose upon the individual. Underlying Alexander's multi-dimensional theory is a commitment to ontological dualism. There are other extremely prominent figures, like Habermas, Foucault and Bourdieu, who are also implicitly committed to a similarly dualistic ontology in a large part of their writings. Thus, Habermas opposes the public, institutional system to the privatised and individual lifeworld (Habermas 1987b; 1991).

Other contemporary social theorists are committed to a similar dualism but employ the concept of structure (or equivalent) in slightly differing ways. They envisage structure as a set of rules which pattern individual action rather than as independent social institutions. In fact, the theorists who employ a 'conceptual' rather than a 'real' definition of structure are closely related since the purpose of structure as a net of concept is to ensure the reproduction of institutional structure. Anthony Giddens' structuration theory is rightly prominent in contemporary social theory and it has also been employed in disciplines as diverse as geography and international relations. There is no doubting the academic importance of structuration theory but it is also a prime example of the ontological dualism of contemporary social theory. The primary task of Anthony Giddens' structuration theory is to explain how the individual contributes to the reproduction of the social system. The central terms in structuration theory are system, structure and structuration. System refers to the social institutions of modern society (which realists call structure), structure (potentially confusingly) to certain rules which pattern individual action and structuration to the moment when individuals act in the light of these rules to reproduce the system. The curious 'stretching' of individual presence of which he writes refers to the way in which individual actions at one point in the system cohere with others elsewhere to reproduce the social structure as a whole. Structuration theory claims that individuals knowingly reproduce the social system, thereby avoiding the 'derogation of the lay actor' (Giddens 1988: 71). For Giddens, the social system is reproduced only by means of knowledgeable individual agency. Nevertheless, the social system has its own autonomous status; it is independent of the individuals who reproduce it. Giddens notes that structuration theory is compatible with a realist epistemology and, to emphasise the point, he insists that 'society is not the creation of individual subjects' (Giddens 1995a: xl). Institutions have structural properties which are not reducible to individuals. Giddens' structuration theory operates around the divide between structure and agency, trying to reconcile the two without falling into either objectivism or subjectivism. In this way, and against many of his critics, Giddens is explicitly committed to ontological dualism; he wants ultimately to preserve both structure and agency. Giddens is one of the most significant examples of dualism in contemporary social theory but he is far from being alone.[1] Although adopting very different political stances to Giddens, Foucault describes the way that modern discourses oppress the individual subject (Foucault 1974a, 1995), while Bourdieu's habitus imposes upon the lone individual (Bourdieu 1984).[2] Contemporary social theory assumes a dualistic ontology. It focuses on the interrelation of structure and agency.[3] Ironically, Giddens' critics share his ontological pre-suppositions. Alex Callinicos has rejected Giddens on the grounds that he has putatively reduced the objective existence of structure to individual agency (Callinicos 1985: 162). Callinicos affirms structure but, at the same time, he defends individual agency: 'The explanatory autonomy of social structures is not inconsistent with the orthodox conception of agents' (Callinicos 1987: 38). For Callinicos, society consists of structure and agents and the purpose of social theory is to reconcile the two distinct elements. Despite his evident disdain for Giddens, in the end, Callinicos promotes a dualistic ontology which is consistent with structuration theory. John Thompson similarly advocates a dualistic ontology against the putative individualism of structuration theory: 'Structure and agency no longer appear to be the complementary terms of a duality but the antagonistic poles of a dualism, such that structural constraints may so limit the options of individuals that agency is effectively dissolved' (J. Thompson 1989: 73). Thompson insists that there is an objective dimension to society, independent of individual interpretation: 'I attempt to situate action within an overall context of social institutions and structural conditions' (J.Thompson 1981: 140–1). Like Callinicos, Thompson replicates the ontological dualism of structuration theory. For these social theorists, society consists of structure and agency.

Indeed, ontological dualism threatens only to become more dominant and, at the moment, the divide between structure and agency is being emphasised ever more strongly. For some social theorists, structure has become the exclusive focus of attention, while, for others, individual agency has become analytically primary. In European sociology, Niklas Luhmann is becoming an increasingly important figure. His writings demonstrate an elaborate commitment to ontological dualism. However, in his work, the objective side of this dualism, the system, threatens to obliterate the individual. Luhmann accepts that any social system must be made up in the first instance of individuals and their actions (Luhmann 1995: 215) but he rejects the argument that sociological analysis can limit itself merely to human social interaction (Luhmann 1997: 47).

> Even the idea, initially attractive for sociologists, of an 'intersubjective' constitution of the world no longer helps; it is too self-evident and insufficiently theoretically productive. We employ the concept of a world as a concept for the *unity of the difference between system and environment.*
>
> (Luhmann 1995: 208)

For Luhmann, society cannot be analysed by reference to human social relations. Luhmann is concerned ultimately with the dialectic between the social system and the environment in which that system exists. As the system transforms, the environment in which it operates also transforms, producing a spiralling process of change. The environment is not an objective given which is independent of the system but the kind of environment which a system faces is partly a product of the character of the system itself. The world which confronts a system depends at least partly on what a system is trying to achieve. There is a dialectical relationship between system and environment. This immanent dialectic of system and environment is the central point of Luhmann's sociology and from it follow the other key arguments of Luhmann's system theory.

For Luhmann, the basis of all interaction between the system is communication. The system receives information about the environment through communication and therefore communication determines the way in which the system can evolve. For Luhmann, the evolution of the system is a critical focus which distinguishes his systems theory from Parsons' structural-functionalism. While Parsons' structural-functionalism prioritises systemic equilibrium through the interrelation of whole and parts, Luhmann emphasises differentiation (Luhmann 1995: 18). The system subdivides itself in the face of the environmental pressure created by its current relation to the environment. Yet, this differentiation necessitates further dialectic transformation because each differentiated subsystem is confronted by a new environment; the environment of each new subsystem now consists of the other subsystems. Luhmann calls this immanent dialectic between systems and their environments 'autopoiesis'; the term refers to the fact that the system makes itself. As the system receives new information about the difference between itself and the environment, it resonates with this new information, stimulating self–transformation.

> System resonance, then, is always in effect when the system is stimulated by the environment. The stimulation can be registered by the system if it possesses a corresponding capacity for information processing permitting it to infer the presence of an environment.
>
> (Luhmann 1989: 22)

When resonance reaches a certain pitch, the (sub)system is forced to adapt to the new situation, usually involving functional differentiation (Luhmann 1989: 107–8).

According to Luhmann, the autopoietic process is structured by certain codes which underlie each (sub)system. Each subsystem is oriented around a binary code which mediates its relationship with its environment (Luhmann 1989: 36; 1995: 231–34; Luhmann 1997: 52). Thus, the legal system is structured by the code legal/illegal, the economic by the code possession/non-possession (Luhmann 1989: 36) and every single system or subsystem is ultimately constituted by these transcendental binary codes: 'Codes are invariant for the system which identifies itself by them' (Luhmann 1997: 52). Crucially, these codes determine the kinds of communication any system can receive or send and therefore the kind of autopoietic adaptations which can occur. These codes also structure the individuals operating in that system. The codes precede social action in any particular system. For Luhmann, the binary codes allow the system to 'interpenetrate' the human subject. Luhmann uses the word 'interpenetrate' because he sees the social system and the human subject as a relationship between two systems and their respective environments. Both consequently influence or interpenetrate each other. However, although Luhmann might argue that the individual interpenetrates the social system, the latter is primary. The social system has determination over the individual whom it socialises by means of the imposition of these binary norms. Luhmann is explicit that interpenetration is the optimum concept because it 'avoids reference to the nature of human beings, recourse to the (supposedly foundational) subjectivity of consciousness, or formulating the problem as "intersubjectivity" (which presupposes subjects)' (Luhmann 1995: 216). Individuals are socialised into the roles required by the social system through the internalisation of certain binary codes. In modern societies with particular kinds of systems, these codes produce a specific kind of person: 'binary schematisms are the precondition for the emergence of a figure that in modern philosophy has gone by the name of the subject' (Luhmann 1995: 233). Luhmann usefully summarises his discussion of the relationship between the individual and the system: 'All socialisation occurs as social interpenetration; all social interpenetration, as communication' (Luhmann 1995: 243). The steering of any system is not consequently the result of conscious social interaction but rather the automatic, self-transforming responses of the system to the communication it receives. In Luhmann's sociology, human social interaction is effaced in favour of a self-equilibrating and self-transforming system. Autopoiesis is not reducible to the social relations between humans; nor does it ultimately depend upon human consciousness. Luhmann's work promotes a stern form of ontological dualism in which the individual is subordinated to the objective system. Human social relations, by contrast, are a subsidiary element in his world.[4]

Luhmann's work emphasises the objective side of ontological dualism. In his work, structure or the system, as he calls it, is dominant. Other contemporary social theorists, in contrast to Luhmann, have increasingly focused on the individual agent; they have gone over to the other side of structure and agency dualism. The later writings of Anthony Giddens are a prime example here. From 1987, the concerns and style of Giddens' writing changed from dense theoretical discussions, to breezier discussions of the defining characteristics of late modernity, which Alexander has satirically called 'Giddens lite' (Alexander 1996: 135). For Giddens, modernity involves the disembedding of relations from local settings and their stretching across time and space. In the light of new methods of communication and new expert systems, the face-to-face relations of pre-modern societies have been replaced by long-distance relations which now straddle the globe. Giddens has increasingly described late modern society as post-traditional (Giddens 1995b: 192). In post-traditional society, the individual is no longer committed to one tradition nor restricted to ascribed social relations. Since it is no longer obvious what individuals should do or be, individuals must self-consciously consider their options and make choices about what they should do. Self-identity must be reflexively created by the individual: 'The more tradition loses its hold, and the more daily life is reconstituted in terms of a dialectical interplay between local and global, the more individuals are forced to negotiate lifestyle choices among the diversity of options' (Giddens 1995b: 5). No longer constrained by tradition, individuals have to decide upon what kind of people they will be. 'The self is seen as a reflexive project, for which individuals are responsible. We are, not what we are, but what we make of ourselves' (Giddens 1995b: 75). The individual's autonomy becomes clearest when Giddens discusses the emergence of a new form of sexuality. According to Giddens, the sexuality of post-traditional society is distinguishable from that of former societies by the fact that sexual practices have become divorced from the biological function of reproduction (Giddens 1993: 34). With the development of 'plastic sexuality', Giddens envisages the development of 'pure relations' between individuals. In these pure relations of friendship or 'confluent love' (Giddens 1993: 61–62), individuals are no longer bound to each other by social and moral obligations but only by their personal needs. 'Giving certain conditions, the pure relationship can provide a facilitating social environment for the reflexive project of the self' (Giddens 1993: 139). Once individuals have established certain rules of conduct, they can utilise their sexuality plastically in mutually pleasurable ways. Although Giddens emphasises the plasticity of sexuality, in fact, given the new reflexivity of the individual, the individual's entire selfhood has become plastic for Giddens. For him, new technological developments have broken the shackles of tradition and liberated individuals into a world of choice in which they can freely decide upon the ways in which they can lead their lives and interact with others. Giddens ignores the wider social context in which the new individual is possible and emphasises instead the personal powers of this putatively autonomous being.

Although for the most part Giddens disconnects the post-traditional individual from the system, at certain points in his later writing, Giddens recognises that there is a link between this individual and the wider social structure. At this point, the ontological dualism of structuration theory re-appears as the isolated post-traditional individual reproduces the late modern social system: 'the overriding stress of the book [*Modernity and Self-Identity*] is upon the emergence of new mechanisms of self-identity which are shaped by – yet also shape – the institutions of modernity' (Giddens 1995b: 2). For Giddens, the post-traditional individual adopts practices which reproduce the very systems that promote the individual in the first place. The liberated individual now reproduces a system which thrives on the emancipation of the plastic individual. Giddens' individual is freer than Luhmann's but both theorists operate around the two poles of structure and agent. Luhmann emphasises the social structure, Giddens agency, but their sociologies are contoured by these two concepts.

Giddens is a particularly prominent example of individualistically oriented dualism but there are many other examples of creeping individualising in contemporary sociology.[5] According to Scott Lash and John Urry, one of the distinctive features of the present era is the increasing significance of the individual: 'Structural change in the economy forces the individual to be freed from the structural rigidity of the Fordist labour process' (Lash and Urry 1994: 5). For Lash and Urry, the individual, freed from structural constraint, has more agency and autonomy in post-Fordist society:

> This accelerating individualization process is a process in which agency is set free from structure, a process in which, further, it is structural change itself in modernization that so to speak forces agency to take on powers that heretofore lay in the social structures themselves.
>
> (Lash and Urry 1994: 5)

Lash and Urry do not entirely ignore structural factors, as their monographs on political economy reveal (1987, 1994), but the significance of structure has receded. Individuals have increasing autonomy to choose their own social existence. Stuart Hall has similarly argued for the emancipation of the individual in contemporary society. In promoting his 'new times' project, Stuart Hall disparages his former structuralism: 'For a long time, being a socialist was synonymous with the ability to translate everything into the language of "structures"' (Hall 1990: 120). In place of structure, sociologists should now focus their attention on the individual agent, who now enjoys more powers than was previously the case: 'One boundary which "new times" has certainly displaced is that between the objective and subjective dimensions of change. This is the so-called "revolution of the subject" aspect' (Hall 1990: 119). His current promotion of the individual is particularly striking since his early work on youth culture and the media employed a structuralist Gramscian approach which subordinated the individual to wider historical and institutional conditions (e.g. Hall *et al.* 1978; Hall and Jefferson 1976). Hall has oscillated precisely between the twin ontological poles of contemporary social theory, once emphasising structure, now the agent. Hall, Lash and Urry are important examples of individualising in sociology. They promote a positive vision of contemporary society in which the individual is increasingly freed from structure. These sociologists are still dualistic but they, like Giddens, now emphasise the individualistic side of that polarity. Other commentators have concurred with their ontology but disputed their optimistic account of contemporary social reality. Jean Baudrillard is prominent here. He has argued that post-Fordist society constitutes a new departure in the history of humanity. The television, in particular, has transformed social reality. It has replaced normal social interaction with powerful images which have become more real than reality itself. These 'hyperreal' images now dominate society, imposing themselves upon lone individuals absolutely: 'For information and the media are not a scene, a prospective space, or something that's performed, but a screen without depth, a tape perforated with messages and signals to which corresponds a receiver's own perforated reading' (Baudrillard 1990b: 65; see also 1990a). Individuals no longer have any external referent beyond these images and consequently know of no other reality. They are completely determined by media images to which their view of the world inexorably corresponds like a roll of music on a pianola. The individual stands alone before these images.[6] Baudrillard presents a pessimistic account of structure and agency in contemporary society. Indeed, he asserts that individual agency has been obliterated by the development of new media structures. Yet, he shares ontological convictions with Giddens, Lash, Urry and Hall. For him, modern society is understood in terms of structure and agency.[7]

In contemporary social theory, the dualistic ontology of structure and agency is hegemonic. Social reality has been reduced to the agent, on the one hand, and structure, on the other. There is ultimately no social context in contemporary society, just structure and agency. Certainly, there is a growing divide between contemporary theorists. Some, like Luhmann, adopt an almost exclusively objectivist view, focusing only on structure, while others, like Giddens, emphasise the new powers of the agent. Yet, in both cases, the social relations between human beings have become irrelevant. The specifically social reality which makes human existence what it distinctively is has been forgotten. This is not the first time this has happened in sociology. In the 1930s, Karl Mannheim proposed the sociology of knowledge as a form of critical theory (Mannheim 1976). For Mannheim, social beliefs could be broadly divided into two forms. 'Ideology' referred to the legitimating beliefs of dominant groups, 'utopia' to the subversive beliefs of subordinate and resistant groups. Mannheim suggested that true intellectuals could attain a disinterested position by recognising the structural origins of the beliefs of subordinate and dominant groups. Intellectuals effectively floated free from structural imperatives. In his well-known criticisms of Mannheim, Karl Popper complained that Mannheim's so-called sociology of knowledge was a misnomer. Mannheim ignored the actual social processes by which groups produced knowledge. The social interaction by means of which humans mutually developed their understandings was absent from his analysis. Instead, he focused merely on the way in which isolated individuals adopted pre-existing ideologies consistent with their position in society. There was no social process here, mere inculcation.

> The sociology of knowledge is not only self-destructive, not only a rather gratifying object of socio-analysis, it also shows an astounding failure to understand precisely its main subject, the *social aspects of knowledge*...Scientific objectivity can be described as the inter-subjectivity of scientific method. But this social aspect of science is almost entirely neglected by those who call themselves sociologists of knowledge.
>
> (Popper 1976: 216–17)

Contemporary social theory is marked by the same fault. Human social relations have been effaced by a dualistic picture in which structure confronts the individual. The infinite richness of shared human life is reduced to a mechanical model; structure imposes upon the agent, the agent reproduces structure. Yet, society is nothing but human social relations. Society consists precisely of the complex web of social relations between people. These social relations are the social reality. Yet, contemporary social theory ignores these social relations. It ironically ignores the very phenomenon which validates the discipline to which they have nominally committed themselves. It is extremely unfortunate that contemporary social theory has descended into ontological dualism. This dualism is philosophically untenable and vitiates empirical research. It has misdirected sociology away from the detailed analysis of human social relations into abstract theorising, of the kind which Luhmann demonstrates, or celebratory individualism, evinced in the later work of Giddens. Although comprehensively fallacious, the current adherence of the discipline to this ontology is perhaps explicable. Such an explanation may begin to provide the first steps towards a new theoretical consensus in sociology today.

The Rise of the State

Towards the end of the fifteenth century, Ferdinand and Isabella in Castile, the Tudors in England and the Valois in France reformed the medieval monarchies to

which they succeeded by centralising existing bureaucratic procedures. The inno-
vations of the new royal houses have been widely recognised as the origins of the
modern state (Anderson 1993; Tilly 1975; Van Creveld 1999; Corrigan and Sayer
1991; Williams 1970; Kennedy 1999). In each case, old dynastic medieval monarchies began to administer their territories with increasing directness from the
throne itself. Certainly, the sixteenth century states were diffuse in comparison
with what they would become in the twentieth century but, from the beginning of
sixteenth century, the rise of a new kind of political entity was evident over much
of Europe. Increasingly, this nascent state did not simply claim theoretical
sovereignty over its domain, as medieval monarchs had sometimes done. It actually administered its sovereign territory with its own representatives. Until the
nineteenth century monarchs often accepted the local appropriation of office by
tax-farmers so long as these tax-farmers ensured the authority of the state there.
Yet, slowly, the state began to emerge as a unified sovereign entity over increasingly closely administered territories. As the state developed, it broke down old
medieval corporations, estates, guilds and civic councils so that individuals
emerged from formerly solidary social relations. These increasingly isolated individuals were confronted by a powerful new political entity which towered over
each of them; a Leviathan, which coiled itself about the individuals over whom it
ruled. From the sixteenth century, accelerating after the second half of the seventeenth, European society was characterised by a twin development: the
emergence of a unified state and the concomitant atomisation of individuals,
sundered from medieval social solidarities.

Norbert Elias has captured this double development of state and individual
by tracing the emergence of manners and etiquette in European court society
from the High Middle Ages. For most of the Middle Ages, European culture was
dominated by the barbaric culture of a warrior nobility. Eating, drinking and
various bodily motions were natural functions subject, according to Elias, to no
social control. Food was eaten with the hands, spitting at will was normal and
nostrils were evacuated without any attempt to conceal mucus. Individuals
performed basic biological functions without the mediation of cultural
constraint.[8] Towards the end of the Middle Ages, especially the late fifteenth and
early sixteenth centuries, a concern with bodily conduct and control emerged in
the courts around Europe. Here, uncontrolled body movements – spitting,
sneezing, farting – were deemed increasingly inappropriate. According to Elias,
the emergent bourgeoisie and professional middle class (employed especially in
the nascent state bureaucracies) introduced new forms of conduct into court
society (Elias 1978: 22, 26–29). At the same time as manners developed,
European states began to become more centralised. Above all, monarchs began
to monopolise violence (Keegan 1994; Howard 2000; Weber 1978). Monarchs
began to raise their own armies, while feuding, which had characterised the
Middle Ages was restricted. The reformation of manners from the late fifteenth
century constituted an important part of in this process of pacification. In
controlling and limiting the individual and especially the formerly volatile
nobility, manners were an element in the historical development of the state.

Manners assisted in centralising violence in the hands of the sovereign, by reforming the everyday conduct of subjects:

> Here the individual is largely protected from sudden attack, the irruption of physical violence into his life. But at the same time he is himself forced to suppress in himself any passionate impulse urging him to attack another physically…. The transformation of the nobility from a class of knights into a class of courtiers is an example of this.
>
> (Elias 1982: 236)

Elias concludes:

> Physical violence is confined to the barracks; and from this store-house it breaks out only in extreme cases, in times of war or social upheaval, into individual life. As the monopoly of certain specialist groups it is normally excluded from the life of others.
>
> (Elias 1982: 238)

Through his analysis of manners, Elias illuminates the way that the emergence of the self-disciplined and autonomous individual parallels the development of the modern state; they are alternative sides of the same historic movement.[9] In early modern Europe, a distinctive political ontology emerged of individual and state.

This political ontology of isolated individuals under an overarching state was recognised by European writers as this new regime began to emerge. One of the earliest examples of this is provided by Alexis de Tocqueville's discussion of the new kind of society forged by the French Revolution. In his analysis of the Revolution, de Tocqueville argued that the turmoil that followed 1789 did not undermine the political order in France so much as rationalise it. The French Revolution was promoted most strongly by the emergent urban, industrial and professional bourgeoisie, particularly those employed in the growing bureaucratic machinery of the state. Although there were moments of near anarchy for short periods, the overwhelming effect of the Revolution was to demote a superfluous aristocracy, engaged merely in trivial struggles for honour and prestige at the court in Versailles. The Revolution assaulted this anachronistic social group but did not reverse the trajectory of French political development; on the contrary, it accelerated the centralisation of the state and for the first time unified a national population beneath it (de Tocqueville 1955). Significantly, de Tocqueville noted that the corollary of the state's appearance was the increasing isolation of individuals.

> That word 'individualism', which we have coined for our own requirements, was unknown to our ancestors, for the good reason that in their days every individual necessarily belonged to a group and no one could regard himself as an isolated unit.
>
> (de Tocqueville 1955: 96)

For de Tocqueville, European modernity involved a novel political situation in which the individual was now freed from former social solidarities, but this was not a moment of untroubled liberation. On the contrary, in this individualism, de Tocqueville saw the potential for tyranny since 'all were quite ready to sink their differences and to be integrated into a homogenous whole, provided no one was given a privileged position and rose above the common level' (de Tocqueville 1995: 96). The new individualism demanded equality in place of the graded hierarchy of the medieval Estates system but this equality threatened to create equal oppression of all under the monolithic state. In this political order, the individual now isolated from various social groups was defenceless against the state. As Max Beloff describes:

> The demand for individual liberty played in the long run, as we have seen, straight into the hands of the State, since the State was the instrument through which the older collective caste or group liberties were destroyed.
>
> (Beloff 1954: 53)

De Tocqueville's writing was an early statement of the dualistic political ontology of modern Europe. He presciently recognised the double historical movement which brought both the individual and the state to the fore and the political problems which this new ontology posed. Following de Tocqueville's diagnosis of the political ontology of modernity, Durkheim similarly emphasised the distinctive individualism of European society. Like de Tocqueville he was similarly pessimistic about the social implications of this dual development; 'While the state becomes inflated and hypertrophied in order to obtain a firm enough grip upon individuals, but without succeeding, the latter without mutual relationship tumble over one another like so many liquid molecules' (Durkheim 1952: 389). Echoing de Tocqueville, Durkheim saw this dual development of state and individual as socially and politically dangerous, threatening not only political oppression but personal anomie as well. In modern European society, human social relations had been replaced by the cold dualism of individual and state.[10]

The dualistic ontology of individual and state described by Elias, de Tocqueville and Durkheim is extremely attractive to the social scientist. It is analytically elegant and it does accord with certain aspects of the modern experience. The individual experience of being confronted by a distant institution is a familiar one in modern societies. The dualistic political ontology has some manifest empirical grounding. Yet, this ontology in no way represents an accurate picture of modern social reality. It focuses only on one experience of this reality, raising it to an axiomatic level. Ultimately, sociologists have taken this beguiling image of individual and state and transformed it into a sociological ontology. Society rather than the state now confronts the individual. In contemporary social theory, this dichotomy is expressed in distinctive terms; the opposition of society and the individual is described as structure and agency. This dualism dominates the discipline as society is consistently comprehended in terms of a relationship between structural realities and individual agency. Given the historic importance of the double development of the state and individual in western history, it is understandable why sociologists should have converted this political ontology into a sociological one. All academic disciplines are inevitably influenced by the historic circumstances in which they arise. However, although the prevalence of the dualistic ontology is historically understandable, this does mean that such a dualism is defensible. It is not. This ontology is sociologically false. Despite the appeal of the dualistic ontology, the institutional reality of modern society can be adequately explained by reference to social relations alone. Society does not consist of structure and agency but of the social relations between human beings. Life is not the struggle of the individual against structure, nor the reproduction of the structure by the agent, but an eternal round of interactions through which social relations between humans are made, transformed and destroyed. Even the vast and apparently faceless institutions of modern society are ultimately reducible to the social relations between humans. In every case, these institutions involve groups of humans in social relations co-ordinated in special ways and with access to certain resources. In this way, these social groups have the extraordinary powers which are so recognisable to individuals in modern society. The reality which individuals confront is human; it is others, even when these others are gathered into very large and powerful groups. In every instance, society consists of human social relations, which are the basis of even the most powerful associations. Just as structure has been consistently misperceived so has the individual in modern society been misunderstood. It is an error to conceive of the modern individual as genuinely autonomous. The modern individual may enjoy greater personal rights than a medieval subject; it is also possible that in certain cases individuals have greater freedom to move between groups. However, the modern individual is a product of new kinds of social relations which emerged in the modern period. Modern society is not characterised by individualism, although as Durkheim famously argued the 'Cult of the Individual' is certainly important, but by the existence of new social networks. Together, these networks make up the institutions which supposedly confront the individual. Similarly, the plastic or post-modern individual is a product of new kinds of social relations. In these relations, a new kind of individual may be emerging; in these social relations, humans may mutually understand themselves and others in different ways. Consequently, the individual may be able to do things which were impossible in previous historical eras. Yet, it is wrong to claim that the individual is more autonomous now. On the contrary, the putative autonomy of the individual is a result of the new social relations in which humans are embedded and which relations allow them certain forms of agency. The trouble is that sociologists have been bewitched by the dualistic image of state and individual. They have exaggerated one kind of experience in modern society – an individual standing before faceless state bureaucracies – and raised it to the level of a sociological axiom. They have tried to understand society in terms of structure and agency because modern society seems to consist of a dualism between social institutions and the individual. They have failed to recognise the reality of modern society, which consists of complex webs of social relations between humans. Instead, social theorists prefer to operate with a conveniently simplified image of social reality; the restless cascade of social relations is reduced to the mechanical opposition of structure and agency.

Beyond Dualism

Current debates in social theory pre-suppose an ontology of structure and agency but even in more empirical areas of research, as the works of Lash, Urry and Hall demonstrate, the concepts of structure and agency predominate. Against this dualism, a social ontology must be promoted. This social ontology does not divide society into structure and agent. It focuses only on social relations between humans. Humans are never isolated, nor are they confronted by an objective structure. Humans exist in social relations with other humans. The focus of sociology has to be these social relations. This social ontology in no way denies the institutional reality of modern society. It recognises the extraordinary powers of modern states and multinational corporations but explains these powers in terms of the social networks of which these entities consist. It does not unthinkingly reify these institutions into objective structures but seeks through detailed empirical analysis to show how certain social groups are able to mobilise themselves in ways which have the most striking social effects. The social ontology understands the reality of institutions by reference to the actuality of social relations which persist there. A sociology based on a social ontology recognises the potency of human social relations but it avoids the reification of ontological dualism. Society is no less real simply because it is believed to consist of social relations. Social theory is currently entranced by a dualism but the reality of social life stands before its eyes.

It is perhaps no accident that this re-orientation of sociology away from its dualist ontology of society and the individual towards a social ontology of interacting humans should appear as necessary now. The historic conditions which made the dual ontology seem so self-evident are unravelling. In particular, the state is undergoing rapid transformation. The political ontology of individual and state is no longer necessarily a fundamental feature of modernity and, consequently, historical conditions allow the dualistic ontology of society and individual to be re-considered. The declining relevance of the individual–state metaphor has allowed social theorists to understand social life in alternative ways.

Current historical transformations do more than merely allow sociologists to recognise the analytical importance of human social relations, however. It is incumbent upon the sociologist to provide an account of these changes. European society is currently undergoing transformations on a scale of a historic significance comparable with the industrial and political revolutions of the eighteenth and nineteenth centuries. The contours of European state society which finally crystallised towards the end of the nineteenth century are being radically re-configured. Global economic forces are undermining the autonomy of nation–states, fissuring formerly stable national unities from above and below.

Waves of mass cross-border immigration are transforming national cultures and demographies. New solidarities and new forms of politics are emerging which are likely to be as historically significant as those changes which characterised the rise of the European state system. The scale of contemporary transformations do not, therefore, merely liberate sociology, allowing it to re-imagine itself, but these transformations demand a radical re-invention of the discipline. Sociology arose precisely in response to the disorientating transformations which Europeans experienced in the early part of the nineteenth century. It will retain its relevance only if it continues to provide compelling interpretations of contemporary social change. It is most likely to be able to provide such interpretations insofar as sociology adopts a social ontology. A social ontology insists that society consists only of social relations; humans interacting with each other on the basis of shared meanings. Sociology should focus precisely on how these social relations come into being and are transformed by the humans engaged in them. They are the fascinating subject matter of this discipline, with their own distinctive properties. Sociology must overcome the dual ontology which is dominant today and turn once again to the reality of human existence: to social relations. In the first instance, this can be achieved only by mounting a critique of contemporary social theory. The manifest and decisive errors of social theory must be demonstrated. The ontology of structure and agency must be refuted. Yet, this critique must also involve a positive element. It must simultaneously illuminate those moments when social theorists recognise the importance of human social relations and renege upon their own formal commitment to the abstractions of ontological dualism.

2 The Relevance of Parsons

At the start of his first major work, *The Structure of Social Action*, Talcott Parsons asked 'Who now reads Spencer?' (Parsons 1966a: 3). Parsons noted the curious fact that a sociologist who had in the previous century been one of the dominant figures was by 1930s all but irrelevant. Parsons' monograph was partly concerned with demonstrating why Spencer's evolutionary interests were now obsolete to sociology. It is no small irony that by the beginning of the twenty-first century, Parsons may have shared a similar fate to his own predecessor. Who now reads Parsons? Certainly, Parsons' work has not declined to the level of Spencer's. Luhmann, for instance, has drawn heavily upon Parsons to produce his neo-functionalism. The significance of Parsons' writing will endure as his works are still drawn upon in contemporary debates. Yet, while some sociologists still take account of Parsons, Parsons is generally read less and less and an inaccurate stereotype of his work has ossified around him. In contemporary accounts, if his politics does not automatically disqualify him, Parsons is swiftly dismissed for his putative objectivism and his ignorance of individual agency. Consequently, for many contemporary social theorists, Parsons has nothing to teach us about the study of society. His voluminous work stands merely as a warning for sociologists today; he is not a resource but a foil against which sociologists react. Anthony Giddens, for instance, exemplifies the standard critique of Parsons: 'functionalism is a teleological theory which, however, allows for only a limited and deficient explication of purposive human action' (Giddens 1977b: 106). In particular, functionalism 'papers over various basic problems concerning the nature of intentional action' (Giddens 1977b: 108). Functionalism explains social action by reference not to individual agents but to systemic needs which have to be met. Against such a reification, Giddens maintains that social systems 'do not have any need or interest in their own survival, and the notion of "need" is falsely applied if it is not acknowledged that system needs presuppose actors' wants' (Giddens 1977b: 110). For Giddens, functionalism makes the fatal error of reducing individuals to mere cogs in the objective social system; it reduces 'human agency to the "internationalization of values"' and fails 'to treat social life as *actively constituted* through the doings of its members' (Giddens 1976: 21). Although some of these criticisms are valid, Parsons should not be totally dismissed on the basis of them. Jurgen Habermas is correct when he insists that 'no social theory can be taken seriously today if it does not at least situate itself with respect to Parsons' (Habermas 1987b: 199). Moreover, the image of Parsons generally current in contemporary social theory has very little to do with what Parsons himself actually wrote. As Joas has noted, 'The protest against the hegemony of Parsons' theory essentially engendered by the social movements in the sixties curbed any serious reception [of his work]' (Joas 1996: 7–8). Unfortunately, this initial reaction to Parsons still predominates today, preventing any serious consideration of his work. Consequently, a re-reading of Parsons may serve much more than a negative purpose; he may be more than a mere foil against which sociologists today should react. On the contrary, a re-immersion into Parsonian texts, dry though many are, may provide a crucial initial step to overcoming the dualistic hegemony in contemporary social theory. Parsons may be re-discovered as an important theoretical resource for the social ontology which needs to be established in sociology today. Despite the image which has congealed around him, Parsons may, in fact, offer a route away from the dualism to which the various contemporary social theorists have committed themselves.

Parsons' Social Ontology

The Structure of Social Action was primarily intended as a critique of utilitarian philosophy, which Parsons believed was dominant in the social sciences at the time. For Parsons, utilitarianism was decisively flawed because it could not explain the manifest fact of social order from its own premise of rational individuals. If humans were genuinely independent, utilitarianism could not explain the fact that humans live for the most part in stable and predictable social environments. In the famous discussion of utilitarian philosophy, Parsons examined the first formulation of this problem of order in Hobbes' *Leviathan* and, from there, traced the various ways that modern philosophers had attempted to solve the problem of social order (Parsons 1966a: 90–125). Parsons began with the work of Hobbes not only because Hobbes was one of the first prominent modern political philosophers to grapple with the problem of grounding social order in rational, self-interested individuals but, according to Parsons, 'Hobbes' system of social theory is almost a pure case of utilitarianism' (Parsons 1966a: 90). For Parsons, 'Hobbes saw the problem with a clarity which has never been surpassed and his statement of it remains valid today' (Parsons 1966a: 93). The problem was that once the definition of humans as rational, self-interested and autonomous individuals was accepted, the creation of social order became inexplicable (Parsons 1966a: 93). In the end, Hobbes could only explain the creation of order out of the state of nature by appealing to the concept of Leviathan, the absolute sovereign, which contradicted the premises of utilitarianism. It denied individuals any autonomy whatsoever. Parsons traces the same failure to overcome the Hobbesian problem in the works of Locke (Parsons 1966a: 96–97), Malthus (Parsons 1966a: 103–7), Godwin (Parsons 1966a: 111–15), nineteenth-century evolutionary theory and Marx (with less success) (Parsons 1966a: 109–10).

Parsons brilliantly noticed that the attempt to explain social order from the premise of rational, autonomous actors led to two unacceptable theoretical positions, which he called the 'utilitarian dilemma':

> Either the active agency of the actor in the choice of ends is an independent factor in action, and the end element must be random; or the objectionable implication of randomness is denied, but then their independence disappears and they are assimilated to the conditions of the situation, that is to elements analyzable in terms of nonsubjective categories, principally heredity and environment.
>
> (Parsons 1966a: 64)

If individuals really were rational and free as utilitarianism claimed, then the action of diverse individuals could never be co-ordinated. Their choices would remain random and no regular social intercourse could take place. Social order would be impossible as each individual randomly pursued now this end and now that. In order to explain the co-ordination of ends, utilitarianism has, therefore, to postulate the existence of some external factor which impresses itself upon individuals, directing their choices. Once determined in this way, individuals would no longer choose randomly; their choices would be co-ordinated to the same ends. Social order would then be possible but only at the cost of individual autonomy. Utilitarianism must either assume that rational individuals are themselves determined by objective factors and, therefore, not independent, or the autonomy of individuals is maintained, their choices are random and social order remains inexplicable. On a utilitarian account, social order cannot be explained.

The purpose of *The Structure of Social Action* is to show that a social theory capable of explaining the manifest fact of social order must transcend utilitarianism. To this end Parsons traces the convergence of four major theorists, two economists and two sociologists, towards a shared position, called the theory of voluntary action. The voluntary theory of action overcomes the utilitarian dilemma by rejecting the latter's premise of autonomous and rational individuals. Parsons grandly demonstrates the way in which Marshall, Pareto, Durkheim and Weber all moved towards this voluntarist position.[1] Parsons takes the fact that all these major theorists have converged independently as evidence of the veracity of that position (Parsons 1966a: 723–24). For Parsons, all these theorists come to agree that social order can be explained only by reference to the existence of shared values and understandings. The existence of common normative orientations is essential to the explanation of social order:

> A society can only be subject to a legitimate order, and therefore can be on a non-biological level something other than a balance of power of interests, only in so far as there are *common* value attitudes in the society.
>
> (Parsons 1966a: 670; also Parsons 1966a: 392)

Individuals are able to co-ordinate their actions because they come to agree upon certain common values prior to their actions. For Parsons, common values can be transcendentally deduced from the manifest existence of social order in Kantian fashion. Kant argued that given the fact of experience it was possible to deduce the existence of *a priori* mental categories which made this experience possible. Similarly, given the fact of social order, Parsons deduces the existence of common values which make social order possible. Through recognising the existence of these common values, the existence of social order is explicable without reducing humans to biological entities determined externally. Humans knowingly orient themselves to these common values and consequently form social groups which interact in regular ways. All direct their activities towards the common and shared ends upon which they have agreed. It is important to emphasise that the commitment to these shared values is itself voluntary, giving Parsons' voluntary theory of action its name. Voluntary, here, does not mean that individuals personally choose their values, for this would imply a return to utilitarianism. By voluntary, Parsons means that individuals have to understand the significance of common values. These values do not impose on humans independently of their consciousness. Humans have to understand what the common values which they accept enjoin. These values are meaningful to them. Since social action requires human understanding, Parsons calls it voluntary. It requires conscious understanding on the part of group members about what their common values imply. The centrality of common values to all social action deflects the criticisms which are sometimes made of the so-called 'action frame of reference' (Parsons 1966a: 39). Joas, for instance, has argued that the focus on individual goal attainment in the action frame of reference is a return to utilitarian individualism (Joas 1996: 157–58). The action frame of reference does not, in fact, amount to a retreat to utilitarianism, for in every case the ends which individuals pursue are established by group norms. Individuals agree socially on the ends they pursue together.

Although individuals must understand the significance of the shared values of their group, shared norms imply moral obligation (Parsons 1966a: 383–84). In his discussion of Durkheim, Parsons demonstrates the importance of collective understandings to social life.

> A moral rule is not moral unless it is accepted as obligatory, unless the attitude towards it is quite different from expediency. But at the same time it is also not truly moral unless obedience to it is held to be desirable, unless the individual's happiness and self-fulfilment are bound up with it. Only the combination of these two elements gives a complete account of the nature of morality.
>
> (Parsons 1966a: 387)

Members do not adhere to group norms because it is in their best material interests. They do not act collectively because they maximise their utility by doing so. The motivation for collective action is not derived from a desire to avoid punishment or to gain material rewards. Social interaction induces a sense of moral obligation in and of itself. When, in the course of interaction, individuals publicly consent to certain shared values, they are committing themselves to the other members of the group and to the collective practices of the group. They are mutually accepting the obligation of group membership. The group is held together by nothing more than the members' mutual recognition that they are part of it. Yet, once a person has recognised they are a part of a group, to act against collective norms is to betray fellow group members. Social relations carry with them their own powerful sanctions. Ingeniously, Parsons does not oppose voluntarism and subjectivism against the objective social order, but shows that human understanding is essential to the production of social order. Humans have to commit themselves consciously to the shared values of the group; individuals cannot be dupes in this process. They have to understand that they are now morally obliged to act in certain ways. Having actively accepted group understandings, however, individuals commit themselves to each other. Social relations have their own special and sacred character simply by virtue of the fact that individuals mutually obligate themselves to each other.

Moreover, an 'individual's happiness and self-fulfilment' are themselves dependent on their abiding by these shared understandings. Individuals feel happy and fulfilled insofar at they abide by the values which are regarded as honourable by their social group. As Parsons emphasises, individuals do not create their own values nor decide privately upon the courses of action they will take – that is exactly the error of utilitarianism; these matters are agreed upon publicly by the group and held in common. Consequently, the esteem which follows from abiding by the common values of the group is not primarily personal. The individual's self-esteem arises from the honour which they receive from the group, even if that honour is given only implicitly. People commit themselves to the shared values of their group and are held to those values by the desire for honour and the fear of shame from their fellow group members. Parsons' theory closely echoes the argument made by Weber and Durkheim on which it is based. On this account, the threat of randomness of ends is obviated because individuals pursue common goals which induce social order. In addition, the danger of objectivism is also avoided because individuals mutually agree upon these values, committing themselves to each other. Social order is not determined by factors external to the people who are part of it. Although Parsons' initial purpose was to overcome the utilitarian dilemma, he also believed that the voluntary theory of action overcame the problem of idealism, where social reality was reduced to the individual's opinion of it. He did not deny the importance of human understanding in social life but social life could not be reduced merely to an individual's interpretation of it. Society was not merely a product of an individual's imagination. The reality of social life rested precisely on the fact that humans agreed to common values together. Social order relied not on individual opinion but on the ideas shared by group members. Consequently, and in opposition to idealism, social reality was not simply a matter of individual interpretation.

Although Parsons' target in *The Structure of Social Action* was primarily utilitarianism, his voluntary theory of action in fact solved the problem of ontological dualism. It provided an explanation of social order without dividing social reality into two opposed entities: structure and agency. Parsons promoted a social ontology in which humans interacted on the basis of shared meanings; humans had to understand what their social relations involved and demanded from them. Parsons himself was well aware of the importance of common values in overcoming sociological dualism. In the conclusion of Chapter 2, Parsons stated: 'It is hoped, in transcending the positivist–idealist dilemma, to show a way of transcending also the old individualism–society organism or, as it is often called, social nominalism–realism dilemma which has plagued social theory to so little purpose for so long' (Parsons 1966a: 74). To a great extent, as Alexander emphasises (Alexander 1984: 43), Parsons was successful in his aim; the voluntary theory of action did overcome ontological dualism. The voluntary theory of social action avoided ontological dualism because, instead of explaining social life in terms of the interaction of individual and society, it referred to social relations conducted on the basis of common understandings. The voluntary theory of action thereby avoids the postulation of any objective Leviathan which imposes upon individuals externally. Society is not separate from its members but arises out of the binding social relations between them. The voluntary theory also avoids voluntaristic individualism. Individuals are always bound into social relations through which they mutually empower and constrain one another. In place of ontological dualism or a nominalist–realist divide, the voluntary theory of action focuses on the way which people are together able to co-ordinate their actions by reference to common understandings. At the end of *The Structure of Social Action*, Parsons proposed that 'we have sound theoretical foundations on which to build' (Parsons 1966a: 775) and his optimism was justified in the light of his brilliant extraction of the theory of voluntary action from the works of Weber and Durkheim, in particular. In the light of his discussions in *The Structure of Social Action*, Giddens' criticisms of him are misplaced. Parsons does not here emphasise systemic needs; nor does he ignore human agency. On the contrary, he provides a compelling picture of the special nature of human social relations. This picture decisively and deliberately undermines ontological dualism, explaining society not by reference to structure and agency, but purely by reference to the social relations between humans. With rarely surpassed clarity, Parsons recognised that while human social relations pre-suppose understanding, they also involve obligation. Once they have recognised their relations to each other, humans mutually bind each other to very specific forms of practice. In the *Structure of Social Action*, Parsons lays out a compelling argument for the social ontology. Human social relations have their own special properties which sociology has to recognise.

Parsons' Ontological Dualism

Although social relations are central to *The Structure of Social Action*, even in this work ontological dualism becomes fleetingly apparent. Towards the end of the book, in his criticism of idealism, Parsons claims that society cannot be understood by reference to shared ideas alone. For Parsons, society is real; it consists of actual material facts which are independent of commonly held ideas.

> The position is realistic, in the technical epistemological sense. It is a philosophical implication of the position taken here that there is an external world of so-called empirical reality which is not the creation of the individual human mind and is not reducible to terms of an ideal order, in the philosophical sense.
>
> (Parsons 1966a: 753)[2]

Confirming the point, Parsons insisted that 'it is scarcely more than a truism that society is simply the aggregate of human beings in their given relations to one another' (Parsons 1966a: 354–55) but, taken together, this aggregate produces autonomous phenomena. There are aspects of society, such as institutions, which cannot be fully understood merely in terms of social relations. It seems likely that Parsons argued in this way because he wanted to protect himself absolutely against idealism. He wanted to eliminate decisively the claim that society can be reduced to what someone thinks it is. However, in arguing for the independent status of society, Parsons unwittingly reneged on his voluntary theory of action. Although he did not realise it, his appeal to certain objective institutional realities was at odds with his original account of the distinctive properties of social relations. By the end of *The Structure of Social Action*, he had already turned away from the social ontology of the voluntary theory of action of towards a dualistic ontology. This dualistic ontology eventually became dominant in his middle and later periods.[3]

The dualistic ontology is explicitly espoused in the early passages of *The Social System*, the first major work of this second period:

> The focus of this work, then, is within the action frame of reference as just outlined, on the theory of social systems. It is concerned both with personality and with culture, but not for their own sakes, rather in their bearing on the structure and functioning of the social system.
>
> (Parsons 1952: 18–19)

Although Parsons formally aligns his position in *The Social System* with the voluntary theory of action, his argument has changed decisively. In this statement from *The Social System*, however, Parsons has altered his definition of social order; he has introduced a new ontology. The social order does not now consist of social relations mediated by shared values. Rather, society is a system which consists of functionally necessary roles. According to Parsons, the fulfilment of these roles is fundamental to the maintenance of the system:

> Roles are, from the point of view of the functioning social system, the primary mechanism through which the essential functional prerequisites of the system are met. There is the same order of relationship between roles

and functions relative to the system in social systems, as there is between
organs and functions in the organism.

(Parsons 1952: 115)[4]

Humans do not mutually sustain their social relations through their shared
understanding of them. Humans no longer obligate themselves to each other by
agreeing to certain common values. Now, individuals simply fulfil roles which
sustain an autonomous social system. Significantly, Parsons' biological analogy
in the last clause of the quotation implies that systems have a self-equilibrating
mechanism which operates independently of shared understandings. The social
system has an autonomous ontological status with causal powers over the social
roles of which it is comprised. Parsons explains the equilibrium of the system by
reference to functional needs which impose themselves upon agents, now
merely fulfilling certain roles. In the light of these passages, Giddens' critique of
functionalism becomes valid.

It is important to recognise that values are still central to Parsons' sociology
in his middle and later periods, although their constitution and role has altered
decisively. This can be clearly seen in much of his analysis. For instance, in *The
Social System*, Parsons developed an analytical scheme which he termed 'pattern
variables'. The pattern variables putatively classified every form of social practice by reference to four abstract categories: specificity or diffuseness, neutrality
or affectivity (Parsons 1952: 84ff). Although Parsons went to great lengths to
describe the pattern variables in *The Social System*, the variables became redundant almost on completion of that work. In *Working Papers in the Theory of Action*,
published less than a year after *The Social System*, Parsons committed himself to
the so-called AGIL schema instead of the pattern variables.[5] Parsons was
heavily influenced by Robert Bales' 'interchange' model, which was designed to
describe the structure of all small-group interaction. Bales described the interchange model as involving adaptation to the environment (A), goal attainment
(G), group integration (I) and pattern-maintenance or latency (L). Through
Bales' interchange model, which Parsons called the 'AGIL' model after the first
letters of the four elements of the model, Parsons believed he could create a
general social theory which could be used at any analytical level from the institutional to the personal (Parsons *et al.* 1953: 63). The AGIL schema marks the
apotheosis of Parsons' formalism. From the early 1950s onwards, this schema is
employed to explain (but really only to formalise) everything.[6] Although his
middle to later periods were untenably formal, social norms remained central.
For instance, in the AGIL schema, Parsons explicitly prioritised pattern-maintenance or latency, the subsystem in which cultural norms are created. Although
pattern-maintenance is often described as the final moment of the interchange
model, Parsons himself regarded the pattern as being primary to the whole model.
'The first functional imperative, therefore, is "pattern-maintenance and tension
management" relative to the stability of the institutionalized value system' (Parsons
and Smelser 1956: 17). Parsons affirmed the priority of culture (and therefore
pattern-maintenance) elsewhere in his writings: 'I am a cultural determinist rather

than a social determinist' (Parsons 1966b: 113). However, there was a decisive change in the significance of these norms in his theory.

The maintenance of the system requires values but these values are no longer held in common. Social values have become institutional. Common norms no longer arise in the social relations between humans. They are the product of institutions, attaining an objectivity which transcends human agreement. Individuals no longer agree to abide by shared norms which mutually obligated them to each other. They merely internalise institutional ones:

> It is only by virtue of internalisation of institutionalized values that a genuine motivational integration of behaviour in the social structure takes place, that the 'deeper' layers of motivation become harnessed to the fulfil-ment of role-expectations.
>
> (Parsons 1952: 42)

As the statement demonstrates, the key question for Parsons has become the issue of how individuals are integrated into their social roles. This is possible insofar as individuals internalise these institutional values. Parsons emphasises the point repeatedly. Thus he asks: 'will the personalities developed within a social system, at whatever stage in the life cycle, "spontaneously" act in such ways as to fulfil the functional prerequisites of the social systems of which they are parts…?' (Parsons 1952: 31). The answer for Parsons is predictably that such personalities will be developed so long as individuals internalise the appropriate institutional values for their role:

> The primary structure of the human personality *as a system of action* is organ-ised about the internalization of *systems* of social objects which originate as the role-units of the successive series of social systems in which the indi-vidual has come to be integrated in the course of his life history. His personality structure is thus in sense a kind of 'mirror-image' of the social structures he has experienced.
>
> (Parsons and Bales 1955: 54)

Humans are no longer bound together in social relations directed towards common ends. Rather, individuals are structured by the roles which they fulfil in the social system. They internalise the appropriate values for these roles, making them the kind of individuals they become. The values which they internalise are no longer shared but merely institutional. In this way, the system is reproduced by the fulfilment of its needs.

For Parsons, individuals have to internalise institutional values. Significantly, he maintains that this process of internalisation is Freudian. Individuals absorb role norms privately. They create a superego for themselves which represses the ego and the id. Parsons' Freudianism leads him to reconsider 'the deeper layers of motivation' which render internalised norms obliging. It is important to see how this Freudianism differs from his earlier writing. In *The Structure of Social*

Action, the motivation for abiding by common norms was social; the mechanism of public honour and shame was paramount. Because they were held in common, these values were morally binding. In the earlier writing, the apparently private fact of guilt is given a sociological explanation. Personal guilt is a reflection of an individual's social relations to others. To act against shared values was to renege on the social relations to which individuals had committed themselves. These social processes fade from view after 1953 and internal Freudian guilt mechanisms become the central method by which adherence to institutional values is ensured. A decisive change has taken place in Parsons writing as individualism has become dominant. Individuals now internalise autonomous norms and ensure their own adherence to these norms through private psychological processes of personal guilt and shame.

The individualism of Parsons' middle and later period becomes particularly clear in his discussion of deviance. His analysis of the 'sick role' which he regards 'as a form of deviant behaviour' is particularly significant here (Parsons 1952: 477). Parsons does not mean that the sick are deviant in a pejorative sense but rather that their social position is structurally analogous with those individuals who resist social norms:

> The sick role is, as we have seen, in these terms a mechanism which in the first instance channels deviance so that the two most dangerous potentialities, namely, group formation and successful establishment of a claim to legitimacy, are avoided. The sick are tied up, not with other deviants to form a 'sub-culture' of the sick, but each with a group of the non-sick, his personal circle and above all, physicians. The sick thus become a statistical status class and are deprived of the possibility of forming a solidary collectivity.
>
> (Parsons 1952: 477)

The description seems to accord unproblematically with empirical reality. It is a common political strategy to isolate subversive individuals in order to prevent them from allying into a group. However, the sick role involves a contentious account of the origins of deviance. It implies that deviance arises according to a random distribution, just as pathologies emerge randomly in a human population. Deviants are a 'statistical status class'. At various points in the social system, individuals who cannot internalise the appropriate values rebel. Once they have mounted this personal rebellion, they are then able to ally with similarly mal-integrated persons. A subculture of deviance emerges once individuals have already independently arrived at the same inappropriate values. A subculture thus arises from the random co-ordination of individual actions. This account of group formation is at odds with the voluntary theory of action and reflects a new dualistic account of society. On the voluntary theory of action, deviant subcultures could never emerge from a myriad of private rebellions. Private rebellions would produce only random results. The existence of coherent deviant subcultures can be explained only by reference to the shared understandings which these groups develop and to which all group members orient themselves. As Parsons demonstrated in *The Structure of Social Action*, co-ordinated social action and the production of stable social relations can be understood only by reference to common norms. Humans must together come to agree on how they are to act even if they decide upon deviant action. Parsons' discussion of the sick role reverses his original position. Individual cases of deviancy arise automatically and the wider society must act to isolate these pathological individuals from each other before the random distribution can coalesce. The sick role demonstrates that, in his middle and later periods, Parsons has adopted the very dualistic ontology which he rejected in *The Structure of Social Action*. It envisages a society of independent individuals who privately internalise or fail to internalise institutional values.

In Parsons' later work, his basic theoretical position has changed. His ontology now consists of a social system, on the one hand, and the individual on the other. His problem of order is no longer the question of how people sustain their social relations with each other but how individuals fulfil certain roles to reproduce the social system. The randomness of individual action is avoided not by mutual agreement on common values but by the internalisation of institutional values by isolated individuals. Privately internalised institutional values are the critical bridge between society and the individual. They are the means by which the ontological divide between society and the individual is overcome. This internalisation of functionally necessary values guarantees social order. The dualistic ontology of Parsons' later work is condemned most effectively by his own criticisms of utilitarianism in *The Structure of Social Action*. There, he objected that in order to explain social order utilitarianism had to smuggle in an objective entity, the Leviathan, which contradicted the premises of this theory by obliterating human autonomy. In his later work, Parsons is guilty of exactly the same error. Here, the individual fulfils the functional needs of the system by internalising external norms. Social order is explained only at the expense of human autonomy, as Giddens rightly claims.

A re-consideration of Parsons' writing itself throws up some surprising revelations. Parsons is not the unremitting objectivist which he is purported to be. On the contrary, his early work constitutes a profound and rich vindication of the social ontology. *The Structure of Social Action* demonstrates the distinctive character of human social relations. It is only by recognising the obligatory and yet voluntary character of human interaction that sociologists can hope to understand society. Humans have to understand what their social relations involve but once they have mutually recognised these social relations and the actions they enjoin humans are obliged to act in coherent and predictable ways. Humans mutually sustain social order by binding themselves to shared understandings and collective ends. Yet, Parsons work also stands as a warning of how sociology confuses itself when it adopts a dualistic ontology. This work is an eloquent testament of the route which sociology should not take. In place of the rich analysis of human social relations, only deadening abstractions arising from a mechanical ontology of society and the individual are to be found in this work. The irony is that while contemporary social theorists like Giddens reject Parsons' objectivism, contemporary social theory has followed the route taken by Parsons in his middle and later periods.[7] It has fallen into the very dualism which characterised Parsons' structural-functionalist writings. The case of Anthony Giddens is particularly pertinent here.

Giddens' Structuration Theory

For Giddens, there is absolutely no connection between Parsons' structural-functionalism and structuration theory. Not only does Parsons unacceptably 'derogate the lay actor' but, according to Giddens, structuration theory is concerned with a sociological problem which differs entirely from Parsons' famous problem of order:

> The fundamental question of social theory, as I see it – the 'problem of order' conceived of in a way quite alien to Parson's formulation when he coined the phrase – is to explicate how the limitations of individual 'presence' are transcended by the 'stretching' of social relations across time and space.
>
> (Giddens 1995a: 35)

For Giddens, structuration theory is intended to explain how individuals can reproduce the social system through personal routines, even though there are gaps in time and space between the enactment of these routines. By contrast, Parsons' problem of order was concerned with the co-ordination of individual action through the adoption of common values. Since the social process which Giddens seeks to explain is different, he assumes that structuration theory and Parsonian functionalism are *ipso facto* incompatible. It is certainly true that Giddens' language is very different from Parsons'. Parsons never spoke about individual 'presences' or the 'stretching' of social relations. Yet, despite this linguistic divide and Giddens' confidence that the project of structuration theory is very different to that of functionalism, on closer inspection it is not at all clear that this is the case. For Giddens, the key problem for social theory is to explain why it is that individuals repeat their routines instead of randomly performing one practice one day, and another the next. Individual presence is stretched when individuals engage in these routines over long periods of time while other individuals often in other places and other times respond in similarly routine ways. Social actions and responses are effectively repeated time and time again – even though participants may not be co-present. Out of this routine repetition, the system is reproduced; a recognisable social order emerges. It is true that in *The Structure of Social Action* Parsons was unconcerned – at least explicitly – with institutional reproduction and the fulfilment of roles. His concern was with the co-ordination of human action towards collective goals. Yet, in his middle and later periods, he was explicitly interested in how individuals fulfilled certain roles to reproduce the institutions of which they were part. The Parsonian notion of role-fulfilment assumed routinised and repetitive social action. When individuals internalised the institutional norms for their role, they would perform actions which were appropriate to systemic reproduction. The functions of the system as a whole would be met because the individuals in a society would fulfil their roles appropriately. They would act routinely. The proper performance of roles at one point in the system would then interconnect with their fulfilment at another point to maintain the system as a whole. Thus, role-fulfilment at one point in time and space, interconnected with the activities of role-fulfilment elsewhere. Parsons did not talk about the stretching of individual presence but it was implicit in his account; the stretching of these individual presences in Giddens' lexicon corresponds to role-fulfilment in Parson's language. To stretch individual presences is to convert potentially random individual action into co-ordinated social activity by means of role-fulfilment. The stretching of individual presence refers to the process whereby individuals fulfil their roles routinely and thereby ensure the reproduction of the institution as a whole. When everyone acts routinely the entire social system is reproduced. Surprisingly, the 'problem of order' which Giddens tries to answer is not 'quite alien to Parsons' formulation' but, in fact, a repetition of Parsons' consideration of this problem in his middle and later periods; both try to explain how individuals perform certain repetitive and predictable roles to reproduce the social system as a whole. It is only the differences in language which persuade Giddens that he is doing anything different from Parsons. Significantly, it is not only the problem of order which Giddens shares with Parsons.[8]

One of the key ways in which Giddens divides himself from Parsons is to argue that Parsons ignores the lay actor. Giddens, by contrast, insists that his own structuration theory amounts to '*a recovery of the subject* without lapsing into subjectivism' (Giddens 1988: 44). Structuration theory begins with an account of the knowledgeable individual because 'an adequate account of human agency must, first, be connected to a theory of the acting subject' (Giddens 1988: 2). Elaborating on this recovery of the subject, Giddens postulates a 'stratification model' of personality where an individual has three levels of consciousness which play into their social actions: the unconscious, discursive consciousness and practical consciousness. The unconscious refers to those subconscious motivations described by Freud are recoverable only through psychoanalysis, while discursive consciousness refers to those aspects of knowledge of which individuals are self-consciously aware; they can describe discursively. However, while these levels of consciousness are important, for structuration theory practical consciousness is critical: 'The notion of *practical consciousness* I regard as a fundamental feature of the theory of structuration' (Giddens 1988: 2). He describes practical consciousness in the following way:

> The stocks of knowledge, in Schutz's term, or what I call the *mutual* knowledge employed by actors in the production of social encounters, are not usually known to those actors in an explicitly codified form; the practical character of such knowledge conforms to the Wittgensteinian formulation of

knowing a rule.

(Giddens 1988: 58, emphasis added)

The stocks of knowledge stored in practical consciousness are mutual or shared – they are common values and beliefs – but since they are assumed in social practice, they effectively become invisible. As Giddens notes, the success of Garfinkel's ethno-methodology and Goffman's interactionism lay in uncovering those shared meanings which have effectively disappeared from view because humans never experience a social interaction without already having assumed them (Giddens 1988: 80–1). The feeling of illumination which the writings of Goffman and Garfinkel provide at their best moments stems not from the fact that they have conducted a psychoanalytical uncovering of unconscious motivations but that they have revealed these common assumptions. Humans only note what is taken for granted when someone misjudges appropriate conduct or when a stranger does not know about these mutual stocks of knowledge; the purpose of Garfinkel's breaching experiments was to demonstrate their importance to social life. Giddens' notion of practical consciousness, which he also terms 'tacit knowledge' in order to capture the paradoxically known but unknown nature of this knowledge, refers to this very important area of human consciousness consisting of assumed shared meanings which humans employ in social interaction. Giddens would have clarified matters if he had used the term 'unacknowledged' understandings rather than tacit knowledge. Nevertheless, Giddens' notion of practical consciousness is a recognisable and important feature of human social life. Moreover, it is richer than Parsons' notion of common values because, drawing on Garfinkel and Goffman, it includes the unacknowledged aspect of those values.[9] However, Giddens' notion of practical consciousness refers ultimately to shared meanings which co-ordinate individual action. It refers to the meanings which humans assume in every interaction so that each knows what is expected of them and what they can expect from others. Possessing practical consciousness, the members of a society know what the significance of their actions is likely to be; they know how others will respond to what they do and vice versa. Practical consciousness ensures that individuals interact in mutually acceptable and predictable ways. Consequently, practical consciousness is compatible with Parsons' famous argument for the centrality of common values in social life in *The Structure of Social Action*. Giddens' practical consciousness refers to the common understandings on the basis of which individuals interact. On both accounts, people agree to pursue common ends and orient themselves to common values and understandings. Like Parsons, Giddens regards these shared meanings as essential to social life.

However, although practical consciousness is an important element in structuration theory, the decisive concept for Giddens is 'structure'. 'Structure' rather than practical consciousness finally ensures that individuals will act in a way which will stretch time–space presence to reproduce the social system. For Giddens, structure refers to rules and resources which exist only when they are employed in social practice (Giddens 1995a: 25). Giddens describes structure in Saussurean terms as 'a virtual order of differences' (Giddens 1988: 46) which is 'marked by the absence of the subject' (Giddens 1995a: 25). Saussure argued that *langue* consisted of a system of arbitrary signifiers (sounds) which were given meaning by not being other; the meaning of each signifier arose from its being different to all the other signifiers in that language. By a virtual order of difference, Giddens means that structure is a system of different elements (rules) each of which implies the others; each element exists only because it is different from all the others. Following the Saussurean analogy, structure, like *langue*, is essential to any social act but not known to the agent; it lacks independent existence. Nevertheless, virtual rules necessarily 'structure' individual acts: 'structure exists, as time–space presence, only in its instantiations in such practices and as memory traces orienting the conduct of knowledgeable human agents' (Giddens 1995a: 17). It is not easy to see what Giddens means when he says that structure is virtual. Indeed, at this point there seems to be a contradiction in his writing, for while he asserts that structure is virtual, he simultaneously describes it as 'memory traces'. Even though structure is only a trace in the memory, this phrase seems to suggest that individuals are at least partially aware of it. They know what the rules of structure in fact involve. Yet, at the same time, he insists that structure has some independent existence; it is marked by the absence of the subject. The status of structure is further problema-tised by its relations to practical consciousness. Practical consciousness is still apparently crucial to the way that structure will be operationalised, and Giddens insists that 'the application of semantic rules as interpretative schemes [structure] in actual contexts of interaction normally draws heavily upon tacit knowledge [practical consciousness]' (Giddens 1977b: 133). The mutual knowledge on which individuals knowingly draw informs the way that they will employ structure. Given Giddens' definition of structure, as a 'virtual order of differences', it is not at all clear how practical consciousness informs structure's application for, on Giddens' definition of it, structure precedes social practice just as *langue* precedes an act of *parole*. It has a virtual status so that it always structures practice prior to individual consciousness. Nevertheless, despite its problematic status, Giddens seems to be arguing that structure 'orients' individual conduct so that individuals act in recog-nisable and appropriate ways; just as when humans speak they always draw on a linguistic structure if they are not to talk gibberish. Structure patterns social action even though individuals are not aware of it. Significantly, structure has duality; it is the 'medium and outcome' of social action because social agents simultaneously reaffirm and reproduce the rules on which they draw in their actions. Giddens illustrates this 'duality of structure' by a favourite linguistic example:

> The duality of structure relates to the smallest item of day-to-day behaviour to attributes of far more inclusive social systems: when I utter a grammatical English sentence in casual conversation, I contribute to the reproduction of the English language as a whole.
>
> (Giddens 1988: 77)

Individuals necessarily draw on a linguistic structure – constituted by a set of Saussurian differences – when they speak and, thereby, unintentionally reproduce the entire linguistic system. Similarly, individuals reproduce the whole system of social rules, this absent set of differences, when they act.

In addition to the three different types of consciousness, Giddens argues that structuration theory involves three decisive levels of analysis: the system, structure and structuration. The system is ontologically separate from either structure or structuration and refers to the institutional realities of a society. Giddens himself emphasises the ontological separation of system and structure; one institutional, one conceptual. Indeed, in his 'de-coding' of functionalism, he criticised Parsons precisely because he did not make this ontological distinction between the social system, with its institutions, and structure as a set of virtual rules (Giddens 1977b: 112). Critically, Giddens himself does not maintain this separation. Giddens initially argues only for the 'duality of structure' where the virtual rules are the medium and outcome of practice. Yet, in the course of his discussions of the relationship between structure and system, it becomes clear that these rules are somehow automatically attached to the wider social system. There is a duality of system as well:

> One of the main propositions of structuration theory is that the rules and resources drawn upon in the production and reproduction of social action are at the same time the means of system reproduction (duality of structure).
>
> (Giddens 1995a: 19)

Individuals reproduce the English language as a whole because they draw on a structure (*langue*) which underlies language (*parole*). Similarly, when they perform a social practice they draw on an analogous structure (of social rules), thereby reproducing the social system as a whole. There is simultaneous duality of the objective system and structure. Structure inevitably connects the individual to the objective institutional social system, ensuring the latter's reproduction. Giddens does not justify the claim that there is not only a duality of structure but a duality of system as well, but this conflation is vital to structuration theory.[10] Structure ensures that individuals act in a way which is automatically compatible with that system. Thus, Giddens argues that 'structure forms personality and society simultaneously – but in neither case exhaustively' (Giddens 1988: 70) and that 'the constitution of agents and structures are not two independently given sets of phenomena, a dualism, but represent a duality' (Giddens 1995a: 25).[11] For Giddens, the individual reproduces the social system because the rules of structure which he instantiates in practice are necessarily compatible with the social system. Although he does not explain this relationship, individuals necessarily act in a way which is consistent with the system. In this way, the same ontological dualism which characterised Parsons' middle and later periods is detectable in structuration theory. There individuals internalised institutional values to ensure role-fulfilment and, thereby, systemic reproduction. Here, individuals instantiate structure to ensure routine practice, which similarly reproduces the system. Structure plays the vital bridging role between the individual and the system which institutional norms play in Parsons' work.

The parallel with Parsons is further affirmed in Giddens' discussion of the individual in structuration theory. Significantly, Giddens claims that the motivation for individuals to follow structure is private and internal. Individuals act in a way which is consistent with structure because they desire 'ontological security':

> Ordinary day-to-day life – in greater or less degree according to context and the vagaries of individual personality – involves an *ontological security* expressing an autonomy of bodily control within predictable routines. The psychological origins of ontological security are to be found in basic anxiety-controlling mechanisms…, hierarchically ordered as a components of personality.
>
> (Giddens 1995a: 50)

For Giddens, individuals subjectively sustain themselves as moral beings by submitting themselves to certain routines (informed by structure). To break those routines and ignore the rules of structure would not only produce social chaos but would also produce personal anxiety and breakdown. Consequently, in structuration theory, individuals are personally obliged to reproduce the system if they want to maintain their mental and emotional stability as individuals. The basic personal need for 'ontological security' conveniently serves the dual purpose of sustaining an individual's personality and the social system. This argument parallels Parsons' appeal to Freudian internalisation as an explanation of the adherence of individuals to institutional values. Individuals commit themselves to certain institutional routines because to do otherwise would be to undermine their own sense of selfhood. For Parsons, this induces guilt and shame and, for Giddens, anxiety and purposelessness. Both commit themselves to a dualistic ontology, proposing a similar connection between the individual and the system. For both theorists, systemic reproduction is ultimately explained by the internalisation of institutionalised norms.

The one area where there seems to be a significant divide between the two social theorists is on the issue of functional needs. Giddens explicitly rejects the notion that the system can have needs independently of the individuals who are part of it, while Parsons' structural-functionalism draws heavily upon this idea. Nevertheless, the basic ontological premises are the same.

By penetrating certain linguistic differences, a surprising affinity between Parsons' structural-functionalism and Giddens' structuration theory comes into view. The concepts of institutional values (structure), individual moral obligation (ontological security) and the social system are central to both theorists. Both explain the reproduction of the social system through the private internalisation of autonomous norms. For both theories, institutionalised values provide the crucial bridge between the agent and the system. Giddens himself provides some of the clearest evidence of this close connection:

Parsons understands action in relation to what he calls 'voluntarism' and has sought to reconcile the latter with a recognition of 'emergent properties' of social systems. The reconciliation is achieved through influence of normative values on two levels; as elements of personality and as core components of society. As 'internalised' in personality, values provide the motives or need-dispositions which impel the conduct of the actor; while on the level of the social system, as institutionalised norms, values form a moral consensus that serves to integrate the totality.

(Giddens 1988: 51–52)

In place of normative values which simultaneously form the core elements in individual personality and the social system, Giddens writes that structure ensures the reproduction of the system by creating routines which simultaneously produce 'ontological security' for the individual. Yet, the basic line of argument and the import of the concepts is the same. For both, individuals are bound to the social system by the internalisation of social norms which ensure that individuals act in a way that is compatible with the reproduction of the system and with their personal and psychological well-being. Both Parsons and Giddens promote a dualistic social ontology in which society consists of an objective system and isolated individuals; of structure and agency. This dualism is resolved by the private internalisation of functionally appropriate dispositions. Giddens has not so much transcended Parsons as reproduced the ontological dualism which is characteristic of much of his work.

Parsons' structural-functionalism operates with dualistic ontology. It comprehends society as a system which is reproduced by individuals, who fulfil their roles so long as each internalises appropriate institutional values. As Giddens rightly emphasises, Parsons' work from his middle and later periods is fatally compromised by this dualism. Assuming a divide between society and the individual, Parsons can only explain the maintenance of the system by derogating the lay actor. The system obliterates individual agency to functional need. In this way, Parsons stands as an example of a route which sociology should not take; he ignores social relations in favour of an abstract dualism. Ironically, this is exactly the route which Giddens and contemporary social theory more widely have taken. Yet, the recovery of Parsons work serves not merely the negative purpose of illuminating the shortcomings of ontological dualism; it does not simply instruct sociologists how not to proceed. It also suggests how this dualism might be overcome. Parsons' early work illustrates the actuality of human society; it prioritises social relations conducted on the basis of shared meanings. Indeed, he illustrates the analytic validity of this ontology with a rigour which has rarely been matched. Since contemporary social theory replicates the ontology of Parsons' structural-functionalism, understanding society in terms of structure and agency, it is important that the social ontology advocated in *The Structure of Social Action* is recognised. A recovery of Parsons' social ontology can be used to promote a new consensus in sociology today in which sociologists focus not on the problem of structure and agency but on human social relations. As Parsons demonstrated, these social relations, although dependent on human under-standing, are binding and obligatory. In social relations, humans bind themselves to each other. Humans are able to demand regular social conduct from each other even though this obligation arises only in their mutual recognition of it. Parsons' early work can be recovered as a rich resource for sociology today. This account of social reality fully recognises human agency but it also realises that humans are never free to do whatever they please; humans mutually constrain and enable each other. It recognises the distinctive nature of human social rela-tions. It can assist in superseding the dualistic hegemony in social theory today. Unfortunately, Giddens is unable to recognise the merits of Parsons' early work and it is perhaps for this reason that he unwittingly replicates Parsons' errors.

3 Structure, Habitus, Discourse

Structure

Giddens' structuration theory is characterised by ontological dualism but it is a dualism of a distinctive kind. For Giddens, the term 'structure' refers to a set of rules which bind the individual to the system to ensure its reproduction. Although the intellectual sources upon which Giddens draws are distinctive, this account of social reality is, in fact, widely replicated in contemporary social theory. A similar explanation of social reproduction is found among other sociologists who are not immediately associated with Giddens. For instance, Pierre Bourdieu's work involves a rich empirical critique of French society and, in particular, its class structure. His work attempts to describe the reproduction of class through central social institutions, such as the state, education and cultural taste. The consistent empiricism of Bourdieu's work and its active political engagement are absent from almost all of Giddens' sociological work. In Giddens' writings, and in particular in his structuration theory, there is no engagement with empirical social reality; nor is there any obvious political or critical perspective. Even in works like *The Class Structure of Advanced Societies* (1977a), Giddens lays out only an abstract theory of class analysis which attempts to synthesise Marxian and Weberian approaches. There is no consideration of how class distorts the educational system or imposes certain visceral tastes upon different groups. Similarly, although more grounded, there is little detailed empirical or historical material in either of the two volumes of his *A Contemporary Critique of Historical Materialism* (1981, 1985). It is true that in the mid-to late-1990s, with his 'Third Way' publications, Giddens has become overtly political, but these writings are manifestos not sociological monographs. Yet, although the style and concerns of Anthony Giddens are manifestly very different to Bourdieu's, in purely theoretical terms, both are compatible sociologists. The fundamental ontology of their work is similar; in both cases they appeal to rules – to structure in the conceptual sense – or, as Bourdieu calls it, the habitus, to explain systemic reproduction.

The underlying affinity between Bourdieu and Giddens, despite the differences between them, facilitates a more surprising theoretical rapprochement. In particular, although Giddens' liberalism is antithetical to Michel Foucault's radical critique of modernity, in a significant part of Foucault's writing, a similar commitment to an ontology of structure and agency is discernible. Although Foucault is concerned with the absolute oppressiveness of modernity, his explanation of how power courses through this society, crushing resistance, is ultimately very similar to Giddens' structuration theory. Both presume that social order is produced by individual conformity to certain autonomous social rules. In particular, while Giddens calls these rules 'structure', Foucault describes them as 'discourses' which impose themselves upon each historical era, ensuring appropriate conduct. Ontologically there is a surprising alliance between Giddens and Foucault which is concealed by an obvious political division. In spite of these differences, Giddens, Bourdieu and Foucault explain social reality by reference to a set of rules which impose upon individuals to ensure social order. Their work focuses upon the nature and operation of these rules. Structure, as a set of rules, binds the individual to institutional structures. Giddens, Bourdieu and Foucault are important examples of contemporary ontological dualism. In differing ways, they explain social reproduction by reference to structure, defined as conceptual templates, patterns or rules.

The Habitus

One of the central aims of Pierre Bourdieu's writings was to overcome the dualism between objectivism and subjectivism, exemplified in France by Lévi-Strauss and Sartre, respectively (Brubaker 1985: 746; Jenkins 1993: 18).[1] Bourdieu famously developed the concept of the habitus to overcome this impasse:

> These two moments, the subjectivist and the objectivist, stand in dialectical relationship. It is this dialectic of objectivity and subjectivity that the concept of the *habitus* is designed to capture and encapsulate.
>
> (Bourdieu 1988b: 782)

The habitus overcomes subject–object dualism by inscribing subjective, bodily actions with objective social force so that the most apparently subjective individual acts necessarily assume broader social significance. Individuals have agency but the kind of agency which they have is prescribed by the culture of which they are part. Following Lévi-Strauss, Bourdieu insisted that this culture cannot be understood in individualistic or voluntaristic ways. The culture forms a determinate framework in which any individual can act. Bourdieu calls this rigid cultural framework the habitus and he describes its interesting origins:

> The conditionings associated with a particular class of conditions of existence produce *habitus*, systems of durable, transposable dispositions, structured structures predisposed to function as structuring structures, that is, as principles which generate and organize practices and representation.
>
> (Bourdieu 1990a: 53; also 1977a: 78, 84, 85)[2]

The habitus comprises perceptual structures and embodied dispositions which organise the way individuals see the world and act in it. The habitus is derived directly from the socio-economic or structural position in which individuals find themselves: 'the cognitive structures which social agents implement in their practical knowledge of the social world are internalised, 'embodied' social structures' (Bourdieu 1984: 468). Individuals unconsciously internalise their objective social conditions, such as their economic class, so that they have the appropriate tastes and perform the appropriate practices for that social position: 'the principle of division into logical classes which organises the perception of the social world is itself the product of the internalisation of the division into social classes' (Bourdieu 1984: 170). Thus, Bourdieu argues that individuals demonstrate an *amor fati* (a love of destiny) (Bourdieu 1984: 244) wherein they automatically fulfil the appropriate role for their objective situation. The habitus facilitates the reproduction of social structure by imposing certain dispositions onto the individual.

Bourdieu argues that the tastes which the habitus produces are deeply inscribed into the very bodies of individuals. The tastes imposed by social class are not merely intellectual judgements but instinctive bodily reactions against those things which do not fit that class's habitus (Bourdieu 1984: 486, 478). Humans feel intense embarrassment and even nausea when confronted with social practices which do not fit their habitus. The habitus even moulds the human physique. In *Distinction* (1984), Bourdieu notes how the working class value functional clothing and food, making a cultural virtue out of an economic necessity. The economic position of the working class conditions them to view the elaborate habits of the bourgeoisie with visceral contempt. To indulge certain tastes would be physically repugnant to the working class. Elsewhere, Bourdieu describes the bowed deportment of Kabylian women, which physically denotes their political subordination in that society (Bourdieu 1979). Bourdieu's emphasis on the body is a useful antidote to the intellectualist emphasis of much social theory and his discussion of the physical manifestations of taste and of the symbolism of the body in social practice are illuminating. It is true that the way humans conduct themselves corporally is central to social life and that, in fact, bodily conduct has to become second nature to be successful. Humans have to act 'naturally' to be taken seriously as social actors. However, although Bourdieu is correct to highlight the centrality of the body to social life, his account of how the society inscribes itself on the human body is objectivist and determinist.[3] The habitus imposes certain conduct on individuals, who unknowingly embody this 'structuring structure'. Bourdieu's ontology is resolutely dualistic.

According to Bourdieu, the habitus operates within a wider institutional setting, which Bourdieu calls a 'field'.[4] A 'field' refers to the structure of social relations in which an individual is located. Bourdieu argues that 'to think in terms to a field is to think relationally' (Bourdieu and Wacquant 1992: 96), but it would be an error to think that Bourdieu refers here to social relations between humans. On the contrary, as far as Bourdieu is concerned, the field has an objective status very similar to Giddens' system:

> What exist in the social world are relations – not interactions between agents and intersubjective ties between individuals, but objective relations which exist 'independently of individual consciousness and will', as Marx said…In analytic terms a field may be defined as a network, or a configuration, of objective relations between positions.
>
> (Bourdieu and Wacquant 1992: 97)

Here, Bourdieu is explicit; he is not discussing the social relations between humans. The field refers to an alternative level of reality. In particular, it denotes the institutional structure of a society, consisting of a myriad of roles and the interconnection between these roles. Above all, in Bourdieu's work, the field refers to the class hierarchy of modern societies, itself a product of economic forces. Bourdieu's concept of the field is intended to enrich the concept of the habitus so that it becomes less static. In a field, groups struggle for supremacy and social distinctiveness. Superior groups try to monopolise certain cultural practices, while subordinate groups attempt to adopt these practices in order to subvert the status of their superior. By adopting the practice of superiors groups, subordinate groups undermine the distinction of superiors, thereby subverting the social hierarchy. The struggle for social distinction is an empirically verifiable process which Bourdieu usefully illuminates. Nevertheless, the field implies an objectivist account of social structure. The structure of social relations is independent from the individuals in the field. This structure pre-exists individuals and decisively determines the nature of any social struggle. Ultimately, individuals merely fulfil their already allotted position in the field. The habitus then imposes upon the individual in order to ensure that the individual acts in appropriate ways to reproduce this field. The habitus imposes certain forms of practice on individuals. Individual action is pre-directed towards certain forms of conduct which are appropriate for the social position which individuals occupy. The habitus is an important example of ontological dualism in contemporary social theory. The habitus is a set of cultural templates which imposes certain 'durable dispositions' upon the individual in order to reproduce the social structure or field. For Bourdieu, society consists of objective institutions, like class or the state on the one hand, and individuals on the other. These individuals are connected to the social institutions by means of the habitus. In this way, Bourdieu's reproduces the ontological dualism which is evident in the work of Giddens.

Discourse

Between the early 1960s and his premature death in the early 1980s, Michel Foucault produced an impressive corpus, whose originality goes some way to offset the frequent empirical lapses in his work. Foucault's work is an example of

Weber's useful aphorism that an ingenious error is often more illuminating than a prosaic truth (Weber 1961). Even when in manifest error, as for instance in his discussion of the Renaissance attitude to madness, Foucault's mistakes were unusual enough to be useful. Foucault attempted to illuminate the distinctive character of European modernity by reflecting upon its repressed aspects. He focused almost exclusively upon those social practices which were marginalised and excluded in public culture and discussion. By analysing madhouses, prisons, medical practices and sexuality, Foucault questioned the apparent 'normality' of modern existence. He sought to display the arbitrariness of modern normality. The analysis of the strange was intended to de-familiarise the commonplace (e.g. Baert 1998: 114–31). It is interesting that, although the second and third volumes of *The History of Sexuality* (Foucault 1986, 1990b) examined sexuality in classical Greek and Roman society, he had intended to write a history of child sexuality (including paedophilia) in the nineteenth century. However, this study of Greece and Rome was part of the same strategy of de-familiarising modernity. The alternative sexual mores of the Greeks and Romans provided a useful counterfoil to the sexual 'normality' of modernity.

For Foucault, history did not involve progress and, indeed, history had no intrinsic unity. The progressive unity of history was a product of the liberal social sciences, whose central role was to vindicate modernity. Foucault subscribed to a discontinuous historical ontology. History was traversed by ruptures which divided epochs from one another absolutely. Different epochs operated according to different principles, which transformed at decisive moments. Historians have to recognise these historical divides in order to avoid the error of interpreting one era according to the principles of another. Although the full significance of the term 'archaeology' will be discussed below, his use of this term to describe his method in his early writings clarifies this discontinuist reading of history. History consists of discrete but internally coherent chronological layers. The artefacts from each layer of the historical excavation must be understood in relation to each other but have absolutely no bearing upon the artefacts in another layer. Although Foucault denied that he was a structuralist, since he never claimed any universal underlying matrix to human culture, it is not difficult to see why he has often been so described. Like Saussure or Lévi-Strauss, he sought to uncover the underlying pattern which determined the forms which cultural phenomena have taken. He framed his studies around the critical historical breaks of 1650 (which denoted the end of the Renaissance and the beginning of the 'Classical' Age) and 1800 (which marked the start of the modern period), analysing these periods as self-referential cultural wholes. Foucault's archaeology might be described as a historical structuralism.

The central concept of his archaeological method was the 'discourse'. The discourse does not refer to the meaningful discussion between people. Indeed, discourses are not even necessarily official, institutional statements concerning the treatment of the insane, the criminal or the ill, although their existence can be detected in the archival record. Rather, the discourse refers to the principles of organisation by which empirical statements in particular fields are organised.

The discourse refers to more than empirical statements then. It consists of the underlying principles and rules which constitute the fields of inquiry in which these statements make sense. Foucault's discourses are transcendental categories which make the institutional reality of any historical period possible:

> I would like to show with precise examples that in analysing discourses themselves, one sees the loosening of the embrace, apparently so tight, of words and things, and the emergence of a group of rules proper to discursive practice. These rules define not the dumb existence of a reality, nor the canonical use of vocabulary, but the ordering of objects... Of course, discourses are composed of signs; but what they do is more than use these signs to designate things. It is this *more* that renders them irreducible to language (*langue*) and to speech. It is 'this' more that we must reveal and describe.
>
> (Foucault 1972: 48–49)

Although, of course, comprised of recognisable signs and symbols – words, phrases, terminology, formulae – discourses do not simply point to objects which already exist. Discourses are not ostensive. On the contrary, discourses are constitutive of the reality in which humans live, determining human perception and practice. Natural and social reality is constituted through discourses. Discourses create the reality which humans encounter in their everyday life. This is the 'more' with which Foucault was concerned. For Foucault, the liberal human sciences have failed because they have taken the objects constituted by discourses of modernity as somehow self-evident. They have assumed that madness, criminality and individuality are self-evident when these very entities are, in fact, the product of specific historical discourses. The fundamental victory of modernity was to establish the discourses which positioned the mad, the ill, the criminal and the sexual in those places which have now become so familiar that these objects have become concrete and unquestionable. Foucault does not want to analyse sexuality itself but the underlying rules which make modern sexuality what it is.

The centrality of the discourse to Foucault's critique of modernity is illuminated in the Preface of *The Order of Things* (1974a). There Foucault discusses Borges' satirical 'Chinese Encyclopaedia', which categorised animals as 'divided into: (a) belonging to the Emperor, (b) embalmed, (c) tame, (d) sucking pigs' and so on. According to Foucault, Borges' imaginary system of classification was germinal to his thinking about the human sciences:

> This book first arose out of a passage in Borges, out of the laughter that shattered, as I read the passage, all the familiar landmarks of my thought – *our* thought, the thought that bears the stamp of our age and our geography – breaking up all the ordered surfaces and all the planes with which we are accustomed to tame the wild profusion of existing things, and continuing

long afterwards to disturb and threaten with collapse our age-old distinction between the Same and the Other.

(Foucault 1974a: xv)

Each culture and each historical period has its own contingent discourses which order all the natural and social objects of any particular society. The very insanity of Borges' Chinese Encyclopaedia highlights the randomness of all classification systems, including the apparently rational modern one. The social and natural worlds are not in themselves ordered and regular – but wild profusions of diversity. The discourses of each culture bring a historically specific order to this profusion of no more objective value than dividing somethings from others on the basis that they are 'drawn with a very fine camelhair brush' (Foucault 1974a: xv). Although Foucault would not employ the same language, discourses constitute the fundamental codes of any culture pre-existing the definitions and terminologies which people in any historical period employ:

> I tried to explore scientific discourse not from the point of view of individuals who are speaking, nor from the point of view of the formal structures of what they are saying, but from the point of view of the rules that come into play in the very existence of such discourse.
>
> (Foucault 1974a: xiv)

Discourses are not only irreducible to human subjects but they determine what a subject can say or do. They are the basis of individual existence:

> Strangely enough, man – the study of whom is supposed by the naïve to be the oldest investigation since Socrates – is probably no more than a kind of rift in the order of things, or, in any case, a configuration whose outlines are determined by the new position he has so recently taken up in the field of knowledge…It is comforting, however, and a source of profound relief to think that man is only a recent invention, a figure not yet two centuries old, a new wrinkle in our knowledge and that he will disappear again as soon as that knowledge has discovered a new form.
>
> (Foucault 1974a: xxiii)

The individual whose existence and whose capabilities are imputed to be primordial is no more than the effect of a particular kind of classification system, of no more intrinsic worth than Borges's schema. When, in the future, the modern order of knowledge becomes a mere archaeological layer, the modern self will be similarly forgotten in a great historical divide. The individual subject is ultimately an effect of discourse.

Discourses are the codes out of which world-constituting knowledge arises but discourses do not simply have an epistemological function. They are also inherently political. In particular, drawing especially in his later work on Nietzsche's radical perspectivism, Foucault maintains that orders of knowledge are inseparable from regimes of power. The kinds of knowledge which emerge at any particular historical period facilitate the development of a specific political order. Foucault's point is partly Weberian. European modernity was substantially defined by the development of state bureaucracies whose principal role was to gather and store knowledge about the population over whom these emergent regimes ruled. Knowledge became a key tool of the state in manipulating its own population and Foucault has no doubt that knowledge operates in this instrumental way. His discussion of Bentham's panopticon in *Discipline and Punish* (1995) is only the most obvious example of this instrumental use of knowledge for political purposes. The panopticon was an edifice designed for the collation of knowledge about the criminals under its view. In knowing everything about its inmates, the prison had power over them.

Yet, the relationship between knowledge and power is closer than this. Power is constituted by knowledge. The kind of knowledge which is produced in any historical period does not merely record a social reality which already exists. Knowledge brings this social reality into being. The particular ways in which people and groups are defined in any age constitutes their very existence. His account of the 'Great Instauration of the insane in the Classical Age' provides a useful example of the way that knowledge constitutes a political order. In *Madness and Civilisation* (1977b), Foucault claims that during the Renaissance the insane were free to roam the country as a ship of fools. The insane were given individual freedom because they were looked upon as 'touched' by divinity. Their madness was not seen as the absence of reason but as the perception of an alternative level of reality. They were consequently employed as a means of communicating insights from another form of reality, which might be higher than the mundane world of the sane: 'In the Middle Ages until the Renaissance, man's dispute with madness was a dramatic debate in which he was confronted with the secret powers of the world' (Foucault 1977b: xii). With the constdruction of the Hopital Général in 1656 in Paris, the age of confinement had begun and the understanding of madness was transformed. No longer were the insane conduits of transcendent insights. They lived only in a world of illusions outside the cold realm of reason. His exaggerations about the Renaissance's view of insanity can be explained as an overzealous attempt to demonstrate a sustainable theoretical point. The social status of the insane in a society is not self-evident; the wider social and political regime interprets and reacts to their insanity in a particular way. The way they are understood and defined determines the kind of social beings which they actually are. Foucault emphasises the point with his analysis of the case of Pierre Riviere, who murdered his entire family in an apparently random psychopathic act (Foucault 1982b). Examining the letter which Pierre Riviere left explaining his actions, Foucault illustrates the way in which this apparently individualistic and random action reflected wider social understandings. The discourses which structured Riviere's life impelled him to perform these murders. Power does not merely use knowledge instrumentally. The very kind of regime which exists in any historical era is a product of the way that this particular society understands itself and its world. The political order is a product of knowledge.

Foucault eventually became dissatisfied with his archaeological method and in the early 1970s promoted a self-consciously Nietzschean methodology, which he termed 'genealogy' after Nietzsche's famous analysis of Judaeo-Christian morality. Foucault's shift to genealogy involves some significant transformations which certain commentators have taken to demonstrate a decisive break in his work (Smart 1983, 1985). In particular, the genealogical method emphasises conflict within contemporaneous orders of knowledge. In place of a single coherent episteme, genealogy emphasises the conflict between discourses:

> The forces operating in history are not controlled by destiny or regulative mechanisms, but respond to haphazard conflicts...Chance is not simply the drawing of lots, but raising the stakes in every attempt to master chance through the will to power.
>
> (Foucault 1977a: 154–55)

The emphasis on political struggle and conflict between different discourses, each envisaging a different regime of power, amounts to an important qualification of Foucault's archaeology, which was reductively monolithic (Merquior 1985: 61; McNay 1992: 43). Emphasising the conflict within different orders of knowledge, Foucault discusses power and its close link to those orders of knowledge more explicitly in his genealogical period. *Discipline and Punish* (1995) and *The History of Sexuality* (1986, 1990a, 1990b), which are the two chief examples of this later genealogical period, demonstrate this concern with internal conflict. Yet, despite these qualifications, there is continuity between Foucault's archaeological and genealogical periods. History still consists of radically incommensurable eras which are divided by untraversable diremptions: 'Genealogy does not pretend to go back to restore unbroken continuity that operates beyond the dispersion of forgotten things' (Foucault 1977a: 146). Genealogy, like archaeology, rejects the pursuit of all essences and origins and therefore any teleological account of historical progress. History is not a tale of the evolution of modernity but a counterfoil against which the contingency of modernity can be seen: 'History becomes "effective" to the degree that it introduces discontinuity into our very being... "Effective" history deprives the self of the reassuring stability of life and nature' (Foucault 1977a: 152–53). Genealogy is an effective form of history because by confronting modernity with alternative political orders it undermines modern assumptions:

> The purpose of history, guided by genealogy, is not to discover the roots of our identity but to commit itself to its dissipation. It does not seek to define our unique threshold of emergence, the homeland to which metaphysicians promise a return; it seeks to make visible all those discontinuities that cross us.
>
> (Foucault 1977a: 162)

In addition, genealogy also disparages any apparently humanistic appeal to the individual. Under genealogy, discourses are still sovereign:

> Emergence is always produced through a particular stage of forces...Consequently, no one is responsible for emergence; no one can glory in it, since it always occurs in the interstice. In a sense, only a single drama is ever played in this 'non-place', the endlessly repeated play of dominations...It establishes marks of its power and engraves memories on things and even within bodies.
>
> (Foucault 1977a: 148, 150)

Humans do not produce discourses. New discourses emerge independently in the gaps which emerge in the conflict of already existing ones. The discourses themselves provide their own logic of development. Having emerged independently of human intervention, the discourses then impose themselves not only on the natural world but on human beings themselves, structuring them in a way which is consistent with the discourse itself. With genealogy, Foucault's lexicon becomes more overtly Nietzschean and there is a greater emphasis on conflict but the central features of archaeology and genealogy are the same; this is a historical method which dismisses historical evolution and knowledgeable human agency. The members of any society are always already structured by the discourses under which they live before they can act in the world. Any agency they have is the product of these autonomous discourses, inscribed within their very persons (Philp 1985: 68; Sheridan 1980: 115; Dreyfus and Rabinow 1982: 104–05).

In the major part of his writing in both his archaeological and genealogical periods, Foucault presented a dualistic social theory. Discourses imposea themselves upon isolated individuals so that they acted in ways which produce and reproduce modern institutions. The enduring image of Foucault's work is Bentham's panopticon, in which prisoners were separated into private cells around a central observation tower which provided a total but unseen view of a prisoner's every moment (Foucault 1995: 200–09); the lone individual, on the one hand, and inexorable power, on the other. For Foucault, the panopticon symbolises a new social order. There are other important passages which overtly commit Foucault to this dualistic ontology where the individual stands against discourse. It has been widely noted that Foucault's critique of modernity necessarily assumes an alternative, liberating vision of human existence which provides a measure against which modernity's shortcomings can be judged (Philp 1985: 79; Taylor 1984: 173). Although Foucault might claim that he does not set up any standard by which modernity is judged, for that would be to produce just another discourse and therefore more oppression, in the interstices of his work an alternative, liberated social existence is fleetingly observable. Significantly, this vision is individualist. The liberation of which Foucault dreams is personal and immediate; it is unfettered fulfilment of personal desire. Foucault's existential ideal becomes apparent when he discusses the case of a cretinous peasant, called

Jouy, who was convicted for the sexual molestation of a number of local children in Lorraine in the nineteenth century (Foucault 1990a: 31–32). Foucault disparages this oppression of evidently innocent and free sexuality. Jouy, whose name is a homonym for 'joy' in French, represents the liberated and de-centred existence which Foucault regards as authentic. It is uncommitted and unrationalised expression, free of all discourse and institutional interference. Foucault's brief discussion of individual liberation from the tyranny of the discourse is important because he envisages a personal liberation. Individuals free themselves of the unifying shackles of the modern episteme and assert random and de-centred aspects of their character. This vision of liberation illuminates the underlying ontology of much of Foucault's work. For Foucault, individuals are oppressed or liberated singly; they submit to or occasionally evade monolithic discourses alone. On Foucault's account, humans establish social relations with each other. Compliance is imposed upon them from above. Foucault's ontology is dualistic, comprising objectivist structure in the form of discourses and isolated individuals who are constituted through the internalisation of these discourses: 'Foucault's non-dialogical conception of the individual leads to a false dichotomy between the individual and the social' (McNay 1992: 190).

Although the political and stylistic differences between them could hardly be greater, Foucault's work is traversed by an ontological dualism which is compatible with Giddens' structuration theory and Bourdieu's habitus. According to all three, individuals are integrated into the modern social system by means of an independent conceptual 'structure' which constitutes them as agents. Giddens' vision of this social order is more optimistic, for the individual is freer, but there is a close ontological affinity between all these theorists. Their writings are oriented around the twin poles of structure and agency. Giddens, Bourdieu and Foucault are prominent representatives of a wider hegemony in social theory. There is no doubting the importance of their contribution to sociology. The empirical work of Bourdieu and Foucault is particularly rich, inspiring new and innovative lines of research. More particularly, the ontological dualism which all three espouse seems unobjectionable. Their explanation of social order seems plausible and many academics have found it useful to draw upon the concepts of structure, habitus and discourse in their own work. Indeed, these concepts have become commonplace in the discipline today, referring to apparently self-evidently valid processes. It is unusual to find a work in sociology or related disciplines which does not draw on one or other of these concepts, thereby knowingly or not accepting the dualism which they imply. Nevertheless, despite their apparently self-evident strength, these concepts are deeply problematic. The dualism which Giddens, Bourdieu and Foucault promote must be exposed and rejected for it prevents any true understanding of social reality.

Rule-Individualism

Bourdieu and Foucault overtly give the habitus and discourse determinism over individuals. Habitus and discourse programme certain behaviours into individuals, independently of their understanding, so that individuals are channelled into recognisably similar forms of social practice. Individuals do not follow habitus or discourse but are determined by them. To use Parsons' phrase, 'the randomness of ends is overcome by the postulation of an external determinism', certain ingrained mental or bodily programmes pre-direct and co-ordinate individual action. Such an objectivism is explicit in the works of Foucault and Bourdieu but it is actually implicit in Giddens' work, despite his equivocations. Giddens' agents may technically be free to do otherwise but, for most of the time, agents merely follow the routines prescribed by a structure. Moreover, as Giddens himself emphasises, the virtual order of differences of which structure consists is 'marked by the absence of the subject' (Giddens 1995a: 25). Individuals are unaware of structure and it imposes on them unknowingly. At this decisive point in his structuration theory, Giddens reneges on the very individualism upon which he formally insists. He derogates the lay actor in favour of an abstract structure of rules. Although the theoretical possibility of random action is emphasised more strongly by Giddens, structuration theory in fact describes a model of systemic reproduction which draws him close to the determinism of the habitus or discourse. Systemic reproduction relies on individuals being oriented by structure independently of their knowledge.

This rule-deterministic account presents each of these theorists with very serious problems for it threatens to curtail, if not obliterate, human agency. Humans are no longer conscious and intentional beings; they are merely programmed to act in certain ways. They are not finally aware of the significance of their actions. Bourdieu seems to espouse this kind of view explicitly, suggesting the habitus is internalised by 'organisms (which one can, if one wishes, call individuals) lastingly subjected to the same conditionings, and hence placed in the same material conditions of existence' (Bourdieu 1977a: 85). For Bourdieu, humans become mere biological entities, on whom the habitus inscribes certain actions. It is notable that critics have rejected Bourdieu's habitus precisely because it seems to deny human agency in favour of a mechanistic account of human responses (e.g. Garnham and Williams 1980: 222; Gorder 1980: 344; Swartz 1977: 554; Wacquant 1987; 81; Brubaker 1985: 759). Despite Bourdieu's claim that the habitus enables 'agents to cope with unforeseen and ever-changing situations' (Bourdieu 1977a: 72), if his definition of the habitus is taken at its word, then it is difficult to see how individuals could respond flexibly to new situations. They are externally determined by a habitus which is the product of their economic position. The habitus imposes itself upon them 'willy-nilly' (Bourdieu 1977a: 79). On this account, social practices are determined by *a priori* rules, embodied unknowingly by social agents, and consequently individual flexibility and creativity are severely curtailed if not eliminated entirely. Individuals can never construct new strategies because the habitus has already determined their response to any situation. Moreover, since everyone in society has a habitus, individuals will never actually be faced with unforeseen and ever-changing situations, because everyone else, informed by their habitus, would simply go on repeating their social practices and reproducing their social relations. Giddens' concept of structure (despite his claims to the contrary) and Foucault's notion of discourse similarly deny agency. Both structure and discourse pre-form individual agency and they consequently rule out the possibility of individuals developing new practices. As long as Giddens, Bourdieu and Foucault retain an objectivist notion of rule-following, they obliterate human agency even against their own intentions. Humans do not consciously respond to situations which confront them. Their reactions are already programmed into them by prior rules.

Although it is possible to interpret these three theorists as promoting a rule-deterministic explanation, they also implicitly provide the means by which this objectivism can be avoided. There is a way of reading Giddens, Bourdieu and Foucault which interprets structure, habitus and discourse not as a set of codes which determine individual action but as rules which individuals only follow. This more open account of rule-following is particularly promoted by Giddens with his structuration theory. Individuals are not determined by structure but rather they knowingly instantiate it in practice. They know how to go on because they know how to apply structure in any particular situation by reference to practical consciousness. Individuals actively follow rules; they are not determined by them. An individualistic account of rule-following of this kind would certainly avoid the problems of rule-determinism by allowing individuals conscious agency. Structure exists but the way it is applied is the product of individual understanding. Bourdieu's annoyance at critics who fail to see the potential flexibility of the habitus suggests that he himself envisages the habitus in this way. For instance, when questioned by Loic Wacquant about the criticisms made about the determinism of his habitus, Bourdieu has simply denied this determinism:

> LW: You thus reject the deterministic schema sometimes attributed to you with the formula 'structures produce habitus, which determine practices, which produce structures'…; that is, the idea that position in structure directly determines social strategy.

> PB: Circular and mechanical models of this kind are precisely what the notion of habitus is designed to help us destroy.
> (Bourdieu and Wacquant 1992: 134)

Despite his often unfortunate descriptions of the habitus, Bourdieu evidently sees the habitus as allowing room for slippage, so the habitus constrains social action without finally determining it. Individuals have agency even under the habitus because they choose how to follow the habitus. It is harder to see any flexibility in Foucault's concept of discourse. However, Foucault does recognise that certain individuals such as the peasant Jouy exist outside discourse (Foucault 1990a: 32). Moreover, it is perhaps possible to infer a rule-following rather than rule-determinist account from his own critical position. Foucault regards modern discourses as absolutely determining. Yet, he believes that his own writing appears from outside this discourse and offers the possibility of overcoming the tyranny of modernity. If he personally is able to escape discourse, then it is logical to assume that other individuals are also capable of freeing themselves of it. This suggests that discourse does not determine individuals without their knowledge but that they, like Giddens' agent, choose to follow discourse. Foucault's later concept of 'governmentality' effectively confirms this point. Individuals themselves collude in their own oppression; they choose to follow the rules inscribed in discourse. Although Giddens, Bourdieu and Foucault formally commit themselves to rule-determinism to a greater or lesser extent, there is also at least implicitly in their work an individualistic rule-following account. Individuals are not determined by structure, habitus or discourse. They knowingly choose to follow certain rules. Such a rule-individualistic account is more plausible as it facilitates the possibility of individual agency. It allows individuals to develop new strategies and adopt new courses of action. It also seems more empirically defensible to claim that individuals follow rules rather than being determined by them. Such an account seems to accord recognisably with how social action is often described; an individual decides how he will act in the light of certain rules of conduct. Unfortunately, while avoiding determinism, this individualistic account of social action involves equally serious difficulties which invalidate the dualism of these theorists.

The problem is that the individualistic rule-following which Giddens, Bourdieu and Foucault sometimes advocate could never, in fact, produce co-ordinated social action. Individually internalised rules could never ensure the social conformity which these social theorists assume. If individuals merely choose to follow rules independently, then the structure, habitus and discourse would not order human agency at all. They would not produce routinised and predictable social action. Ultimately, structure, habitus and discourse would never in fact reproduce modern society in the way in which these theorists assume. Institutional reproduction simply could not occur on this account. The problem with this kind of rule-individualist account, which Giddens, Foucault and Bourdieu are ultimately forced to adopt, has been illustrated most famously by Ludwig Wittgenstein. In his later philosophy, Wittgenstein criticised the account of language promoted by philosophers like Russell and, indeed, Wittgenstein himself in the *Tractatus*. For them, language-use was determined by the existence of certain putatively prior and universal rules which individuals necessarily followed when they spoke. There was only one way in which an individual could follow a linguistic rule and the rule necessarily applied in all cases; an individual was effectively able to apply these rules independently of other language-users since their meaning was self-evident. Consequently, philosophy could understand language use by a purely logical analysis of it. This style of philosophy envisaged a rule-individualistic account of word use. The prime purpose of the *Philosophical Investigations* (Wittgenstein 1976) was to illustrate the fallacy of this approach to language-use. This work sought to demonstrate that the rule-individualistic accounts of positivist philosophy simply could not explain the very phenomenon which was under investigation; co-ordinated and comprehensible language use. The rules which positivist philosophy attempted to elucidate did not self-evidently direct individual action. On the contrary, the rules in themselves suggested no obvious course to the individual. Wittgenstein insisted that word usage could be explained only by reference to the specific social context in which it arose. For him, there were no prior rules which determined individual usage in every case. In different circumstances, language-users together agreed upon the meaning of words. These local agreements were binding in that particular context but they were not absolute and they were resolutely social; they had to be publicly recognised.

The essential argument against an individualistic account of rule-following is described in a famous paragraph in the *Philosophical Investigations* (1976) which has become known as the 'sceptical paradox' (Kripke 1982: 4):

> This was our paradox: no course of action could be determined by a rule, because every course of action can be made out to accord with the rules. The answer was: if everything can be made out to accord with the rule, then it can also be made out to conflict with it. And so there would be neither accord nor conflict here.
>
> (Wittgenstein 1976: §201)

As Kripke has emphasised, Wittgenstein's argument against rule-individualism is philosophical. His scepticism is hypothetical. In practice, it never occurs to anyone to question how to follow a rule. The description of the individual following rules independently seems to provide a convincing account of everyday life. This is instinctively what humans seem to do. Wittgenstein himself is fully aware of this. For instance, in paragraph 85, Wittgenstein admits that in certain circumstances it is self-evident how an individual should follow a rule. In this case, when there is no doubt how an individual should follow a rule, 'this is no longer a philosophical proposition, but an empirical one'. There are certain cases where philosophical objections become practically irrelevant and the activities of individuals can usefully be examined only in their empirical detail. Yet, even here, Wittgenstein makes a decisive critical proviso. Although it is empirically true that in certain cases the way to follow a rule seems to leave no doubt, at a philosophical level this is never the case. It is never in fact obvious how a rule should be followed. A course of action could always be envisaged which would conflict with the rule. In his later philosophy, Wittgenstein employs a number of examples to communicate the inadequacy of rule individualism: 'A rule stands there like a sign-post. – Does the sign-post leave no doubt open about the way I have to go?' (Wittgenstein 1976: §85). In the *Philosophical Investigations*, the use of the hyphen at the beginning of a sentence is significant. A large part of the *Philosophical Investigations* takes the form of a dialectic between Wittgenstein and an imaginary interlocutor who adopts precisely the kinds of philosophical positions which Wittgenstein wants to refute. The hyphen denotes Wittgenstein's replies to his imagined interlocutor or the interventions of the interlocutor to which Wittgenstein responds. Here the interlocutor gives a standard account of rule-following. Given the existence of a rule, it is self-evident what action is implied; it is obvious what the individual should do. Individuals follow rules, just as they follow a sign-post. Wittgenstein refutes this account. A sign-post in itself does not determine how a traveller should interpret it. It does not necessarily show the way to go: 'Does it show which direction I am to take when I have passed it; whether along the road or the footpath or cross-country?' (Wittgenstein 1976: §85). The sign-post itself has no determination over the way it is actually applied in practice. A series of individual travellers could interpret the sign in any number of ways. Car-drivers may use the sign to point them along a road which winds to a village, but for cross-country runners it might be a sign that they should now leave the road and head across the fields. For lovers, the sign-post may denote a meeting point. When humans follow a rule, the rule itself does not direct their action. It could theoretically be applied in an infinite number of ways.

Significantly, even those rules which seem utterly self-evident are subject to the sceptical paradox. According to Wittgenstein, even mathematics cannot be comprehended in rule-individualistic terms. Wittgenstein's interlocutor represents the position of positivist philosophy and, typically, insists upon a rule-individualist account of mathematics: 'But mathematical truth is independent of whether human beings know it or not!' (Wittgenstein 1976: 226). For Wittgenstein's interlocutor, individual mathematicians pursue a logic which self-evidently points them all in the same direction. Wittgenstein rejects this: 'Well, I could imagine, for instance, that people had a different calculus, or a technique which we should not call "calculating". But would it be *wrong*?' (Wittgenstein 1976: 226–27). Wittgenstein is not denying the validity of mathematics. Mathematics is not random but the sceptical paradox reveals that even in this sphere, where abstract logic seems to dominate and where, therefore, rule-following appears self-evident, shared human agreement is actually decisive. Logic in the end involves shared understanding. Mathematicians share certain pre-suppositions about what they are trying to do, from which their reasoning follows. Those pre-suppositions are not given by logic but actually precede the logical deduction which subsequently occurs (see Wittgenstein 1964). It could be theoretically possible to have a different type of mathematics in alternative circumstances and with alternative pre-suppositions. Even here, when an individualistic account of rule-following seems self-evident, predictable social action cannot be accounted for by reference to individual rule-following alone. It is *theoretically* possible that an individual could in any given case follow a rule in an alternative way. The sceptical paradox is radical and it demonstrates the logical incoherence of the concept of individual rule-following. If individuals genuinely followed a rule privately, there would be no coherent social practice. Any rule could be interpreted in an infinite numbers of ways. Consequently, the same rule could produce entirely different kinds of behaviour. Following a rule individualistically could theoretically lead not to coherent social practice but in fact to the most infinite range of acts.

A rule could be followed in an infinite number of ways. Yet, in reality, human action is typically regular and predictable; humans seem to follow rules routinely. Since human practice is predictable but a rule-individualist account is untenable, social action has to be explained by reference to some other process. Co-ordinated rule-following – predictable social action – is a fact, but the model of individualistic rule-following is inadequate to it. Individuals cannot follow rules alone if the co-ordination of social action is to be explained. There must be some other process or factor which explains how humans are for the most part able to go on in a predictable fashion. Famously, Wittgenstein claimed that co-ordinated rule-following could be understood only so long as philosophy recognised the centrality of 'forms of life' to human existence: 'What has to be accepted, the given, is – so one could say – *forms of life*' (Wittgenstein 1976: 226). The 'form of life' is a critical concept in Wittgenstein's later philosophy but it is not immediately obvious to what he is referring. Nevertheless, it is possible to infer the meaning of this concept from the way he uses it. For Wittgenstein, it is important to recognise the priority of the form of life; it precedes and underpins all subsequent practice. Wittgenstein tries to communicate the precedence of the form of life through a number of metaphors and at, this point, the meaning of the form of life begins to become clear. He describes the form of life as the point at which 'I have reached bedrock, and my spade is turned' (Wittgenstein 1976: §217) or at which 'here we strike rock bottom, that is we come down to conventions' (Wittgenstein 1989: 24). The form of life refers to 'conventions': to the public agreements on the basis of which humans in any particular society conduct themselves. It refers to the customs of a society. More broadly, the form of life could be defined as the common culture in which humans live in the anthropological sense; the forms of life refer to the shared understandings and the everyday practices of particular human groups. It is notable that while Wittgenstein made no reference either to Dilthey or Weber in his work, both employed the term 'life' to refer to shared culture. The interpretation seems to be confirmed elsewhere, such as when he emphasises the priority of the form of life in an exchange with his interlocutor.

> 'So you are saying that human agreement decides what is true and what is false?' – It is what human beings *say* that is true and false; and they agree in the *language* they use. That is not agreement in opinions but in form of life.
>
> (Wittgenstein 1976: §241)

Humans can disagree and they can dismiss each other's opinions as false, but such disagreement pre-supposes a prior agreement – in the form of life, as Wittgenstein calls it. In order to have a meaningful disagreement, humans must share basic understandings on the basis of which they interact with each other. They must understand themselves in terms of shared ideas in order that their disagreement has any significance. The form of life refers to the taken-for-granted assumptions on the basis of which any humans act. It is this fundamental agreement at the level of cultural pre-suppositions which allows humans to co-ordinate their actions. In any particular case, rule-following pre-supposes a form of life. Individuals are able to follow rules consistently because they are already embedded in a common culture which orients them to particular ends in the first place. In the light of this common culture, it becomes obvious how humans should act in certain situations. Individual rule-following pre-supposes a common culture which orients the individual to the particular ways of life in this group, ensuring that a rule which could be taken an infinite number of ways is in fact followed in only one way.

The priority of the form of life explains Wittgenstein's potentially misleading comments that 'I obey the rule *blindly*' (Wittgenstein 1976: §219) or that 'one does not feel that one has always got to wait upon the nod (the whisper) of the rule' (Wittgenstein 1976: §223). This has led certain commentators (e.g. McGinn) to interpret Wittgenstein as a individualist. Individuals learn to follow rules habitually and, consequently, no longer need to think about them (McGinn 1984: 200). McGinn claims that individuals ultimately internalise rules so well that they follow them automatically. It is understandable why McGinn should have interpreted Wittgenstein in this way but this interpretation runs against the entire tenor of the later philosophy. Wittgenstein is not returning to a modified individualist model in which individuals habitually rather than consciously follow rules. On the contrary, his comments about the instinctiveness of rule-following are intended to illuminate the importance of the form of life. So integrated are humans in their form of life that in any particular situation they simply act. They do not need to 'wait on a rule'. Their cultural pre-suppositions will automatically illuminate a course of action so that it seems as if they obey a rule instinctively and without thinking. They know what the sign-post means. The common culture, which is already assumed by the people in a form of life, creates the illusion that there is only one way to follow a rule and that individuals automatically converge on the same kinds of rule-following. Since humans always live in one form of life or another, it is easy for them to think that they follow rules individualistically. They forget the centrality of the form of life to their conduct because it is always there. So familiar do the shared understandings on the basis of which they conduct themselves become, that they disappear from view. They become mere background and only the rule and the individual remain until the sceptical paradox illuminates again the transcendental importance of the form of life. The form of life, unseen and assumed for the most part, determines how any rule will be taken by the individual. The individual, then, follows any rule in reference to the other humans in this form of life. In order to illustrate the point, Wittgenstein draws a useful distinction between meaning and interpretation: 'What one wishes to say is: "Every sign is capable of interpretation: but the *meaning* mustn't be capable of interpretation. It is the last interpretation' (Wittgenstein 1989: 34). Alone individuals can theoretically interpret rules in any number of ways and, indeed, the sceptical paradox demonstrates the philosophical significance of such a possibility. However, once established in a form of life, a sign is not open to interpretation. It has a meaning. Humans mutually agree to take it in a particular way and ultimately they do not then need to think about it any more. They simply act in reference to it. It means something to them. Indeed, to interpret the rule at this point rather than following it blindly would mean that the common cultural pre-suppositions were under threat. Humans in this form of life are unsure how it should be taken and they need to think how to apply the rule. Humans are able to co-ordinate-their practices-they follow rules-when they are integrated in a particular form of life. They have already developed certain shared understandings on the basis of which they act. Rule-following only appears self-evident to the individual in the light of this common culture.

Rule-following occurs in a form of life but it is important to recognise that, even then, rule-following is limited. In a form of life, humans can follow rules apparently automatically over a finite series of cases. In standard and constantly repeated situations, it is empirically obvious what to do (although philosophically there is always doubt). Beyond those cases, however, there is uncertainty. In the face of new circumstances, the rule will not suggest how individuals should act. The group will have to decide in these cases how it is appropriate to go on (Bloor 1983, 1997).[5] The empirical application of rules is always finite. These cases of uncertainty illuminate only the fundamental reality of even apparently self-evident rule-following. In every case, to follow a rule assumes shared understandings which suggest appropriate action. Rules seem decisive in this social context. This social context stabilises rules but it is a serious error to assume, as individualists do, that the application of a rule is self-evident. Only the form of life makes rule-following obvious and, even then, only in a limited number of cases.[6]

If individual action can be co-ordinated only if there is a public culture which establishes what constitutes rule-following, Giddens, Bourdieu and Foucault confront a problem. Structure, habitus and discourse, at best, assume a rule-individualist model; individuals knowingly follow the rules embodied in structure, habitus and discourse. Yet, if individuals followed structure, habitus and discourse individually in this way, the most diverse forms of social practice could follow. Structure would not ensure the reproduction of the system, habitus would not reproduce class and discourse would not produce the modern political regime. Individuals could apply structure in the most diverse and random ways. They could take apparently self-evident precepts wrongly. In order to explain the way that individuals are bound into regular and predictable practices which reproduce the social institutions of which they are part, Giddens, Bourdieu and Foucault all have to implicitly assume the existence of 'forms of life' in which individuals are already integrated. These forms of life suggest to the individual appropriate courses of action; indeed, certain types of conduct are expected and even demanded from others if a person is to take part in this particular culture. Structure, habitus and discourse presume prior shared understandings on the basis of which humans in modern societies interact. This shared culture co-ordinates individuals so that they act in predictable ways. Humans mutually establish and sustain appropriate forms of conduct in reference to each other. Modern society is not reproduced as individuals follow rules, but only insofar as the members of this society mutually sustain their social relations with each other, all agreeing to certain common forms of conduct. The decisive failure of these three theorists is that for the most part they ignore the specifically social aspect of human existence. The institutional reality of modern society is a vast and complex social network, at each point of which humans do not act in ways to reproduce the system by following rules, but by reference to their colleagues, their families, their friends and their associates. Humans sustain the extraordinary reality of modern society by reference to common understandings which bind them together. Despite their error of rule-individualism, the work of Giddens, Bourdieu and Foucault is not obsolete though. Not one of them is inexorably committed to this individualistic account of rule-following or to the dualistic ontology. Their work is not totally dominated by the model of structure and agency. On the contrary, each implicitly recognises the centrality of shared agreement to co-ordinated social action. All finally appeal to a social ontology. On this social ontology, social relations between humans are primary. It is possible to extract this genuinely sociological account of human interaction from their work. In this way, Giddens, Bourdieu and Foucault can be utilised to overcome social theory immanently.

Giddens' Practical Consciousness

In the work of Anthony Giddens, the concept of practical consciousness refers to the unacknowledged shared understandings upon which partners in social interaction necessarily draw. It is created mutually and leads to expectations about appropriate social conduct. Giddens sees a close link between this unacknowledged knowledge and Wittgenstein's later philosophy. In particular, Giddens believes that the application of practical consciousness in everyday life accords with Wittgenstein's descriptions of rule-following as knowing how to go on. As Porpora (1993) has noted, Giddens draws heavily on Winch's interpretation of Wittgenstein to develop his structuration theory. Consequently, a consideration of Winch's discussion of Wittgenstein usefully highlights the implications of Giddens' concept of practical consciousness. In perhaps the most famous line of *The Idea of a Social Science* (1977), Winch stated that: 'All behaviour which is meaningful (therefore all specifically human behaviour) is *ipso facto* rule-governed' (Winch 1977: 52). As the discussions in the rest of the book demonstrate, rule-governed behaviour and meaningful behaviour are synonymous for Winch because meaningful behaviour refers to those activities which others understand as appropriate and, therefore, rule-following. An activity follows a rule when it has some meaning in a particular social context; it is has an intention which is discernible to others in this form of life. Crucially, rule-following is determined by the reactions of other individuals in a form of life: 'One has to take account not only of actions whose behaviour is in question as a candidate for a category of rule-following, but also the *reactions of other people* to what he does' (Winch 1977: 30). To follow a rule and, therefore, to act appropriately in social life is not to apply a formula individually but to perform acts that others can understand.[7] Highlighting the fact that by 'rule-governed' Winch means social practices based on common understandings, Winch strongly opposes Oakeshott's notion of habits where individuals simply perform certain social practices instinctively and, therefore, mechanically (Winch 1977: 62). Winch does not deny that individuals sometimes act in a way that is 'habitual' – they do not self-consciously think what they are doing – but Winch's objection to Oakeshott is that the latter's reduction of human practice to habit threatens to efface the inevitably meaningful nature of social practice. Although certain habitual practices do not involve an explicit interpretation in themselves, these habits do have some meaning in the social context in which humans resort to them. Others understand them. Human habits – as opposed to the conditioning of animals – always involves a meaningful dimension even if the act of explicit interpretation seems to be absent on a particular occasion. Shared understandings are crucial to the determination of any practice. When an act is understood by both the perpetrator and the recipients in the same way, it follows a rule.

Practical consciousness refers to the shared understandings on the basis of which humans interact. For the most part, humans take these understandings for granted and simply act habitually, but even then their actions 'follow a rule' insofar as a meaning can be imputed to them by the other members of that person's group. Human social relations are decisive to every individual action. On the account promoted by practical consciousness, sociologists need to focus on the social relations between humans in which each sustains the actions of the other. In point of fact, Giddens gives no empirical example of practical consciousness at work, although it is implied in his discussion of Garfinkel and Goffman. There, at least, he begins to recognise the dynamism of social interaction. However, it is possible to develop an account of institutional reality from practical consciousness. Humans are always embedded in social relations and these social relations form complex and powerful networks, which comprise the institutional reality of modern society. At every point, these relations are mutually maintained and enforced by humans in reference to common understandings. On this ontology, the system is reproduced not by individuals being determined by or following structure, but by humans in social relations mutually sustaining forms of practice by reference to shared understandings. A social ontology is implicit in Giddens' structuration theory but it is obscured by his commitment to structure and agency. Giddens fleetingly recognises the analytical efficacy of this ontology but, for the most part, he fails to apply it. He favours a dualistic account of social reality where the individual reproduces institutional structures by following private routines directed by virtual rules. Yet in every case practical consciousness is decisive, for it is the basis on which social relations and therefore social institutions are sustained.

Bourdieu's 'Practical Theory'

Despite the dualism of the habitus, Bourdieu, like Giddens, is able to redeem himself; there is a second strand in Bourdieu's writing which lucidly describes a social ontology.[8] In the opening pages of the *Outline* (1977a), Bourdieu argues that the anthropologist's peculiar position as a (putatively) impartial observer who is an outsider to native social processes has had a nefarious effect on the social sciences:

> So long as he remains unaware of the limits inherent in his point of view on the object, the anthropologist is condemned to adopt unwittingly for his own use the representation of action which is forced on agents or groups when they lack practical mastery of a highly valued competence and have to provide themselves with an explicit and at least semi-formalized substitute for it in the form of a *repertoire of rules*, or of what sociologists consider, at best, as a 'role', i.e. a predetermined set of discourses and actions appropriate to a particular 'stage-part'.
>
> (Bourdieu 1977a: 2)

For Bourdieu, the 'objective' and external position, which the social scientist adopts, ensures that the social life under study is misrepresented. Since anthropologists and other social scientists are outsiders to the social realities which they are studying, they invariably construct maps, models and rules by which they orient themselves around this strange cultural landscape. The anthropologist 'compensates for his lack of practical mastery, the prerogative of the native by the use of a model of all possible routes' (Bourdieu 1977a: 2). The anthropologist then takes this map only of use and interest to the outsider in the first place as evidence for the existence of an objective system of rules which imposes itself remorselessly on social interaction. In positing the existence of inexorable rules, anthropologists have not gained an insight into the way individuals actively and knowingly engage in everyday interactions with the skill of virtuosos (Bourdieu 1977a: 79). They have merely imposed their own curious and contemplative relation to that social life onto native practices. Since they, as visiting intellectuals, have to think of social life in terms of rules (because they do not know it properly) they assume that native agents share this curious intellectualising position.

For Bourdieu, social agents are 'virtuosos' (1977a: 79) who do not follow abstract social principles but who know their culture so well that they can elaborate and improvise upon the themes which it provides and in the light of their relations with others. Bourdieu describes social actors as having a 'sense of the game', using football and tennis players as examples of this virtuosic sense. These players do not apply *a priori* principles to their play – only beginners need to do that. In the face of the diverse situations which arise, they have an instinctive understanding of what is appropriate. They know when they should run to the net because they are familiar with what courses of action this form of life would allow (1992: 19, 120–21; 1990b: 62; 1990a: 66–67, 81; 1988: 783). It is important not to think in individual terms here. The 'sense of the game' is not the internal property of the individual. It refers ultimately to a sense of what others in this culture will regard as tolerable, given shared understandings. Players learn appropriate and acceptable moves even in the face of unforeseen circumstances from their intimate familiarity with the social expectations of how players are supposed to conduct themselves. Ultimately, they respond to any situation by automatic reference to others players with whom they have social contact. Bourdieu's discussion of honour among the Kabyle highlights this inter-subjective sense of the game (against individualistic rule-following):

> The driving of the whole mechanism is not some abstract principle (the principle of isotimy, equality in honour), still less the set of *rules* which can be derived from it but the sense of honour, a disposition inculcated in earlier years of life and constantly reinforced by *calls to order from the group*.
>
> (Bourdieu 1977a: 14–15, second emphasis added)

Kabylian men's sense of honour is a shifting agreement established and transformed by Kabylian men themselves. Individuals do not solipsistically consult *a priori* rules which then determine their action independently. Rather members of groups act according to a sense of practice which is established and judged by the group. The final determination of correct action is not whether one rigorously followed an *a priori* rule but rather whether one's actions are interpreted as appropriate and proper by others. Others – the group – decide whether an action is acceptable or sanctionable given their shared sense of honour; they call those individuals to order who have acted against this socially agreed sense of honour. The same emphasis on intersubjective virtuosity is highlighted in Bourdieu's critique of structuralist accounts of gift exchange:

> All experience of practice contradicts these paradoxes, and affirms that cycles of reciprocity are not the irresistible gearing of obligatory practice found only in ancient tragedy: a gift may remain unrequited, if it meets with ingratitude: it may be spurned as an insult.
>
> (Bourdieu 1977a: 9)

Bourdieu rejects Lévi-Strauss' formulaic analysis in which negative and positive exchanges inevitably negate each other in corresponding rounds of exchange. Rather than merely enacting an already established system of exchange by the following of rules, individuals re-negotiate their relations with others by manipulating common understandings about gift exchange in their favour. Social action is not determined by objective rules but developed by reference to the social relations in which any human is embedded. Consequently, as appropriate action is informed by group agreement, which is only a negotiated and temporary settlement; there is an openness to practice:

> If practices had as their principle the generative principle which has to be constructed in order to account for them, that is, a set of independent and coherent axioms, then the practices produced according to perfectly conscious generative rules would be stripped of everything that defines them distinctively as practices, that is, the uncertainty and 'fuzziness' resulting from the fact that they have as their principle not a set of conscious, constant rules, but practical schemes...
>
> (Bourdieu 1990a: 12)[9]

The term 'fuzziness' deliberately refers to Wittgenstein's critique of rule-individualism. Since rules are always the product of public understanding, they are not determinate. In the future, and in the face of new situations, rules can always be followed differently. The application of rules is not determined by their intrinsic logic, as Bourdieu's habitus describes, but by social agreement in the form of life in which people exist. Consequently, group members may be able to justify certain actions to the group which are not, in fact, 'given' by the rules but are recognised by the group as appropriate. In this way, the commonly held sense of honour might change. However, while under 'practical theory' rules do not close action down, the fact that practices have to be continually referred to the informal tribunal of the group means that individuals can certainly not do anything they like. They are constrained by others. Since humans learn how to act from others (rather than being imposed upon by an objective structure as the habitus suggests), their repertoire of what they can do is circumscribed by a particular cultural horizon. That horizon is certainly broad and 'fuzzy' but there is a limit to imaginable action within it because individuals can only decide upon courses of action learned from others. Humans can never invent a purely individualistic and asocial act. Under practical theory, humans act in the context of social relations with others, who mutually demand from each other appropriate forms of conduct. Individuals are not determined by rules; nor do they follow rules alone.

Bourdieu's 'practical theory' promotes a social ontology. In the opening pages of the *Outline* (1977a), Bourdieu rejects ontological dualism; society cannot be understood in terms of structure and agency. In place of these rules which direct isolated individuals, Bourdieu's 'practical theory' highlights social relations between humans conducted on the basis of shared understandings. Society does not consist of a synchronic map which imposes itself upon the individual. By replacing structure and agency with social relations, Bourdieu has overcome the dualism of conventional social theory. On this 'practical theory', there is no longer the individual and society, the subject and the object, but only social interaction between humans on the basis of shared understandings. The predictability of human action is a product of the fact that it always takes place within this social context and is always oriented to others. Class is not reproduced because individuals or organisms have absorbed a habitus but insofar as humans sustain particular kinds of relations with each other by adopting distinctive shared practices. In this way, humans maintain their own 'class' groupings by excluding others. The common cultures and exclusive groupings which Bourdieu analyses with great interest are, in fact, the product of social relations. They are explicable in terms of his practical theory.

Foucault's Power

Although Foucault is the most radical dualist of the three theorists, in the end he too must confront the weakness of his position. The discourse has absolute power over the individual. Yet, Foucault is forced most obviously into self-refutation when he considers the problem of historic change. In trying to explain the transformation of one order of knowledge into another, he invalidates his own definition of discourse. Significantly, at this point, he has to replace his ontological dualism with a social ontology. He has to evoke the very social relations which he formally ignored in order to sustain his empirical explanation of social change. This self-refutation is most obvious in *Discipline and Punish* (1995) when he describes the transformation from the torture of criminals in the early modern period to their confinement in the nineteenth century. The quartering of Damiens in 1757 for his attempt at regicide exemplifies the penal strategy of the early modern period. Damiens offended against the king's person itself with his treasonous attempted regicide and his punishment was a symbolic act of revenge. Foucault notes that by the beginning of the nineteenth century public executions all but disappeared and he successfully illuminates the alternative political regime in which the prison rather than the public execution became the favoured method of punishment. In doing so, Foucault supposedly juxtaposes opposing discursive formations. Yet, he also posits a mechanism by which one discourse of punishment was transformed into another. For instance, in his discussion of Damiens' execution, he notes that, although the crime which he committed was publicly condemned, the sight of his immolation inspired pity among the gathered assemblage. The purpose of the public execution was to demonstrate the power of the monarch over his subjects but, in the end, it threatened that very absolutism. These public gatherings, stirred by the extreme sights which they witnessed, often provided a very effective site of public protest and social disturbance (Foucault 1995: 61). Indeed, the condemned could exploit the event to impugn the monarch and the wider political system rather than exemplify its unyielding authority: 'If the crowd gathered round the scaffold, it was not simply to witness the sufferings of the condemned man or to excite the anger of the executioner: it was also to hear an individual who had nothing more to lose, curse the judge, the laws, the government and religion' (Foucault 1995: 60). The criminal could become 'a hero by the sheer extent of his widely advertised crimes' (Foucault 1995: 67). In the light of the potential subversiveness of the public execution, the new penal system of modernity did not necessarily represent a more humane form of punishment. It was simply a more expedient system of social control; the prison system eliminated the possibility of public protest. The account of the discursive transformation which Foucault provides in *Discipline and Punish* (1995) is cogent and is empirically verifiable; there is documentary evidence that precisely the kinds of discussion which Foucault describes did in fact occur. The problem is that his description of penal reform is incompatible with his formal definition of discourses. Discourses structure the world and indeed human consciousness itself. Social change does not, on this ontology, involve human understanding or political negotiation. The possibility of change is given logically by the gaps which appear between existing discourses. Yet, Foucault's own explanation of the rise of the modern penal system explicitly involves reference to the understandings and interventions of certain social groups. The state bureaucracy, with its *noblesse de robe*, and the monarchs recognised that the public execution was a liability. Consequently, they transformed the system of punishment. Crucially, these groups self-consciously developed new 'discourses' about crime in response to their specific political needs, which they fully recognised. The discourse of crime did not operate autonomously. New interpretations of crime and criminals were knowingly mobilised by these bureaucrats to transform political relations between citizens and state. The new form of punishment involved a dramatic transformation in the relationship between the state, the criminal and, in fact, the population as a whole. This transformation was precipitated actively by bureaucrats but its final success was only possible insofar as the population as a whole and the criminals themselves understood the significance of these new forms of punishment. The population itself had to recognise and accept kind of conduct which was expected of them; they had to understand and accept new forms of state authority and the punishment that they could expect if they transgressed against it. In order to explain social change, Foucault himself has to introduce a social ontology into the heart of his model. He explains social change by reference to the way particular political elites were able to transform their relations with subordinate groups by reference to new shared understandings. In every case, humans had to understand what these new relations actually involved and, out of these social relations, the grand regimes of power emerged. The concept of the discourse is redundant here. Discourses have no autonomous status; they do not impose upon individuals. At most, the concept of discourse can refer broadly to the common cultural pre-suppositions or understandings on the basis of which humans interact in any particular historical era. Power cannot be comprehended in terms of independent discourses which merely impose upon the individual. Power cannot be understood without taking into account they way humans actually conceive of their relationships to each other.

In his later work, Foucault elaborates further on this account of power, which is implicit in *Discipline and Punish* (1995). Foucault no longer suggests that discourses impress themselves on the individual from above. Power seeps unseen into every part of the social formation. Power is capillary; it arises out of the most insignificant social relations. A regime's power does not derive from its unassailable distance. On the contrary, a regime is powerful when all these social networks mesh together to support each other to ensure universal conformity:

> For let us not deceive ourselves; if we speak of the structures or the mechanisms of power, it is only insofar as we suppose that certain persons exercise power over others. The term 'power' designates relations between partners.
>
> (Foucault 1982a: 217)

Power does not impose upon individuals from outside. Rather, subordination and super-ordination arise out of interactions in which the partners are active participants. Power operates as the partners in social relations mutually create the hierarchy in which they consent to live. The political regime as a whole arises from all these apparently trivial and everyday moments of consent and compliance. Power does not deny human agency but, on the contrary, relies absolutely upon it:

> When one defines the exercise of power as a mode of action upon the actions of others, when one characterises these actions by the government of men by other men – in the broadest sense of the term – one includes one important element: freedom. Power is exercised only over free subjects, and only insofar as they are free.
>
> (Foucault 1982a: 221)

In contrast to Foucault's discussion of discourses, here power exists only by virtue of human agency. It is important that this agency is not interpreted in individual terms. The human agency out of which power arises is decisively shared; it is a product of their social relations in which each mutually empowers the other. In the first volume of the *History of Sexuality* (1990a), Foucault elaborates upon this interactive account of power. 'Power is not something which is acquired, seized or shared' (Foucault 1990a: 94); power is not a thing. Power exists only in and through human social relations; it appears 'in the machinery of production, in families, limited groups and institutions' (Foucault 1990a: 94). Crucially, Foucault insists that 'power relations are both intentional and non-subjective' (Foucault 1990a: 94), directed at 'a series of aims and objectives' (Foucault 1990a: 95). At first sight, the claim that these relations are intentional and yet non-subjective seems contradictory. It is more usual to think of intentions as arising in individual consciousness and, yet, Foucault seems to be claiming that intentions are objective; they do not arise from individual consciousness. In this way, Foucault seems to have returned to a dualistic ontology. Once again discourse merely imposes objectively upon the individual. Individuals orient themselves to intentions which are not their own but which are presumably the product of discourses. In fact, this is a misperception. Foucault emphasises that intentions are non-subjective because he wants to avoid any relapse into individualistic liberalism. Power relations do not arise by individuals personally considering their interests, but this does not mean that power is an objective force independent of human agency. Social relations are constituted by reference to the common understandings which those engaged in them have of them. The intentions here are shared. They do not arise privately but are developed in 'families, limited groups and institutions'. Power emerges out of social relations conducted on the basis of shared understandings and power is inseparable from these social relations. Power emerges in social interactions and operates through social relations. On this account, power is not an autonomous institutional force which presses down upon the individual, but arises out of the social relations between people. Power operates only through human consciousness, for the way humans understands themselves in a particular society will determine the kind of power relations which already exist for them. Power is dependent upon how people in that society understand themselves. Thus, when crime and punishment begin to be understood in different ways, when they are no longer personal acts of insurrection and revenge against a monarch but the product of irrationality against new institutions, the criminal became a different entity. The social relations between the criminal and the state changed. The new description of the criminal invokes a new social relationship between the society and the deviant. Above all, since power arises through conscious human activity, it is also open to subversion and to resistance. A political order is always open to transformation:

> In effect, between a relationship of power and a strategy of struggle there is a reciprocal appeal, a perpetual linking and a perpetual reversal. At every moment the relationship of power may become a confrontation between two adversaries.
>
> (Foucault 1982a: 226)

Foucault's discussion of power undermines the dualistic ontology which underpins his concept of the discourse. The discussion of power presumes a social ontology. On this account of power, the development of the carceral society described in *Discipline and Punish* (1995) becomes explicable. The social change involves the development of new social relations and new practices as bureaucrats and the population mutually begin to understand themselves and to interact with each other differently. Power is certainly a feature of social relations but, like those relations, it does not exist independently of the way humans understand it. Power cannot be explained without reference to the way that humans actually conceive of themselves and their relation to others. In this way, Foucault's discussion of power decisively rebuts the discourse, for that concept is explicitly aimed at elucidating the hidden codes which direct public discussions independently of understanding. The discourse refers to the 'more' which underpins all social action. Foucault's later account of power demonstrates that there is no more to society than social relations conducted on the basis of shared meanings. Nor do sociologists need to refer to anything more. These social relations can in and of themselves explain the grand institutional reality.

Practical Consciousness, Practice, Power

The reproduction of modern society cannot be explained by reference to rules which individuals follow, as Giddens, Bourdieu and Foucault sometimes assume; the ontology of structure and agency is inadequate to it. On a rule-individualist account, regular social practice remains mysterious, for, unless individuals are determined by rules, they could follow the rules in the most diverse ways. In fact, humans engage in regular social practice because they are already bound into social relations which suggests appropriate action in any particular situation. Together, mutually deferring to each other, humans sustain predictable social practices over time. In this way, humans are able to sustain the largest and most complex institutions of modern society. This social ontology avoids the dangers of objectivism and individualism. It explains how social institutions can persist over time without in any way appealing to objective factors which merely impose upon the individual, but it also prevents the individual from merely doing what they please. At each point, humans mutually constrain – and empower – each other. Institutions persist so long as the humans who are part of them mutually sustain their social relations and they change as humans transform their social relations with each other. Although, for the most part, Giddens, Bourdieu and Foucault ignore the social ontology in favour of a dualistic one of structure and agency, this ontology, nevertheless, finds expression in their writing. In the works of Giddens, it is present in his concept of practical consciousness. In Bourdieu, it is represented by his emphasis on practice; and, in Foucault, the social ontology appears in his later definition of power. These three concepts, practical consciousness, practice and power, can be used to overcome the unfortunate dualism implicit in the rest of their work. In contemporary social theory more widely, these three concepts should become the shared terms on the basis of which sociologists carry out their research. These terms, practical consciousness, practical theory and power, should replace the contemporary totems, structure, habitus and discourse. As long as these false gods remain central to social theory, the dualistic hegemony will persist.

4   The Reality of Realism

Giddens, Bourdieu and Foucault each conceive of social reality as a dualism of rules which individuals follow to ensure social order. Their work, for the most part, focuses upon the nature and operation of these rules. Yet, ontological dualism is to be found much more widely in contemporary social theory, although the form which it takes is slightly different. Typically, the focus is on how 'real' social institutions confront the individual. Structure no longer refers to the rules which direct action but to institutions; it refers to the objective social reality of state bureaucracies, class hierarchies and economic systems. Structure no longer refers to conceptual phenomena but to real ones. In fact, there is a close affinity between those theorists, like Giddens *et al.*, who define structure as a set of rules and other theorists who use the term to refer to objective institutional orders because, as the examination of Giddens, Bourdieu and Foucault showed, the purpose of structure as a set of rules was always to reproduce structure as an institutional order. Nevertheless, in contemporary sociology, the concept of structure is frequently used to refer to objective institutional realities alone. In this case, structure and agency refer to the divide between the individual, on the one hand, and objective social institutions, on the other. Lash, Urry and Hall have employed the term 'structure' in exactly this way. However, in contemporary social theory, this ontological definition of structure is best represented by realism and particularly by Roy Bhaskar (see also Archer 1995; A. Sayer 1992; Outhwaite 1987; Keat and Urry 1982; Savage *et al.* 1992; Porpora 1993; Gimenez 1999). However, other important contemporary theorists have adopted a realist ontology, even though they never formally describe themselves by this term. Above all, although the parallel is rarely drawn, Jürgen Habermas adopts a very similar position to Bhaskar and, indeed, once the terminological differences between the two philosophers is overcome, their theoretical proximity to each other is striking. Both promote ontological dualism.

Bhaskar's Realism

Bhaskar's critical realism emerged out of his earlier contributions to the philosophy of science (e.g. 1978) in which he posited the existence of an intransitive 'real', dimension to the natural world where generative mechanisms exist that

make 'actual' events and 'empirical' experiences possible (1978: 13, 15).
Following this differentiated natural ontology, Bhaskar has argued for a similar
ontological stratification of social reality. Social relations have an intransitive,
material aspect just as the natural world also has a reality which is irreducible to
human experience of it. Bhaskar insists upon a real dimension to social reality:
'the *conditions* for phenomena (namely social activities as conceptualized in experience) exist *intransitively* and may therefore exist independently of their
appropriate conceptualization' (Bhaskar 1979: 66). Bhaskar emphasises the ontological autonomy of these intransitive aspects of society. Bhaskar claims that:

> There is more to coping with social reality than coping with other people.
> There is coping with a whole host of social entities, including institutions,
> traditions, networks of relations and the like – which are irreducible to
> people.
>
> (Bhaskar 1991: 71)

For Bhaskar, an institution does not simply consist of individuals but has
powerful properties far extending those of the individual. Society has an
enduring and objective existence; it has a structure. Bhaskar insists that human
agency and society 'cannot be reduced to or re-constructured from one another'
(Bhaskar 1986: 124) and that 'there is an ontological hiatus between society and
people' (Bhaskar 1979: 46). Society may emerge out of individual action but, in
the end, society is ontologically autonomous of individuals. The division of
society into individuals and structures is an ontological fact rather than a mere
analytical device. Bhaskar further emphasises this ontological definition of structure at other points in his writing where he elaborates upon what he means by a
social structure:

> We need a system of mediating concepts, encompassing both aspects of the
> duality of praxis, designating 'slots', as it were, in the social structure into
> which active subjects must slip in order to reproduce it; that is, a system of
> concepts designating the 'point of contact' between human agency and
> social structures. Such a point, linking action to structure, must both endure
> and be immediately occupied by individuals.
>
> (Bhaskar 1979: 51)

The term 'slots' in this passage might be more typically called social roles. For
Bhaskar, individuals have to fill roles if the social structure is to be reproduced
but roles pre-exist and are independent of the individual. The social structure as
a whole consists of a network of roles which individuals occupy. The network of
roles is not reducible to individuals.

The claim that society consists of more than its members is plainly problematic. It raises the spectre of a metaphysical entity which exists independently of
humans. Bhaskar is keenly aware of this danger of reification but he believes that
he has avoided any such accusation by appealing to the concept of emergence.

Bhaskar defines emergence in the following way: 'a property possessed by an entity at a certain level of organisation may be said to be emergent from some lower level insofar as it is not predictable from the properties found at that level' (Bhaskar 1986: 104, footnote 1a). Thus, water has emergent properties which are irreducible to its constituent molecules of hydrogen and oxygen. Analogously, in society, the accumulated activities and conceptions of individuals produce a wider social context which although dependent upon individuals is irreducible to any of those individuals' activities and conceptions. Society as a whole has features which are not predictable from the properties of individuals, even though, like the hydrogen and oxygen molecules in water, there could be no society without individuals: 'society, as a real object of possible scientific study, possesses properties irreducible to those of people' (Bhaskar 1979: 124). Society arises out of the conceptions and activities of individuals but finally consists of cumulative emergent or structural properties which are more than those practice and beliefs alone. Certainly, Bhaskar's appeal to emergence is intuitively sensible. Although individuals contribute to society and there could not be any society without them, society is plainly more than any individual. Moreover, it is self-evident that an individual's understanding of society is inadequate to social reality as a whole; society exists whether any particular individual understands it or not. Emergence seems to capture the fact that social reality, which precedes and is definitively more than the individual, is simultaneously only the result of individual action. Consequently, a social structure arises out of the cumulative action of all individuals to confront every and any individual as an objective institutional reality. It is on this basis that Bhaskar is able to claim that there is more to institutions than mere individuals. As an emergent phenomenon, structure, consequently, has three unignorable properties: it pre-exists individual action, it is autonomous of it and it has causal powers over it.

Despite the importance of these intransitive aspects of social life, Bhaskar always emphasises that social life has a conceptual element. The understandings of humans are critical and have to be recognised. Society has a transitive dimension: 'Any adequate account of social science must be able to do justice to Winch's intuition that the subject matter of social science is concept-dependent' (Bhaskar 1979: 173). Bhaskar accepts Winch's hermeneutic argument that the definitions which social actors put on their relations make them what they are. Yet, he rejects the idea that hermeneutics could in itself be an adequate philosophical basis for the social sciences. Although the meanings which individuals put on their relations are important, individual understandings must ultimately be 'corrigible' against objective realities: 'social life has a material aspect and agent's conceptualizations are corrigible' (Bhaskar 1979: 175). For Bhaskar, those aspects of reality which have obvious and indeed disastrous effects on people's lives demonstrate the inadequacy of hermeneutics, for these features of reality impose themselves upon people however they might understand them:

> Being in prison or fighting in a war is not just (or even perhaps necessarily) possessing a certain idea of what one is doing: it is being physically sepa-

rated from the rest of society or being party to an armed conflict; and without the separation and the conflict the concepts would lack the material substrate, as it were, that is essential for their correct application.

(Bhaskar 1979: 174)

Bhaskar's complaint is that Winch obliterates the manifestly material aspects of social action, reducing everything to mere personal interpretation.

For Bhaskar, then, social structure is irreducible to individual belief and action. Nevertheless, individual practice is essential to the maintenance of the social structure and ultimately Bhaskar's 'transformational model of social activity' attempts to reconcile these two aspects of social reality.

> It is no longer true to say that men *create* it [society]. Rather one must say: they *reproduce* or *transform* it. That is, if society is always already made, then any concrete praxis or, if you like, act of objectivation can only modify it.
>
> (Bhaskar: 1979: 42)[1]

Individuals are confronted by an institutional reality which imposes upon them. However, although this structure has causal power over the individual, the structure is only reproduced by the individual. Since individuals are conscious agents, they are able to re-interpret their situation and consider new forms of actions. By altering their own practice, the social structure as a whole can be transformed. In particular, individual actions have unintended consequences which recreate or transform structure:

> People, in their conscious activity, for the most part unconsciously reproduce (and occasionally transform) the structures governing their substantive activities of production. Thus people do not marry to reproduce the nuclear family or work to sustain the capitalist economy. Yet it is nevertheless the unintended consequence (and inexorable result) of, as it is also a necessary condition for, their activity.
>
> (Bhaskar 1979: 44)

Bhaskar illustrates this stratified ontology as three different moments or levels of social reproduction (Bhaskar 1979: 46). In the first, structure pre-exists and has causal power over the individual, socialising the individual in ways which are consistent with structural imperatives. In the second, the individual acts consciously and meaningfully in the light of this socialisation so that individuals not only reproduce structure through their actions but also transform it. The reproduction or transformation of structure constitutes the third and last moment of Bhaskar's transformational model of social activity. For Bhaskar, this model overcomes the shortcomings of the 'Durkheimian' reified stereotype in which society merely impresses upon the individual or a 'Weberian' voluntaristic stereotype in which individuals create society through their intentional action (Bhaskar 1979: 40). The transformational model of social activity allows for structural constraint and individual agency without either reifying society or eliminating the individual. The institutional reality which confronts the individual is open to some re-interpretation and alteration. However, although individuals are capable of consciously changing their actions and therefore transforming their social structure, structure cannot be reduced to them and has determination over them. Indeed, even when individuals transform structure through consciously choosing new forms of practice, structural transformation outruns their volition. They alter only their practice but this may have structural effects of which they are completely unaware. Structural change is ultimately independent of the private decisions of many individuals. Thus, economic crashes are the result of the conscious actions of many individual share-holders but crashes cannot be explained merely by reference to individual share-holders. An economic crash occurs when individuals begin to sell stock, concerned that prices are about to decline. As these individuals sell their stock the overall value of shares declines, propelling others to sell their own shares. At every moment, individuals make rational and conscious decisions but the overall result is disastrous for everyone and is unintended by anyone. Individual consciousness is unignorable but it cannot account for structural transformation which occurs at a level independent of the individual through a process of unintended consequences. Bhaskar's transformational model of social activity is an eloquent statement of ontological dualism. It rigorously defends the ontological separation of the agent and structure.

Habermas' Realism

Like Bhaskar, Habermas has always insisted that there is a meaningful dimension to human social life.[2] Indeed, Habermas has not simply emphasised the meaningful dimension of social life but he has provided a profound critique of the entire tradition of modern philosophy on the grounds that it has ignored this fact. In *The Philosophical Discourse of Modernity* (1987a), Habermas argues that modern philosophy from Hegel on has fatally limited itself to individual consciousness. Modern philosophy has rejected theological appeals to God or any other metaphysical entity on which human knowledge can be grounded; reason alone must provide its own foundations. *The Philosophical Discourse of Modernity* describes how some of the key figures in western thought, Hegel, Marx, Nietzsche, Adorno and Horkheimer, Heidegger, Derrida, Bataille and Foucault have all in turn failed to provide an adequate basis for the philosophy of consciousness. In each case, these philosophers failed to provide a firm grounding for knowledge because they limited themselves to a subjective philosophy of consciousness. Each remained wedded to an individualistic ontology, which provided no route out of epistemological nihilism and ethical individualism. Alone individuals have no external reference to the world beyond their own experience. They know the world only through their own senses and can never be certain that their knowledge is accurately grounded. Individuals can never reach a grounded position on the basis of their own knowledge alone because that knowledge has no external referent against which to confirm itself; any knowledge they have is the product of the very senses that are suspect in the first place. On this basis, individuals can never know whether their own knowledge is accurate or not. For Habermas, modern European philosophy has failed to recognise that humans are social animals who learn within communities. These communities provide verification for knowledge, which is impossible for the individual alone: 'The concept of communicative reason that transcends subject-centred reason, which I have provisionally introduced, is intended to lead away from the paradoxes and levelings of a self-referential critique of reason' (Habermas 1987a: 341). While the individual cannot confirm their own knowledge, social groups provide the possibility for such verification. Humans can mutually verify their own experience of the world with other members of their social group. Other members of the group can affirm or reject the individual's experience as valid. Other people provide the external reference which is lacking for the lone individual. Group members mutually provide each other with an account of the world which is independent of the others' senses. Certainly, absolute knowledge cannot be achieved through intersubjective agreement. Others can be wrong about their experiences and groups constantly have to consider whether their account of the world is accurate. Nevertheless, although not producing absolute knowledge, intersubjectivity overcomes the self-defeating nihilism of consciousness philosophy. The individual is no longer trapped merely within their own experience. They can affirm their experience against that of others and consequently develop better understandings of the world. For Habermas, intersubjectivity is an unignorable fact of human existence which provides the grounds for reason and knowledge. Communities, not individuals, establish whether certain practices and certain beliefs are reasonable. Reason is always embedded in a particular form of life and is the product of intersubjective understanding and negotiation.

A social ontology has remained an essential part of Habermas' extensive work, although the language which he uses to describe this commitment has changed slightly. Thus, one of the central concepts in Habermas' work from *The Theory of Communicative Action* (1987b) onwards is the notion of the 'lifeworld'. This term was originally invented by Husserl, who was himself influenced by Dilthey's hermeneutic concept of 'life'. Most of Husserl's work concerned itself with a phenomenological analysis of human consciousness. In Cartesian fashion, he did not attempt to analyse the world itself but, under the somewhat misleading aphorism of 'to the things themselves', he sought to explicate the contents and structure of human consciousness, through which any experience of the world was mediated (Husserl 1931). As Heidegger somewhat brutally pointed out, this solipsistic approach was doomed to self-defeat and ironically, towards the end of his career, Husserl himself finally recognised that he could never explain human communication from the premise of an individualistic phenomenology (Husserl 1970: 155). If human consciousness developed entirely individualistically, then it was impossible to explain how individuals in each culture communicated conscious experiences to each other. Husserl effectively admitted that he had started at the wrong end of human experience and working forward from the individual he could never explain the fact of shared consciousness among social groups. He realised that any philosophy of consciousness had in fact to start with the social group which created shared understandings, meanings and finally consciousness itself. This shared consciousness explained any individual consciousness rather than the other way around. Husserl called this shared consciousness the 'lifeworld' (Husserl 1970) and his famous student Alfred Schütz set himself the sociological task of explicating the nature of the human lifeworld. For Habermas, the lifeworld consists of the 'more or less diffuse, always unproblematic, background convictions' in which 'the interpretive work of preceding generations' is stored (Habermas 1991: 70). The lifeworld, therefore, refers to those 'taken-for-granted' understandings the importance of which Schütz's phenomenology exposed. These background convictions are essential for human interaction and the members of any society are always already thrown into a particular lifeworld, in which they have to operate: 'Communicative actors are always moving *within* the horizon of their lifeworld; they cannot step outside it' (Habermas 1987b: 126). Echoing Bhaskar's argument, Habermas insists that any serious social theory has to recognise the hermeneutic character of human interaction; humans necessarily live within lifeworlds. They are always part of one lifeworld or another, interacting with others on the basis of shared understandings. Indeed, Habermas sees the lifeworld as an essential part of human experience; it provides the arena in which individuals can realise themselves.

In *The Philosophical Discourse*, Habermas demonstrates the centrality of the lifeworld to all human existence. He highlights how modern philosophy might overcome its self-entrapment by grounding itself in social intercourse rather than in the subject. Yet, although Habermas emphasises the importance of the lifeworld, he nevertheless rejects the notion that the lifeworld constitutes an adequate account of social reality in itself. There is, for Habermas, like Bhaskar, more to social reality than intersubjective understanding. Above all, as Habermas stresses with increasing conviction from *The Theory of Communicative Action*, there is 'system'. Habermas 'would therefore like to propose (1) that we conceive of societies *simultaneously* as systems and lifeworlds' (Habermas 1987b: 118). While the latter consists of social relations between people conducted on the basis of understanding, the former refers to the causal operation of institutions. The system refers to the operations of the state and the economy, which pre-exist and dominate the life of every individual. In modern European society, the system, as opposed to the lifeworld, is prior: 'Whereas primitive societies are integrated via a *basic normative consensus*, the integration of developed societies comes about via the *systemic interconnection of functionally specified domains of action*' (Habermas 1987b: 115). Habermas' conviction that there is a distinction between the lifeworld and system constitutes a fundamental tenet of his later work. Certainly, it was effectively already present even in an early piece such as *Knowledge and Human Interests* (1971) when he separated the technical interests ontologically from the practical and emancipatory ones, but this ontological divide between the lifeworld and system becomes central to *The Theory of Communicative Action*. For Habermas, although sociologists have to recognise that individuals interact with each other on the basis of meanings, society itself does not function on the basis of shared meanings. Certain institutional relations and imperatives operate at a structural level which are not explicable in terms of shared beliefs; social actions at this level are oriented by abstract codes so that they become systemic. These rationailsed rules create problems of alienation and exploitation. Individuals mechanically follow impersonal rules to produce an objective social system. Consequently, certain areas of society cannot be explained by individual interpretation alone – they cannot by 'semaniticised'. On the contrary, these objective spheres of institutional interconnection provide the background for any possible lifeworld. For Habermas, a critical social theory has to recognise this material dimension to social life:

> It has to opt for a theoretical strategy that neither identifies the lifeworld with society as a whole, nor reduces it to a systemic nexus. My guiding idea is that, on the one hand, the dynamics of development are steered by imperatives issuing from problems of self-maintenance, that is, problems of materially reproducing the lifeworld; but that, on the other hand, this societal development draws upon structural possibilities and is subject to structural limitations that, with the rationalisation of the lifeworld, undergo systematic change in dependence upon corresponding learning process. A *verstehende* sociology that allows society to be wholly absorbed into the lifeworld ties itself to the perspective of self-interpretation of the culture under investigation; this internal perspective screens out everything that inconspicuously affects a sociocultural lifeworld from the outside.
>
> (Habermas 1987b: 148)

Habermas' 'guiding idea' is that society consists of both lifeworld and system. In the lifeworld, individuals influence each other in the course of their interactions conducted on the basis of common understandings. The system, by contrast, operates on the basis of causal function. In particular, the system consists of the media of money and power which encode a purposive-rational attitude, by-passing the consensus-oriented communication of the lifeworld (Habermas 1987b: 183). Individuals do not mutually agree to certain forms of conduct on the basis of shared understandings but, on this account, they merely enact rationalised codes. All of these individual purposive-rational acts taken together produce an objective social system which operates functionally. In contrast with primitive society, the lifeworld becomes almost superfluous in modern society, existing separately to the functioning system which threatens to crush it (Habermas 1987b: 186, 201). The lifeworld no longer provides the background for every interaction but becomes dependent upon the economy and state bureaucracy. The lifeworld diminishes until it survives only in the private sphere of the family, where individuals create their own personal forms of social interaction: 'Familial lifeworlds see the imperatives of the economic and administrative systems coming at them from outside, instead of being mediatized by them from behind' (Habermas 1987b: 387). As the system predominates, the lifeworld becomes fragmented. It no longer underpins the social order through powerful ritualistic affirmations but becomes dispersed across a fragile archipelago of private spheres. Each home provides a temporary haven from a heartless world but the system, which provides the material basis of each island of meaning, functions remorselessly. Habermas' account of the social system is more sophisticated than Bhaskar's but it is committed to the same ontological dualism.

The Social Ontology of Realism

Bhaskar and Habermas both assume that institutions have an objective reality independent of human understanding. The objective context of social action consists of phenomena like class or bureaucratic institutions which persist in the face of any individual volition. Institutions have an independent ontological status. However, although institutions are extremely powerful, irreducible to any individual in them, Habermas and Bhaskar never finally prove that these structures are autonomous. They assume that they are autonomous because they are not reducible to individual action and understanding but they never prove that they are independent of all the individuals in a society taken together. They assert the existence of structure. Despite the assurances of Habermas and Bhaskar, it may be possible to re-consider the nature of social structure more carefully in order to demonstrate that Habermas' and Bhaskar's dismissal of human social relations is too hasty. A closer examination of social structure may demonstrate that apparently objective social institutions can be explained by reference to the social relations between humans. It may also be possible to see that this reduction of apparently objective and autonomous social structure to a network of social relations in no way denies the manifest reality of society.

In his discussion of the relevance of Wittgenstein to social theory, David Bloor has examined rules as a fundamental social institution (Bloor 1983, 1997). Following Wittgenstein, Bloor argues that if individuals inferred the meaning of rules by reference to their own logic, then a rule could enjoin any action. For Bloor, rule-following must be a social institution. The group agrees upon what constitutes rule-following in the light of shared understandings. Rule-following necessarily implies a social group which defines publicly what rule-following is. Bloor's claim that rule-following is a social institution can be usefully re-applied to criticise Bhaskar's realism. In particular, it can be employed to show that Bhaskar's argument that there is more to coping with institutions than 'coping with other people' is simply untenable (Bhaskar 1991: 71). Bhaskar believes that the roles – or 'slots' – in these institutions exist autonomously of individuals. Thus, Bhaskar asserts that, although individuals have to fill roles if the social structure is to be reproduced, roles pre-exist the individual. Since any role self-evidently precedes its particular occupant and institutions consist of a structure of roles, institutions as a whole are independent of the individual's activities and understandings; they have ontological autonomy. The concept of the independent role is therefore crucial to Bhaskar because it constitutes the basic ontological unit from which structure is built. If it can be shown that roles are not autonomous in the way which Bhaskar believes, then his entire notion of structure begins to subside. It is here that Bloor's argument can be usefully employed.

It is true that roles pre-exist and are autonomous of any individual who fills them and Bhaskar is right to emphasise this point. Yet, it does not follow that roles are independent of all the individuals. A role only exists because a wider network of individuals recognise a role's existence and have certain expectations about what the role's purpose is. They decide what someone who takes on that role should do. Only colleagues can tell any individual what a role involves and ensure that the role is, in fact, fulfilled properly. Thus, the position of bank manager certainly pre-exists any particular incumbent but it does not pre-exist, nor is it autonomous of, all the other individuals who work or have worked in the bank. The role of bank manager exists insofar as this role's function is recognised by others. Bank managers who fill this role are judged on whether they perform their duties adequately by the other workers in the bank and by customers. A role is independent of the particular individual filling it but not of the wider social network in which it is embedded. This network consists only of other humans who mutually influence each other and ensure that all act appropriately. Individuals can fulfil a role only insofar as they take their cues from and are supported by other members of this particular institution. Roles are dependent upon a wider network of social relations, just as rules operate only within forms of life. When Bhaskar argues that roles are autonomous, he simply fails to recognise this wider network which in fact sustains any particular role. He effectively argues for a form of role-individualism. For him, an individual is able to fulfil a role, independently of any one else. Bhaskar detaches roles from their proper social and institutional context. Once detached from the networks which sustain them, he assumes that they are truly independent because they cannot manifestly be reduced to any particular incumbent. Having wrongly asserted the independence of the role, he then defines social institutions as the accumulation of all these independent roles. He compounds the initial error of isolating the role from its proper social context in the first place. Roles exist in social networks; they are mutually sustained by the humans who work in any institution. They are certainly not reducible to the individual, but nor does any reality other than a social and human one need to be invoked to explain them. Institutions persist because the humans in them mutually ensure that everyone performs their role properly. Ultimately, institutions are themselves just human social networks and groups.

Bhaskar defends the concept of structure by reference to the concept of emergence; social structure arises out of individual action but it is more than all these actions taken together. In order to refute realism, it is necessary to demonstrate that even the concept of emergence is untenable. The appeal to emergence seems initially plausible. Social class is often taken by realists to be an emergent property (Porpora 1993). Class exists only by virtue of the actions of individuals in a society and yet class as a whole is irreducible to any particular individual. Sociologists are often able to identify general social trends which can be defined as 'class' responses and which have dramatic effect on the historical transformation of a society. These class movements require different individuals in a class to act in certain ways but none of the individuals in a class may be aware of the activities of others. Classes typically have unintended social effects of which their members may be ignorant. Class seems to possess properties which are irrefutably emergent. While initially plausible, Bhaskar's concept of emergence ultimately involves a misperception of social reality of a similar type to that which he makes when he describes social roles as independent. The error can be analogously rectified by reference to an ontology of social relations. The social phenomena which Bhaskar describes as emergent are, in fact, simply collective phenomena involving many individuals. These phenomena cannot self-evidently be reduced to the individual but they cannot at the same time be described as being more than all the humans involved in them. It is notable that even the emergent properties of class can be understood in terms of a human collective. For instance, large numbers of people unaware of each other may respond to certain economic pressures in the same way, thereby causing society as a whole to develop in certain ways. This 'class' response is not reducible to the individual. Yet, this does not mean that it is independent of the individuals in this class considered together by the sociologist. The 'class' response simply refers to all their social actions, each undertaken knowingly, when they are taken together. Although individuals may be ignorant of the response of others, each is aware of their own response. The fact that others elsewhere are responding similarly does not make the social effect more than the humans involved. Those other individuals in other locations are similarly aware of what they are doing. Collective phenomena simply are all the social actions undertaken by a group of humans, each act understood by those who performed them. The collective events are certainly more than any particular individual, but they are not more than all the humans involved in them. It is precisely the collective nature which lends them such extraordinary potency. An individual walking up a street is a different phenomenon from a crowd, but a crowd is not more than its members; a crowd refers precisely to all the people who are part of it. A crowd does not have properties separate from all its members even though it is manifestly irreducible to any particular individual in this gathering. The appeal to emergence confuses the fact that a 'class' response or a collective phenomenon more generally is irreducible to *any* particular individual with the claim that it is independent of *all* individuals. The reality of collective phenomena is not denied but their status as ontologically independent is rejected. There is no evidence that structure as it is ontologically conceived by Bhaskar actually exists, and even the appeal to emergence renders the concept of structure no more defensible. In every instance, the concept of structure in fact refers to complex chains of social relations enacted in an infinitesimal myriad of everyday interactions: 'The appropriate image of the social world is a bundle of individual chains of interactional experience, criss-crossing each other in space as they flow along in time' (Collins 1981b: 998). At each point, apparently objective structures are reducible to this social ontology of social relations. When people act together, it is different from when they are on their own, but this does not mean that society has properties which cannot be understood in human terms.

The reducibility of apparently objective structure to wide-ranging networks of social relations illuminates an important point about Bhaskar's realism. Bhaskar appeals to the concept of structure because he takes a peculiar and inadequate view of it. Institutions are assumed to be autonomous by Bhaskar only because he analyses these 'structures' from the perspective of a single individual. From this perspective institutions indeed seem autonomous. From the individual's point of view, social reality is objective; it manifestly exists independently of what an individual thinks or does. From individual experience, structure is prior, it is independent and it does have causal powers. Yet, although compelling for the individual, this view is a solipsism. It takes the individual perspective as the basis of sociological analysis. It looks resolutely out from the contemplative perspective of the isolated individual. It ignores others and transforms the social networks between other humans which extend beyond the individual's knowledge and power into independent entities. Since these relations are independent of the individual, Bhaskar, operating from a parochial solitude, reifies them into objective structures. Bhaskar needs to de-centre his viewpoint from that of the individual to encompass other people. Once that wider perspective is taken, social life becomes no less real. Each individual is still confronted by a genuinely independent social reality but this reality consists only of others. At every level, there are humans in social relations, mutually binding each to each. Humans are mutually engaged in these never-ending social relations, sustaining, transforming and sometimes breaking them off. This is the reality of social life, not a social structure which is independent of the individual. Society is certainly more than any one particular individual but it is never more than all the members of this society bound together in complex webs of social relations. Once a social ontology is adopted all the problems of dualism are avoided, while the manifest reality of society is in no way denied.

Habermas' assertion of the autonomy of the system is open to a similar line of criticism. At each point, the system which Habermas describes can always be reduced to the social relations between humans. However, Habermas does not merely claim that the system is autonomous. He also asserts that there is a fundamental ontological divide between the modern institution and the social organisation of 'primitive' societies (Habermas 1987b: 115). Modern institutions do not interact with each other on the basis of shared meaning. They are 'functionally specified domains of action' which interconnect with each other causally as the individuals in them act according to abstract, rationalised codes. The institutions of modern society affect each other independently of the understandings of their members. It is certainly correct that modern institutions have powers which operate independently of any particular individual's understanding. It is self-evidently the case that many people are simply unaware of the resources which certain institutions have at their disposal and what they are able to do with them. However, while the claim that institutions can exist independently of the understanding of some individuals is valid, it is simply untrue to claim that an institution operates causally as individuals merely follow purposive-rational codes. Institutions do not interact with each other independently of shared human understanding. The interaction of institutions relies precisely on the members of one institution mobilising themselves and their resources to act in certain ways, while the members of other institutions respond knowingly to these actions. The interaction of institutions is certainly a real phenomenon but it cannot occur without at least some of the members of each institution understanding what relations between these institutions involves. The functional relation can, in every instance, be reduced to the relationship between humans and groups in which shared understandings are mobilised. There is, for instance, an institutional relationship between the judiciary and the government. The judiciary is the executive branch of the government, which is intended to affirm the legitimacy of the laws. In this way, the judiciary sustains the government by ensuring the legality of the laws which it enforces. Habermas would describe this relationship as functional; the judiciary supports the government institutionally. It is certainly true that this relationship cannot be reduced to the personal relationship of certain judges and members of governments. The institutional relations extend beyond any personal connection between single individuals in either institution. Yet, this relationship cannot be independent of the understanding of the members of the judiciary and government taken as a whole. The relationship between these bodies depends precisely upon how these two groups understand it and respond to each other's different needs and powers. The institutional relationship here is real but, at every point, it is reducible to the social relationship between two powerful groups of people; a social relation which itself pre-supposes shared understandings. For instance, the institutional relationship is symbolically represented by the relationship between the Lord Chief Justice and the Prime Minister and it is through their actual persons, as representatives of the wider institutions, that these institutions supposedly functionally interact with each other. Despite Habermas' assertion, the interaction between modern institutions is no different from the interaction of groups and individuals in primitive societies. In every case, the social reality is reducible to the social relations between humans, and these humans must understand what their relations actually involve. The Lord Chief Justice (and the rest of the judiciary) and the Prime Minister (and the government) must recognise what the law is and what actions it allows them to perform. Representatives from these institutions are in constant communication so that they continually reaffirm what they take to be the law and, therefore, what each regards as legitimate action. There is no abstract code here which produces independent institutional functions. The supposedly functional relationship is reducible to a social relationship in which the participants interact with each other on the basis of shared understandings. The relationship between the judiciary and the government may demand responses from other groups or institutions located in other parts of societies but this demand is not the product of systemic need; or determined by abstract code. It is a result of knowledgeable activity of these social groups, the judiciary and the government. Social function is, in fact, the interaction of social groups with each other.

Ironically, both Bhaskar and Habermas implicitly commit themselves to the social ontology. One of the key points of Bhaskar's 'Transformational Model of Social Activity' is that individuals reproduce and transform the objective social reality that confronts them (Bhaskar 1979: 42). According to Bhaskar, individuals in the present re-create and transform the prior social structure, which only continues to exist through them. Thus, individuals in the future will be confronted by an autonomous social structure which is irreducible to them because they did not create it. Yet, on his own admission, the structure which confronts individuals in the future is actually only produced by the practices of individuals in the present. Although autonomous of people in the future, current society consists of the actions of its members now. His 'Transformational Model of Social Activity' stresses that without this social activity in the present, structure will not be reproduced. This social interaction produces the material reality which Bhaskar then defines as structure. Although Bhaskar is unaware of it, the necessity of social action by individuals in the present – the second moment of the transformational model – entirely undermines the transformational model of social activity, for it renders the appeal to objective structure superfluous. If Bhaskar extrapolated back from his description of what happens in the present to the past, it would be evident that humans in the present are confronted only by ok social actions of individuals in the past. Just as future generations will be confronted by the results of social relations and practices conducted now, so are humans today confronted by the actions of past generations. There is nothing structural about these relations. Humans today did not perform those actions and some of them may not know about them, but individuals in the past must have both performed these actions and known about them or such actions could not have occurred. Individuals do not re-create autonomous social structure but, rather, through their interactions and over time, humans maintain, change and re-negotiate social relations with others. All of these relations together constitute social reality and society transforms as these relations between its members change in the course of their interactions with each other. Bhaskar has ontologised the social interactions of the past into an autonomous structure. He assumes that these past interactions become objective merely because they pre-exist and are independent of individuals in the present. Yet, the supposedly objective social structure consists simply of those social relations between individuals in the past and the practices they undertook. In order for realism to explain the reproduction of structure, it must invoke a social ontology. Bhaskar accepts that the present consists of social actions without which structure cannot persist. Yet nowhere does he begin to explain how this social interaction in the present is transformed into structure in the future. It seems that, simply by being in the past, human acts somehow become structural. Once again, Bhaskar is a victim of his own solipsistic perspective. Because he always sees society from the perspective of the individual confronted by a prior structure, he fails to see the reality of the past. He views the past from the perspective of the individual now. This individual is confronted by a reality which is independent of him, but trapped within this perspective he cannot see that this past consists simply of other individuals engaged in social relations in another time and place. He cannot see the past merely as the historical accumulation of social relations between other humans but he has to endow this manifest reality with an unten-able objectivism. Bhaskar imposes an unnecessary dualism on social reality when in every case society both past and present is best understood in terms of human social relations. The recognition that society consists only of social relations means that it no less real for all that, however.

Habermas is similarly committed to a social ontology. In *The Philosophical Discourse* (1987a), Habermas insists on the priority of intersubjectivity. For Habermas, there is no human reality which is not social and any philosophy which fails to recognise the significance of social relations is necessarily flawed. The priority of meaningful human relations has been a consistent feature of Habermas' work up to the present time, even though its significance is often obscured by his emphasis on the system. In *The Theory of Communicative Action* (1987b), following Lockwood's famous distinction, Habermas insists that it is equally important to consider social integration: 'The fundamental problem of social theory is how to connect in a satisfactory way the two conceptual strategies indicated by the notion of "system" and "lifeworld"' (Habermas 1987b: 151). Social theory must not simply consider how the system sustains itself functionally but how individuals are integrated into this system as part of social groups. Without that social integration which is effected at the level of shared under-standing, the reproduction of the system is threatened. The members of a society need to orient themselves consciously to collective ends; they have to share common understandings and direct their various actions in particular co-ordinated directions. Only in this way will there be a social or institutional coherence or, in Habermas' language, will the system function. Significantly, exactly this account of social reality is prominent in Habermas' work. One of Habermas' chief aims has been to create a critical theory which, he has variously developed by means of the ideal speech situation, the theory of communicative action and discourse ethics. For instance, in the ideal speech situation (and in the theory of communicative action and discourse ethics), the members of a society come together to discuss the basis on which they will organise themselves trans-parently, away from all political and economic interest. In the ideal speech situation, the social consensus is established by reference to the unforced force of the better argument. Habermas claims that this ideal speech situation produces certain universal principles of social consensus which can form the counterfac-tual basis of a critical theory. Yet, the ideal speech situation is not merely a means of creating a critical theory. It is directly related to actual political arrangements ,although the relationship between the ideal speech situation and social reality is not entirely specified. In particular, it is not clear whether this situation is an actual historical moment which once occurred in modern society

(1996), the continuing process of political discussion in modern societies (1995a: 86) or a transcendental condition which underlies all public debate in any society (1979; 1995a: 57). Habermas seems to commit himself to all three of these positions in his writings. However, it does seem that Habermas regards the ideal speech situation as an actual political reality whereby the legitimacy of any particular regime is established. It is a means by which a new political consensus could be reached which would underpin the system. The collective goals towards which the system is oriented are established in these moments of communal debate. There is evidence for this. For instance, he suggests that a real equivalent of the ideal speech situation has grown empirically out of the transformation of the public sphere (Habermas 1996), while in *Legitimation Crisis* (1976) Habermas postulated the ideal speech situation as a means of overcoming the crisis of the post-war Fordist settlement. With the ideal speech situation, Habermas attempts to provide a collective normative basis for the system. He creates a public life-world which reconnects all the archipelagos of private lifeworlds to produce a normative grounding for the entire system. Individuals are no longer oppressed by the system but in Hegelian fashion they are an intrinsic part of it; they subject themselves only to the normative requirements that they have created: 'We do not adhere to recognised norms from a sense of duty because they are *imposed* upon us by the threat of sanctions but because we *give* them to ourselves' (Habermas 1995a: 42). Echoing Parsons, Habermas recognises the obligatory nature of common norms; once accepted they bind humans to each other in mutually recognised social relations. The ideal speech situation provides a normative basis for the system, therefore, and by means of it Habermas is able to recouple social integration with system integration because once individuals have willingly consented to these norms they are obliged to act in accordance with them. In this way, collective action is enjoined on the part of every member of the society and the steering problems which threatened the legitimacy of the society are overcome.

Although Habermas avowedly assumes a dualistic ontology, the ideal speech situation reveals that the system relies at each point on communal agreement. Despite his claims that interpretive sociology cannot account for institutional social realities, the entire edifice of the theory of communicative action (and his subsequent discourse ethics) is based on the assumption that shared understandings do in fact preceed all forms of social life, including institutional ones. As Habermas himself states: 'Communicative actors are always moving within the horizon of their lifeworld; they cannot step outside it' (Habermas 1987b: 126). Even the most rigid and apparently objective institutions pre-suppose a common culture among those who work in these institutions. Faceless institutions are, in fact, completely human even though they may well be inhumane. The basis of even the most rigorous institutions in shared communication does not deny the enduring material reality of these institutions. However, the means and content of the communications will determine what any institutional reality is. Habermas rejects any reduction of society to a lifeworld, that is, to the social relations between humans. Yet, his social theory ultimately rests upon exactly this ontology. For him, modern society is always the product of prior social agreement which orients the members of that society to the same collective ends. Despite Habermas' claims to the contrary, the system ultimately assumes a broader lifeworld which determines what kind of system will in fact exist. Like Bhaskar, Habermas unwittingly vindicates the social ontology. At each point, their social theories ultimately appeal not to objective structures or to isolated individuals but to human social relations. In every case the vast and complex institutions of modern society are reducible to the social relations between the members of this society. Yet this sociological reduction denies these institutions none of their reality, nor any of their extraordinary powers.

After Social Theory

Contemporary social theory is currently dominated by a dualistic paradigm in which society is understood as the relation between structure and the agent. There are alternative definitions of structure, and social theory today can broadly be divided into two main streams: those theorists who define structure conceptually as a set of rules and those theorists who use the term structure 'realistically' to refer to objective institutions. In both cases, society is explained in terms of the *interaction* of structure and agency. Both strands are closely related because, even when structure refers to rules, the purpose of these rules is to reproduce an institutional reality.[3] In contemporary social theorists, the concept of structure is fundamental. Yet the apparently self-evident status of structure is a mirage; it only seems to exist when sociologists take a peculiar and solipsistic perspective on society. Consequently, although contemporary social theorists assumes the existence and even the priority of structure, it never actually demonstrate's its existence. In each case, whether structure is conceived as rules or as institutions, structure is only ever asserted. Thus, when they talk of structure, habitus and discourse Giddens, Bourdieu and Foucault describe nothing more than the shared understandings on the basis of which humans interact. In important parts of their works, Foucault, Bourdieu and Giddens all recognise this and, indeed, they describe the reality of social relations eloquently. Similarly, while Habermas and Bhaskar are confident of the existence of certain independent institutional structures, in every case structure can be reduced to social relations. Although overtly dualistic, contemporary social theory in fact presumes a quite different ontology. Contemporary social theory immanently operates with a social ontology in which society consists of social relations between humans.

In order to set sociology on its feet, it is necessary to elucidate and illuminate this social ontology. It is necessary to bring social reality into relief by clearing away the thick undergrowth which has grown over it. The recovery of this landscape will allow sociology once again to view contemporary social change with a clarity which is currently choked by dualism. Contemporary social theorists have drawn upon shared traditions, embodying shared understandings, to create the dualistic ontology which is now hegemonic. In particular, a canon has been created which legitimates ontological dualism and which gives this dualism a powerful tradition. Thus, Bhaskar draws upon Marx as a critical resource for his realism. Giddens draws on the works of all the major classical social theorists in his writings but his structuration theory is specifically a synthesis of Parsonian and interactionist approaches. Habermas similarly draws on classical sociology, on Weber and Marx, in particular, but also upon Mead and Parsons, to create his ontology of lifeworld and system. Bourdieu's work is an avowed attempt to synthesise Lévi-Strauss and Sartre but he draws on Kant, Wittgenstein, Merleau-Ponty, Heidegger and Marx to do this. Foucault draws upon Nietzsche and Weber to produce his radical critique of modernity. These theorists draw upon the diverse sociological traditions in different ways, but in all of their writing a broad common tradition is evident. The sociological canon provides the totems of these social theorists, orienting each to a common academic approach. For them, this tradition seems to vindicate ontological dualism. In the light of this tradition, a social ontology cannot be established simply by demonstrating the theoretical inadequacy of the dualism. The destructive work of critique is necessary but it is equally important to re-create a new common tradition for sociologists today. It is essential that new traditions are collectively produced to legitimate new forms of research. In particular, classical sociology must be re-appropriated to become not a totem of dualism as it currently is but as the embodiment of the social ontology. In the sociological tradition, the social ontology which is implicitly assumed in contemporary social theory is expressed with unparalleled clarity. As Giddens himself claimed, sociology can be developed most effectively by reconsidering the classical texts of Marx, Weber and Durkheim (Giddens 1992: vii). A reappropriation of the elements of these texts can provide the theoretical groundwork for contemporary sociology. Assuming a dualistic ontology, Giddens substantially failed to provide that grounding. However, his claim that contemporary sociology could advance most effectively by drawing on its past is correct. Sociology can develop as a coherent discipline most effectively by reinvigorating its shared origins and traditions. By orienting ourselves to common sources and texts, sociologists can enjoin common academic practices among themselves. This sociological tradition can be positively recovered to orient sociologists collectively to the actuality of social reality. Through a re-examination of classical sociology, social reality in all its rich colour can be rediscovered. Thus sociology is destined to open a new way to the human sciences (Durkheim 1976: 447).

Part II
Classical Sociology

5 Hegel and the Concept of *Geist*

The Origins of the Social Ontology

The origins of sociology are usually traced back to Auguste Comte, very substantially because he invented the term 'sociology' (Comte 1974; Aron 1965). It is true that in Comte's works the outlines of a new discipline which submits society to a scientific enquiry is evident. Yet, while Comte's contribution cannot be dismissed, his invention of the term 'sociology' has, perhaps, led to the over-estimation of his significance to the origins but more especially to the development of the discipline. For instance, of the now recognised founders of sociology, Marx, Weber and Durkheim, only Durkheim was ever seriously influenced by Comte but even in Durkheim's case the influence was quite subsidiary and, more often than not, negative. Durkheim was much more directly influenced by Renouvier and in his writings most of the comments directed specifically at Comte were critical. Even in his early writing when Durkheim seemed to adopt some of Comte's positive method, he rejected most of his specific claims. Moreover, after 1895, when Durkheim 'found' religion, Comte was all but irrelevant to Durkheim's work. If Marx, Weber and Durkheim are considered to be the major classical figures in sociology, then the origins of the discipline might usefully be traced back not to Comte but rather to Hegel. The entire *oeuvre* of Karl Marx is written with the deliberate intention of inverting Hegel's dialectic. Yet, while Marx rejected Hegel's idealism, he never disputed the power of his dialectical method which sought to identify the contradictions within historical cultures which necessitated their transformation:

> I therefore openly avowed myself the pupil of that mighty thinker…With him it [the dialectic] is standing on its head. It must be turned right side up again, if you would discover the rational kernel within the mystical shell.
>
> (Marx 1977b: 29)

Following Hegel, Marx claimed that humans must be understood in a specific social and historical context. Since, Max Weber's work was predicated by a desire to refute Marx's economism and to demonstrate the importance of other factors and, above all, religion, in the course of the human history, Weber's work can be interpreted as an indirect response to Hegel. Interestingly, although

Durkheim was not influenced by Hegel and the meagre references to him are negative (Durkheim 1957: 5; 1978: 118), in fact, Hegelian themes, developed autonomously by Durkheim himself, are evident in his work. Like Hegel's, Durkheim's work is based on the premise that humans are social beings. Moreover, *The Division of Labour* (1964) demonstrates an implicit Hegelianism wherein society develops from an unsatisfactory universalism (mechanical solidarity), to an inadequate particularism (organic solidarity), culminating in a moment of reconciliation with the rise of professional social groups.

Of course, Hegel's influence has extended well beyond the classical social theorists and has had a profound impact upon the development of the discipline in the twentieth century, especially among Marxist circles. Gramsci's sociology is an explicit attempt to re-Heglianise Marx, emphasising the cultural pre-suppositions which give rise to economic forms. In addition, while the Frankfurt School rejected Hegel's concept of Absolute Mind, it developed critical theory from Hegel's dialectic (Adorno 1990). Hegel's influence extends beyond these obvious examples. If Simone de Beauvoir's *Second Sex* (1988) is taken as the seminal work in contemporary feminism, then Hegel's influence must be acknowledged in the development of one of the most important movements in sociology in the post-war era. De Beauvoir's account of woman is underpinned by Hegel's famous 'master–slave' dialectic. Similarly, in identity politics and the study of racism, Hegel's 'master–slave' dialectic informs much of the discussion of the fight for recognition by subordinate groups (e.g. Fanon 1968). By contrast, Comte has become a mere curiosity. His texts, when they are studied, do not inspire living ideas but are used as historical examples of a kind of sociology which is now outmoded; his writing yields no more insight into social reality than Tylor's anthropology provides reliable insights into tribal society. Consequently, although more usually analysed for his contribution to philosophy and to German idealism in particular, it is appropriate to consider the seminal contribution of Hegel's work to the origin sociology. This re-examination of Hegel can begin to create a new tradition for sociology today. This tradition, in contrast to currently hegemonic dualism, prioritises a social ontology; social relations are the social reality.

The Concept of *Geist*

Synthesising the work of Kant and Fichte, Hegel produced the first thorough-going social philosophy even though Montaigne, Vico and Montesquieu anticipate some of Hegel's arguments. As Collingwood has noted (1992), Hegel's philosophy was derived from existing philosophical traditions but it was a synthesis of extraordinary originality and richness. Hegel's work was a reaction against modern philosophy which culminated with his great German predecessor, Immanuel Kant. Above all, Hegel rejected the individualism and ahistoricism of the western tradition. Western philosophers, especially since Descartes, had attempted to build a philosophical system from an examination of subjective consciousness. For Hegel, individualistic contemplation ignored the dynamic reality of existence. It ignored the fact that humans, including philosophers, were historical beings whose thoughts and actions arose within a social context. This context provided the grounds for any philosophy in the first place. In the Preface to the *Phenomenology of Spirit*, Hegel excoriated philosophy for desiccating life (Hegel 1977: 31). Western philosophy stultified life by producing categorical systems derived from the contemplation of the philosopher's own private experience. The purpose of the *Phenomenology of Mind* and, indeed, Hegel's entire system was to re-invigorate philosophy, re-immersing it into life and history.

Hegel did not emphasise life merely to make philosophy more interesting. Hegel regarded modern post-Cartesian philosophy as hopelessly dualistic. Either rationalist philosophers emphasised subjective consciousness and ignored the reality of the object, or empiricist philosophers looked upon the mind as a blank slate upon which the objective world made its mark. For Hegel, both of these traditions were fatally one-sided. The empiricists recognise the 'colourful show of the sensuous' but fail to explain how this experience is ordered in human consciousness or communicated to others. The rationalists, by contrast, and Kant in particular explain the adequacy of human knowledge only by reference to a 'super-sensible beyond'. For Kant, experience pre-supposes a noumenal realm of things-in-themselves which humans can never know. The certainty of human knowledge is, on this account, guaranteed by the postulation of a speculative level of reality which is beyond human cognition. Consequently, the central task of Hegel's philosophy was to unify the subjective and objective sides of reality, which Kant and the empiricists fail to do. Through the concept of the *Geist*, Hegel believed that he could reconcile empirical and rational philosophies by unifying the subject and object. Through his philosophy Hegel intended to demonstrate that human existence was reaching a stage where human knowledge of the empirical world and that world itself were becoming compatible. For Hegel, *Geist* was the means by which the philosophical dualisms might be overcome. Unfortunately, it requires extensive exegesis before it is possible to gain a proper understanding of what Hegel actually meant by *Geist*.

The meaning of *Geist* can begin to be inferred from Hegel's discussions of his dialectic. Hegel derived this dialectic from the logical syllogism in which a universal premise combined with a particular empirical case produced an individual deduction. There is a standard philosophical example of this logical form: man is mortal (universal), Socrates is a man (particular), therefore Socrates is mortal (individual). For Hegel, this syllogism is replicated at the general level of human cultures. The culture or consciousness of each human society develops triadically through moments of universality, particularity and individuality, though it is important to see this triad fluidly. For instance, Hegel opposes it directly to Kant's dialectic precisely on the grounds that Kant is too formal:

> Of course, the *triadic form* must not be regarded as scientific when it is reduced to a lifeless schema, a mere shadow, and when scientific organization is degraded into a table of terms. Kant rediscovered this triadic form by instinct, but in his work it was still lifeless and uncomprehended.
>
> (Hegel 1977: 29)

Hegel openly admits that he derived the idea of his dialectic from the famous chapter in Kant's *Critique of Pure Reason*, 'The Antinomy of Reason'. There Kant tried to mediate between four irreconcilable philosophical claims: the world is infinite and finite, composite substances are either composed and not composed of simple parts, causality and freedom are compatible or incompatible and, finally, there is or is not a necessary being in the world (Kant 1992: 396–415). Kant claimed that these antinomies could be overcome by reference to the noumenal and phenomenal realms. The noumenal realm referred to the domain of thing-in-themselves which underlay the reality which humans experienced but which they could never know. The phenomenal realm referred to that level of reality of which humans were actually aware. Thus, freedom might exist in the noumenal realm about which humans had no knowledge but in the phenomenal realm of human experience freedom could not be said to exist. The other antinomies could be similarly solved. For Hegel, this solution failed to relate these different premises to human life. Instead Kant imposed a formal categorical system on to the antinomies. Kant recognised the potential of dialectical thinking but could not overcome the divide between the subject and the object. Ultimately the subject knew only the contents of its own experience, the noumenal realm, beyond which lay a more profound level of reality. Kant in no way overcame the dualism which had characterised modern philosophy. However, by re-invigorating the dialectic, through which process *Geist* developed, Hegel believed he could overcome the diremption of subject and object.

In his description of the dialectic, the nature of *Geist* appears for the first time. The dialectic refers to consciousness and, according to Hegel, this consciousness can transform itself over time. In this way, through a dialectic process, the division between the subject and the object can be overcome. Hegel's dialectical development of consciousness involves three interdependent moments. In the first, 'the will contains (a) the element of pure indeterminacy': which is 'the unrestricted infinity of absolute abstraction or universality' (1967b: 21). It is the moment of the unpredicated 'I', unrestricted by any determinate content to its consciousness; 'the pure undifferentiated "I" is its first immediate object' (Hegel 1977: 110). This is a moment of complete freedom. Having not fixed itself on anything, consciousness is unrestricted – it has no content – but it is also the emptiest and most unsatisfactory moment of consciousness. Consciousness is only free because it is vacuous. The inadequacy of the first universal moment of consciousness necessarily drives it forward to a second moment. Consciousness demands a content. It has to give itself a form in order to overcome the empty liberty of the first moment. In the second moment of consciousness, therefore, it becomes differentiated (1967b: 22). It focuses on a particular object or practice. It takes a particular form and limits itself to that concrete actualisation; it becomes particular. Yet, this second moment of consciousness is equally unsatisfactory for the very reason that consciousness is limited to the particular. Consequently, a further movement towards a higher unity is necessary:

The will is the unity of both these moments. It is particularity reflected back into itself and so brought back to universality, i.e. it is individuality. It is the self-determination of the ego, which means that at one and the same time the ego posits itself as its own negative, i.e. as restricted and determinate, and yet remains by itself, i.e. in its self-identity and universality.

(Hegel 1967b: 23)

When consciousness posits itself in a particular form, it recognises that this particular manifestation does not embody its full potentiality. It recognises that it is more than its particular manifestation. There is a separation between this particular embodiment of consciousness and consciousness itself. Human consciousness is able to divide itself from itself: 'Consciousness has for its object one which, of its own self, posits its otherness and difference as a nothingness, and in so doing is independent' (Hegel 1977: 110). When it splits itself from itself, consciousness becomes aware that its particular focus on one object is but one expression of itself. It is aware of itself as a separate and independent nothingness even though it can simultaneously hold this object in its attention. Consciousness, in short, becomes aware of itself; it becomes self-conscious. The moment of self-consciousness is extremely important because when a consciousness is aware of itself it can satisfactorily limit itself to a particular manifestation because it is not entirely encompassed by this particularity. This particularity is only one limited expression of a total individuality. It is a particular expression of consciousness within an encompassing self-consciousness. Particularity, encompassed within this wider whole, does not restrict consciousness but gives it individuality. It is important to recognise, as Kojeve (1969) has emphasised, the inherent dynamism of consciousness. The triadic dialectic is not merely a formal structure. The self-transformation of consciousness is necessary. Consciousness must have an object. It must be conscious of something, but in the course of being aware of something, humans also become aware that they are aware of this object. In this way, they automatically become self-conscious. In this moment of self-consciousness, however, consciousness of the object itself is necessarily transformed. The moment of self-consciousness in and of itself transforms what the object is for consciousness. The object is no longer the sole focus of consciousness, but one moment in a wider whole. The relationship between object and consciousness is transformed immanently by processes internal to consciousness itself. At this moment, self-consciousness demands that consciousness reconsiders its original relation to the object and deepens its understanding of it. As a result of self-consciousness, human consciousness propels itself on a self-transforming spiral of awareness. For Hegel, consciousness is able to supersede (*aufheben*) itself because, although it surpassed inadequate, particular expressions of itself, it was nevertheless able to retain and remember them. The particular moments were preserved in a higher unity.

In the course of Hegel's discussion of the dialectic, the meaning of *Geist* begins to become clear. For Hegel, the dialectical movement of consciousness overcomes the subject–object dualism of western philosophy. Subject–object dualism is superseded by the inevitable development of consciousness. Gradually, through a dialectical process, subjective consciousness develops by repeated encounters with the object. Consciousness continually recognises that it grasps the object only partially. At each moment of self-consciousness, it is apparent that consciousness has only an inadequate and particular concept of the object. Consciousness sets itself on a spiralling relationship with the object so that gradually inadequate concepts of the object are replaced. Eventually the concept of the object and the object itself are reconciled; both become adequate to each other. The subject's knowledge of the object becomes exhaustive. The object offers no more material for consciousness and consciousness itself has reached its highest expression. At this moment, which Hegel termed Absolute *Geist*, the subject and object are reconciled. Consciousness of the world and the world are one. Consciousness has developed to a sufficient degree that nothing in the world is alien to it. *Geist* has posited itself in all its possible forms so that it has a complete understanding of itself and the world. Its own potentialities and the world are recognised and each inadequate expression of consciousness is preserved in the self-consciousness of *Geist*. Consequently, all the inadequate particular moments of the *Geist* are incorporated into an overarching self-consciousness. *Geist* has reached the ultimate moment of individuality where differentiated particularity and undifferentiated universality are synthesised; humanity is finally aware of every possible one of its manifestations and has drawn these into itself. With little modesty, it is evident that Hegel believed not only that *The Phenomenology of Spirit* traced the historical development of *Geist* from initially empty universality to the divine individuality of Absolute Spirit but that this book itself was the embodiment of Absolute Spirit. Hegel's system, arising at this decisive historical moment, was the expression of the crowning of human consciousness in a moment of total self-consciousness. The *Geist* was this consciousness and by means of this consciousness Hegel genuinely believed he had overcome the subjectivism and objectivism of western philosophy.[1]

The Critique of *Geist*

Hegel's attempt to transcend dualism is ingenious but concept of the *Geist* has been severely criticised. Many of Hegel's critics have argued that *Geist* is a metaphysical entity and that his philosophy therefore descends into incoherent mysticism (Russell 1961; Popper 1976). Marx's criticisms are probably the most well known, however: 'To Hegel, the life process of the human brain thinking, i.e. the process of thinking, which under the name of 'the Idea' he even transforms into an independent subject, is the demiurgos of the real world' (Marx 1977b: 29). In his *Critique of Hegel's Doctrine of the State*, Marx objected that the Idea of the state was prioritised above the actuality of the state. The state became the mere reflection of rational necessity: 'Logic does not provide a proof of the state but the state provides a proof of logic' (Marx 1992: 73). For Marx, Hegel mistook the things of logic for the logic of things. Thus, for instance, Marx notes that in his discussions of the family and civil society, which he considers to be the one-sided moments of undifferentiated immediacy and differentiated particularity, Hegel wrote as if the Idea determined the form which the family and civil society took:

> The Idea is subjectivized and the *real* relation of the family and civil society to the state is conceived as their *inner, imaginary* activity. The family and civil society are the preconditions of the state; they are the true agents; but in speculative philosophy it is the reverse. When the Idea is subjectivized the real subjects – civil society, the family, 'circumstances, caprice etc.' – are all transformed into *unreal*, objective moments of the Idea referring to different things.
>
> (Marx 1992: 62)

Although Hegel may attempt to overcome the dualism of western philosophy, on Marx's account, his reconciliation fails. *Geist* overcomes the difference between the subject and the object only by obliterating the subject entirely. The subject is unknowingly directed by *Geist*, which uses the world for its own expression. Subjective volition and consciousness are irrelevant. They are the unwitting expressions of *Geist*, whose logic demands certain actions from humans at certain moments in the course of its development. *Geist* is not so much human consciousness as a divine consciousness which precedes all human existence.

There is ample evidence in Hegel's writing to support the reading of *Geist* as a transcendent being which directs human history from above. Indeed, Hegel explicitly describes *Geist* as a deity:

> It was for a while the fashion to admire God's wisdom in animals, plants and individual lives. If it is conceded that Providence manifests itself in such objects and materials, why not also in world history? Because its scope seems to be too large. But the divine wisdom, or Reason, is the same in the large as in the small. We must not deem God too weak to exercise his wisdom on a grand scale. Our intellectual striving aims at recognising that what eternal wisdom *intended* it has actually *accomplished*, dynamically active in the world, both in the realm of nature and that of the spirit. In this respect our method is a theodicy.
>
> (Hegel 1953: 18; also 1956: 457)

Geist is God and history is only the self-expression of this God. Hegel's philosophy is a theodicy which explains the often mysterious and cruel manifestations of this deity. The *Geist* is a deity which becomes incarnate in actually existing human subjects in order to develop itself (Hegel 1956: 109). The priority of the *Geist* seems to be emphasised elsewhere:

> The spiritual alone is the *actual*; it is essence, or that which has *being in itself*; it is that which *relates itself to itself* and is *determinate*, it is *other-being* and *being-for-self*, and in this determinateness, or in its self-externality, abides within itself; in other words, it is *in and for itself*.
>
> (Hegel 1977: 14)

Geist is the essence of human history because it alone is capable of self-consciousness. Only *Geist* is a being which is both in and for itself; *Geist* is a coherent independent entity which recognises its own identity. Only *Geist*, therefore, is a real individual, while humans are the merely subordinate and particular moments of this independent self-consciousness. This is true for normal human beings (Hegel 1967: 217) but even 'world-historical' figures who display more self-awareness than the average human seem to be the servants of *Geist* according to Hegel:

> The historical men, world-historical individuals, are those [who grasp just such a higher universal, make it their own purpose, and realize this purpose in accordance with the higher law of the spirit].
>
> (Hegel 1953: 39)

For Hegel, Julius Caesar and Napoleon stand at the front rank of world-historical individuals. Thus, Hegel admires the anti-republican spirit of Ceasar because at the moment he became emperor the republic was dead. By putting 'an end to the empty formalism of this title' (Hegel 1956: 313), Caesar was in fact driving human history forward to higher levels. The empire he would create gave rise to Christianity, with which the first glimmer of freedom and un-alienated consciousness appeared. However, even though Hegel regards world-historical figures as deeply significant in the development of *Geist*, there is more than a suggestion than even these visionaries are only pawns in a historical drama. Although Caesar and Napoleon grasp the meaning of their age in their actions, they do not see the wider significance of their actions. Even world-historical figures in the end do not know what contribution they are making to mankind. They act in accordance with the higher law of *Geist*. Human history is finally directed not by men but by the 'Cunning of Reason' (Hegel 1953: 44), whereby *Geist* works towards its ends through unwitting human activity. Thus, the cunning of reason 'sets the passions to work for itself, while that through which it develops itself pays the penalty and suffers the loss' (Hegel 1953: 44). Julius Caesar destroyed the Republic but he was unaware of the significance of this act in world-historical terms. He had no idea that his imperial accession would allow for the development of Christianity. Behind the contingent slaughter of history, there is a deeper purpose at work which is distinct from it and which is working all the time to its own end. The accusation that Hegel is a mystic transcendentalist who believes in a consciousness which hovers over human history and determines it externally certainly appears well grounded. Subject–object dualism is overcome only because Hegel posits the existence of a consciousness which already knows everything. The human subject is replaced by a divine one who is able over time to incorporate all objects, including human knowledge, within itself. The human is not the subject of the dialectic but only an object which must itself be incorporated into a divine consciousness.

Confirming the untenable status of *Geist*, Hegel's philosophy often assumed an arbitrary formalism. Especially in Hegel's later writings, this autonomous consciousness takes exactly the form of the rigid logical structure which he derided in the Preface of the *Phenomenology*. History was conveniently ordered according to the dictates of the triadic structure of the dialectic. In the *Philosophy of Mind*, the third part of the *Encyclopaedia*, the description of the development of *Geist* is at each stage arbitrarily forced into a triadic structure of universality (α), particularity (ß) and individuality (γ). Similarly, there is no reason why the Prussian state should be seen as the highest expression of Absolute Spirit simply because it has a monarch. Hegel seems to value the actual person of the Prussian king simply because his dialectic operates with a third moment of individuality. The presence of an actual individual on the throne seems to prove the operation of the *Geist*. At certain points, Hegel did ontologise the *Geist*, transforming it into a consciousness which existed independently of humans. Humans were but the vehicle for the inevitable synthesis between *Geist* and the world, when God finally knew himself and his world in its entirety. Human consciousness and understanding itself was subordinate to *Geist* and the reconciliation of subject and object ultimately occurred independently of merely human understanding. At best, humans were limited to particularistic understandings of their own petty activities but only *Geist* encompassed these particularities in a wider self-conscious whole. The subject–object dualism at the heart of western philosophy was overcome only in a dialectic process which subordinated human consciousness at every moment to a divine one. *Geist* was this divine consciousness.

Re-Thinking *Geist*

Marx's critique of Hegel is certainly sustainable. There are times in Hegel's writing when *Geist* is evidently described as a force above humanity which reveals itself through individual action; the Idea does seem to become the subject, while humanity is the mere predicate. Yet, there are a number of other passages in Hegel's works which suggest that Hegel was not a transcendental idealist and that *Geist* was not a divine consciousness. For instance, Hegel explicitly describes the *Geist* as 'the spirit which not merely broods *over* history as over waters, but lives in it and is alone its principle of movement' (Hegel 1894: 153). Elsewhere, Hegel explicitly contrasts his discussion of *Geist* with Leibnizian metaphysics because the 'justification of God, which Leibniz attempted metaphysically, in his way by undetermined abstract categories' (Hegel 1953: 18), was inevitably flawed. Hegel rejects those philosophies which try to understand the world merely by applying formal *a priori* categories to it. The inseparability of *Geist* from actually existing humans is suggested elsewhere. In the previous section, it was noted that Hegel seemed to describe the actions of even world-historical individuals as subordinate to an already existing *Geist*. However, if these passages are re-contextualised, the priority of *Geist* with its cunning of Reason becomes questionable:

> The first glance at history convinces us that the actions of men spring from their needs, their passions, their interests, their characters and talents.
>
> (Hegel 1953: 26)

Nothing therefore happens, nothing is accomplished, unless those concerned with an issue find their own satisfaction in it. They are particular individuals; they have their special needs, instincts and interests. They have their own particular desires and volition, their own insight and conviction, or at least their own attitude and opinion.

(Hegel 1953: 28)

If Hegel regarded *Geist* as a genuinely autonomous entity standing outside history and imposing itself upon it, his powerful descriptions of human practice and the resulting 'slaughter-bench' of history would be superfluous. If *Geist* were really intended transcendentally, then human history would be a mere detail in Hegel's system, unworthy of serious attention. The actual course of human history would be irrelevant and Hegel would focus on the final form which the *Geist* logically assumes. Yet, Hegel always emphasises human volition.

The Christian leitmotif of paradise, sin and redemption which appears throughout his work is significant here. Hegel emphasised that Christians redeem themselves not by fleeing from the world but through acting in it, reconciling themselves to their sins. Against the 'beautiful soul' who 'flees from contact with the actual world and persists in its self-willed impotence' (Hegel 1977: 400), the evil will acts in the world. This is the means by which the spirit transforms itself to a higher state. By sinning and wickedness, the evil will learns it has done wrong. It does not preserve itself in ignorant innocence. While the evil will acts in ways which will lead to eventual self-knowledge, the beautiful soul, 'instead of proving its rectitude by actions, does so by uttering fine statements' (Hegel 1977: 403). For Hegel, the evil will is superior because, while the beautiful soul is ignorant of existence, the evil will immerses itself into life and comes to a conscious understanding of sin. It does not reject sin theoretically but knows that sin involves forms of activity in which human potential cannot be fulfilled. Hegel's support for the evil will suggests that actual human history is essential to Hegel. Human activity and human history may not be supererogatory, *Geist* already existing without it. On the contrary, these passages suggest that *Geist* can become what it is only insofar as humans engage in actual social practices in the course of human history. Although commonplace, it may be an error to think that the *Geist* is ever separate from this visceral and often brutal reality. It is necessary to re-consider what *Geist* actually means more carefully.

The celebrated discussion of the master–slave dialectic is critical to this re-interpretation of the *Geist*. There, the inseparability of *Geist* from the actuality of human history begins to become clear. In order for *Geist* to reach a higher level, human self-consciousness is required. Crucially, human self-consciousness first appears in the interaction between the master and slave. It is this social relation at the beginning of human history which drives human consciousness to a new level. Hegel begins the master–slave dialectic lyrically, emphasising the social origin of self-consciousness: 'Self-consciousness exists in and for itself when, and by the fact that, it so exists for another: that is, it exists only in being acknowledged' (Hegel 1977: 111). Self-consciousness can be developed only in human social interaction when individuals see that others recognise them. Only then, when human beings become aware not simply of objects in the world but of the existence of beings who simultaneously recognise them, do they become self-conscious. They are able to see themselves as beings-for-themselves not simply as beings-in-themselves. This self-consciousness is possible precisely because humans are recognised by others. Effectively humans internalise the recognition they receive from others so that they are able to see themselves as others see them. The master–slave dialectic elaborates on the dynamic potential of social relations. The master–slave dialectic begins with a struggle to the death between two antagonists; 'In so far as it is the action of the *other*, each seeks the death of the other' (Hegel 1977: 113). Both demand recognition from the other but in the end only one is prepared to risk annihilation in the pursuit of that recognition. The other submits. This individual is not willing to risk death and is forced into a position of subordination. Initially, the master embodies the highest point of human consciousness at this moment of human history. He is the most self-conscious being and *Geist* finds its most developed expression in him. Significantly, although the development of self-conscious is extremely important in the struggle between the would-be master and slave, this social relationship does not remain static at this level. Having established himself as the superior, the master finds that in fact his role is unsatisfactory and empty (Hegel 1977: 116–17). He has gained recognition but his recognition is now provided by an inferior; an individual the master does not recognise. The object for his consciousness is inadequate to it: 'it is clear that this object does not correspond to its Notion, but rather that the object in which the lord has achieved his lord-ship has in reality turned out to be something quite different from an independent consciousness' (Hegel 1977: 116–17). The lord achieves only a pyrrhic victory; his development is stultified for he is no longer engaged in a self-propelling relationship of mutual recognition. The slave is a mere object for him; not another consciousness for whom the lord can be something. The lord is accepted automatically as lord and, providing no challenge, his slave cannot demand greater self-awareness from him. By contrast, the slave, although apparently the loser in the struggle for recognition, has the advantageous position. The slave must work. He must immerse himself in the world to produce for the master and in these moments of practical enterprise the slave externalises himself (Hegel 1977: 117–18). Consequently, the slave is able to become an other for himself and to develop his self-understanding. He is able to undergo dialectic development, differentiating himself in particular moments of labour but then re-incorporating those moments into his identity in a higher moment of individuality. The development of consciousness is indivisible from the social role and practical activities of the slave. Crucially, the development of the conscious-ness of the master and slave is not directed from outside. Their consciousness specifically develops in their interactions with each other. These humans mutu-ally transform each other and themselves. There is no external force here at all; the dynamic of development is internal to the social relation.

Nevertheless, although the self-transformation of the consciousness of these individuals is internal to their social relations, Hegel sees the master–slave dialectic as crucial to the development of *Geist* as a whole. As these humans develop themselves in their interactions, so does *Geist* also develop. If Hegel genuinely conceived of *Geist* as a divine consciousness, there would be a contradiction here. Hegel would be insisting on the importance of actual human history but at the same time he would be dismissing it as wholly superfluous. Human interaction is crucial to the development of *Geist*. This contradiction suggests that Hegel never in fact intended *Geist* as an independent and divine consciousness. Indeed, this contradiction can be reconciled only if another interpretation is put upon *Geist*. The master–slave dialectic begins to suggest that *Geist* is not a divine consciousness. *Geist* does not drive these social relations from above, always already fully formed, knowing the end of history. *Geist* is not a separate and prior idea, of which human consciousness is a supererogatory expression. On the contrary, *Geist* refers precisely to actually existing human consciousness at any particular point in history. This consciousness undergoes immanent, dialectical transformation in the course of human interaction. For him, human consciousness was inseparable from human activity and, in the course of their activities, humans are able to develop their consciousness of themselves. As humans transformed themselves, they engaged in new practices and social relations. The development of *Geist* referred precisely to this social process by which, in the course of history, humans were gradually able to understand themselves and their world better. In the course of their social interaction, humans reconcile themselves to the world; through historical development, humans – as subjects – knowingly reconcile themselves to the object.

The structure of the *Phenomenology* provides severe exegetical problems. Because of the abstract and often obscure way in which Hegel writes, it is not always clear which historical period Hegel is talking about. As Taylor has noted, each section does not begin from where the last left off (Taylor 1975: 139). In addition, Hegel wants to unify three separate processes into a single developmental account. He wants to trace the development of *Geist* philosophically as it becomes more coherent but he maps this conceptual development onto the historical development of humanity and his own personal, autobiographical intellectual development. Consequently, it is often not clear which process he is specifically discussing in any one section of the *Phenomenology* or whether, indeed, he is discussing two or even all three processes at any one time. Comments about the structure of the *Phenomenology* cannot be definitive since the work itself makes suggestive and speculative connections between philosophical, historical and autobiographical developments. Nevertheless, the position of the master–slave dialectic in the structure of the *Phenomenology* seems to confirm the immanence of *Geist* to human history. The first three chapters discuss consciousness, examining sense-certainty, perception and understanding. Typically, the first three chapters of the *Phenomenology* have been read as an account of the dawn of history as humanity gradually came to consciousness of the world or as the birth of consciousness in the human baby. Since Hegel argues in the Preface that human biological and historical evolution map each other, such readings are not without foundation. However, there are certain anomalies in reading the opening chapters of the *Phenomenology* like this. Firstly, in sense-certainty, Hegel demonstrates that the rich particularity at which this consciousness aims is inevitably vitiated by the appeals which it makes to language ('Here' and 'Now') to express this particularity (see Taylor 1975). As Taylor has noted, Hegel argues that in order to express the particular contents of its consciousness the human must draw on universal concepts like 'Here and now'. These universal terms cannot express the particular. This contradiction drives consciousness to a higher level. Taylor's reading is plausible and interesting. However, it is strange that if Hegel regarded this chapter as referring to the earliest humans or, indeed, to a human baby he would suppose that these beings would have a language with universal concepts at their disposal. They would not yet have developed these sophisticated concepts. It is perhaps significant that, in the next chapter, 'Perception', Hegel, describes this form of consciousness as 'sound common sense'. It is, of course, possible that this phrase simply refers to the practical orientation of humans at the beginning of history but it seems also to be an oblique reference to British empiricism, which prioritises experience as the basis of all proper understanding. Finally, the last chapter in the section, 'Force and Understanding', explicitly discusses the rise of certain forms of science and Kantian transcendental philosophy. It is curious that if Hegel intends the *Phenomenology* as a philosophy of history he would have inserted the rise of science here before the development of slavery, Greek and Roman civilisation and Christianity. The anomalous content of these chapters, which discuss arguments and concepts which arise only later in modern European philosophy, suggests that the first three chapters may not denote the historical birth of human consciousness. Rather, these chapters might be read more usefully as introductory remarks intended to demonstrate why neither empiricist nor rationalist philosophy could provide an adequate account of human cognition. These early chapters may not be so much an account of early human evolution as a critique of contemporary philosophy.

There are other reasons for interpreting these chapters as epistemological critiques, rather than as descriptions of the earliest moments of the dialectic. It is also notable that, as an account of the earliest development of human consciousness, these chapters are manifestly inadequate:

> The greater part of the book is taken up with historical dialectics, hence arguments which are not self-authenticating. But, in fact, these only start after the strict dialectic with which the work opens, that of consciousness. The dialectic of self-consciousness with its underlying notions of life, human self-consciousness and the desire for recognition builds supposedly on the results of the first part. In this respect the *PhG* resembles the system laid out in the *Encyclopaedia*. But when we look at it in this light, the first three chapters are much too weak and sketchy to support the rich superstructure of historical and anthropological interpretation that Hegel has erected.
>
> (Taylor 1975: 220)

While the first three chapters fail as descriptions of early human consciousness, they do make some pertinent critiques of empiricism and rationalism. If Hegel's intention in these earlier chapters is indeed epistemological critique, then this would at least explain why there is so little connection between this first part of the *Phenomenology* and the 'rich superstructure of historical and anthropological interpretation' which appears in the rest of the work. Hegel, perhaps, intended no developmental connection. The first three chapters illuminate merely the fallacies of western philosophy which tried to explain human understanding from the perspective of subjective consciousness. They may not be the starting point of the development of *Geist* but, on the contrary, a theoretical foil which Hegel's philosophy sought to overcome. In contrast to empirical and rationalist philosophy, Hegel recognised that human understanding arises only within social reality. Any valid epistemology must be grounded in a social ontology. Consequently, the philosophical argument begins in Chapter IV with the rise of self-consciousness in human society. Hegel's philosophy can begin only when human society itself appears and begins to develop.

There is further evidence that *Geist* refers to human consciousness when the opening chapters of the *Phenomenology* are compared with the *Philosophy of History*. These two works are extremely similar and ultimately the *Phenomenology* is a more philosophical and abstract version of the *Philosophy*. Consequently, a comparison of these two works allows the reader to map the specific historical development of humanity onto the philosophical intricacies of the *Phenomenology*. This comparison seems to confirm the point that human self-consciousness emerges at the dawn of human society. In *The Philosophy of History*, Hegel places the master–slave dialectic at the beginning of human development, as humans arise from mere bestial existence. Discussing the low level of existence in Africa, where tyranny and cannibalism are present, he notes that 'the standpoint of humanity at this grade is mere sensuous volition with energy of will' (Hegel 1956: 96). He claims that Africa has never risen above this level of existence and consequently has played no role in world history (Hegel 1956: 99). Even so, in connection with Africa, he comments: 'Slavery is in itself injustice for the essence of humanity is Freedom: but for this man must be matured' (Hegel 1956: 99). Africa may not have played a significant role in subsequent human development but it usefully illuminates the earliest experiences of humankind. Although debased, slavery is the initial social form out of which humanity eventually develops its self-conscious freedom. The master–slave dialectic marks a historic dividing point. It denotes the emergence of distinctively human society from the bestial herd. Significantly, social development and the development of human self-consciousness are indivisible. As these understandings change and develop, human relations with each other are simultaneously transformed. If this reading is correct, then the structure of the *Phenomenology* implies that human knowledge in essence is social and consequently its origins must always be linked to human historical development. The master and slave dialectic is the first moment in human history and constitutes the initial rise of human consciousness. All this supports the claim that *Geist* refers to human not divine consciousness.

Yet, it is still difficult to sustain this argument for the first three chapters of the *Phenomenology* definitively. However, even if the first three chapters of the *Phenomenology* were intended only to describe the emergence of the most basic level of human consciousness, the subsequent development of *Geist* is still dependent on social developments. Significantly, when Hegel moves on to self-consciousness and the master–slave dialectic in Chapter IV (Hegel 1977: 119–36), all developments of consciousness are explicitly linked with historical epochs. Minimally, therefore, Hegel claims that the development of human self-consciousness is inseparable from social development. While some basic consciousness may be possible outside society, human self-consciousness can be reached only in the context of actual historical and social developments. Human understanding is inseparable from human social development. Consciousness itself is inexorably bound up with human social relations. As humans develop new relations and new practices, they simultaneously develop new understandings of what they are doing. Consciousness and social activity are indivisible. If this is the case, then a re-interpretation of the *Geist* is necessary against conventional criticisms. *Geist* is not a divine consciousness; it does not determine individual action in history. *Geist* does not determine the social forms which arise in each era. On the contrary, *Geist*'s development is dependent upon the historical transformation of human social relations. Actual historical social relations are primary in Hegel's system but these relations necessarily involve a conscious element. In the course of interaction, as the master–slave dialectic revealed, human understanding undergoes necessary and immanent transformation. *Geist* is that consciousness which is an indivisible part of the human social world at any point in time, changing as humans interact with each other to develop new kinds of understanding. Ultimately, the development of *Geist* and human consciousness are indivisible; *Geist* just is human consciousness as it develops in the course of social interactions.

It is important that *Geist* is not interpreted as individual consciousness. In *Reason in History*, Hegel inserts a phrase of deceptive import: 'But each individual is also the child of a people at a definite state of its development. One cannot skip over the spirit of his people any more than one can skip over the earth' (Hegel 1953: 37). The world–historical figures do not embody individual consciousness. They are not solitary actors. Their status as historical figures is because they are able to express the understandings and intentions of the communities in which they live; the 'spirit' of their people. The distinctive historical phases represented by world-historical figures cannot be ignored by philosophers because *Geist* exists precisely and purely at the level of these communities; *Geist* just is the collective consciousness at various stages of history. This consciousness is, of course, not static, but in the course of human interaction undergoes inevitable transformation, as humans alter their understandings of themselves. This interpretation of *Geist* as shared consciousness renders certain obscure phrases explicable. When Hegel claims that 'it [*Geist*] is the spirit which not merely broods over history as over waters, but lives in it' (Hegel 1894: 153),[2] he means only that human understanding is an integral part of human history: the way humans understand themselves, the way they are conscious of themselves, is decisive to what they actually are in any historical era. *Geist* refers to this collective human consciousness as it develops through history in the course of social interaction. It is not a force which determines human existence from outside.

In the light of this discussion, it might be possible to suggest a different translation of the word *Geist*. In the first English translation of the *Phenomenology*, Bailey rendered it as 'Mind' (Hegel 1967a). Although an understandable translation, the word 'Mind' is unsatisfactory; it is abstract, denoting purely cognitive processes. Consequently, the translation 'Mind' communicates an intellectualism which was quite the opposite of Hegel's intention. In the more recent translation, Miller has tried to remedy this abstraction, rendering *Geist* as 'spirit' (Hegel 1977). It is a more accurate translation and it expresses the immanence which Hegel intended. *Geist* is deep within humanity; it refers not merely to cognitive or mental faculties but to emotions as well. Moreover, the word 'spirit' connotes a sense of fluidity which is certainly central to Hegel's writing. Consequently, it also communicates some of the vivacity of Hegel's concept.[3] Yet, the word 'Spirit' in English is so evidently foreign that it too finally relapses into an abstraction it simply does not have in Hegel's German. *Geist* is a word which finally defies easy translation but this does not mean that the significance of the concept cannot be rendered in English. For Hegel, the *Geist* referred not to any individual mind or spirit. It referred neither to individual cognition of the world nor to the categories which underlay that individual cognition. For Hegel, individual perception was in fact dependent upon the pre-existing *Geist*. *Geist* referred broadly to the consciousness of a people of itself and the world in which they lived. It referred to a people's self-understanding. It denoted the practices which a people regarded as appropriate, the kind of social intercourse in which that people engaged and, finally, the kind of world there was for that people. This consciousness was not just a system of logical categories; it was the living force of this people, sustaining them as a coherent social group, motivating every belief and action. Although a much looser translation, *Geist* might be better rendered as 'culture' in the anthropological sense. It refers to the distinctive lifestyles which various human groups have historically adopted, and to the shared understandings which underpin them. Indeed this is effectively what *Geist* came to mean later in Germany; the term *Geisteswissenschaften* refers to the sciences concerned with the study of human culture, the humanities. For Hegel, philosophy's primary concern was not individual cognition but human culture, in all its empirical colourfulness, since all human existence took place within the horizon of one culture or another. All human existence was a manifestation of *Geist*. *Die Phenomenologie des Geistes* is, therefore, the study of the historical manifestation of human cultures. It examines how human culture has developed in the course of world history.

The ontological immanence of *Geist* does not entirely absolve Hegel, however, for while he cannot be interpreted as an ontological dualist who believed that the Idea preceded its historical manifestation, Hegel's vision of *Geist* wrongly restricts itself to ideal cultural forms. Despite claiming that *Geist* finds its expression in the passions of particular individuals and is played out on the slaughter-bench of history, in fact his discussion of the *Geist*'s various forms refers almost invariably to the major philosophical positions in each period. Hegel's philosophy of history is ultimately only a history of philosophy. Thus, in the *Phenomenology*, Hegel describes the development of human consciousness through Greek philosophy, Christianity and modern philosophy, including utilitarianism and Kantianism. Indeed, even when he discusses a specific political event such as the Terror during the French Revolution, the reality is interpreted in terms of its underlying philosophy. Hegel intended his phenomenology of *Geist* to be a concrete history of the forms which human consciousness had assumed in actual human practice, but he only ever considered one small element of the totality of human historical practice: philosophical contemplation. Given this tendentious over-emphasis on the beliefs of a small literate elite in European society, it is not surprising that Marx and others should have interpreted *Geist* as a divine consciousness and Hegel's philosophy as a form of mystical dualism.

The *Geist* does not impose externally upon individuals but lives between them in the eternal round of social interactions. It is human culture; the medium of social interaction. It refers to the shared understandings on the basis of which humans interact with each other and with the world. These understandings determine the relation between any human subject and the object, but because humans are self-conscious they are able to transform their understandings and therefore their relationship to the object immanently. Once the import of the concept of the *Geist* is properly recognised, a genuine social ontology is recoverable from Hegel's philosophy. Humans live in social relations the reality of which depends upon their collective understanding of them. Social relations are sustained only insofar as humans recognise them and understand what they involve. In the course of their interactions, both social relations and human consciousness are transformed. The master–slave dialectic stands as a brilliant exemplification of this social philosophy. In this way, Hegel overcame the dualism of western philosophy. Human consciousness could not be understood by reference to the individual subject confronting an isolated material object. On Hegel's description, the world which existed for humans was invisible from their culture. Their social existence was necessarily implicated in any interaction with material objects. Consequently, the object did not merely stand before the individual but was already dependent on the way that humans in any particular culture oriented themselves to each other. The object was not pristine but partly depended upon the way humans understood themselves. In their social development, as humans understood themselves and their relationship to the world differently, the object also altered. For Hegel, a new and better way of understanding the world emerged, until at last, in modern western culture the potential of human consciousness has been reached. Human consciousness of the object becomes adequate to the object itself. It is certainly possible to reject Hegel's teleological story of human perfectability. It would be entirely possible to claim that humans did not improve their knowledge of the world but simply changed what they knew about it and their relation to it as they lived in different social forms. Nevertheless, Hegel's work offers a compelling account of the self-propelling nature of human social life. At the heart of this account lie human social interactions conducted in reference to shared consciousness. It is precisely this conscious element of human relations which imbues them with such flexibility. In the course of their relations, humans can mutually transform their understanding of themselves and, therefore, the very reality in which they exist. Hegel was not an idealist who subordinated the world to a divine Idea. His philosophy recognised only the priority of human culture, of human social relations. In this way, Hegel could prove to be an extremely rich resource for contemporary social theory, illuminating a clear route away from ontological dualism. In place of structure and agency, human history should be comprehended as the restless intercourse of conscious human beings.

6 From Praxis to Historical Materialism

Praxis

Ludwig Feuerbach employed Hegel's theory of objectification to claim that religion was the mystified externalisation of humanity. In creating gods for itself, humanity had falsely transposed its own activities onto a higher being and thereby alienated itself from itself. Humans deludedly deferred to a divinity which they had in fact created. Feuerbach did not merely reject religion, however. He refuted the power of ideas totally, promoting a rigorous natural materialism in which human existence was determined by biological imperatives. Feuerbach's critique of religion and his materialism played a significant role in the development of Marx's philosophy, especially in relation to Hegel. However, although Feuerbach's materialism offset the excesses of Hegelian idealism, Feuerbach's position was itself unacceptable to Marx. In the end, Feuerbach descended into the crudest form of biological materialism in which the putatively unmediated natural human appetites, the need to eat, to shelter and to procreate, ultimately determined all human existence.[1] In this way, as far as Marx was concerned, Feuerbach's materialism failed to comprehend the distinctive nature of human activity: 'The chief defect of all hitherto existing materialism – that of Feuerbach included – is that the thing, reality, sensuousness is conceived only in the form of the object or of *contemplation*, but not as *human sensuous activity*, *practice* not subjectively' (Marx 1978: 143). This was a crucial development. Marx did not want to replace Hegel's dialectic with an equally reductionist material one in which humanity was determined by biology rather than divinity. For Marx, social reality was distinctive because it could not be explained without considering the role which human consciousness played in it. Social reality was never independent of how the humans involved in it understood it. Humans did not, therefore, simply behave. It was an intrinsic element of their species being that they were capable of practice (*Praxis*); their activities had meaning for them. They understood their activities 'subjectively' and this subjective meaning made the practices what they were. *Capital* features a well-known remark in which the conscious element of human practice is affirmed:

> We presuppose labour in the form that stamps it as exclusively human. A spider conducts operations that resemble those of a weaver, and a bee puts to shame many an architect in the construction of her cells. But what distinguishes the worst architect from the best of bees is this, that the architect raises his structure in the imagination before he erects it in reality. At the end of every labour-process, we get a result that already existed in the imagination of the labourer at its commencement.
>
> (Marx 1977b: 174)

In both this passage and in Thesis I, human practice is distinguished by the fact that it has a meaning for those performing it. The way humans understand what they are doing is decisive to what any act actually is. However, either passage could be interpreted individualistically. Marx writes that practice is understood 'subjectively' in Thesis I, while the architect or labourer seems to conceive his work in his own private imagination. Yet, in fact, it is evident that, despite these potentially misleading phrases, Marx never conceives of praxis in individual terms. Individuals attach meaning to their activities and their consciousness of what they do is an essential part of their work, but the understandings which inform their work are not dreamt up alone. For instance, in Thesis IX, he explicitly rejects individualism: 'The highest point attained by contemplative materialism, that is materialism which does not comprehend sensuousness as practical activity, is the contemplation of single individuals in civil society' (Marx 1978: 145). Materialism is reductive precisely because it operates from individualistic premises. It examines the experiences of the individual alone. Marx distinguishes his own approach from Feuerbach's because he regards practice as intrinsically social. Although Marx writes that humans understand their practices 'subjectively' in Thesis I, he in fact means that they understand what they do intersubjectively. Together, not individualistically, humans understand the significance of their actions; human practice is conducted on the basis of shared understandings. Human practice is not independent of what the humans involved in it mutually take it to be. For Marx, practice always occurs within a matrix of social relations. Throughout the *Theses*, this social ontology is critical and the fact humans live in social relations decisively divides Marx's approach from Feuerbach's materialism. Marx's is explicit about this difference:

> The materialist doctrine that men are products of circumstances and upbringing, and that, therefore, changed men are products of other circumstances and changed upbringing, forgets that it is men who change circumstances and that it is essential to educate the educator himself.
>
> (Marx 1978: 144)

Materialism assumes that there are certain external circumstances which impose automatically upon humans. Materialism fails to recognise that even these social circumstances which confront humans now are themselves the product of human activity, even if that activity was in the past or in another place. The conditions which confront humans – the 'circumstances and upbringing' – are themselves social. The social circumstances are a human product. Indeed they consist only of the actions and interactions of humans; the educator is himself the product of the human social relations in which he was born. Against Feuerbach, Marx promotes a social ontology which in every case looks to the social relations between humans rather than to apparently independent material factors. Feuerbach, by contrast, understood humans in individualistic terms. He conceived humans as isolated individuals confronted by material facts. Marx rejected this dualistic account of social reality, interestingly arguing that 'the abstract individual whom he analyses belongs in reality to a particular form of society' (Thesis VII, Marx 1978: 145). Feuerbach took the modern abstract individual as evidence that humans are genuinely isolated and alone. He raised a culturally specific concept of the individual to the level of a theoretical axiom. Since there manifestly is a reality outside this individual, Feuerbach concluded that humans were determined by objective and material forces independent of them. For Marx, by contrast, the individual is not alone, confronted by an objective material reality. Rather, the individual is always bound into social relations and the institutions which confront humans themselves consist only of networks of other humans. Humans everywhere are the product of their social relations and social reality consists precisely of these relations.[2]

This emphasis on social relations in no way implies a reversion to idealism, even though Marx recognises that social practice involves a conscious element. As Marx stresses: 'Social life is essentially *practical*. All mysteries which mislead theory into mysticism find their rational solution in human practice and in the comprehension of this practice' (Marx 1978: 145). This is a deceptively important passage because in it, Marx overcomes the dualism of individual and society and materialism and idealism. Human existence is social; the relations into which individuals are integrated provide the conditions of their existence but these conditions have a peculiar quality. They, of course, involve a material element. They involve real human practices which produce food, clothes, shelter, goods, art-work and finally hierarchies of inequality. Yet, these practices are also meaningful. Practices also necessarily involve human understanding. Social practices do not exist independently of what the humans engaged in them believe them to be. Humans have to understand what their practices actually involve. Social practices, therefore, inevitably involve a conscious element. The way humans understand what they are doing makes these activities what they are. By extension, human social relations involve a similarly conscious element. Humans are certainly confronted by a real world, as Feuerbach insisted, but that world has a distinctive character. It is a practical social reality in which material and ideal elements are indissolubly fused. Social practices are decisively constituted by the way these humans understand them but this makes them no less real. Marx explicitly rejects the ontological dualism of Feuerbach's materialism: 'Hence, this doctrine [Feuerbach's materialism] necessarily arrives at dividing society into two parts, one of which is superior to society' (Marx 1978: 144). Marx rejects Feuerbach's dualism which envisages the isolated individual confronting a prior material reality. For Marx, society consists of human social relations involving practical activities with real effects. In the *Economic and Philosophical Manuscripts*, he similarly prioritises social existence as the species being of humans there. Human existence is explicable only in terms of the social relations in which people live. Although he is unaware of it, Marx reproduces the social ontology proposed by Hegel. Like Hegel, Marx claims that human social relations constitute the only substance of history. Both Hegel and Marx advocated a social ontology; human history involves the dynamic transformation of the social relations between humans in the course of which new practices are developed. It is somewhat ironic that in order to return to the 'Master', Marx had to overcome Feuerbach's materialism, which misrepresented Hegel in the first place.

Marx's similarity to Hegel goes further. In *The Theses on Feuerbach*, Marx already sketched the outline of a theory of historical change: 'The coincidence of the changing of circumstances and of human activity can be conceived and rationally understood only as revolutionising practice' (Marx 1978: 144). Human society changes when new activities and social relations develop. This seems to be a statement of the merely obvious but, in fact, the ontological import of this sentence is profound. Historical transformation is not a process which is independent of human understanding; its course is not inevitable, determined by forces beyond human volition. Rather, society transforms itself as humans together develop new practices out of old ones by understanding themselves in different ways. Social relations are themselves revolutionary. They can be transformed immanently by the humans engaged in them because these humans have to understand what they are doing to make these relations what they are.

In various passages in Marx's writing, he applied this social ontology to the empirical analysis of particular moments in human history. The two most prominent examples are *The Eighteenth Brumaire* and the description of the rise of capitalism in the last part of the first volume of *Capital*. In *The Eighteenth Brumaire*, Marx analysed the counter-revolutionary coup of Louis Napoleon III in December 1851. His coronation defied the reality of French society at that time and Marx sought to explain this farcical historical reprise. Marx's central point is that although Bonaparte represented the peasantry (Marx 1977c: 171, 176), the most reactionary group in French society – as inert as 'potatoes in a sack' (Marx 1977c: 170), his accession was facilitated by a bourgeoisie, who prioritised social and political order above their immediate economic interests. Louis Bonaparte's policies might have been inconsistent with the economic interests of the progressive bourgeoisie but his political authority at least ensured the suppression of radicals who threatened the entire social order. According to Marx, the French bourgeoisie applauded 'with servile bravos the *coup d'état* of December 2' (Marx 1977c: 164) on expedient grounds: '*Rather an end with terror than terror without end!*' (Marx 1977c: 161). This political compromise of the bourgeoisie created a contradiction within French society whereby the state was directly opposed to the interests and activities of the most important social group, the bourgeoisie (Marx 1977c: 176). The result was that 'Bonaparte throws the entire bourgeois economy into confusion' (Marx 1977c: 178). Marx concludes with the suggestion that this contradiction will ultimately be resolved by the eventual overthrow of Louis Bonaparte (Marx 1977c: 179).

The Eighteenth Brumaire is an example of the application of Marx's theory of practice to the analysis of a particular historical event. In line with this method, Marx situates the accession of Louis Bonaparte in 1851 in a broad historical and social context. This event is explained by reference to the wider social 'circumstances'. These involve the economic dominance of the French bourgeoisie in nineteenth-century France, the threat posed by the radical urban proletariat and the powerful but inert interests of the French peasantry. Bonaparte's coup is explicable only when the social relations between these three groups are considered. It is important to note that, while Marx uncontroversially emphasises the economic dominance of the bourgeoisie, the monopoly enjoyed by the bourgeoisie did not ensure political authority. Pure economic power did not ensure hegemony even in capitalist society. Bonaparte was able to attain the crown because social and political stability was possible only on the basis of an appeal to common collective traditions embodied in the idea of the countryside. While the economic dominance of the bourgeoisie could not be doubted, social conditions were not finally determined by market forces alone. Other social groups were necessary to create a stable regime. It was necessary to gain the political support of the mass of the peasants in order to buttress this regime. *The Eighteenth Brumaire* provides an empirical exemplification of the theoretical position Marx described in the *Theses*. Human history is not determined by independent material facts. It is the product of social relations, in which human understanding is an unignorable element. In 1851, the French bourgeoisie and French peasantry understood their social situation in a particular way and made political alliances which seemed appropriate to them. They were not simply determined by economic forces.

This practical ontology is also demonstrated in Marx's account of the rise of European capitalism in the last part of *Capital*. The most interesting chapters here are Chapters 27 to 29, although the final sections of Chapter 26 are also relevant, when Marx describes the agricultural revolution in England (and briefly in Scotland) as the necessary precursor to the rise of capitalism. Marx focuses on the enclosure of common land, which created a rural proletariat which would form the basis of the urban working force. As Marx notes, in England the immense majority of the population in the fifteenth century were free proprietors (Marx 1977b: 671) but by 'about 1750, the yeomanry had disappeared' (Marx 1977b: 676). The historical importance of this rural transformation is hard to overestimate and, consequently, it is imperative that Marx provides some explanation of how the Enclosure movement occurred. Interestingly, given Weber's famous argument about the connection between Protestantism and the rise of capitalism, Marx notes that the 'process of the forcible expropriation of the people received in the 16th century a new and frightful impulse from the Reformation' (Marx 1977b: 675). Unlike Weber, he does not suggest that the new theologies of the sixteenth century provided any impetus to accumulation. The Reformation propelled the agricultural revolution because 'the consequent colossal spoliation of church property' (Marx 1977b: 675) enriched the aristocracy which annexed church lands. Marx maintains that the initial impulse for the agricultural revolution was economic, noting that the 'rise in the price of wool in England, gave the direct impulse to these evictions' (Marx 1977b: 672). However, Marx also suggests – admittedly briefly – that this economic incentive cannot be separated from the wider social conditions of the time. Notably, 'the old nobility had been devoured by the great feudal wars' (Marx 1977b: 672), while the new rural elite no longer prioritised military honour but rational economic accumulation as the ultimate value. The enclosure of the lands was not an inevitable historical event; it only became rational once a new consciousness emerged among the English aristocracy. This economic activity must be conceived as a practice involving 'subjective' understanding, as Marx called it in Thesis I. The rise in the price of wool was significant only given the new way the English aristocracy understood itself. They no longer recognised old feudal obligations to their peasantry but considered themselves to be free to exploit any economic opportunity whatever the social implications. Marx notes: 'they abolished the feudal tenure of land' and 'vindicated for themselves the rights of modern private property' (Marx 1977b: 676). From the sixteenth century, this re-definition of social relations proceeded informally until it received legal sanction after the Stuart Restoration (Marx 1977b: 676). The new English aristocrat was free to exploit his property for its full financial value with no consideration for the welfare of the peasants to whom his forebears had once been bound. The freeing of the lords was a decisive cultural moment in English history but, for Marx, it was paralleled by a more ominous manumission: the creation of a 'free', landless labour force (Marx 1977b: 686). The market became the dominant principle of social relations, transforming the aristocracy into a landed bourgeoisie and the peasantry into a labour force. For Marx, the hegemony of the market constitutes the decisive moment in European history because, for the first time, it facilitates the absolute exploitation of the nascent working class:

> The organisation of the capital process of production, once forcefully developed, breaks down all resistance. The constant generation of a relative surplus population keeps the law of supply and demand of labour and therefore keeps wages in a rut that corresponds with the wants of capital. The dull compulsion of economic relations completes the subjection of the labourer to the capitalist. Direct force, outside the economic conditions, is, of course still used, but only exceptionally. In ordinary run of things, the labourer can be left to the 'natural laws of production'.
>
> (Marx 1977b: 689)

Market forces are disciplinary because they compel labourers to compete with each other for their subsistence until they are oppressed beyond a point of political engagement. Free labourers are free to starve. Crucially, reflecting his rejection of Feuerbach's materialism, Marx does not believe that the market is a necessary or universal reality. It does not constitute an autonomous economic order to which humans must submit. On the contrary, the very belief that the market economy is 'natural', independent of all human volition or understanding, precisely denotes the triumph of capitalism as a new form of social relationship. The capitalist economy was secure when this consciousness had established itself as the unshakeable basis on which social relations between the bourgeoisie and labourers were conducted: 'The advance of capital production develops a working-class, which by education, tradition and habit, looks upon conditions of that mode of production as self-evident laws of Nature' (Marx 1977b: 689). Capitalism involves real social practices, the production and exchange of goods, out of which arises an unequal social order, but these practices pre-suppose the understandings of those involved in them. Capitalism always involves the understandings and beliefs of the people who are part of this society because, at every point in history, humans have to understand what their social relations actually enjoin. In the case of capitalism, the development of the bourgeoisie and the working class necessarily involved the growing acceptance that social relations should be conducted by reference to the concept of the market.

Historical Materialism

The theory of praxis which Marx outlines in the *Theses* suggests that society consists of human social relations each involving ideal and material elements. Economic activity itself necessarily takes place within social relations. In his account of the extraordinary coup of Louis Bonaparte and the agricultural revolution in England, Marx is faithful to this theory of praxis. The economic factor, while necessarily important to the emergence of modern European society, is not necessarily the dominant one. Moreover, economic practice is not purely material. Capitalism, in fact, involves social relations in which certain concepts about private property and the free market orient individuals to interact with each other in particular kinds of ways. This theory of praxis overcomes the dualism between the individual and society by seeing humans as irremediably social beings but it also demands a particular methodological orientation. It demands immersion into the actual, empirical historical reality of any particular society. In order to analyse any historical moment, the interrelation of the various social relations in society cannot be determined *a priori*; models and abstractions might occasionally be useful as rules of thumb but the use of them runs the constant risk of reification. Since practice always involves the consciousness of the people performing it, it is essential that analysts understand that consciousness; such an understanding cannot be achieved in advance for human consciousness varies from period to period and from group to group. The theory of praxis rejects the violence of abstraction (D. Sayer 1987).

Unfortunately, although it is possible to draw a social ontology from Marx's work, as indeed many commentators have (e.g. Carver 1982; D. Sayer 1987; Avineri

1968; Rubinstein 1981; Kitching 1988; Hook 1936; Kolakowski 1978; Gould 1978), Marx did not remain faithful to this ontology throughout his writing. Indeed, the bulk of his writing is characterised by a commitment not to this theory of praxis but rather to a more rigid historic materialism. Ironically, Marx returned to the very dualism for which he rejected Feuerbach. It seems incorrect to argue, as some commentators have done, (e.g. D. Sayer 1987) that Marx is essentially a practical theorist and these moments of materialism are mere aberrations. When commentators argue like this, they are forced into contrived re-interpretations of those passages in which a dualistic ontology appears. These passages are violently re-interpreted until they are made compatible with Marx's theory of praxis. For instance, the famous passage from *The Poverty of Philosophy* in which Marx's claims 'the hand-mill gives you a society with a feudal lord; the steam-mill, a society with the industrialist capitalist' (Marx 1984: 102) is more than a little inconvenient for those commentators who argue for an essentially practical Marx. Kolakowski – and other commentators – has interpreted this famous phrase as loosely rhetorical: 'we are clearly not meant to take this literally' (Kolakowski 1978: 363). While the bluntness of the statement does seem to support Kolakowski's reading, there is extensive evidence to show that, while Marx might have descended into reductive technological determinism only for literary effect here, the implications of this clause are consistent with the position which Marx generally adopted in his writing. It is evident in *The German Ideology*, *The Grundrisse*, *A Contribution to the Critique of Political Economy*, especially in its famous Preface, and, of course, in large parts of *Capital*. While exegetically impressive, these interpretations are unnecessarily convoluted. By contrast, Kitching's position on these problematic passages is more sustainable. At certain points, Marx did in fact descend into the very reductionist materialism which he rejected in the *Theses* (Kitching 1988: 40–43).[3] Accepting that Marx did not always remain faithful to his earlier theoretical principles relieves some exegetical pressure; it is no longer necessary to have to re-interpret inconvenient passages against the grain of the words Marx actually wrote. Moreover, it explains why certain theorists such as Althusser, Poulantzas, Miliband and Cohen have maintained a structuralist and materialist reading of Marx. It is certainly possible to disagree with their reading to promote those elements of Marx's writing which point to a practical theory, but it seems evident that large passages of Marx's writing do support the kinds of interpretation which Cohen *et al.*, put upon him. It is possible to find a similar contradiction in the works of both Marx and Hegel. Whereas Hegel descended into idealistic dualism, Marx retreats into materialistic dualism. The individual is not confronted by a transcendent Idea but by an objective material reality. In much of Marx's writings, individuals are confronted by an economic base which exists independently of them and determines their existence.

The evidence for the descent into materialistic dualism is widespread in Marx's writing but one of the most prominent earlier examples of it is *The German Ideology*. The tone is set from the outset when Marx's rejects the 'child-like' fancies of Hegelian idealism: 'Once upon a time a valiant fellow had the idea that men were drowned in water only because they were possessed with the idea of gravity' (Marx 1977a: 37). For Marx, Hegel was guilty of the most facile form of idealism: reality was dependent upon what any individual took it to be. By contrast, Marx insists that humans are confronted with a reality which exists independently of what they think. As the drowning analogy suggests, society exists independently of human understanding, determining human existence irrespective of their beliefs about themselves. The text which follows this statement confirms this retreat from the social ontology: 'It has not occurred to any one of these philosophers to inquire into the connection of German philosophy with German reality, the relation of their criticism to their own material surroundings' (Marx 1977a: 41). In marked contrast to the *Theses*, where Marx employs the word 'praxis', in *The German Ideology* he employs the word 'material' to describe his position. Material circumstances now confront the individual, while social relations have faded from view. Marx continues in assertive vein to propose that human species being lies in the fact that they 'produce their means of subsistence'. Significantly, this productive labour is 'conditioned by their physical organisation' (Marx 1977a: 42). Practical activity is conditioned not by consciousness but by brute facts of material reality. Thus, Marx lists the fundamental needs of humanity: 'The first historical act is thus the production of the means to satisfy these needs', the satisfaction of which 'leads to new needs' (Marx 1977a: 48). In the first instance, man is an economic producer of subsistence and shelter in response to external imperatives. His consciousness of himself arises out of this productive confrontation with material reality. Marx has altered his position. Where he once emphasised that sensuousness had to be understood as a form of social practice in the *Theses*, basic material need – mere sensuousness – now assumes primacy. Economic production precedes social activities. The point is affirmed elsewhere:

> The fact is, therefore, that definite individuals who are productively active in a definite way enter into these definite social and political relations. Empirical observation must in each separate instance bring out empirically, and without any mystification and speculation, the connection of social and political structure with production.
>
> (Marx 1977a: 46)

Marx may well advocate empirical observation in each case but such observation illuminates only the alternative ways in which production is primary in different societies. The priority of economic production arising from biological need is assumed. Marx usefully summarises this shift from a social ontology to a dualist one in a famous phrase: 'Life is not determined by consciousness but consciousness by life' (Marx 1977a: 47). This phrase could be interpreted to make it compatible with the *Theses*. In the *Theses*, consciousness was not a dependent reflection of a social world which already existed. The particular social form was dependent on the way a group understood itself; human social existence and their consciousness of it were not separable. Following the *Theses*, this phrase could be read to mean that human consciousness is a reflection of human social relations. The way humans understand their relations to fellow humans determines their entire consciousness. However, the context in which the sentence arises renders a different and more problematic reading more likely. The phrase is found in a passage which explicitly prioritises production in the face of material necessity as the underlying essence of mankind. It ultimately stands as a summary of Marx's argument about the primacy of biological needs to human development. The economic facts which confront humans determine the kind of understandings which they can develop of themselves and thus the kinds of social relations they can have with each other.

Of course, Marx's belief that economic production takes ontological precedence is elaborated most famously in the 1859 Preface to *A Contribution to the Critique of Political Economy*. Marx himself called this passage his 'guiding thread' (Marx 1971: 21) since he viewed it as a condensed description of the central points of his method:

> In the social production of their life, men enter into definite relations that are indispensable and independent of their will, relations of production which correspond to a definite stage of development of their material productive forces. The sum total of these relations of production constitutes the economic structure of society, the real foundation, on which rises a legal and political superstructure and to which corresponds a definite form of social consciousness. The mode of production of material life conditions the social, political and intellectual life process in general.
>
> (Marx 1971: 21)

In the *Theses*, the social conditions which confront humans are produced by them and are dependent on their collective understanding of themselves. Here, in the Preface, Marx's ontology has become a duality; material conditions confront humans and impose on their consciousness. Society is divided into a material base and a super-structure which is determined by it. Consciousness no longer actively constitutes human social relations. Humans no longer need to understand what their social relations involve in the first instance. This understanding has become subordinate to a prior reality. Social relations are a mere mirror of a material reality and take a form independently of what humans actually think about them. The conscious element has become subordinate. Where Marx's theory of praxis promoted a social ontology, he now commits himself to a dualistic ontology. Individuals are now confronted by material conditions over which they have no control; they are 'independent of their will'. Having overcome ontological dualism in the *Theses*, Marx reproduces it. Here the individual is confronted by objective material circumstances; he is not embedded in a network of social relations which presume human understanding.[4]

Although Cohen's reading of Marx may be one-sided because he ignores important passages like the *Theses*, which his opponents invest with decisive significance (e.g. Carver 1982: 30–1; D. Sayer 1987: 41; Kitching 1988: 53), he provides a lucid elucidation of Marx's ontological dualism. Cohen shows that there is ample evidence that Marx proposed the existence of a socially unmediated productive sphere (G. Cohen 1988). Cohen draws particular attention to the division which Marx made between 'labour-power' and labouring activity (G. Cohen 1988: 42). 'Labour-power' refers to an essential though abstract capability which workers actually sold to the capitalist. This was the fundamental unit of economic production unmediated by social factors. The worker possessed labour-power as an essential individual capacity. Labouring activity, by contrast, referred to the actual activities which were performed in the factory by the workers as they were set to work. In his analysis of capitalism, 'labour-power' was a crucial concept on which Marx's analysis of exploitation was based. The capitalist bought labour-power not labouring activity and the worker was paid the proper price for this labour-power: 'Every condition of the problem is satisfied, while laws that regulate the exchange of commodities, have in no way been violated. Equivalent has been exchanged for equivalent. For the capitalist as a buyer has paid for each commodity, for the cotton, the spindle and labour-power its full value' (Marx 1977b: 189). The capitalist bought labour-power. However, he profited from labouring activity and it was this discrepancy, concealed by the originally fair exchange of wages for labour-power, that produced surplus value for the capitalist: 'Yet for all that he withdraws 3 shillings more from circulation than he originally threw into it' (Marx 1977b: 189). For Marx, the new technologies of production were critical in this exploitation of surplus value: 'by incorporating living labour with their dead substance, the capitalist at the same time converts value, i.e. past, materialised and dead labour into capital, into value big with value, a live monster that is fruitful and multiplies' (Marx 1977b: 189). The capitalist bought labour-power at its true derisory, value but by employing it in mechanised activities, he converted it into highly productive forms of labouring activity. The problem was that the workers were not paid for their mechanised labouring activity but only for their abstract labour-power. Marx considered this process to be the secret dynamic of the capitalist system. The conversion of labour-power in to profit was the alchemy at the heart of the factory system.

According to Marx, the process of exploitation was conveniently concealed by 'commodity fetishism'. The value of commodities seemed to be decided in exchange:

> The mystical character of commodities does not originate in their use-value…A commodity is therefore a mysterious thing, simply because in it the social character of men's labour reappears to them as an objective character stamped upon the product of labour; because the relation of the producers to the sum total of their own labour is presented to them as a social relation, existing not between themselves, but between the products of their labour…There it is a definite social relation between men, that assumes, in their eyes, the fantastic form of a relation between things.
>
> (Marx 1977b: 76)

The money economy obscures the origin of value by providing commodities with an autonomy which they do not possess. Commodities seem to attain their value from each other in exchange, not from the labour which was originally put into them. Marx's commodity fetishism argument has been rightly celebrated. It is an intriguing description of capitalism. Moreover, it echoes some of the elements of his theory of praxis. Against appeals to the existence of autonomous material objects (commodities in this case), he grounds these objects in the social practices out of which they arose. The value of a commodity is derived from its social basis of production, the factory system and the relationship between capitalist and labourer. Marx is correct to illuminate this connection between the system of production and the processes of exchange which the latter presumes. However, in his discussion of commodity fetishism, Marx no longer conceives production in the same way as he previously defined it. In particular, the social relationship between bourgeoisie and working class does not accord with the way Marx defined them in the *Theses*. The relationship of capitalist and worker is no longer a social one based on shared understandings. The commodity is specifically a product of labour-power. Labour-power has the same value whatever the relationship between capitalist and worker. Labour-power is not a social product but an essential entity which exists abstractly.

In Marx's critique, labour-power and its obscured transformation into profitable labouring activity by means of technology are the heart of the capitalist system. Yet, it is precisely at this point that Marx reneges on the position laid out in the *Theses* most decisively. Indeed, the sociological explanation he proposes here can be criticised from the very position which he himself elaborated in the *Theses*. The process of exploitation can, in fact, be understood not by reference to any essential labour-power but by reference to social relations; that is, to the social ontology which his practical theory illuminated. Despite Marx's confident assertions, it is far from clear whether commodities do in fact receive their value from an unmediated labour-power. In the last part of *Capital*, Marx does not mention surplus value or commodity fetishism as the mechanism of exploitation. Rather, the market provides a very efficient and independent form of oppression. Through the creation of free labour, those people who had no land or capital were forced to sell their labour. For the very reason that there were many workers offering the same good, the price which they could ask for their labour was extremely low. The mass of impoverished workers mutually undermined the value of each other's labour. Once social relations were conducted on market basis – once the bourgeoisie and labourers understood themselves in these terms – exploitation necessarily followed. In this section of *Capital*, Marx provides an account of capitalist exploitation in the nineteenth century without the appeal to the essentialist concept of labour. As Karl Popper noted: 'The laws of supply and demand are not only necessary but also sufficient to explain all the phenomenon of "exploitation" which Marx observed' (Popper 1976: 175–76). Workers could be exploited simply because the supply for their labour far outstretched the demand. Consequently, their wages could be held at a derisorily low level. Capitalist profit could be explained by reference to the same market process. The price of commodities was set by the demand for them. Capitalists aimed at selling their commodities at the highest price, while at the same time suppressing wages as low as they could given the laws of supply and demand. The greater the market for commodities and the lower the market for labour, the greater would their profit be. Significantly, when the market position of the labourers changed, the value of labour also changed. Crucially, the alteration in market position did not involve any essential change in the individual properties of the workers. They were the same individuals performing the same jobs and since labour-power was an essential property it must have remained unchanged. Significantly, however, they began to form themselves into unions. For the first time, they recognised that they shared collective interests and were able to encourage each other to act in ways which furthered those interests. Individual workers no longer competed in a free market, but a union monopolised the labour market, driving up the amount which capitalists, as the purchasers, had to pay for it; the workers had altered their social relations with each other and, therefore, their (market) relations with the factory owners. Decisively, the social circumstances in which they worked had changed – simply because workers began to understand themselves in different ways and to recognise the special bond which now bound them together. This proves an important point. As Marx proposed in the *Theses*, the economic realm is not autonomous. Production is embedded within a network of social relations. The value which is placed on the labour of any group is not determined by reference to the essential labour-power of individual workers but by this group's relationship to other groups. These relations, even in the sphere of production, involve collective understandings on the basis of which workers and capitalists interact with themselves and each other. When humans understand their relations with others differently – as workers started to do when they formed themselves into unions – they actually transform their material conditions and indeed the material conditions of the whole society. Social groups have a decisive role in every aspect of production and these groups exist only by virtue of the understanding which group members have of themselves and their fellow members. Marx's error for the greater part of his writing was to give the economic sphere and labour, in particular, an unmediated priority which it did not deserve. He forgot his own greatest insight, that all human practice is social. Human activities must be explained by reference to the social relations in which they occur and, consequently, in every case the sociologist has to consider how humans actually understand these relations. The possibility of social mobilisation relies upon them.

The Two Marxs

The work of Karl Marx has often been interpreted as being divided into two basic periods: an early one up to 1846 in which Marx was primarily concerned with philosophical issues, the critique of Hegel and human alienation, and a later one from 1846 until his death when Marx focused on the critique of the capitalist economy. Although the argument for a substantive break in Marx's work is feasible, noting his shift from philosophical concerns to empirical analysis, Kolakowski has cogently argued that no such break is discernible (Kolakowski 1978: 263). The themes of alienation which are first articulated in the 1844 *Manuscripts* plainly underpin the analysis of capitalism in *Capital* itself; the concepts of surplus labour and commodity fetishism are empirical exemplifications of the process of alienation. In terms of thematic interest, Marx's *oeuvre* forms a coherent whole. His central theme is the alienation of human labour and its social and political effects. However, while Kolakowski is correct to question the validity of the 1846 break, it seems clear that there is another, more invidious tension in Marx's work which is not so easily periodisable. This tension involves the contradiction between Marx's theory of praxis and his historic materialism. The first theory, found generally though not exclusively in works such as *The Theses* and *The Eighteenth Brumaire*, promotes a social ontology. Society consists of the social relations between human beings. These relations involve both material and ideal dimensions. The 'circumstances' which confront individuals are social and, therefore, dependent upon how the people in this culture understand themselves. Moreover, in the course of human interaction, human societies undergo inevitable transformation as new forms of practice and understanding arise, effacing the old. In promoting a social ontology, Marx was much closer to Hegel than he ever realised.

The second ontology which appears in Marx's writing contrasts markedly with the social ontology of the practical theory. This second theory ironically succeeds in inverting Hegel but in doing so it falls into an inverse dualism which is no less pernicious. In place of Hegel's dualistic idealism, Marx promoted a material dualism, where production exists independently of the individual. The unmediated forces of production determine the course of human history, imposing themselves on the individual and determining the form which social relations take. Basic material needs give rise to specific forms of economic production which determine the rest of the social order. Reflecting the priority of production in the capitalist economy, labour-power becomes an abstract and essential entity. The social circumstances are no longer the product of conscious human relations but the mere reflection of objective material fact. Where Hegel adopted a conceptualist dualism where the Idea imposed upon the individual, Marx promoted a realist dualism where the economy preceded the individual. Yet, Hegel and Marx simultaneously supersede their own dualistic tendencies. In this way, both Marx and Hegel offer contemporary social theory a clear route away from the currently dominant ontological dualism. Human history should not be understood as the imposition of the *Geist* and or the economy on the individual. The reality in which humans live is not characterised by an opposition between the society and the individual. Rather, humans live in fecund and dynamic social relations eternally open to transformation. These social relations involve a material dimension but they are not independent of the way that the humans engaged in them understand them. When humans think about their relations with each other differently or when they form new social relations based on new understandings, the social reality itself changes. Hegel and Marx provide a genuinely sociological vision. Unfortunately, for the most part contemporary social theory has drawn upon the most unsatisfactory part of Marx's and Hegel's work. It is necessary to redress that balance in order to recover from Marx's work the profound proposal of a social ontology which is contained there. This social ontology will set contemporary sociology on its feet, just as Marx wanted to ground Hegel's philosophy in the actual social relations between humans.

7 Status Groups and the Protestant Ethic

In his editorial essay for the new journal *Archiv fur Sozialwissenshaft*, Weber stressed his opposition to Marxism: 'The so-called "materialistic conception of history", as a *Weltanschauung* or as a formula for the causal explanation of historical reality is to be rejected most emphatically' (Weber 1949: 69). For Weber, 'Marxian laws' were ideal types which could be analytically useful as long as they were not thought of as 'real' or 'effective' forces (Weber 1949: 103). In fact, it is not an exaggeration to claim that a very large part of his writing was an empirical elaboration of this anti-materialism. The entire *Sociology of Religion* (1965) (comprising some 500 pages of *Economy and Society* (1978)), which effectively culminates in the Protestant Ethic thesis, is a direct attempt to show how religion hindered the development of capitalism in the Orient while Christianity provided the necessary conditions for Occidental capitalism. It might in fact be argued that *The Religion of China* (1964) constituted a further example of Weber's anti-Marxism since it demonstrated the significance of cultural and political institutions to the possibility of capitalism. Moreover, while the *General Economic History* (1961) discusses various developments which were necessary to the development of capitalism, the work concludes with *The Protestant Ethic* (1958d), which is identified as 'in the last resort the factor which produced capitalism' complementary to 'rational permanent enterprise, rational accounting, rational technology and rational law' (Weber 1961: 260). Even in Weber's general historical writings, his opposition to Marx is evident.[1] Material facts alone cannot explain historical development. Weber's interpretive sociology proposed an account of social life which was opposed to those reductive passages in Marx, where the economy became the driving force of history.

Status Groups

In *Economy and Society*, Weber defined the main characteristics of his 'interpretive' sociology: 'Sociology... is a science concerning itself with the interpretive understandings of social action' (Weber 1978: 4). Sociology, for Weber, must focus on 'action', which he defined as that activity by which 'the acting individual attaches a subjective meaning to his behaviour' (Weber 1978: 4). For Weber, although causal and functional explanations of social life constituted an appropriate introductory form of analysis, sociology only reached a level of explanatory completeness when its analysis operated at a level which was 'adequate on the level of meaning' (Weber 1978: 12). Although Weber talks of 'subjective' meaning, the meanings which individuals attach to their actions are, in fact, a product of the social groups of which they are part; these meanings may be understood in subjective individual consciousness, but they are in origin always shared. A human action necessarily involves others and, consequently, for it to have the effects which it does others must understand what the actor intended by this act. Social actions pre-suppose shared understandings. *Economy and Society* is thus an encyclopaedia of interpretive sociology in which social groups are the primary focus. There, Weber stresses the importance of 'lifestyle' and 'status honour' to emphasis the fact that the meanings which inform individual action are shared. Sociological analysis for Weber must be adequate at the level of shared not individual meaning. This becomes clear in other texts. For instance, in his essay '"Objectivity" in Social Science and Social Policy', the ontological premises of his interpretive sociology are promoted with unusual lucidity. Since social relations presume human understanding, they cannot be reduced to positivistic laws, be they economic, psychological or biological (Weber 1949: 76–77). Sociologists must understand the meanings which historical actors give to their activities: 'Our aim is the understanding of the characteristically unique reality in which we move' (Weber 1949: 72). At the end of the essay, Weber describes exactly what it is that sociologists should study:

> Life with its irrational reality and its store of possible meanings is inexhaustible. The *concrete* form in which value relevance occurs remains perpetually in flux ever subject to change in the dimly seen future of human culture. The light which emanates from those highest evaluative ideas always falls on an ever changing finite segment of the vast chaotic stream of events which flows away through time.
>
> (Weber 1949: 111)

Weber rarely found a poetic voice but here he expresses his interpretive position sonorously. The object of social science is not some dead matter impressed by the mindless forces of nature. It is life. The concept of 'life', derived from Dilthey, refers to the shared understandings which underpin human existence in any historical era. Crucially, for Dilthey and for Weber, life was an irreducible unity in which particular human social relations arose and from which they derived their significance. Life consists of shared understandings which define social relations in any particular society. Life is the way humans mutually understand their social relations, thereby making them what they are. Life denotes the values and meanings by which people live and die. These understandings shape every activity, economic or otherwise. Life is the medium of existence, not the mere tablet on which external forces write themselves, because humans have actively to understand what their social relations actually involve.

The centrality of 'life' to Weber's sociology emerges with special clarity in his

definition of status groups. Weber's discussion of status groups is usually interpreted as merely one type of collectivity in modern society, alongside classes and
parties. This interpretation is entirely understandable since in *Economy and Society*
Weber's discussion of status groups is framed in exactly this way. It does appear
that the status group is simply one possible form of social group, with no more
theoretical significance than class or party. In fact, to read Weber's discussion of
the status grown groups in this way is to miss its profound theoretical importance. Weber's discussion of the status group does not merely illuminate one
possible form of social grouping. It describes the way in which all human groups
come into being. Crucially, his discussion of status groups demonstrates that
purely economic explanations of group formation are inadequate; prior material
facts can never in and of themselves explain the creation and maintenance of
human social relations. Weber does not deny that status groups may have
economic ends. Indeed, some status groups may be formed purely for the
purpose of exploiting economic resources, yet, even if this is the case, the formation of a social group still cannot be understood purely in economic terms.
Economic interests do not simply determine group formation. In his famous
definition of status groups Weber claims that status groups always monopolise
certain 'ideal and material goods or opportunities'. In order to do this, any
would-be status group has to exclude others (Weber 1978: 935). The status group
has to form itself into a unified entity closed to outsiders. The members of the
group have to recognise the special relationship which binds them to each other
to the exclusion of others; they have to recognise their *collective* interests. It is at
this point that economic explanations fail. No prior economic facts can finally
determine group formation because economic facts will never automatically
force humans to recognise their social relations with each other. The economic
facts cannot force humans to recognise collective interests. In the face of competition for the same material resources, humans could form themselves into a
range of groups, depending on which relations humans mutually decide to establish and which humans they seek to exclude. There is nothing in the prior
economic reality which finally determines this process of selection. Any one
could theoretically be included in a group and, similarly, any one could be
excluded. The rise of specifically collective interests – even if these are purely
economic – has to be explained by reference to non-economic processes.

As Weber stresses, in order for a group to emerge its members have to recognise that they share something in common. The group has to select certain
criteria for group members which all consciously recognise. These criteria are
not imposed upon group members by prior economic facts. They are ultimately
arbitrary: 'It does not matter which characteristic is chosen in the individual
case: whatever suggests itself most easily is seized upon' (Weber 1978: 342). They
are established only insofar as the group itself recognises them. Lifestyle, skin
colour, language or gender could all be used to distinguish group members from
non-group members and, indeed, these criteria have historically been employed.
Ultimately, these criteria of group membership can be established only insofar as
would-be group members engage in social intercourse. Weber consciously

stresses the importance of 'intercourse which is not subservient to economic or any other purposes' (Weber 1978: 932). In order for a status group to emerge, the members must engage in non-instrumental activity with each other in the course of which they can begin to recognise their special social connection to each other. During these periods, group members mutually establish or affirm their social relations with each other. They understand themselves to be part of a group and define the criteria of group inclusion and exclusion. In these periods of exclusive social interaction dedicated to the affirmation of social relations, collective interests are recognised for the first time. The group as such emerges. Collective interests do not exist before this interaction has taken place. A group cannot exist until its members recognise their common bond to each other. For Weber, the group emerges as a unified entity with collective interests as it develops a 'status honour'. Status honour refers to the central values of the group and the common lifestyle which the group adopts. The status honour is also vital in sustaining the group because it provides incentives for acting in accordance with collective interests and sanctions for acting against them. Group members are honoured when they act in accordance with the collective interests of the group – they gain status honour – but to breach group norms involves the loss of status honour and, ultimately, exclusion from the group. It is important to recognise that Weber is not denying that status groups are always engaged in real practices or that they will require certain material resources to sustain themselves. Indeed, some status groups, only purpose is economic; it is to monopolise certain economic opportunities. Yet, even in this case, the existence of groups cannot be understood without accepting the critical role of human understanding and social interaction, which enables humans to orient themselves to collective ends. Groups only emerge when their members develop a common status honour to which all are knowingly oriented. Humans create collective interests insofar as they recognise their special social relationship with one another and exclude others. That recognition arises in the course of social interaction; it cannot be determined by prior economic reality. Humans have to recognise their collective interests. They are not simply imposed upon them by a prior economic reality. They could exploit economic opportunities in any number of ways.

Weber's discussion of class emphasises the point. There, Weber suggests that a class situation is a product of an individual's market position, which is overwhelmingly determined by his property (Weber 1978: 302, 928). Weber recognises that in modern society the market has become increasingly important in determining social position (Weber 1978: 306). However, although the market may be important and although it might be loosely possible to argue that individuals who share broadly similar market positions represent a class, the theory of status groups refutes the claim that the market determines the formation of class as a social group. Even if individuals found themselves in the same market position, they would only constitute themselves into a 'class' if they consciously recognised their special relationship with one another. There is nothing in their shared market position which in itself would determine that they should do this.

There is no intrinsic reason why they should ally with other individuals in that position to form a group. Alternatively, selected individuals in the same market position might ally themselves with each other to the exclusion of others in the same position. In other words, individuals might form a group which specifically cut across supposedly objective class interests. There are historical examples of this occurring. When the English working class formed unions in the middle of the nineteenth century, they specifically sought to exclude women and children from the factory even though it might be argued that all labourers of whatever sex and age shared the same market position. A class analysis would have predicted group formation on these inclusive lines but such an inclusive group is precisely what did not emerge. A particular masculine status group arose in response to economic competition. Masculinity became the arbitrarily selected criterion on the basis of which adult male workers unified themselves. It might be possible to use the concept of social class to refer broadly to a range of people in more or less the same economic position but it is important to recognise that this market position cannot determine the formation of exclusive status groups.

Indeed, empirically the market never operates purely and humans are never simply assigned a class position on the basis of their position in the labour market. As Randall Collins has demonstrated (1990), Weber's theory of status groups in fact involves a profound re-consideration of the very concept of an individual having a purely market position. As Randall Collins notes, status groups are 'the natural form in which economic interests can act socially' (Collins 1990: 129). The economy does not precede status groups. On the contrary, the economy itself is constituted in the first instance by a complex hierarchy of status groups interacting and competing with each other. These groups are formed through interaction in which a particular kind of status honour is established. The economic interests of status groups depends upon the lifestyle and the status honour of these groups. The interests of a group are not given self-evidently but are a product of the way a group collectively defines its interests. Crucially, the existence of status groups oriented to a particular status honour produces the material conditions in any era. There is no prior economic reality before the existence of these groups. The material reality of any society is decisively contoured by the groups which actually exist. The nature of these groups and their relationship to each other determines the character of the supposedly autonomous economic base. The social relations within and between groups define the material reality of any society. Individuals never simply occupy a market position, for any position they occupy is created as a result of the existence of social groups oriented to collective interests and status honour in other parts of the society.

Weber's theoretical discussion of status groups is illuminated in his analysis of the Junkers of Prussia. Weber examines the historically important example of the role which the Prussian rural aristocracy, the Junkers, played in the development of the German economy. The Junkers rose to pre-eminence in the course of the eighteenth century, especially under the monarchy of

Frederick the Great. His regime was founded on a modern army, the officer corps of which consisted exclusively of aristocrats, the Junkers. In return for this honourable service to the state, the Junkers consolidated their political power. They became the most culturally prominent group in Prussia, enjoying a hegemonic position over it:

> These Junkers imprint their character upon the officer corps, as well as upon the Prussian officials and upon German diplomacy, which is almost exclusively in the hands of noblemen. The German student adopts their lifestyle in the fraternities in the university. The civilian 'officer of the reserve', a growing part of all the more highly educated Germans belong to this rank – also bear their imprint.
>
> (Weber 1991c: 373)

The dominance of the Junkers remained into the nineteenth century (and beyond) and Weber noted their continued political influence: 'The class of rural landowners of Germany, consisting particularly of noblemen residing in the region east of the Elbe, are the political rulers of the leading German state' (Weber 1991c: 373). These landowners were not especially wealthy. Weber notes that unlike Western Germany, where urban industrial capitalism was strong and the agriculture consisted of market-oriented small properties, in the east, on the black soils of Prussia, the land was divided into large estates owned by the Junkers. The different form of agricultural ownership and production had important economic implications: 'The western landlord used the peasants as a taxpayer, while the eastern landlord, by becoming a cultivator began to use the peasants as a labouring force' (Weber 1991c: 376). In the west, landlords subdivided their property and rented it out to peasants, who exploited its produce for market value. In the east, the Junkers retained control of their estates but they required an agricultural labour force to work the fields. Although the Junkers wanted to create a mass of landless rural labourers, like the English aristocracy, they were 'a very different social product than the English landlord' (Weber 1991c: 380); because they did not want a total marketisation of agricultural production. Although the Junkers demanded protection from the international free market in the sphere of agricultural production, they were totally market-oriented as hirers of agricultural labour, encouraging the migration of cheaper slave labour into Prussia to undercut the native peasant workforce (Weber 1991c: 381–82). Yet it would be wrong to understand the Junkers in purely economic terms. Their significance as an economic group was itself dependent on the fact that they were able to establish themselves as a dominant social group with a distinctive status honour. The Junkers' existence was not a product of prior economic facts. On the contrary, the economic orientations and interests of this group were a reflection of its status honour. The collective understandings of the Junkers, which unified them as a group, demanded certain forms of conduct from them. The Junkers developed only those economic activities which were consistent with the militaristic honour culture of this group. The collective cultural ends towards which this group directed itself decisively contoured the economic reality which emerged in Germany in the nineteenth century. As Bendix has noted:

> Weber emphasised that the collective actions of the *Junkers* as well as of farm workers could not be understood in economic terms alone. It also was necessary to analyse the ideas derived from the subculture of each group – in Weber's terms, its 'style of life' – which entered into the evaluation of its economic interests.
>
> (Bendix 1960: 105)

Weber does not reduce economic reality to a matter of opinion. However, a prior economic reality does not automatically determine the formation of social groups. Social groups can be developed only as humans come together and mutually orient themselves to certain common ends. They develop a status honour. Prior economic factors cannot determine the conscious process whereby the *social* relations between people are recognised. Once group members recognise their social relations to each other, the status honour they develop then enjoins particular economic practices which are deemed appropriate. The economic reality of any society cannot be comprehended without a consideration of the social groups operating in that society. There is simply no independent economic reality which can be identified independently of the status groups which exist in a society. Humans are confronted not by a pristine economic reality but by a hierarchy of status groups which make this society what it is.

The Confucian bureaucrats of China provide another example of the centrality of status groups to human history. During the period of the Warring Kingdoms, capitalist money-lenders and purveyors existed in China (Weber 1964: 84) but, in a historical process which was directly opposite to Europe's, this incipient capitalism was stifled after the imperial unification of China. This empire prioritised political stability over economic development. The state bureaucracy did not seek to promote economic growth but merely to raise taxes on stagnant economic practices which sustained the patrimonial interests of the state. While the cities of China were suffocated by the imperial bureaucracy, the villages which remained more independent were dominated by the '*sib*', the kin group. The *sib* itself was dominated by tradition and by the authority of the elders and ancestors, which blocked development as effectively as the state. For centuries, China was constricted and underwent minimal historical transformation. The curious historical stasis of China demonstrates a number of important points. It highlights that economic factors are not necessarily the determining factor of history; capitalism developed and then disappeared in China. Above all, it also emphasised the role of status groups with distinctive styles of life in human history. The Chinese imperial bureaucracy was administered by an elite status group, the *literati*. Entry to this group was restricted by adherence to

Confucianism and a series of difficult examinations. Unlike the *noblesse de robe* in Europe, who were among the most important agents for change from the sixteenth century onwards, the culture of the Chinese status group emphasised not dynamism and innovation but tradition: 'The examinations of China tested whether or not the candidate's mind was thoroughly steeped in literature and whether or not he possessed the *ways of thought* suitable to a cultured man' (Weber 1964: 121). This status group did not prioritise critical or speculative thinking and the concept of logic remained foreign to it (Weber 1964: 125–26). On the contrary, 'puns, euphemisms, allusions to classical quotations, and a refined and purely literary intellectuality were considered the conversational ideal of the genteel man' (Weber 1964: 132). The *literati's* opposition to development was supported by the population, for the various regions competed in producing candidates for the bureaucratic examinations and would take honour from having their own candidates accepted. Although Weber does not elaborate, it seems likely that regions did not merely attain honour from the appointment of their candidates but that, once in office, a region's candidate could usefully manipulate the state bureaucracy in favour of his region. *The Religion of China* (1964) demonstrates the centrality of status groups to human history. The historic development of Chinese society cannot be explained by reference to some autonomous economic base which determined the social forms which arose. Rather, Chinese society consisted of status groups, the most important of which were the state bureaucrats. These status groups and above all the state *literati* were oriented to particular forms of status honour which emphasised certain kinds of collective ends. The status honour of these groups directed them to certain kinds of appropriate economic activities. The economic activities which characterised Chinese society were not given prior to the existence of these groups. Rather, they were a reflection of these social groups. In the case of China, the power of the *sib* groups and the *literati* ensured economic stagnation, for the status honour of groups promoted not economic development and enrichment but traditionalism and erudition. The trajectory of Chinese development was a function of the social groups which existed in this society. No independent economic base is remotely discernible.

Weber's sociology does not simply provide an account of the theoretical importance of status groups. His writing offers some striking examples of the historical significance of status groups and, in particular, the way in which the interaction and competition of status groups is a critical element in historical development. As Bendix noted, 'Weber's approach conceived of society as an arena of competing status groups, each with its own economic interest and orientation toward the world and man…This emphasis upon the struggle among different social groups was at the core of Max Weber's personal and intellectual outlook on life' (Bendix 1960: 270). Weber's interpretivist focus on status groups with distinctive lifestyles offers a sociological perspective at radical odds with ontological dualism. Human society and historical development are not explained by reference to a material base which determines social reality. The individual does not confront an autonomous society. On the contrary, society consists only of social relations conducted on the basis of shared meanings. These social relations involve economic elements but are not reducible to them. Ironically, although Weber's interpretive sociology was conceived as a reaction against Marxism, his discussion of status groups echoes Marx's argument in the *Theses* almost exactly. There, Marx similarly argued that there were no pristine economic or material realities. Human existence is social, involving a conscious dimension of understanding. Humans have to recognise their social relations with each other and understand what they demand. The sociologist must similarly recognise that human understanding is central to any explanation of society.

The Protestant Ethic

A large part of Weber's *oeuvre* remained faithful to this social ontology but, like Marx and Hegel before him, Weber slipped away from this position in certain texts. It is particularly unfortunate that this slide away from genuine interpretivism is demonstrated most obviously in a work for which he is most famous, *The Protestant Ethic and the Spirit of Capitalism*. There, Weber noted the striking fact that throughout Europe the leading capitalists and the most economically innovative societies from the sixteenth century were Protestant:

> It is a fact that Protestants – both as ruling classes and as ruled, both as majority and as minority, have shown a special tendency to develop economic rationalism which cannot be observed to the same extent among Catholics, either in one situation or in the other.
>
> (Weber 1958a: 39–40)

Weber famously claimed that there was an elective affinity between the ethics of Protestantism and capitalism so that, while a wholly unintended consequence, the religious belief of the reformers was the ultimately necessary, if not the sufficient, condition for capitalism. The Protestant businessman was distinguished from his medieval forebear by a new kind of ethic. The Protestant businessman was involved in rational acquisition which prioritised long-term capital increase over conspicuous consumption. For Weber, the Protestant businessman was not to be confused with the Fuggers, the Medicis or the other famous merchant families of the medieval world. Crucially, for Weber, the origin of this new business ethic could be traced directly back to Protestantism and, in particular, to the severe doctrines of John Calvin. Martin Luther rejected the authority of the Church: insisting that Christians could find their salvation through faith alone and through thorough immersion in Biblical texts. Luther believed that the private interpretation of God's word could provide salvation. Calvin equally emphasised the centrality of the Bible and similarly insisted on unmediated communication with God. However, his doctrine rejected the notion that individuals could somehow save themselves through demonstrations of their faith. Faith was essential but it was not adequate to salvation. Since God was omniscient, he must, according to Calvin, know which individuals would be saved and which damned. Salvation or damnation had to be pre-destined, for if humans could alter their destiny, then God was neither omniscient nor omnipotent. Consequently, for Calvin, the world consisted of the Elected and the damned and no action in the world could affect God's judgement, which was already passed. Humans were only fulfilling the destinies which had already been decided at the Creation.

For Weber, the doctrine of pre-destination placed an unsupportable psychological strain on Calvinists; it was intolerable that they should not know whether they were damned or saved. Consequently, the question 'Am I one of the elect?' (Weber 1958a: 110) had 'far-reaching psychological consequences' (Weber 1958d: 160) for Calvinists and this question was the essence of the Protestant Ethic in particular 'the influence of those psychological sanctions which, originating in religious belief and the practice of religion, gave a direction to practical conduct and held the individual to it' (Weber 1958d: 97). For Weber, the psychological pressures which Calvinism produced led logically to capitalism. In order to demonstrate their Election, Calvinism demanded that individuals – be they entrepreneurs or artisans – toil as hard as possible at their chosen profession. This work was not carried out for selfish reasons but rather made 'labour in the service of impersonal social usefulness appear to promote the glory of God and hence to be willed by Him' (Weber 1958a: 109). To submit oneself to the discipline of work was to conduct one's life according to religious principles. In relation to the Calvinist entrepreneur, there was no longer a mere brute acquisitiveness; the end of accumulating money was not important. Only the Calvinist entrepreneur's regular and methodical work mattered. Weber postulated that if Calvinists were able to submit themselves to their professional duties, they could take their success as a sign of Election; successful work could be used to alleviate the psychological pressures which Calvinism purportedly placed on its believers. In the case of the Calvinist entrepreneurs the attempt to alleviate the psychological pressures which their religion placed upon them had a convenient effect on their business activities. Because they worked methodically and rigorously in order to prove themselves Elect, Calvinist businessmen were extremely likely to be successful. This led to one of the most ingenious parts of Weber's thesis. Although Protestants were likely to be rewarded materially for their labour, to indulge in worldly goods and luxury was against God's will. It was a sign of damnation. Consequently, although Calvinists were very often successful in accumulating capital, they could not indulge themselves. The only pious course of action was to re-invest the fruits of their labour into the 'service of impersonal social usefulness'. Accumulated capital was re-invested in the capitalist enterprise, which subsequently became larger and larger (Weber 1958a: 170–71). The Protestant Ethic postulated a purely psychological explanation for the rise of capitalism. Given certain theological assumptions, individuals were psychologically driven towards certain forms of conduct which were conducive to the development of capitalism.

The Critique of the Protestant Ethic

On its publication it 1904, Weber's essay was subjected to severe, though always respectful, criticism from Fischer and Rachfahl (see Harrington and Chalcraft 2001). Perhaps suggesting how central the thesis was to Weber, his own responses were, by contrast, assertive and *ad hominem*, though they equivocated on the issues. The basic criticisms forwarded by Fischer and Rachfahl were straightforward but damning. Firstly, the capitalist spirit existed before the Reformation in cities like Florence (Harrington and Chalcraft 2001: 28, 57). The Fuggers and Medicis were certainly rational businessmen. Secondly, Protestant and particularly Calvinist ethics had no elective affinity with capitalism. Calvinism was explicitly opposed to wealth *per se*, railing against the dangers of Mammon (Harrington and Chalcraft 2001: 56, 90). Throughout the twentieth century there were periodic debates about the thesis after the initial exchanges between Weber, Fischer and Rachfahl (Lehmann and Roth 1993: 241–42), many of which stimulated very useful general discussions about the development of modern Europe (Trevor-Roper 1967; Pellicani 1994). Yet, while valuable on broader historical issues, in their analysis of Weber's text itself these debates only elaborated upon Fischer and Rachfahl's initial criticisms. All subsequent critiques (Trevor-Roper 1967; Marshall 1982; Samuelson 1957; Pellicani 1988, 1989, 1994; Piccone 1998; Hennis 1988; Bendix 1960; Alexander 1983; Lehmann and Roth 1993; Turner 2000; Burger 1976) have similarly focused on these two fundamental criticisms, as have Weber's defenders (Hill 1961; Oakes 1988, 1989).[2] Following Fischer and Rachfahl, critics have argued that the rational accumulation of capitalism manifestly existed before the Reformation. Medieval and Renaissance merchants were as rational as any Protestant businessmen. It is also simply untrue to claim that Protestant businessmen were not ostentatious. There are numerous examples showing that Protestants demonstrated their new wealth and status as publicly as the apparently irrational Fuggers. In addition, the psychological pressure which Weber imputes to Calvinist theology simply does not persist; Calvin rejected material accumulation of any sort and economic development was stifled in Geneva as a result of his authoritarian regime. Calvin never suggested that adherents should seek signs of election in profane, business activity and Weber's thesis that Calvinism suggested that business should re-invest the fruits of their labour was entirely hypothetical. Election involved the rejection of that world. In the end, the historical criticisms are decisive and no causal connection can be drawn in the specific way in which Weber attempts between Protestantism and capitalism.[3]

The Protestant Ethic thesis is historically false but this error is not of primary concern here. The empirical error of assuming that there was no capitalism before 1517 and that Calvin legitimated profit-making is of less importance than the fact the Protestant Ethic thesis promoted a vision of social transformation which was at fundamental odds with Weber's interpretive sociology. Weber's interpretive sociology had emphasised 'life', referring to the shared understandings on the basis of which humans interacted. His empirical analysis of status groups demonstrated 'life' at work. Status groups emerged in the melee of social interaction as people came to agree upon a unifying status honour. These groups existed only insofar as their members oriented themselves to common ends. Group members had to recognise what the collective ends were. Therefore, no sociological explanation can ignore the shared understandings towards which group members oriented themselves. This ontology does not ignore the economic or material dimensions of society but it insisted that any account of social reality has to recognise the special character of social relations. Everywhere, this involves a conscious element, whereby humans understand what is expected of them from others. In his work on status groups, Weber explicitly describes a social ontology. Individuals mutually agree to orient themselves to collective interests. They recognise their social relations with each other and enjoin each other to act in mutually beneficial ways.

The Protestant Ethic presumes a different ontology. In place of this social ontology, Weber commits himself to a dualistic one in which rationalised ideals impose upon now isolated individuals. Individuals are submitted to psychological pressures which impose upon them alone; individuals are directed by an autonomous idea. Others are irrelevant. In order to relieve intolerable psychological pressures, Protestant businessmen were driven to entrepreneurial success, the fruits of which were re-invested in their businesses. The Protestant ethic postulates an individualistic account of social change. The Protestant ethic is a psychological mechanism. Weber himself emphasised the point: '*My* chosen task laid out as clearly as possible in my essay – was first and foremost to establish not where and how strongly but *how*, through what psychological structures of motivation, particular forms of Protestant belief came to exert the effects they did' (Chalcraft and Harrington 2001: 70).[4] Weber imagines how an individual Calvinist must have felt in the face of this merciless universe and proposed a soteriology which each adherent must have developed. There are no status groups nor any social relations here; only an idea and the individual.

Yet, the development of capitalism was not an individualistic phenomenon. It did not involve individuals all independently adopting a new business ethic as a result of internal psychological pressure. Capitalism involved the development of new bourgeois groups and institutions. A capitalist enterprise was a social institution whose success depended on its interconnection to and support from other similar enterprises. In this context, entrepreneurs did not primarily invest the fruits of their own labour but rather the capital of other members of the bourgeoisie. Their work precisely involved gaining the trust of other entrepreneurs. Entrepreneurs would offer credit to others only if they were able to establish mutually obliging social relations with one another which ensured that neither would renege on the other. In the light of these mutually supporting networks, the pressure for hard work, rational practice and re-investment came not from internal psychological sanctions but from the social pressure which entrepreneurs exerted on each other. In particular, the pressure to re-invest rather than to squander profit may be more plausibly explained by reference to the mutual desire for profit. Entrepreneurs could attract capital investment most successfully by offering potential investors the prospect of profit on their shares. Ultimately, the emergent bourgeois group developed standards of business practice which were expected of those who would be members. These business standards benefited the entire group by creating stable capitalist companies, the profit of which could be enjoyed or employed as capital for further investment. The sanction for not abiding by those standards was not existential torment but social exclusion and, therefore, economic marginalisation. The problem with a profligate businessman was not that he was damned but that it was unlikely an investment in his activities would show a return.

It is noticeable that in his empirical account of Protestant sects in America, psychological sanctions play no part. On the contrary, Weber specifically describes a social process. Individual Protestant businessmen were not honest and hard-working simply because their theology demanded it of them personally. Rather, these Protestant sects of which these businessmen were members enforced integrity as a status honour (Weber 1991c: 305). The probity of group members was important for the sect because the group was able to exploit its position in business only insofar as the population trusted them (Weber 1991c: 309). The Protestantism of these sects was an external symbol of honesty, which was enforced internally as the status honour of the group. The success of Protestants in America was not a result of private psychological sanction but the product of the status honour of this social group, which its members mutually enforced. Protestant businessmen were able to enjoy the collective benefits of group membership by acting with integrity and ensuring that other group members similarly acted in this way. It is not inconceivable that these business groups could have developed the kind of theology which Weber describes and could have oriented themselves to rational accumulation because they thought this demonstrated their Election. However, in this case, the pressure to engage in disciplined work would still not have been psychological. The true pressure would have been social. The concept of Election would have been used as the status honour of the group; it would refer to those activities which the business group regarded as acceptable and it would have distinguished members of the group from non-members. In such a hypothetical sect, Election would define group membership and this membership, not psychological sanctions, would compel businessmen to conduct themselves in certain ways. Group members would have mutually expected certain kinds of 'rational' action from each other; they would work methodically and re-invest the fruits of their labour because this was what was expected of group members.

An important, though subordinate, strand in Weber's argument was that Calvinism legitimated business activities for the first time and thereby gave a decisive impetus to them. Although this argument is plausible and has been employed by some commentators to defend the thesis (e.g. Oakes 1988, 1989), it is questionable whether it is an accurate account of why the bourgeoisie gained in social status after 1500. It is particularly noticeable that capitalism arose in parallel to the state. From the sixteenth century, emergent states were locked into competitive political relations with other states. Since states either hired mercenary armies or had to create their own professional standing force, they required increasing financial support. Consequently, in each country, states encouraged the development of new markets and economic activities from which they might benefit. The competition and conflict between states provided the decisive ground on which capitalism could develop. Weber himself was well aware of the importance of this rivalry between states: 'This competitive struggle created the largest opportunities for modern western capitalism' because 'the separate states had to compete for mobile capital' (Weber 1961: 249). As Weber notes, 'out of this alliance of the state with capital, dictated by necessity, arose the national citizen class, the bourgeoisie in the modern sense of the word' (Weber 1961: 246). In the light of this alliance between business and the state, the increasing legitimacy of business after the Reformation cannot be explained primarily by theological reasons. Business did not become acceptable because its validity was implicit in Protestant theology. It became legitimate precisely because it was indispensable to the state. The status of businessmen and their activities transformed as their social relations to political elites became stronger. Any doubts or guilt which Weber presumes that businessmen may have felt about their pursuit of profit were eliminated not by a new theology but by their new position in society. This new position could also explain Weber's claim that businessmen began to act more rationally after the Reformation. Rather than desiring to demonstrate their Election to themselves, successful business activity would result in growing status and political power in this world. It is likely that these tangible rewards, on offer in a new social context, motivated Protestant businessmen rather more decisively than any putatively psychological sanction.

While *The Protestant Ethic* is the most celebrated example of Weberian dualism, it is not the only example. On the contrary, throughout Weber's work there are important passages which fall into a similar dualism. While *The Protestant Ethic* itself ignored the historical significance of the emergent European state system, Weber was, of course, always fully conscious of the importance of the state. Indeed, the rise of the modern state induced in Weber a profound pessimism which infiltrated much of his writings about modernity; the 'iron-cage' or 'steel-hard housing' (Scott 1997: 562) of modernity has remained one of the enduring images of his sociology, inspiring the work of the Frankfurt School, Foucault and Zygmunt Bauman. Weber prophetically recognised that the rational bureaucratic state constituted a unique historical development. These bureaucracies harnessed human and technological capabilities on a scale never witnessed before even under the tyrannies of Egypt and Ancient Rome. Weber's analysis of bureaucracy remains a living resource in contemporary debates, providing a useful insight into some of the main characteristics of these institutions. Weber gives a compelling description of the importance of rules, files and above all knowledge to bureaucracies. Weber was right to recognise the importance of the modern bureaucracy but, while powerful as an initial analytical sketch of the ideal administration, this propaedeutic is not ultimately a sustainable account of how bureaucracies actually operate.

Pre-modern bureaucracy operated on a patrimonial basis. Monarchs appointed individuals to particular functions, in return for the rewards which that administrator was able to wring from his office. Offices were called 'benefices' because privileges accrued to the holder; they were gifts. The modern bureaucracy differs markedly from the patrimonial system. Modern bureaucracy involves domination through knowledge. Bureaucrats have become salaried individuals, separated from the offices which they performed. Offices were not to be appropriated by them for personal gain but were to be fulfilled according to strict and formally established rules. These rules regularised the bureaucracy and ensured an efficient division of labour, in which each role was clearly defined, culminating in a single monocratic head (usually a minister). The file was the critical innovation for the modern bureaucracy since it allowed for the transparent application of rules, irrespective of person or rank. Moreover, since the bureaucracy operated according to rules, the bureaucrats themselves had to undertake training and examination so that they became reliable instruments of the state, devoted to impersonal function (Weber 1978: 956–1003). According to Weber's description, individual bureaucrats simply follow the rationalised procedures they internalised as a result of training and examinations. For Weber, the rule-following is individualistic and automatic. The rules in themselves ensure appropriate action.

In his discussion of bureaucracy, Weber does discuss the significance of bureaucrats as a status group. Educational certificates limit entry to this form of employment and have therefore become the prime method by which this status group sustains itself and its 'claims to the monopolization of socially and economically advantageous positions' (Weber 1978: 1000). He also notes that 'the possession of educational certificates or patents…is usually linked with qualification for office; naturally this enhances the "status element" in the social position of the official' (Weber 1978: 960). As in China, the appointment to the state bureaucracy is not simply an economic matter; it raises an individual's social prestige. Moreover, once in this privileged position, bureaucrats act appropriately because their status in wider society is dependent upon their impartial professional conduct. This is an important and relevant observation. In order to sustain their privileged position, they have to act with probity. Interestingly, Weber describes how certain forms of exclusive social interaction have developed among this group, such as intermarriage. Weber recognises the way that the status group sustains itself by excluding others socially. All of this accords with his interpretive sociology. Nevertheless, he assumes that the bureaucratic procedures which he describes are themselves applied rationally and automatically. Although acting as a group externally, Weber's account assumes that this status group becomes irrelevant in the performance of its work. Individual bureaucrats ultimately work in isolation, following apparently self-evident procedures alone. Yet, the status group of bureaucrats plays a much more significant role than this in sustaining the bureaucracy. The reality of any bureaucracy will depend upon the culture of the elite status group which works in it. This group determines how exactly the bureaucracy will operate. The apparently decisive rules which Weber describes do not in themselves explain the functioning of the bureaucracy. Individual bureaucrats could interpret the same rules differently to produce an incoherent system. With different ends in mind, with a different organisational culture and with different relations between bureaucrats, rational rules could be implemented in quite different ways. The coherence of the bureaucracy pre-supposes a unified culture among bureaucrats. The rules have power only insofar as they are understood to imply certain courses of action; the group finally determines how rules are to be applied. The status group is essential to the persistence of the bureaucracy as an institution. In his sociology of the Chinese *literati*, Weber demonstrated exactly this point. The Chinese administration which persisted over centuries as a culturally exclusive group imposed appropriate social conduct on initiates. Would-be members of the *literati* in China had to abide by the erudite status honour of this group and this status honour was continually and actively sustained by this group. The bureaucratic status group continually decides how the work of the bureaucrat will be performed. In the course of exclusive interactions, the group re-affirms its mode of operation and its central values. No bureaucracy is ultimately run exclusively according to its rules but rather according to the wider understandings or 'life' of the bureaucratic status group. Bureaucracies require periods of exclusive social interaction where the way the rules are to be taken is communally decided. Bureaucracies require formal meetings in which collective understandings of how the work will be done are developed but they also need informal periods of interactions where collective norms are constantly re-affirmed. In these settings, problem cases, questions and criticisms can be aired. In these periods of interaction, the collective ends of the group and the means by which those ends should be achieved are re-affirmed and re-negotiated. The interpretive sociology of Weber suggests that a modern bureaucracy is a far more interesting and lively place than Weber's pessimistic vision allows (see Allbrow 1970). Like the Protestant ethic, the analysis of bureaucracy reduces interactive social reality to a dualism of idea and individual; in both *The Protestant Ethic* and his discussion of bureaucracy, the individual follows independent rules.[5]

In *The Protestant Ethic* and in his description of bureaucracy, Weber resorted to a dualistic ontology, in which independent concepts demanded certain types of action from the individual. At these points in his writing, Weber reneged on his interpretive sociology, in which social groups were primary. Instead, ideas detached themselves from their natural social context to determine individual action autonomously. In a famous passage, Weber summarised this idealistic and dualistic approach:

> For the meaning as well as the intended and actual psychological quality of redemption has depended upon such a world image and such a stand. Not ideas, but material and ideal interests, directly govern men's interests. Yet very frequently the 'worked images' that have been created by 'ideas' have, like switchmen, determined the tracks along which action had been pushed by the dynamic of interest.
>
> (Weber 1991: 280)

Although there is the characteristic equivocation, Weber's point is explicit: in the end, ideas determine human history and these ideas are divorced from their social context. They no longer have their existence only within the life of a status group but take on an autonomy and force of their own, imposing on the individual from above. Weber's interpretive sociology certainly prioritised ideas as part of a group's cultural consciousness, but those ideas were always inseparable from the group. Ideas are important sociologically only insofar as the members of social groups orient themselves collectively to them. Groups exist only insofar as humans consciously recognise their membership of them. Shared understandings are consequently decisive in human social life. Humans have to recognise their social relations with each other and understand what these relations enjoin. In much of Weber's writing, he successfully demonstrated the sociological decisiveness of status groups with their common understandings but in decisive elements in his oeuvre, in *The Protestant Ethic*, *The Sociology of Religion*, and in much of his description of ideal types in *Economy and Society*, he fell into the very reductive dualism for which he berated Marx.

The Sociology of Religion

Weber's interpretive sociology offers a route away from ontological dualism. It can be re-discovered to re-invigorate contemporary social theory. His work on status groups, in particular, demonstrated the distinctive qualities of human social life. Above all, he recognised that, in the social groups in which all humans must live, ideal and material strands were indivisible. Social relations necessarily involve the understandings of those engaged in them. The way social relations are collectively understood defines what they are. This genuine insight is immediately relevant to contemporary debates in social theory. There, social relations are ignored. Instead, the individual confronts a reality which is independent of human understanding. Structure imposes itself upon individuals. By recognising the sociological profundity of Weber's comments on status groups, contemporary social theory relieves itself of the burdens of ontological dualism. Through the work of Weber, contemporary social theory can become genuinely sociological. In place of deadening and dualistic abstractions, it would look to life 'with all its irrational reality and its store of possible meaning'. In turning to life, contemporary social theory would usefully illuminate the historic transformations which are occurring today instead of painting life grey on grey, reducing everything to the mechanics of structure and agency.

In employing Weber to re-invigorate the discipline today, it is also necessary to recognise the moments when Weber himself fell short of the standards of his own interpretive sociology. Sometimes, Weber himself was not sociological. In his *Sociology of Religion* and *The Protestant Ethic*, in particular, Weber returned to the very dualism he sought to supersede by ossifying the reality of religion into theologies which imposed upon the individual. Weber's study of religion was intended to demonstrate the inadequacy of Marx's economism, which claimed an independent status for production. Yet, in rejecting Marx, Weber re-instituted only another form of dualism. Weber replicated the kind of dualistic idealism for which Hegel was criticised. He postulated the existence of independent ideas which determined individual action. Weber reduced living religion to formal logic with its own internal dynamic. Yet, theology is inseparable from what the group understands it to be. Theology is ultimately only an expression of the group's understanding of itself. If Weber had recognised that religion refers to the collective consciousness of particular social groups, created and re-created in periods of exclusive interaction, then he would never proposed the Protestant ethic. He would never have suggested that an independent idea could determine action individually. If Weber had applied his theory of status groups consistently to religion, he would always have seen that the power of religion is dependent upon the group. The group determines what religion is and what practices it demands of group members. Religious precepts themselves determine nothing. The individual does not stand naked before theology. The social group collectively decides what practices religion enjoins. Humans in social relations together decide upon appropriate courses of action. Significantly, almost contemporaneously with Weber, Emile Durkheim proposed exactly this line of argument. His work provides one of the most important resources for overcoming ontological dualism in contemporary social theory.

8   Society and Ritual

Although Weber and Durkheim recognised the sociological significance of religion, there was no dialogue between them during their lives even though their professional careers overlapped. Durkheim died in 1917, five years before Weber's own death. It is striking that two individuals central to the development of sociology at the turn of the twentieth century could have been so mutually ignorant of each other. There are indications that Weber may have been aware of some of Durkheim's writing and it is possible that he dismissed it as Comtean positivism without engaging with it (Runciman 1972: 30). He may have been put off by Durkheim's claims that society had a *sui generis* and independent existence. Durkheim, in turn, may have disparaged Weber's ideal types as dangerously abstract (Bendix and Roth 1971: 283, 286). It is also possible that the political hostility between their two countries during the working lives of Durkheim and Weber may have prevented any intellectual relationship between them. Whatever the reasons, the mutual ignorance of these great intellectuals of each other's work is strange especially given the similarity of the position which they both eventually adopted. Parsons, of course, highlighted the affinities between Durkheim and Weber in order to create his voluntary theory of action but this close connection has been all but forgotten in contemporary social theory. This may be because Parsons found Weber's argument for shared norms in his discussion of charisma when it is evident that the argument is made much more powerfully in his discussion of status groups. Nevertheless, there is a close affinity between the sociologies of Weber and Durkheim, the illumination of which is of potentially enormous benefit to social theory today. The convergence which Parsons highlighted in 1937 may be of no less relevance in 2003.

Durkheimian Dualism

> Social phenomena are things and ought to be treated as things.
> (Durkheim 1966: 27)

Durkheim's aphorism has been frequently taken as evidence that his sociology is self-evidently dualistic; society is an independent entity – a thing – which confronts the individual. Indeed, the phrase has often been taken as clear evidence that Durkheim held a metaphysical conception of society. This interpretation of the phrase is certainly sustainable within the context of *The Rules of Sociological Method* (1966), from which it is taken. The central purpose of that book was to demonstrate the special status of society, which could not be accounted for by references to the individuals of whom it consisted. Society was an irreducible reality. Durkheim described the social phenomena which were to be treated as things as 'social facts' and these social facts took several different forms. For instance, he described customs as a social fact because 'such reality is still objective for I did not create them' (Durkheim 1966: 1):

> Here then are ways of acting, thinking and feeling that present the noteworthy property of existing outside the individual consciousness. These types of conduct or thought are moreover not only external to the individual but endowed with coercive power, by virtue of which they impose themselves upon him, independent of his individual will.
>
> (Durkheim 1966: 2)

Durkheim cited the example of the education of a child, which 'gives us in a nutshell the historical fashion in which the social being is constituted' (Durkheim 1966: 6); the child is a blank slate on which society impresses its customs and morals. Following this line of thought, Durkheim also believed that law, historical monuments, fashions and artistic taste, which are material expressions of a society's customs, are all examples of social facts for the very reason that they 'tend towards an independent existence outside the individual consciousness, which they dominate' (Durkheim 1966: 30).

Somewhat obscurely, he also described social facts as 'social currents' which run through society, imposing themselves upon individuals but without 'such crystallized form' as a custom (Durkheim 1966: 4). At other moments, Durkheim describes these social currents as a 'substratum', insisting that this 'can be no other than society' (Durkheim 1966: 3). This substratum produces 'social currents' which impress upon the individual. For Durkheim, a crowd is a useful example of how 'social currents' develop and circulate. When a crowd forms, it takes on an existence of its own and, as members of the crowd, individuals become deeply sensitive to its sentiments. However, these sentiments are not those of any individual within the crowd but impose themselves upon each member of the crowd. In order to emphasise that the social currents which pass temporarily through the crowd are not to be explained in individual terms, Durkheim notes: 'once these social influences have ceased to act upon us and we are alone again, the emotions which have passed through the mind appear strange to us and we no longer recognise them as ours' (Durkheim 1966: 5). As uncrystallized 'currents', social facts press upon individuals, sweeping them into appropriate behavioural channels. Perhaps surprisingly, in *The Rules of Sociological Method*, Durkheim is explicit that these social currents and social customs as social facts are not simply external to each individual but are in fact external to all individuals in a society. The social fact is an identifiable entity which exists separately from individuals:

> A social fact is every way of acting, fixed or not, capable of exercising on the individual an external constraint; or again every way of acting which is general throughout a given society, while at the same time existing in its own right independently of its individual manifestations.
>
> (Durkheim 1966: 13)

Durkheim notes that 'currents of opinion with an intensity ranging according to the time and place, impel certain groups to more marriage, for example, or to more suicides or to lower birth rates' (Durkheim 1966: 8). These social facts manifest themselves in particular individual cases which may very well take somewhat idiosyncratic forms but behind each embodiment, the fact exists as an independent reality. Social facts emanate from a prior, independent reality. It is difficult to read these passages of *The Rules of Sociological Method* without concluding that Durkheim has explicitly committed himself to a dualistic ontology: 'When the individual is eliminated, society alone remains. We must, then, seek explanation of social life in the nature of society itself' (Durkheim 1966: 102). This independent entity, society, apparently surpasses the individual in time and space and it is this totality which exerts pressure on the individual.

Throughout Durkheim's career, the French sociologist Gabriel Tarde, who was one of his major opponents, rejected Durkheim's sociology on the grounds that it reified society into a thing; individuals were confronted by society. Tarde opposed the dualism which he thought was the basis of Durkheim's sociology. Tarde, by contrast, insisted that society consisted only of individuals and could therefore be explained in every case by reference to these individuals alone: 'There can only be individual actions and interactions. The rest is nothing but a metaphyscial entity and mysticism' (Gabriel Tarde, cited in Lukes 1973: 313). To that end he promoted a form of sociology called 'interpsychology', which examined the individual psychological processes which gave rise to certain forms of interaction (Tarde 1969; Durkheim 1952: 308; Lukes 1973: 302–13; Nisbet 1967: 95). Tarde's interpsychology was individualistic, explaining all social phenomena by reference to individual characteristics. Tarde rejected the idea that there was anything distinctive about social interaction or about social groups. Although Tarde's individualism was deeply problematic his criticism of Durkheim seems valid. Society certainly has no existence apart from the individuals who are part of it. Durkheim's claim that society has an independent status is self-evidently wrong. It is manifestly false that society can exist independently of the people who are part of it.

The Rules of Sociological Method certainly denotes the highpoint of Durkheim's sociological dualism. There he commits himself to the claim that society has an existence independent of the individuals on whom it imposes itself. Yet, this ontological dualism which contrasts the social and the individual is evident in other parts of his writing and it is consequently not possible simply to dismiss *The Rules* as an aberration. Most obviously, *Suicide* (1952) formally follows the precepts laid out in *The Rules*. *Suicide* is intended to demonstrate that even the most apparently personal act – self-immolation – is determined by society. Durkheim notes that in each society the suicide rate is stable over long periods. From this statistical fact, he concludes the existence of certain 'suicidogenetic currents' which flow through society independently of individual volition, impelling a certain number of unfortunates to kill themselves each year. Each society effectively requires these deaths, which are an effect of its moral coherence:

> These currents are plainly social facts. At first sight they seem inseparable from the forms they take in individual cases. But statistics furnishes us with the means of isolating them. They are, in fact, represented with consider-able exactness by rates of birth, marriages and suicides... The average then expresses a certain state of the group mind.
>
> (Durkheim 1966: 8)

The application of the method laid out in *The Rules* is clear. Social statistics record the regularity of certain practices which are the effect of social currents emanating from the underlying social fact. The insignificance of individual consciousness to this apparently most personal of all acts is strongly emphasised by Durkheim in one of the most important passages in the book, the first chapter of Book Three, 'The Social Element of Suicide'. There Durkheim rejects Tarde's argument that suicide can be explained by imitation. He notes that Tarde claims that 'anything social...passes from an individual... to another individual' (Durkheim 1952: 308). The distribution of suicides demonstrates that Tarde's theory of imitation is false:[1]

> Victims of suicide are in an infinite minority which is widely dispersed, each performs his act separately without knowing that others are doing the same, and yet, as long as society remains unchanged the number of suicides remains the same. Therefore, all these individual manifestations, however independent of one another they seem, must surely actually result from a single cause or single group of causes, which dominate individ-uals...There must be some force in their common environment including them all in some direction whose greater or lesser strength causes greater or lesser number of individual suicides.
>
> (Durkheim 1952: 304–05)[2]

Against Tarde, suicide cannot be understood by reference to individuals alone. The collective life of social groups has some autonomous power which surges through society, causing certain individuals, situated at weak points in the social order, to kill themselves. For Durkheim, the suicide rate remains stable so long as society remains stable and this conjunction demonstrates the direct causality between the state of the collectivity and the incidence of suicide:

> These tendencies of the whole social body, by affecting individuals, cause them to commit suicide…It all depends on the intensity with which suicido-genetic causes have affected the individual.
>
> (Durkheim 1952: 300)

The collectivity impels individuals to kill themselves. Social currents run through society independently of whether individuals are aware of them or not:

> We think it a fertile idea that social life must be explained not by the conception of it created by those who participate in it but by profound causes which escape awareness; and we also think these causes must principally be sought in the way in which associated individuals are grouped.
>
> (Durkheim 1978: 127)

Individuals formulate reasons for their own or other's suicide's but the real cause of immolation lies outside their consciousness. It seems clear that Durkheim espouses ontological dualism. Individuals are determined by a social entity whose existence is independent of them and about which they are not necessarily fully conscious. The independence of society is manifested in social facts which take two principal forms. Social facts refer either to collective representations (customs and so on) or to certain social pressures (currents) which circulate around society. In either case, these facts are independent of individual volition and understanding.

Durkheim's Social Ontology

It is somewhat surprising that in the very chapter in *Suicide* in which he seems to assert the existence of society most forcefully, he denies that he ever made such a claim:

> Nothing is more reasonable then, than this proposition at which such offence has been taken; that a belief or social practice may exist independently of its individual expressions. We clearly did not imply by this that society can exist without individuals, an obvious absurdity we might have been spared having attributed to us. But we did mean: 1. That the group formed by the associated individuals has a reality of a different sort from each individual considered singly; 2. That the collective states exist in a group from whose nature they spring, before they affect the individual as such and establish in him a new form of purely inner existence.
>
> (Durkheim 1952: 320)

Although Durkheim seems to think that the claim he makes here is compatible with his earlier comments in the chapter, by any reasonable interpretation this passage proposes a very different account of social life to those laid out only a few pages previously. Here, he argues that individuals come together to form groups which cannot be understood by reference to isolated individuals; this is an empirically verifiable proposition. There, by contrast, society was given a *sui generis* status separate from individuals and existing without their knowledge. The simplest and most generous explanation for this contradiction is to argue that Durkheim was never genuinely committed to ontological dualism but that at certain unfortunate moments his writing was poor, implying a position which he never, in fact, held (see Lukes 1973; Douglas 1973; Parsons 1966a: 367). Although difficult to prove, it is possible that in these problematic sections of his writing he rhetorically overemphasised the existence of society in order to distinguish his *sociological* position from individualistic accounts of social life. It is, perhaps, not coincidental that the most dualistic passages of Durkheim's writing are explicitly intended as a riposte against Tarde's interpsychology. If this is the case, in rejecting individualistic sociology as forcefully as he could, Durkheim raised an equally egregious sociological spectre; a social *deus ex machina* which confronts the individual. Durkheim's dualism in these passages should not mislead, however. These passages should not be taken as evidence that he was an ontological dualist. It is notable that in much of his writing he explicitly opposed social dualism, disparaging those who proposed the existence of an autonomous society which confronted the individual. It is important to read Durkheim more sympathetically and to re-consider those passages which seem to promote ontological dualism so evidently.

This rejection of dualism is clear, for instance, in his perceptive analysis of Rousseau. In his political writings, Rousseau maintained that human civilisation constituted a corruption of the natural existence. Through an examination of the state of nature, Rousseau attempted to describe a political order which might be able to exploit the benefits of civilisation while avoiding its corrupting aspects. In the state of nature, savages were noble because they were independent of their fellow humans. Uncorrupted by human social intercourse, savages developed their own potential in the face of the brute forces of nature. Savages confronted a force outside themselves. In Rousseau's ideal society the situation of the noble savage would be replicated. Individuals would not be undermined by the interference of other individuals but would submit themselves to the general will, which was an independent entity even though it was the sum of all wills. This entity imposed upon each individual separately. Individuals were subordinate to this *force majeur* but they were not the slaves of other individuals and, consequently, they were free (Durkheim 1965b: 135). Durkheim's analysis of Rousseau is striking and the position which Rousseau adopts accords with the claims which Durkheim seemed to make in *The Rules of Sociological Method* and *Suicide*. In both those works, Durkheim, like Rousseau, seemed to conceive of society as an independent entity which imposed on the isolated individual. It might be expected that Durkheim would support Rousseau. Yet, Durkheim decisively rejects Rousseau's account of civil society. For Durkheim, civil society could not be explained if individuals remained independent of each other.

If, however, a society is formed of isolated, atomised individuals, one is at a loss to see where it comes from…So unstable is its foundation in the nature of things that it cannot but appear to us as a tottering structure whose delicate balance can be established and maintained only by an almost miraculous conjunction of circumstances.

(Durkheim 1965b: 137–38)

In order to explain the stability of civil society, social relations between humans had to be recognised. Individuals could never form themselves into groups unless they established regular social relations with each other. Durkheim rejected Rousseau because he ignored this specifically social interaction in favour of an image of isolated individuals imposed upon by a force beyond any of them. For Durkheim such a dualistic image was only a 'tottering structure' which could never account for social order. For Durkheim, the *force majeur* of human life was precisely social interaction, not nature or the general will. Durkheim effectively inverted Rousseau. While Rousseau regarded human social relations as corrupting, preferring a reality in which humans confronted objective forces alone, Durkheim's sociology prioritised them. Social interaction and the social relations which arose from it were the necessary medium of all human existence. These relations could never be explained in terms of the properties of individuals but had to be comprehended in their own terms. Social relations and therefore society arose between individuals but they were not reducible to the individual alone. The mere interaction of humans produced a reality which had to be understood at the specifically social level. Durkheim's advocacy of social relations against Rousseau begins to suggest that he was not a dualist after all and that there was nothing metaphysical about his advocacy of society.

He elucidates his position in *Moral Education*. There he rejects the notion that social morality can be explained by reference to the individual. Morality cannot arise out of individual psychology because morality precedes any particular individual; humans are born into societies, whose moralities they must learn. Moreover, even though as individuals humans are biologically almost identical, moralities differ dramatically. If morality really arose in individual psychology, there would either be one morality for the entire human species arising directly from biological adaptations or there would be infinite moralities developed by each individual. It is clear that, although there are diverse moralities across different human societies and across history, each morality is a reasonably stable entity. Morality, therefore, has properties which are irreducible to the individual (Durkheim 1973: 60). Nevertheless, although not an individual product, morality is a human creation. It may not be produced by single individuals who happen independently of each other to follow the same morality, but it arises out of social interaction. This interaction produces joint creations which are irreducible to any single individual and are far more powerful than each individual. Yet, they are not in any way metaphysical. The creation of morality is an empirically identifiable procedure. Durkheim gives the example of tin and copper, whose combination produces a substance, bronze, which has properties entirely different from those of its constituent elements. Bronze is hard. Similarly, in social life, when individuals interact they create social relations, which, while consisting only of their individual members, nevertheless have properties which exceed the isolated individual. When individuals come together, they mutually empower each other through the act of association. Social facts do not necessarily imply a dualistic ontology. Through their co-operation, individuals both create a social group with distinctive powers and also transform themselves. They are not what they were outside the group; only the group allows them to perform certain practices. Consequently, 'a whole may be something other than the sum of its parts' (Durkheim 1973: 61; also 1978: 50). The whole – the social group – is entirely empirical. In their intercourse with each other humans are able to produce a distinctive social reality. Durkheim's problematic term 'social fact' referred to the powerful properties of human social relations and human groups.[3] In Durkheim's writing, social facts took two main forms. He characterised them either as 'substratum' or as 'collective representations'. Substratum referred to the currents which underlay the performance of certain regular social practices, such as crime or suicide. Collective representations referred to those apparently objective entities such as morality, laws and customs which imposed upon the individual. It is worth examining each in turn to show that neither is metaphysical. On the contrary, in the case of both types of social fact, social currents and collective representations, they can be understood in terms of the social ontology of human relations.

The Substratum

It is certainly true that the concept of the substratum appears mysterious at first. The notion of a reality underlying individual activities, of which the latter are only expressions, seems manifestly dualistic. Durkheim seems to conceive of society as a reality which is independent of and prior to the individual. A closer consideration of what Durkheim actually means by the substratum is necessary. In his discussion of collective representations in *Suicide*, a useful description of the substratum emerges:

> We refuse to accept that these phenomenon have as a substratum the consciences of the individual, we assign them another; that formed by all individual consciences in union and combination. There is nothing substantival or *ontological* about this substratum, since it is merely a whole composed of parts. But it is just as real.
>
> (Durkheim 1952: 319, emphasis added)

Explicitly, the substratum is not ontological. It is not separate from the members of society; nor does it have any autonomous status. Rather, the substratum refers to those moments of social interaction when the members of a society come together and commit themselves to common values. The substratum is the 'union' of individual consciences. It denotes the social milieu in which individuals interact with each other, mutually orienting each other to common ideas and practices.

Although there are reifications in *Suicide*, one of the most lucid examples of the substratum is also to be found there when Durkheim describes the gathering of a crowd. This description of the processes of social interaction is explicitly intended as a refutation of Tarde's individualistic idea of imitation.

> A number of men in an assembly are similarly affected by the same occur-rence and perceive this at least partial unanimity by the identical signs through which each individual feeling is expressed. What happens then? Each one imperfectly imagines the state of those about him. Images expressing the various manifestations emanating, with their different shades, from all parts of the crowd, are formed in the minds of all...A new state is thus formed, less my own than its predecessors, less tainted with individu-ality and more and more freed, by a series of repeated elaborations analogous to the foregoing, from all excessive particularity.
>
> (Durkheim 1952: 125–26)

If humans merely imitated each other in their interaction, then nothing new would arise in interaction. Interaction would merely repeat and affirm individual propensities and potentialities. Yet, in gatherings, this does not happen. There, each individual mutually responds to others, thereby setting a dialectical process of self-propulsion in motion. In the crowd, individuals are mutually influenced by those around them. They all begin to act differently, each empowering others and in turn being empowered by them. A self-propelling context is created. Durkheim does not mean an objective social fact which has existence indepen-dent of social interaction. On the contrary, the substratum consists of 'mutual reactions'; it refers precisely to the dynamic round of social interaction. The substratum does not impose on people externally. Rather, the substratum refers to that organic process of social interaction in which humans exert a mutual influence on each other. The substratum refers to the everyday and eternal round of social relations. This is not a dualistic social theory, in which society as an independent entity imposes upon isolated individuals. Rather, Durkheim's sociology focuses on the self-transforming potential of human social relations. The substratum refers to the ceaseless flow of myriad social interactions of which every society consists. The substratum is this vast and endless stream of everyday, often apparently meaningless, social relations.

The interpretation of the substratum as the dynamic and never-ending process of social interaction facilitates a re-reading of Durkheim's apparently curious claim in *The Division of Labour* when he writes that 'there is, then, a social life outside the whole division of labour but which the latter presupposes' (Durkheim 1964: 277). This suggests that there is an unknown social entity beneath the division of labour which is a strange and apparently dualistic claim. In the light of the re-interpretation of the concept of the substratum proffered above it is possible to re-consider this statement in a way which does not imply dualism. The division of labour in a society develops as individuals specialise into particular functions to avoid direct competition with others (1964: 266–69). However, Durkheim notes: 'when competition places isolated and estranged individuals in opposition, it can only separate them more' (Durkheim 1964: 275). An increase in competition would drive individuals apart if they were not already bound together by some prior relationship. There would be no division of labour but simply diffusion. The fact that competing individuals stay together and specialise proves for Durkheim the existence of prior commitments:

> For a number of theorists, it is a self-evident truth that all society essentially consists of co-operation… We have just seen that this so-called axiom is contrary to the truth… What brings men together are mechanical causes and impulsive forces, such as affinity of blood, attachment to the same soil, ancestral worship, community of habits etc. It is only when the group has been formed on these bases that co-operation is organised there… In short, association and co-operation are two distinct facts and, if the second, when developed, reacts on the first and transforms it, if human societies steadily become groups of co-operators, the duality of the two phenomenon does not vanish for all that…If this important truth has been disregarded by the utilitarians, it is an error rooted in the manner in which they conceive the genesis of society. They suppose originally isolated and individuals, who, consequently enter into relations only to cooperate.
>
> (Durkheim 1964: 278–79)

Human beings are not isolated individuals who agree to co-operate due to certain self-interested motives. That is the error of utilitarianism. Co-operation is a secondary and dependent fact in human history. In the first instance, humans simply associate; they come together and interact. They form social relations. Durkheim notes, in an extraordinary echo of Weber's discussion of status groups, that the specific basis of that interaction is unimportant; the criteria of group membership is arbitrary. They could come together because they consider themselves to be kin, or because they share the use of a piece of land or they believe in the same God or they have similar ways of doing things. The communal grounds of gathering are diverse but as humans interact they will gradually agree upon shared collective understandings and interests so that they become oriented to the same ends. At this point, they begin to develop social relations with each other and to form themselves into social groups. These groups, formed once humans recognise their social obligations to each other, will determine the kinds of practices in which people in that society can engage. Below the division of labour exist certain prior social links between the members of modern society which bind them together prior to their economic specialisation. The term 'substratum' refers to the process of association which is the fecund basis of all social life.[4] It constitutes the social relations in which humans inevitably have their being. The substratum is a powerful entity and it is not reducible to the individual. Yet, this in no way suggests that it is metaphysical.

The substratum refers to the great round of social relations, all of which taken together comprise society. By means of this vast network, individuals are bound to each other, mutually influencing each other. The social pressures which arise in the substratum are completely empirical, therefore, even though they cannot be understood individualistically. These pressures refer to the mutual pressures which individuals put upon each other, demanding particular kinds of actions from themselves and from other group members.

Collective Representations

The other key social fact to which Durkheim refers is collective representation. At first appearance, these representations seem to presume a similarly dualistic ontology. In numerous passages Durkheim describes the autonomy of these collective representations and the power which they exert over the individual. For instance, in *Suicide*, collective representations which are not fully known to individuals propel suicidogenetic currents through society, causing random individuals to kill themselves. Yet, although the dualistic passages cannot be ignored in *Suicide*, it is possible to re-interpret the concept of collective representations. As Douglas (1973) has shown, Durkheim's argument does not stand up on its own terms. In order to explain how collective representations impose upon the individual and how suicidogenetic currents course through society, Durkheim must refer to the shared beliefs of the members of a society. At the outset of the work, Durkheim dismissed the possibility of knowing the intentions of the individual suicide; any motive recorded by the official statistics was almost certainly misleading. Consequently, Durkheim dismissed individual intention from his explanation of suicide and proposed instead to understand suicide in terms of external factors. Yet, in every case, be it egoistic, altruistic or anomic suicide, the explanation of suicide surreptitiously re-introduced individual self-understandings. In the case of egoistic suicide, individuals were afflicted by existential doubt as a result of their Protestantism. They could not bear the weight of the world which their religious beliefs put on them. Altruistic suicide occurred when individuals recognised that they had dishonoured their social group and that redemption was possible only through their own deaths. Anomic suicide occurred when individuals had no direction to their lives because they were free to do whatever they wished. In the face of this indeterminacy, life loses all meaning and they destroy themselves in despair. As Douglas notes, while Durkheim claims that he ignores all self-understanding in his explanation of suicide, he must despite himself appeal to certain recognisable intentions if the acts are not to be explained purely by the mechanical operation of biological or physiological factors.

In each type of suicide, the act of self-immolation becomes understandable within a particular cultural context which gives individuals a reason for killing themselves. Durkheim, then, does not replace intentions and meanings with the objective operation of social currents emanating from certain collective representations; he merely substitutes the intentions recorded in the official statistics with his own interpretation of the actual intentions of the suicides:

In place of such 'objective' measures and the meanings to the individual involved, he substituted the meanings of the associations to himself as a member of the society and as a social observer. *He relied upon his own common sense knowledge of social action in European society to provide most of the superficial meanings of the associations*...Durkheim was then using his common-sense understanding of his everyday social experience to provide the most important part of data to be used to test his theory.

(Douglas 1973: 68)

Durkheim had to refer to the motivation of suicides even if he himself wanted to give a rigorously positivist explanation of the phenomenon. At some point, the intentions of those people who commit suicide have to be considered. Douglas is correct that it is impossible to argue for an account of suicide which ignores the motivations which are attributed to the act. He is also right to note that, in the end, Durkheim merely asserts what these intentions must have been. Yet, there is evidence that Durkheim always recognised that social meanings were essential to this process. It may be possible to re-interpret Durkheim's concept of collective representations to demonstrate that, like the substratum, it refers to an identifiable social process. On this re-reading, *Suicide* does not ignore the role of human understanding in the act of self-immolation but it rejects the idea that the relevant understandings here are private and personal.

Durkheim illustrates what he means by collective representations through the example of religion. Although 'religion seems merely like the development of individuals states of mind and private feeling' (Durkheim 1952: 312), Durkheim insists that the origin of religion lies in a very different reality. 'Religion is, in a word, the system of symbols by which society becomes conscious of itself; it is the characteristic way of thinking of collective existence' (Durkheim 1952: 312). Anticipating the argument of *The Elementary Forms* (1976), Durkheim claims that religion is in fact society in a 'hypostatic form'; religion is a collective representation which symbolises society. The origin of religion as a collective representation is not to be found in individual psychology. Individuals do not converge automatically on the same beliefs. On the contrary, religion is a system of symbols which come to represent a society insofar as the members of that society mutually invest those signs with shared meaning. The power of religious collective representations rests on this communal recognition. Collective representations impose upon individuals but their power is not metaphysical. Their power arises as humans mutually invest them with significance. In the course of association, individuals together create signs which symbolise their social relations and what actions are appropriate for these humans given their social relations to each other. The collective representation is closely connected with the substratum, for these representations arise in social interaction between people and they represent their relations to each other. The collective representations symbolise the substratum, those fundamental social relations on the basis of which all social life is conducted. Ultimately, the collective representations are signs of the mutual expectations which the members of any society have of each other and they denote the pressure which humans exert over each other; they represent social currents, as Durkheim calls them. It is possible to re-read the potentially problematic passages of *Suicide* once the social origin of collective representations is recognised.

When Durkheim dismisses individual intentions in the early sections of *Suicide*, he is not thereby dismissing all appeals to meaning. He is not suggesting that suicidogenetic currents course through society independently of the social relations between members of this group. He is suggesting only that individual psychological peculiarities should not be taken as the fundamental cause of suicide, especially since statistics record these idiosyncrasies inaccurately. Meaning and intention are always crucial to suicide, as they are to all social action, but these meanings are not private. On the contrary, social relations are conducted in the light of shared meanings symbolised by certain collective representations. The causes of suicide in each society are to be sought not in personal experience but rather in those collective meanings on the basis of which individuals interact. *Suicide* is not a positivistic analysis of this phenomenon but an interpretation of how different social milieus (Catholic, Protestant, married, unmarried, civilian and military) provide a ground in which self-murder becomes a meaningful option for individuals. Crucially, the work recognises that this option has a different significance in alternative milieus and it notes the way that in different social milieus humans put pressures on each other which drive some to suicide. It is true that Durkheim in fact produced no convincing evidence to prove that his particular interpretations were correct. The best that can be said about Durkheim's argument on the suicidal tendency of Protestants, for instance, is that it is a stimulating hypotheses. Nevertheless, while empirically questionable, the theoretical approach which he was forwarding in *Suicide* is compelling. Society consists of people interacting with each other to produce social groups which unify themselves by the creation of certain publicly recognised symbols. These symbols become central to the lives of the members of these groups, denoting members' relations to each other. Above all these symbols express what action is expected of them. Since these relations are signified by a symbol, certain ideas or representations can appear to drive the individual to extreme acts, including suicide, to fulfil the obligation placed upon them by their social relations. The power of society, manifested in symbols, to influence the individual is real but this power is only the pressure which humans mutually impose on each other in their social relations. Despite the apparent objectivism involved when Durkheim talked of collective representations, he never intended collective representations, as social facts, to have any ontologically independent status. Collective representations were always rigorously embedded in the context of social interaction. In his final major work, *The Elementary Forms*, the significance of Durkheim's social ontology emerged fully for the first time, unobscured by deceptively objectivist claims.

The purpose of *The Elementary Forms* was not simply to provide an explanation of an important social phenomenon, religious beliefs and practices, by examining their simplest manifestations among aboriginal tribes. Nor was it to demonstrate that the apparently irrational practices of tribal peoples were understandable in their own terms, although the work certainly achieved these subordinate ends. Durkheim's aim in *The Elementary Forms* was to explain the origin of human social groups. For Durkheim, religion was not a matter of arcane theology but the basis of human sociability *per se*. Early in the work, Durkheim consciously gave religion the widest possible definition; it was not necessarily a belief in the divine or supernatural since there were various religions which knew nothing of these things. Rather, Durkheim defined religion simply as the sacred; it referred to those practices and beliefs which were opposed to the profane. Religion was 'a unified system of beliefs and practices relative to sacred things, that is to say, things set apart and forbidden – beliefs and practices which unite into a single moral community called a Church, all those who adhere to them' (Durkheim 1976: 47). Having defined religion merely as the sacred, Durkheim rejected previous accounts of aboriginal religion as inadequate. In particular, he was intent on demonstrating the rationality of even the most apparently bizarre religious beliefs and practices. For him, it was impossible that religion could have maintained its grip on humanity so powerfully if it were a mere tissue of lies (Durkheim 1976: 83). The persistence and power of religion ensured that there must be some dimension of reality to which it referred and which it represented accurately.

For individuals to form a social group they must create common values and understandings which co-ordinate their actions and unify their interests. Humans have to demonstrate their unity publicly and demonstrate what constitutes appropriate action in this group. In short, humans have to recognise their social relations and understand what they involve. Human social relations are ultimately grounded on the apparently fragile basis of conscious human understanding. Consequently, in publicising these common values objective symbols are crucial since they fix mere beliefs in a bodily form. They give an external reality to mere human understanding:

> Individual minds cannot come into contact and communicate with each other except by coming out of themselves; but they cannot do this except by movements. So it is the homogeneity of these movements that gives the group consciousness of itself and consequently makes it exist. When this homogeneity is once established and these movements have once taken a stereotyped form, they serve to symbolize the corresponding representations. But they symbolize them only because they have aided in forming them. Moreover, without symbols, social sentiments could have only a precarious existence.
>
> (Durkheim 1976: 230–31)

Because social relations are dependent on human understanding, they require objectification to give them an enduring reality. They need to take a physical form in order to establish them in collective consciousness. In the course of the ritual, these symbols often take on a reality of their own in the eyes of the participants. So viscerally do participants feel these common attachments that they presume that they derive from the totems themselves. In fact, the totem comes alive only when the clan is gathered and it is experienced as sacred only in the ecstatic presence of the other members of the group. The feelings of awe are produced by these others, especially when they are engaged in ecstatic celebrations, and not the totem itself. However, understandably, the natives transfer this feeling of awe, which they themselves mutually create, onto the symbol itself:

> Since religious force is nothing other than the collective and anonymous force of the clan, and since this can be represented in the mind only in the form of the totem, the totemic emblem is like the visible body of the god.
>
> (Durkheim 1976: 221)

The natives may reify the symbol, which only exists through them, but the power which they feel in the ritual is real. Once gathered together and unified, the clan constitutes an extremely powerful entity which transforms the members themselves. Durkheim emphasises the dialectical character of society:

> Social life, just like ritual, moves in a circle. On the one hand, the individual gets from society the best part of himself, all that gives him a distinct character and a special place among other beings, his intellect and moral culture. If we should withdraw from men their language, sciences, arts and moral beliefs, they would drop to the rank of animals. So the characteristic attributes of human nature come from society. But, on the other hand, society exists and lives only in and through individuals. If the idea of society were extinguished in individual minds and the beliefs, traditions and aspirations of the group were no longer felt and shared by the individual, society would die.
>
> (Durkheim 1976: 347)

Through their interactions, people produce social groups and social groups cannot exist without their members. However, in social interaction, humans mutually influence and thereby transform each other. In social relations, in the course of social interaction, group members can mutually develop potentialities of which they would have been incapable alone. Durkheim emphasises the internal dynamic of social interaction yet further. For the ritual to have its powerful social effects, the clanspeople must be aware of the significance of the totem. It is the clanspeople's understandings of themselves, their relations to each other and to their totem which inspire effervescence and this re-affirmation of their social group. Durkheim emphasises that 'there is one division of nature where the formula of idealism is applicable almost to the letter: this is the social kingdom' (Durkheim 1976: 228). Social interaction and social groups have the power they do only so long as group members invest these social relations with significance. Thus, social groups exist only as long as they are actively recognised by the people who are part of them. However, although the active understanding of group members is essential, it is false to suppose that groups are a matter of mere individual opinion. Once they have come into being through the consciousness of group members, the social relations of which they consist are real and binding. Fellow members are bound to each other only because they consciously recognise their bond, but this makes it no less of a bond: 'Yet the powers which are thus conferred, though purely ideal, act as though they were real; they determine the conduct of men with the same degree of necessity as physical forces' (Durkheim 1976: 228). Social interaction has an extraordinary property. It relies on the conscious understanding of humans but, once established, these shared understandings demand certain forms of practice from group members. The ritual is the moment, essential to all forms of social life, these collective understandings actively re-affirm these beliefs and bind group members together. In participating in the ritual, group members physically demonstrate their allegiance to each other. They create binding social relations.

For Durkheim, there was indeed a tangible and immediate reality which religion did reflect, society:

> But from our point of view, these difficulties disappear. Religion ceases to be an inexplicable hallucination and takes a foothold in reality. In fact, we can say that the believer is not deceived when he believes in the existence of a moral power upon which he depends and from which he receives all that is best in himself; this power exists, it is society.
>
> (Durkheim 1976: 225)

Aboriginal groups spent most of the year dispersed into smaller family groups involved in profane subsistence activities. Periodically, however, these families came together for clan or tribal gatherings. At these times, the clan would congregate at a special site and before the totem of their tribe they would engage in ecstatic (and often orgiastic) celebrations. In the 'effervescence' of the ritual (Durkheim 1976: 216), the aborigines genuinely felt a force outside themselves which pressed upon them and which inspired the most intense emotions:

> One can readily conceive how, when arrived at this state of exaltation, a man does not recognise himself any longer. Feeling himself dominated and carried away by some sort of external power which makes him think and act differently than in normal times.
>
> (Durkheim 1976: 218)

The aborigines believed that the force which imposed upon them was their totem, their God, who was entering them in these heightened moments. In fact, this force which they felt was not their totem but the clan itself, which was gathered bodily about them in this sacred spot and with whom the members of the tribe always experienced their totem. The totem and this visceral feeling of communal solidarity were indissoluble in the minds of the aborigines.

Durkheim noted an important point about ritual and social solidarity. When the clan gathers, its members respond reciprocally to each other, heightening emotions and producing a sense of communal effervescence. This feeling is symbolised by the totem, the memory of which demands certain actions of them even after the ritual. However, away from the group, the once powerful totem and the social sentiments it inspires are corrupted by the profane world:

> Though very strong as long as men are together and influence each other reciprocally, they exist only in the form of recollections after the assembly has ended and when left to themselves, these become feebler and feebler: for since the group is now no longer present and active, individual temperaments easily regain the upper hand.[5] The violent passions which may have been released in the heart of the crowd fall away.
>
> (Durkheim 1976: 231)

Consequently, since collective representations persist insofar as they are re-affirmed by the re-convening of social groups, groups must periodically gather together. This is an extremely important point because it decisively refutes any suggestion that Durkheim considers society to be external to humans, with its own independent ontological status. Society can exist only insofar as the members of a group come together to re-affirm their allegiance actively to one another. Social relations have to be re-affirmed periodically and this can be achieved only insofar as humans recognise their bond to each other. The point is forcefully re-emphasised at the end of *The Elementary Forms*:

> A society can neither create itself nor recreate itself without at the same time creating an ideal. This creation is not a sort of work of supererogation for it, by which it would complete itself, being already formed; it is the act by which it is periodically made and remade.
>
> (Durkheim 1976: 422)

Social groups persist only when humans together recognise themselves to be part of the group, and that recognition can be achieved only if the group periodically gathers and members publicly affirm their commitment to each other.

It is very important that *The Elementary Forms* is not read merely as a piece of ethnography. It is a work of sociological theory which describes the fundamental features of social life. Human groups arise out of social interaction when humans mutually recognise each other and the collective interests which they have. Although arising in the first instance only on basis of collective understanding, these social relations are not simply ideas. They are not reducible to individual opinion; they cannot be made to appear or disappear simply because a single individual thinks about them. Human social relations involve human understanding but once humans together recognise them they have tangible and unignorable existence. Once humans have recognised their social relations to each other, individuals are bound to each other. Human society can be understood only when the distinctive nature of social relations is comprehended. At various points, Durkheim points to the wider significance of this study. For instance, in his discussion of the creation of symbols in the ritual, he hints at the universal applicability of his analysis: 'Thus social life, in all its aspects and in every period of its history, is made possible only by vast symbolism' (Durkheim 1976: 231). All forms of social life involve the same process whereby collective representations which signify the social relations between humans are periodically created and re-created. *The Elementary Forms* is radical here. An important subsidiary theme in the work is that the creation of symbolic orders of classification by native Australians is in form no different from the production of science by professional experts in the west. Both involve ecstatic social interaction between the members of the groups which gives rise to a common understanding of collective interests. Both create collective representations which facilitate the achievement of practical ends, be it subsistence in the wilds of Australia or comprehending the universe. These representations direct the members of these groups towards the appropriate kinds of action.

It has become conventional to read Durkheim as an ontological dualist. Thus, in describing the substratum as a social fact, he seemed to suggest that society was independent of the individual in it. Similarly, when discussing collective representations he seemed to imply that there were ideas which imposed upon the individual. His dualism seemed to take a realist form in some of his work and a conceptual form in others. Yet, in both cases, these readings are unsustainable. Neither the substratum nor collective representations were ever intended to refer to anything metaphysical. Even a passing knowledge of *The Elementary Forms* would reveal that social interaction is paramount in Durkheim's work. Yet, this social ontology is not limited merely to Durkheim's most important work. A social ontology is present throughout his writing, sometimes obscured below purportedly dualistic passages. Above all else, Durkheim prioritised social interaction. In the course of interaction, humans transform themselves into groups and mutually constitute themselves as agents through conscious understanding. Social life is not reducible to individual psychological explanations but this did not imply that society had an existence independent of its members. Society consists of social relations. Durkheim was not an ontological dualist. On the contrary, he was sensitive only to the extraordinary character of human social life. Durkheim's emphasis on social relations – on life – accorded closely with Weber's interpretive sociology. Both recognised that human social life consisted of an irreducible conscious element. Humans had to recognise their social relations with each other and what those relations enjoined. Those relations did not exist independently of the understanding of humans but were precisely constituted by what humans mutually took them to be. Neither Durkheim nor Weber reduced society to individual opinion but they demonstrated that the nature of a particular social order depended upon what the humans involved in it took it to be. Durkheim and Weber converged on this decisive point. Even more strikingly, both recognised the sociological importance of status groups, and especially professional ones, in modern European society (e.g. Durkheim 1964: 278–79).

Given these theoretical and empirical affinities, it is even more extraordinary that Durkheim and Weber passed each other in the intellectual night.[6] However, although Durkheim and Weber may have been ignorant of the similarities between their work, a recognition of the parallels between them is extremely useful for contemporary social theory. Above all, the convergence of Durkheim and Weber illustrates the analytical power of the social ontology. Against ontological dualism, a focus on human social relations rigorously grounds sociology in social reality. It demands from sociology an attention to empirical reality in place of its current predilection for abstraction.

The Lessons of Classical Sociology

The close similarity between aspects of Weber's and Durkheim's work illuminates a significant thread running through classical sociology. The work of Hegel, Marx, Weber and Durkheim contains passages in which ontological dualism is espoused. At certain moments, Hegel's concept of *Geist* described a prior and independent idea which imposed upon individuals. *Geist* was a divine consciousness which structured history. Weber ultimately invokes a similarly conceptualist form of dualism: ideas provided a historical switch-point which channelled individuals in certain directions. Thus, Calvinist theology or bureaucratic rules prescribed particular forms of action, which were logically followed by the individual. When Durkheim discussed collective representations he seemed to be similarly drawn towards this conceptualist dualism in which a prior idea directed the individual from outside. However, in other parts of his writing where social facts referred to 'currents', Durkheim seemed to adopt a realist position. Society was an independent and material force which pressed on the individual from outside. Marx committed himself to a similar form of realism with his notion of the priority of production. In various passages, the economy determined the social forms. In Marx's work a materialistic dualism is evident in which economic forces, existing independently of human understanding, determine individual existence. The conceptual or realist dualisms which have become established as hegemonic in contemporary social theory are detectable, therefore, in classical sociology. In this way, Giddens, Foucault and Bourdieu echo the work of Hegel, Weber and some of Durkheim's writing, while the realism of Habermas and Bhaskar has affinities with Marx and with the realist parts of Durkheim's work. At certain points, classical sociology ignored the social ontology, promoting the ontological dualism which is hegemonic in contemporary social theory today. Yet, when the classical sociologists did recognise the social ontology, they described it with force and clarity. In the master–slave dialectic, in *The Theses on Feuerbach* (MacIntyre 1972), in the analysis of status groups and in the study of religion, the explanatory power of a social ontology is highlighted with unsurpassable rigour. Here, humans interact with each other on the basis of shared meanings to produce social relations. These relations are binding and obligatory, even though they depend finally only on human understanding. They have decisive influence over individual conduct and provide the real substance of human history. Only in these social relations are real and often brutal human activities explicable. These passages of classical sociology constitute the models which sociology should follow today. These texts should become the new totems of sociology today. Social relations between humans, not the abstract reproduction of social structure by agency, must be the focus of attention. Although philosophically sophisticated, the social ontology demands a rigorously empirical approach which classical sociology, including Hegel, demonstrated at its most successful moments.

For the most part, contemporary social theory has unfortunately forgotten the lessons of classical sociology. It has forgotten the reality of human social relations, in favour of theoretical abstractions about structure and agency. Indeed, while classical sociology saw dualism as an embarrassment even though it sometimes descended into it, contemporary social theory embraces this ontological dualism (e.g. Habermas 1987b; Bhaskar 1979). Social theorists today insist that the ontological division of structure and agency is essential; it cannot and should not be ignored (e.g. Mouzelis 1995; Layder 1981). For social theorists today, society has a self-evidently dual character. On the one hand, there are structures (institutions or rules) and, on the other, agency. Sociologists today need to create a new common sociological tradition in which the social ontology is paramount. To this end, classical sociology can be revived and re-invigorated as a collective memory for sociologists working today. Operating with a social ontology derived from classical sociology, sociologists will be able to recognise the distinctive properties of human social relations.

Yet, it is not enough for contemporary social theory merely to re-discover classical sociology as a source for the social ontology. The social ontology can be usefully recovered from classical sociology only so long as this social ontology is also established as a paradigm for contemporary sociology. In order to draw on classical sources, it is necessary for contemporary social theory to recognise this social ontology as well. A new theoretical paradigm must be established in social theory today. Operating from within this paradigm, classical sociology can become a rich resource for the super session of contemporary social theory. Significantly, a new paradigm is already available to contemporary social theory. Indeed, contemporary social theory is extremely familiar with this new paradigm. Social theory does not need to be re-built from the ground up. It does not need to import alien concepts and methods; it requires no major transformation. In order to explain the reproduction of society, all the major social theorists have finally to resort to a social ontology. They have to explain society in terms of social relations. Indeed, in the works of Giddens, Bourdieu and Foucault this social ontology is described eloquently, while it is rigorously defended by Habermas at the philosophical level. Although for the most part they do not recognise it, contemporary social theorists fully recognise the special quality of human social relations and draw upon this recognition at decisive points in their writing. The social ontology can certainly be recovered immanently from contemporary social theory. Contemporary social theory already draws implicitly upon this paradigm even to support its putatively dualistic ontology.

From the 1960s, the interpretive dimension of human social life began to be emphasised in opposition to the objectivism of functionalist theory. Reacting against their teacher, Talcott Parsons, both Irving Goffman and Harold Garfinkel tried to demonstrate the centrality of understanding to human social life. The interactionist and ethnomethodological traditions re-emphasized the fact that social life presumed human consciousness because people involved in interactions had to understand the significance of what they were doing. In the Anglophone world, partly through the work of Peter Winch, the relevance of Wittgenstein's later philosophy to the social sciences was also becoming evident. The rule-following which was essential to human social life finally rested on the particular forms of life in which humans existed. Together humans publicly established what constituted rule-following on the basis of their shared understandings of themselves. Heidegger's existential hermeneutics were also beginning to have an impact on the academy, despite the troubled political implications of his work. These developments in the social science came to be collectively termed 'the linguistic turn' and, although Wittgenstein, Goffman and Garfinkel never themselves used the term, this turn to meaning could ultimately be described as the rise of hermeneutics. Hermeneutics was specifically concerned with interpreting meaning and consequently became the general term which was applicable to those social sciences concerned with the significance of shared understandings to human existence. Hermeneutics has had a major impact on the social science and, as the work of Giddens, Bhaskar and Habermas demonstrates, contemporary social theory has accepted that hermeneutics – the interpretation of the shared meanings in social life – must feature in any credible social theory. Although implicit in these different traditions, in the contemporary era the social ontology can be recovered most effectively from the hermeneutic tradition, especially expressed in the work of Hans-Georg Gadamer. Gadamer's hermeneutics was derived from Martin Heidegger's existential phenomenology and has constituted one of the most important contemporary resources for hermeneutics. A recovery of hermeneutics involves the rectification of the misrepresentation of hermeneutics in contemporary social theory. Contemporary social theorists have accepted the significance of hermeneutics to sociology but rejected its theoretical adequacy on the grounds that it is idealist. It reduces objective social reality to individual interpretation of that reality. Following on from this claim, hermeneutics is regarded as individualistic; it reduces social reality to the individual. Finally, hermeneutics is accused of being uncritical. Since it does not seek to transcend individual interpretations but insists that social reality is never independent of the way humans understand it, hermeneutics must accept the account of reality provided by any individual no matter how deluded or interested. It has denied itself access to any wider social reality. Against its contemporary critics, it must be shown that hermeneutics is not idealist, it is not individualist and it does not prevent critique. In the following chapters, each of these criticisms will be refuted in turn. Once these criticisms are recognised as false, a proper account of hermeneutics can then be established against the caricature which is prevalent in

contemporary social theory. At that point, hermeneutics can be openly acknowledged as the theoretical basis of sociology. Sociologists can commit themselves to
hermeneutics in full knowledge that the social ontology which it promotes
provides the most coherent account of the reality which they seek to study.
Promoting a social ontology, hermeneutics is able to comprehend the manifest
reality of social reality, which the ontology of structure and agency only
obscures.

Part III

Towards a Hermeneutic Sociology

9 Hermeneutics and Idealism

Habermas' Critique of Gadamer

Contemporary social theorists generally recognise the validity of hermeneutics. Thus, Bhaskar insists that social action always involves a meaningful dimension, while Giddens has emphasised the importance of the hermeneutic tradition in English-speaking countries. Hermeneutics is discussed at length especially in the *New Rules of Sociological Method* (1976). However, although accepted as a necessary adjunct to sociology by contemporary theorists, hermeneutics is regarded as inadequate as an independent social theory. Institutions cannot be understood solely in hermeneutic terms. All the dualistic theorists cited in the opening chapter are similarly convinced of the inadequacy of hermeneutics. According to contemporary social theory, hermeneutics cannot be an adequate social theory in itself because, if interpretation alone were considered, society would be reduced to an individual's understanding of it:

> The thesis of hermeneutic universality commits, once again, the epistemic fallacy...from the fact that interpretative processes are a significant part of what goes on in the social world, and that our access to the social world is necessarily via our understanding of these interpretative processes (Giddens' double hermeneutic), it does not follow that this is all that exists, or can be known to exist.
>
> (Outhwaite 1985: 75–76)

> These contradictions of the historical context of tradition, expressed in criticism and coercion, are the very factors which hermeneutic methods have always failed to take into account.
>
> (Wellmer 1974: 48)

> We must go beyond language and other ideal factors to the material base of existence and the social relations underlying it.
>
> (J. Wolff 1975b: 124; see also J. Thompson 1981: 120, 140; Eagleton 1983: 73; Bleicher 1980: 156)

The common position is clear: hermeneutics is a necessary but insufficient social theory.

In his debate with Gadamer, Habermas has replicated the standard contemporary interpretation of hermeneutics. While recognising the importance of hermeneutics, he regards it as fatally flawed. In itself, it cannot provide an adequate philosophical basis for the social sciences. He has claimed that Gadamer's hermeneutics is untenably idealist:

> There is good reason to conceive language as a kind of metainstitution on which all social institutions depend. For social action is constituted only in ordinary-language communication. But clearly this metainstitution of language, as tradition, is dependent in turn on social processes that cannot be reduced to normative relations.
>
> (Habermas 1988: 172)

Against Gadamer, Habermas claims that there are fundamental aspects of society which determine the very nature of language. Words describe a reality which has an independent existence:

> The nonnormative forces that enter into language as a metainstitution derive not only from systems of domination but also from social labour. The instrumental sphere of action monitored by success structures experience that can give rise to specific linguistic interpretations and subject traditional patterns of interpretation to the constraints of the labour process.
>
> (Habermas 1988: 73)

Interpretations do not determine material facts. On the contrary, objective material practices give rise to new linguistic expressions: 'a new practice is not set in motion by a new interpretation' (Habermas 1988: 173). Given the dependence of hermeneutics on these economic facts, Habermas concludes that Gadamer falls into voluntaristic and subjectivist idealism:

> An interpretive sociology that hypostasizes language as the subject of life forms and of traditions binds itself to the idealist presupposition that linguistically articulated consciousness determines the material being of life-practice. But the objective context of social action is not reducible to the dimension of intersubjectively intended and symbolically transmitted meaning.
>
> (Habermas 1988: 173–74)

For Habermas, Gadamer reduces society to the idea which individuals have of it, but it is self-evident that society exists whatever an individual may think of it. If social relationships were only a matter of interpretation, then merely by thinking differently about their relations, individuals could transform their social worlds. Individuals could change their reality simply by re-interpreting it.

Yet, it is manifestly the case that merely thinking differently about the world does not alter the world for an individual. An individual can re-interpret the world in any number of ways but it will not alter reality a jot. Gadamer seems to be guilty of the idealism which Marx mocked in *The Germany Ideology* when he wrote about the 'valiant fellow who had the idea that men were drowned in water only because they were possessed of the idea of gravity' (Marx 1977a: 37). Humans are born into a social world which has been created independently of them and which cannot be reduced simply to their interpretation of it. Certainly, the individual's interpretation of society is important but that interpretation cannot obviate the fact that there is something objective which exists for them and which constrains them. At certain points, it is irrelevant what an individual thinks about a society. It will continue to determine them whatever they think. By denying the material priority of society, its structure of inequality and its economic system, in favour of interpretivism, Gadamer seems to be obliterating the manifest constraint which society has over humans. He falsely liberates individuals, who are seen to exist in a world where the social reality is only what they think it is.

Furthermore, even those commentators such as Bubner and Misgeld who have sought to reconcile Habermas and Gadamer (e.g. Bubner 1975; Misgeld 1977a, 1977b, 1979) have ultimately concurred with Habermas. Thus Bubner and Misgeld have promoted a 'practical philosophy' which focuses on the material aspects of society which cannot be captured by Gadamer's hermeneutics. They do not think that Habermas' universalising critical theory can capture this practical reality because it ignores the meanings which social agents attach to their situation. Nevertheless, they ultimately share the same social ontology as Habermas; there are material aspects which cannot be reduced to interpretation. It is not all a matter of interpretation as Gadamer seems to claim. Even Ricoeur, who explicitly argues for hermeneutics, believes that Gadamer has ignored real material processes. In a critical discussion of the three cognitive interests which Habermas describes in *Knowledge and Human Interests* (1971), Ricoeur describes the importance of a Habermasian notion of material interest over Gadamer's linguistic idealisation of the social world:

> I take from the concept of interest as an important warning which hermeneutical philosophy must heed – that forgetfulness of the trilogy work – power – languages can always lead to a disastrous retreat into a philosophy of language which would lose its anthropological breadth.
>
> (Ricoeur 1973: 162)

By arguing for the primacy of language and its universal constitution of all social relations, Ricoeur fears that Gadamer falls into an untenable and finally uncritical form of idealism. Against such a relapse, Ricoeur tries to develop a critical hermeneutics which synthesises both Gadamer's philosophical hermeneutics and Habermas' critique of ideology.[1]

The Origins of Hermeneutics

Hermeneutics originally developed in the Middle Ages as a way of assisting monks in the transcription of books, especially the Bible. Before the invention of the printing press, books were reproduced through a laborious process of hand-copying in which mistakes were inevitable; typically words were omitted or copied wrongly. Consequently, in order to recover the original meaning of the texts, a careful process of interpretation had to take place by which the original text was inferred from the copy. Mistakes were erased by a circular process of comparing the part with the whole. The proper meaning of problematic sentences and passages was established by examining the connection between the part and the context in which it was situated. From the wider whole, the meaning of the obscure part could be inferred so that mistakes could be eliminated (Gadamer 1975: 154). From the eighteenth century, this hermeneutic technique was taken up especially in Germany and, stripped of its strictly theological concerns, was promoted as a general technique of textual analysis. As Gadamer has emphasised, Schleiermacher was the pivotal figure in the development of hermeneutics as a general analytical technique. He refused to limit hermeneutics to biblical exegesis or to foreign texts but insisted that this was a universal method of comprehension (Gadamer 1975: 163; Bauman 1978; Mueller-Vollmer 1986). For Schleiermacher, hermeneutics started from a distinctive point: incomprehension. The failure to understand was integral to the entire hermeneutic process but this failure to understand, although the necessary starting point: could be overcome: 'Complete knowledge always involves an apparent circle, that each part can be understood only out of the whole to which it belongs, and vice versa' (Schleiermacher 1986: 84). Superseding traditional biblical hermeneutics, Schleiermacher claimed that the failure to understand could be overcome not simply by trying to understand the texts themselves but by referring to the intentions of the author. For Schleiermacher, hermeneutics involved returning to the original thought which inspired the text in the first instance. This was a quite radical step which reflected the Enlightenment emphasis on humanity and the individual. For him, every author's thought could be understood psychologically in relation to the rest of his life. The unity from which the hermeneutic theorist now began was the life of the author itself. It was this life which gave meaning to any particular text: 'to put oneself in the position of an author means to follow through with this relation between the whole and the parts' (Schleiermacher 1986: 84). Schleiermacher believed that the original intentions of the author could be recovered pristinely and that interpreters could understand any text as it was really intended. Indeed, he argued that hermeneutics should try 'to understand the text at first as well as and then even better than its author' (Schleiermacher 1986: 83; Gadamer 1975: 169). Schleiermacher's hermeneutics pre-supposed a notion of individual genius, whereby the texts were a pure emanation from the author's personality. Schleiermacher had performed a crucial service in liberating hermeneutics from Bible studies but his emphasis on individual creation prevented his hermeneutics from providing a method for the social sciences more generally because he focused too much upon individual intuition.[2]

Schleiermacher's individualistic errors were rectified by the German Historical School, exemplified by Ranke and Droysen, but above all by Wilhelm Dilthey. Dilthey drew a firm line between the social and natural sciences. In the natural world, objects obeyed physical laws which operated causally. The motion of the planets was not dependent on what the planets thought of themselves. The social world of humans operated on a fundamentally different basis. Although human action had to accord with the laws of the physical world, it was not reducible to these laws. Human actions necessarily involved an intentional element. A social action has its effects by virtue of what humans together take it to be. For Dilthey, the human mind was an unignorable fact for the cultural sciences since it invested the objective world with meaning. The human mind was not an individual mind, although it certainly found expression in the individual, but arose in social groups. Dilthey strongly rejected what he regarded as the metaphysical pronouncements of Comte, who promoted the idea of an autonomous social entity. Human society had to be understood in human terms; by reference to the way individuals in any particular historical era understood themselves. However, Dilthey was equally dismissive of Mill and the utilitarians, who insisted on reducing human society to the rational individual (Dilthey 1976: 160). For Dilthey, humans lived in social groups whose primary characteristic was that they were conscious of themselves: 'the world is nowhere else but in the consciousness of such individuals' (Dilthey, quoted in Hodges 1944: 145). Dilthey called this cultural consciousness 'life' and he maintained that 'life' must be the critical focus of the social and cultural sciences. 'Life' referred to the shared meanings with which humans invested their existence and Dilthey rejected all those philosophies which reduced this diverse meaningfulness to dry, logical universalities: 'No real blood flows in the veins of the knowing subject constructed by Locke, Hume and Kant, it is only the diluted juice of reason' (Dilthey 1976: 162). Human existence could not be understood by logical deduction but only by understanding particular lifeworlds which groups created for themselves.

'Life', in particular, distinguished the natural from the social sciences, for whereas the natural sciences developed, according to Dilthey, from a consideration of independent units whose interconnection was explained, the social sciences had to start from the fundamental fact of the unity of human life. Life referred to shared understanding, the broad cultural presumptions on the basis of which humans interacted. It was objectified in the various human monuments such as art and architecture, and the social scientists could interpret the significance of each of these manifestations of the human mind by reference to shared understandings of the group. Life then provided the hermeneutic whole from which any particular objectification could be understood. Life gave a meaning to any of its manifestations and, consequently, the task of the hermeneutic social scientists was decisively different from that of the natural scientist:

> We explain nature but we understand mental life. Inner experience grasps the process by which we accomplish something as well as the combination of individual functions of mental life into a whole. The experience of the whole context comes first; only later do we distinguish its individual parts. This means that the methods of studying mental life, history and society differ greatly from those used to acquire knowledge of nature.
>
> (Dilthey 1976: 89)

In human society, actions do not operate in a purely causal way. Social acts do not have causality independently of human understanding. It is impossible to comprehend social actions or their effects without a consideration of this cultural unity which is assumed in each action. Elsewhere, Dilthey referred to the social sciences as idiographic and the natural sciences as nomothetic. Because the social sciences were concerned with establishing meaning through situating particular activities in the wider horizon of life, they could only offer interpretations of human practice within particular cultures, whereas the natural sciences could establish universal causal laws. This did not make the social sciences inferior. On the contrary, the idiographic interpretations of the human sciences offered the genuine possibility of liberation because they expanded contemporary consciousness. By understanding other cultures, humans became aware of the diversity of human potential. In that way, contemporary consciousness, life itself, became richer. Humans were capable of greater self-understanding and a wider range of possible ways of existing. The parallel with Hegel is clear; both argued that human liberation arose insofar as humanity was aware of the extent of its possibilities, which had already been manifested historically. Dilthey himself was conscious of this similarity but he rejected the rationalism of Hegel's dialectic and its culmination in Absolute Mind. For Dilthey, human life could be enriched by understanding other forms of life but this process could never come to an end (Dilthey 1976: 193–95).

For Dilthey, life provided the interpretive unity from which any particular act could be understood. Social scientists had to recognise the distinctiveness of partic-ular forms of life but the diversity of forms of life was not a bar to interpretation. On the contrary, the fact that humans always and everywhere existed under a particular way of 'life' allowed them to become the possible objects of understanding. The primary feature of human nature was its orientation to understanding. Because all humans themselves live in a particular form of life based on shared understandings humans are *ipso facto* capable of understanding other forms of life. Different under-standings give rise to different forms of life but human understanding is an ineradicable feature of every form of life. In any society, humans have to understand what their social relations involve. Dilthey proposed that there were three key methods by which the human scientists could achieve this understanding: '*Sichhineinversetzen*', putting oneself in other's shoes; '*Nachbilden*', copying; and '*Nacherleben*', re-living (Bauman 1978: 39). For Dilthey, because humans live in a particular form of life, they can empathise with other examples of human life. Understanding could become the 'rediscovery of the I in the Thou' (Dilthey 1976:

207). In this way, Dilthey overcame the individualism of Schleiermacher's hermeneutics. For him, the whole was not the author's psychological life but the public culture in which an author existed. The work derived its meaning from this public culture, the interpretive unity in which this work took place.

Although Dilthey distinguished the natural from the human sciences on the grounds that life had to be understood not explained, he was concerned about the objectivity of the social sciences, particularly after 1900. Although he initially wanted only to understand other cultures, he also paradoxically wanted to produce an understanding which was objective. Thus, where life had once been described by him as the rich and ineffable medium of all human existence, in his later writing he emphasised the structural properties of mental life. In this way, the human sciences became analogous to the natural ones, for while the specific meaning of each objectification of life was singular, each took a universal form. Every objectification of life had the same fundamental structure, which could apparently be identified by the hermeneutic social theorist:

> The elementary logical operations which occur in the sciences and the human studies are the same...These are induction, analysis, construction and comparison. What matters is how they are used in the empirical sphere of human studies. Here too, induction, using observable process for its data, is based on the knowledge of the content. In physics and chemistry this is mathematical knowledge of quantitative relations; in biology it is fitness for survival; in human studies the structure of mental life.
>
> (Dilthey 1976: 262–63)

Although Dilthey eventually retreated into objectivism, his hermeneutics constituted a seminal moment for the human sciences. He demonstrated that human social life had a distinctive ontological status in which social relations could not be comprehended independently of the way participants understood them. The purpose of hermeneutics was precisely to highlight the meaningful dimension of social relations and to offer a way by which the social scientists might interpret those meanings. Hermeneutics recognised a social ontology and attempted to demonstrate the implications of this ontology for the social sciences.

It would, in fact, be possible to create a contemporary hermeneutics from the work of Dilthey alone, rectifying his eventual objectivism, to produce a theoretical standpoint which is adequate to the social ontology. However, the themes of Dilthey's work and especially the concept of life were taken up by Martin Heidegger and used to reject the phenomenology of his one-time mentor, Edmund Husserl. In so doing, Heidegger laid out a seminal account of hermeneutics which has profound importance for the social sciences. The contemporary development of hermeneutics cannot be understood without a consideration of Heidegger's contribution and his work offers the richest source for a hermeneutic sociology today. Against the rationalist argument that thought, and above all abstract and universalising reason, was the primary event, Heidegger insisted on the priority of existence. The central tenet of *Being and*

Time (1967) was that being itself must become the object of philosophical consideration. The distinctive fact of human existence had to be questioned in the first instance. To this end, the focus of Heidegger's attention in *Being and Time* is the *Dasein*, literally meaning the 'being there'. The *Dasein* refers to the human being, for whom existence is an issue (Gelven 1970: 22–23; Steiner 1978: 80; Polt 1999: 31). For the *Dasein*, the meaning of life is a problem which must be resolved. The *Dasein* tries to give life a meaning.

In *Being and Time*, Heidegger divides existence into two forms, ontic and ontological (Heidegger 1967: 31, 34; see Polt 1999: 33; Gelven 1970: 19). Ontic existence refers to everyday, profane existence and he describes this ontic form of existence as *existentiell* (Heidegger 1967: 34). In translation, this ontic existence is rendered as 'being' and as such it is opposed strongly to the ontological existence of the *Dasein*. The *Dasein* has Being, where Being refers to a higher level of existence than the merely ontic. Being is distinctive because it refers to that mode of existence which is concerned with giving that ontic existence meaning. Heidegger further divides existence into authentic and inauthentic modes, which do not correspond with ontic and ontological forms of existence precisely, though they are closely related to this divide. Inauthentic existence refers to mindless involvement in everyday life: chatter, 'idle talk' (Heidegger 1967: 213). Authentic existence, by contrast, is raised to a higher plane wherein everyday activities are situated in an understanding of the meaning of Being. The language which Heidegger employs in *Being and Time* is problematically abstract but also, especially to the analytical philosopher, empty. The entire work seems to be based on the false reification of a predicate, as Heidegger himself was aware; he notes that Kant himself had stated that 'Being is not a real predicate' (Heidegger 1967: 127). Heidegger seems to transform a verb, being, into an autonomous subject when this verb only ever refers to the necessary characteristic of the actual things which exist. Not a few critics have rounded upon exactly this point, among the most prominent of which has been Theodor Adorno (1973). For Adorno, Heidegger's concern with Being is mere metaphysical speculation which falsely detaches the issue of human existence from its social and political context: 'It remains true that the factual particular has meaning to the extent that the whole, above all the system of society, appears in it' (Adorno 1973: 41). For Adorno, Heidegger attempts to describe an authentic existence separate from every ontic form of practice. He attempts to create a sacred grove away from the reality of social life and, in so doing, his philosophy becomes ideological. There is no 'Being' away from actual social life and the postulation of such an individualistic idyll only buttresses a political system in which genuine liberation is impossible. Bourdieu has similarly argued that Heidegger's ontology of authentic existence has affinities with the Nazism with which Heidegger associated himself (Bourdieu 1988a), while Habermas also sees Heidegger's philosophy as a vain pursuit of the universal (Habermas 1993: 199). Although these criticisms are not without foundation, especially given Heidegger's willfully obscure prose, Heidegger's argument about Being and the *Dasein* may not be as circular and self-defeating as it at first appears.

The language which Heidegger employed is unfortunately obscure but his philosophy is not necessarily based on a *non sequitur*. The significance of Being becomes a serious philosophical question when the role of the *Dasein* itself is recognised. It is consequently necessary to consider the *Dasein* first. The *Dasein* has ontic, everyday existence but it also has a special form of existence (Being) because it does not merely act in the world but contemplates what its actions mean. 'Being' relies on everyday existence for it is only through the contemplation of this everyday being that *Dasein* comes to understand the meaning of its life itself. The development of *Dasein* is dependent on its 'being-in-the-world' (Heidegger 1967: 77) and the very concept of '*Dasein*' emphasises the existence of this being in the real world of practical activity. The *Dasein* is there; it exists in everyday life. The *Dasein* tries, however, to interpret the meaning of its 'facticity'. The way the *Dasein* tries to give meaning to its existence is distinctive:

> If to interpret the meaning of Being becomes our task, *Dasein* is not only the primary entity to be interrogated; it is also that entity which already comports itself, in its Being, towards what we are asking about when we ask this question.
>
> (Heidegger 1967: 35)

The statement appears absurd but Heidegger's definition of the *Dasein* in fact describes a recognisable process. The *Dasein* is not simply the focus of philosophical inquiry. The *Dasein* is a specifically philosophical mode of existence which asks what meaning can be attached to ontic existence. That very mode of existence is capable of giving human existence a meaning. Specifically, the *Dasein* is conscious of its everyday existence but can divide itself from it to ask itself what everyday life can possibly mean. The *Dasein* examines its ontic existence from a paradoxically externalised internal perspective. Heidegger describes the *Dasein* as a decisive nothingness: 'It itself, being a basis, *is* a nullity of itself' (Heidegger 1967: 330). Significantly, this nullity is not merely an absence: 'Nullity does not signify anything like not-Being-present-at-hand or not-subsisting; what one has in view here is rather a "not" which is constitutive for this Being of *Dasein* – its thrownness' (Heidegger 1967: 330). The 'nullity' is internal to the *Dasein* and is the means by which it divides itself from itself so that it is able to view its own ontic existence from a distanced perspective. In this way, the *Dasein* is not limited to everyday conscious existence; the *Dasein* is not confined to its ontic existence but recognises its existential possibilities (Heidegger 1967: 331). The *Dasein* can situate its being within a wider sense of its own existence. It can recognise that any specific ontic existence is only one expression of its possibilities. In the light of the discussion of the *Dasein* as a nothingness which can divide itself from everyday being and look on that being externally, it might be possible to describe the *Dasein* in rather more prosaic and less abstract terms. The *Dasein* corresponds to self-consciousness and, echoing Hegel, this self-consciousness transcends actual conscious existence. Only self-consciousness is able to divide itself from itself and to situate its own particular activities in a wider whole. Only self-consciousness is able to hold simultaneously the experience of a particular moment and the wider sense of existence. Self-consciousness is precisely this pregnant nothingness.

Significantly, Heidegger argues that *Dasein*, as self-consciousness, situates everyday being in the wider whole of human existence. It tries to situate being within life, which in the first instance means only the life of the individual. In Part II of *Being and Time* (especially sections 45 to 62), Heidegger describes the way that life provides the finite whole by which the part is given significance. The *Dasein* tries to give a meaning to its life in the full knowledge of the fact that it will die. Every ontic moment is bounded by the fact of birth and the future fact of death. The fact that *Dasein* is always a Being-towards-death necessarily provides it with a whole in which the part has meaning. Certainly humans often try and deny their mortality: 'for the most part *Dasein* covers up its ownmost Being-towards-death, fleeing in *the face* of it' (Heidegger 1967: 295). It is understandable that the anxiety caused by death provokes this response but this does not deny the existential reality of human life. Life necessarily provides a hermeneutic whole for the *Dasein* by which the ontic parts can be judged, for life is finite. Heidegger describes this hermeneutic whole as 'the ecstatical unity of temporality' (Heidegger 1967: 401), where the term 'ecstatical' refers to the way that future existence stands out before humans like a finite promontory offering alternative but always bounded possibilities. Life is authentic when it acknowledges human mortality and is conducted in ways which reconcile everyday existence with its finitude. When Heidegger claimed that he was considering the nature of Being itself, it would have been more accurate to say that he was considering the significance of self-consciousness for human existence. In particular, the *Dasein* is special because it is aware of its existence and, of course, its mortality. If *Dasein* really refers to human self-consciousness, which emerges out of everyday life, then Heidegger's discussions of authenticity and inauthenticity may be less deprecating of normal people than is often thought. Certainly Heidegger emphasised that the concept of inauthenticity was not intended dismissively (Heidegger 1967: 211). People are not inauthentic simply because they are not philosophers but they become inauthentic when they forget their own mortality. When humans forget that their existence is limited and that they must therefore act each day in the knowledge that there will be an end to their activities, then they act inauthentically. They fail to see the relationship of the individual parts of their life to their whole existence. They focus only on the parts, never thinking about the significance of each day to the entire scheme of their lives. They consequently fail to give their everyday life a meaning. They merely act. They are effectively in bad faith because they act in a way which does not recognise that life will come to an end; they accept the waste of their lives on activities which simply cannot be given meaning in the face of death. Heidegger's *Being and Time* and his later philosophy, in a somewhat different way, attend to the creation of meaning which follows from human self-consciousness. Human self-consciousness gives existence a special quality, in particular because they are self-conscious, humans and are able to situate particular activities in the context of their whole life. In this way, their everyday activities gain a significance. They have a place in the whole. When they cohere with that wider whole, contributing to the fulfilment of a life project, they have a meaning and a significance. The whole in turn has a meaning in the light of all the particular activities in which an individual has engaged. Life does not have a meaning prior to these activities but gains one only in the course of human existence.

Heidegger's description of *Dasein* is important because it allows Heidegger's definition of Being more widely to be considered. This is finally the whole by which self-consciousness is able to give meaning to being. His definition of Being draws heavily upon Dilthey's concept of life, and Heidegger's hermeneutic analysis of Being has profound philosophical implications, especially for the social sciences. It is interesting that, at a similar time, Wittgenstein pointed in a very similar direction to Heidegger (see Rorty 1993b: 339, 348). For Heidegger, in order to identify the meaning of existence, it is impossible to operate by deductive reasoning. The meaning of life is not determined by a universal logic. In *Being and Time*, Heidegger first began to argue on these lines in his rejection of Cartesian method (Heidegger 1967: 44; Steiner 1978: 86; Gelven 1970; Polt 1999: 47). For Descartes, the entire span of human existence could be explicated by reference to an *a priori* logic. For Heidegger, contemplation alone was empty. To arrive at self-consciousness, humans have to throw themselves into existence in the first place. Human activity in the world is critical. In analysing this activity, Heidegger distinguished between those aspects of the world which were 'present-at-hand' and those which were 'to-hand'. 'The present-at-hand' referred merely to those objects which happened to exist but were not a significant part in a human's life; humans did not interact with these objects. By contrast, humans have an intimate relationship with those things which are 'to-hand'. These objects decisively become 'equipment'. Heidegger employed the example of the craftsman's hammer to illustrate the nature of 'equipment'. The hammer's uses and properties are not determined by the *a priori* rational properties of the mind. Rather, the hammer's uses are given by the way that the craftsman related to it:

> The less we just stare at the hammer-Thing and the more we seize hold of it and use it, the more primordial does our relation to it become, and the more unveiledly is it encountered as that which it is – equipment.
>
> (Heidegger 1967: 98)[3]

Significantly, the world which gives the hammer meaning is created through the craftsman's work (Heidegger 1967: 99). The world which the craftsman encounters is not there before he has worked in it. That world is given only by his work, which determines the kind of relationship he has with the world. The 'to-handedness' of the hammer can be extrapolated to the question of the meaning of being more generally. The craftsman's work pre-supposes a particular attitude towards the world. Heidegger defines the craftsman's relationship to the world as care. This care denotes the general attitude which the craftsman takes to the world given his employment. Crucially, the world does not itself exist independently of this attitude of care. The 'worldhood of the world' (Heidegger 1967: 92) is constituted by the type of careful attitude which humans take towards it. The world which humans experience is not ultimately an objective present-at-hand entity which exists independently of them. The kind of world in which humans live is constituted by the attitude which they take toward it; the kinds of projects and practices in which they are engaged. The world ultimately is a form of equipment, enlivened only through the relationship which humans develop with it.

Heidegger further illustrates the point by reference to the concept of space. He recognises that as a result of certain scientific discourses, a concept of pure objective space has developed. Against this, Heidegger argues that humans do not live in objective space but in a world of spatiality in which nearness and remoteness are determined by their practical orientations: 'We say that to go over yonder is "a good walk", "a stone's throw" or "as long as it takes to smoke a pipe"…Such a duration is always interpreted in terms of *well-accustomed everyday ways* in which we "make provision"' (Heidegger 1967: 140, emphasis added). At this point Heidegger's concept of Being begins to become clearer. Being is a form of concern or care and it refers to the practical orientations which humans have already taken towards the world. These orientations are neither theoretical nor arcane but familiar and routine: they are 'well-accustomed everyday ways'. The Being which the self-conscious *Dasein* attempts to disclose refers to the understandings by which humans always already orient themselves to the world. Self-consciousness is able to disclose these wider understandings on which existence is grounded because it has the special ability of being able to detach itself from ontic existence; only it can distance itself from itself. Significantly, Heidegger repeatedly describes the *Dasein* as 'ontically "closest" to itself and ontologically farthest' (Heidegger 1967: 37; also 105). At first this phrase is mysterious but it becomes comprehensible in the course of the discussion of equipment and the worldhood of the world. There Heidegger begins to describe the *Dasein*'s mode of Being more concretely: 'When, for instance, a man wears a pair of spectacles which are so close to him distantially that they are "sitting on his nose", they are environmentally more remote from him than the "picture on the opposite wall"' (Heidegger 1967: 141). The *Dasein* is ontically closest to itself because the Being which it tries to explicate is pre-supposed in every activity. Yet, for the very reason that all activities assume this form of Being, it resists interpretation. It is difficult to recognise the specific nature of Being because it is always assumed. Humans consequently focus on their ontic activity, forgetting the careful 'fore-havings' which give rise to their activities in the first place. Being as a form of concern or care refers to the understandings by which humans have already oriented themselves towards the world. It is these fore-given meanings and intentions which ultimately produce the kind of world which there is for humans. As Heidegger argues, 'a person is in any case given as a performer of intentional acts which are bound together by the unity of a meaning' (Heidegger 1967: 73). Being refers precisely to this prior unity of meanings in which human activities always take place. The distinctive quality of human existence is that it is constituted by conscious but often assumed understandings. The projects conducted on the basis of these understandings are decisive to the reality which actually presents itself to humans. The *Dasein*'s role is to elucidate these understandings which underpin everyday activity and, thereby, give those activities a meaning through self-conscious awareness of their connection to human life as a whole.

In an interesting discussion towards the end of the first part of *Being and Time*, Heidegger makes his position explicit. He rejects realism as a philosophical position. The world is not simply there for humans independently of their understandings of themselves. The world or 'entities' do not simply determine human existence. For Heidegger, 'in realism there is a lack of ontological understanding'. By contrast, Heidegger promotes a position which he regards as at least partially compatible with idealism: 'As compared with realism, *idealism*, no matter how contrary and untenable it may be in its results, has an advantage in principle, provided that it does not misunderstand itself as "psychological idealism"' (Heidegger 1967: 251). Heidegger rejects idealism, which reduces the world to individual subjective opinion. His hermeneutics does not reduce existence to a matter of personal interpretation. However, the world cannot be understood without recognising the importance of human consciousness. The world is not whatever any individual believes it to be but the world which exists for humans necessarily involves the understandings on the basis of which they interact with it. In particular, the world in which humans exist is decisively constituted by how humans understand themselves and what they seek to do in it: 'If what the term "idealism" says, amounts to the understanding that Being can never be explained by entities but is already that which is "transcendental" for every entity, then idealism affords the only correct possibility for a philosophical problematic' (Heidegger 1967: 251). Being precedes human experience of objects in the world. It determines the attitude which humans will in fact take towards the world. It refers to the concepts and understandings which make the world what it is for humans. Heidegger consciously avoids a subjective idealism here. The concepts and understandings are not the product of isolated individuals. To postulate that would be to adopt a facile form of idealism. However, if Being refers to *common* cultural understandings, then these can be seen to underpin every form of life 'transcendentally' without reducing the world merely to an individual's opinion of what it is. These common understandings orient humans in that place towards particular kinds of activities and define the kinds of relations in which humans there find themselves. It now becomes clear why Cartesian deduction cannot explicate the nature of human existence. Human existence is primarily constituted by the conscious understandings by which people orient themselves to the world and to each other. These meanings constitute a unity which frames the world that exists for them. In the light of this framing, particular kinds of practices and relationships are possible. In order to understand any specific form of human existence, therefore, it is necessary to understand the common cultural assumptions; the meaningful unity on the basis of which people act. This unity cannot be arrived at by deduction. It can be understood and interpreted only by means of the hermeneutic circle whereby humans begin to recognise their common cultural pre-suppositions through considering their everyday activities. Being cannot be deduced but only 'disclosed' as the wider horizon in which particular activities have their place is revealed. This is why the *Dasein* is the nearest and furthest from human existence. It illuminates those assumed understandings which become invisible because they are taken for granted in every encounter and which therefore become the most difficult and distant objects for contemplation.

The hermeneutic insight of *Being and Time* is obscured by Heidegger's use of the word Being, which seems to suggest some metaphysical essence which precedes actual human existence. Yet, *Being and Time* did not, in fact, seek the metaphysical underpinnings of existence. It sought rather to demonstrate how human life cannot be understood except by reference to human understanding. Philosophy had to recognise that human existence was decisively constituted by the way in which humans understood themselves. This hermeneutic position is described forcefully in *Being and Time*. Yet Heidegger himself recognised certain shortcomings to the work. Above all, although the work rejected the individualism and rationalism of Descartes, it was still overwhelmingly characterised by a similarly individualistic outlook. The work was very obviously the consideration of a single individual and, indeed, could be read almost as an intellectual autobiography of Heidegger himself. Although Heidegger claimed that the concept of inauthenticity was not intended dismissively, it is notable that he described this mode of existence as the 'they' (Heidegger 1967: 298). This implied that authentic existence arose only when the individual established themselves autonomously in Nietzschean fashion. His later work, although in many ways even more abstract, attempted to overcome this individualism by emphasising the role of language in life. The focus on language was an attempt to communicate that the understandings which frame human activities are shared. The very way in which this philosophy was expressed brought it into being. The meaning of this later work is captured by the typically bewildering aphorism 'Language is the house of Being' (Heidegger 1996c: 217). Many critics have taken this and other phrases to imply a hypostatisation of language. Imposing a Saussurian reading, they assume that Heidegger is arguing that language is a prior structure which directs individuals; language, independently of human usage, makes the world what it is. Heidegger's point is not this, however. Language is not a prior entity which transcendentally underpins being. His emphasis on language is intended to re-direct philosophy from its individualistic perspective to a social one. Individuals are not thrown into a world which they have created for themselves. The world which individuals inhabit and into which they are thrown is social; it is constituted through the language which their particular community employs. Any language community creates a world for itself by defining what is in the world for it and determining what projects are appropriate for it. The craftsman learns to use the hammer by practice but the practices he learns are formed by the traditions of the community of which he is part. Crucially these traditions are communicated and indeed constituted in language because the way humans describe them defines their very significance to those humans: 'Language, by naming being for the first time, first brings beings to word and appearance' (Heidegger 1996a: 198). It is important to recognise that Heidegger does not deify language. He is not claiming that there is a prior language which determines human existence. On the contrary, his focus is on actual human practice. Heidegger's response to critics like Sartre who regard his philosophy as degrading to human dignity is significant in this connection: 'Because we say that the Being of man consists in "being-in-the-world" people find that man is downgraded to a merely terrestrial being' (Heidegger 1996c: 249). Against his critics, Heidegger insists that to recognise the priority of being-in-the-world is not to degrade humanity but to emphasise only the nature of human existence. Heidegger effectively employs the term 'language' as a symbol of common culture, which is primary in human existence. References to language are not intended to efface this social reality in favour of a metaphysical one. In the later writings, it becomes further evident why he employs this metaphor of language. He tries to re-create a new tradition for philosophy poetically because poetry is able to create a reality through its very use of language. Poetry is a powerful example of the way in which shared understandings, shared references and meanings, make the world what it is. Poetry does not merely describe. It evokes a world through the meaningful use of language.

In his later work, Heidegger uses metaphors which he draws from his experiences of walking in the Black Forest. The terms 'lightings' and 'clearings' (Heidegger 1996a: 185, 181) in his later writing are intended to communicate this notion of the linguistic constitution of human existence. Language – the culture of which humans are part – illuminates the particular world in which humans live and thereby brings this world into being: 'Beings can be as beings only if they stand within and stand out within what is cleared in this clearing' (Heidegger 1996a: 178). Humans have their existence by virtue of the cultures of which they are part. The common understandings on the basis of which social relations are conducted provide the ground on which humans live. Heidegger emphasises the point: 'Just as the openness of spatial nearness seen from the perspective of a particular thing exceeds all things near and far, so is Being essentially broader than all beings because it is the clearing itself' (Heidegger 1996c: 240). When humans look at a particular object, they ignore the context which facilitates the appearance of this object in this particular way in the first place. Similarly, when engaged in everyday activity, humans focus on that activity, and forget the wider culture in which they exist and which makes this activity what it is. Nevertheless, even though humans take this culture which gives their activities their significance for granted, this culture (Being) is in fact primary and precedes all particular forms of practice (being). This cultural background, embodied in language, brings the reality in which humans exist into being. In Heidegger's later work, the term 'language' refers to the shared understandings which make the reality which confronts humans what it is. Neither language nor these shared meanings are to be detached from the practices in which humans are actually engaged. The point is not to reduce human existence to language but merely to emphasise that no human practice exists independently of the way humans understand it. These understandings expressed in language make a practice what it is: 'Thus, the bridge does not first come to a locale to stand in it; rather, a locale comes into existence only by virtue of the bridge' (Heidegger 1996d: 356). Heidegger insists that the world which exists for humans is constituted by the common culture on the basis of which humans act in the world. Human culture transforms a mere space in the world into a location with meaning and significance. The bridge converts the world into a location in which humans dwell. The way communities understand their relations bring them into existence. In his famous essay 'The Origin of the Work of Art', Heidegger makes a similar point. There he posits an opposition between the earth and the world. The earth refers to objective natural reality, while the world refers to the social existence of humans. The world is necessarily based on the earth (according to its natural laws) but the world is not determined by it. Art expresses and indeed brings the world of the culture into being but great art also re-defines this boundary between the earth and the human world, re-formulating the relationship of a human society and its natural environment. Heidegger famously describes the way in which Van Gogh's painting of peasant shoes communicates these meanings, but he also discusses a Greek temple which ultimately performs the same task.[4] The temple is not simply erected in a world which already exists. Like the bridge which creates a location, the temple embodying the common cultural understandings of the Greek community brings their world into being. It symbolises their social relations with each other, their social practices and therefore their orientation to the natural world. The natural world does not determine the construction of the temple but rather the temple is a symbol of the way this world is for this community: 'To be a work means to set up a world' (Heidegger 1996a: 170). Being refers to the common cultural understanding on the basis of which humans engage with each other and the world. Heidegger is not denying the reality of either the social or the natural worlds but he is arguing that whatever world there is for humans is ultimately dependent on the way they communally understand themselves. Human consciousness and the meanings which arise in it are an unignorable aspect of the reality in which humans live. Heidegger did not deny the practical reality of existence – indeed he emphasised everyday activity so much that some humanist critics thought he was devaluing humanity – nor did he reduce existence to the mere effect of a deified language. For Heidegger, philosophy had to start from the premise that human life is not independent of the way that humans themselves understand it. For all its abstractness, Heidegger's hermeneutics promotes a rigorously empirical social ontology. Humans live in social relations and engage in social practices. This social reality cannot be comprehended without recognising the way in which humans in this particular form of life actually understand it.

Heidegger's most important student, Hans-Georg Gadamer, has elaborated upon the centrality of understanding to human life to demonstrate the relevance of Heidegger's philosophical hermeneutics to the social and political sciences today. Gadamer's work stands as one of the most important statements of contemporary hermeneutics and as such it offers a prime resource for the re-invigoration of sociology today. The key source here is, of course, Gadamer's *magnum opus*, *Truth and Method* (1975). In that work, Gadamer elucidated the historical origins of hermeneutics in order to establish it as the philosophical basis of the social sciences. The work is divided into three parts. In the first, Gadamer examines the relevance of hermeneutics to aesthetics; in the second part, Gadamer describes the application of hermeneutics to the study of history; and, in the final part, Gadamer demonstrates how the hermeneutic process is an essential part of human existence. In this third and final part of *Truth and Method*, Gadamer, following Heidegger's later work, elaborated upon both the nature of human existence and the appropriate form for an adequate social philosophy. Like Heidegger, Gadamer emphasised the centrality of meaning to human existence. Gadamer dismissed the notion that the world which humans confronted had a self-evidently objective status. Human under-standings and human concepts did not simply reflect a reality which already existed. On the contrary, the way that humans understood themselves made the world what it was for them; in particular, it defined their social existence. Following Heidegger, Gadamer expresses these arguments by a linguistic analogy. It is important that Gadamer's discussion of language, like Heidegger's, is properly understood. In this way, it is possible to tease out a social ontology from his writing.

In Part III of *Truth and Method*, Gadamer initiates his argument that hermeneutics is universal. Gadamer rejects (like Wittgenstein) the notion that language is merely ostensive:

> The interpreter does not use words and concepts like an artisan who takes his tools in his hands and then puts them away. Rather, we must recognise that all understanding is interwoven with concepts and reject any theory that does not accept the intimate unity of word and object.
>
> (Gadamer 1975: 365)

Humans cannot put language down and confront an unmediated, objective world, for the very world which confronts them, the kinds of interests they have in it and practices they perform in it are given by their language. Humans never escape this language. For Gadamer, language is a form of incarnation:

> There is, however, an idea that is not Greek and that does more justice to the nature of language and prevented the forgetfulness of language in Western thought from being complete. This is the Christian idea of incarnation.
>
> (Gadamer 1975: 378)

In the Christian tradition, language is not something which simply stands for the world that is already created, but rather the Word (of God) creates the world.

Being comes to life through the Word and is the Word embodied. The word brings the object into being, not just naming something that already exists for humans. Consequently, word, thought and object are not separate:

> The object thought (the species) and the word belong as closely together as possible. Their unity is so close that the word does not occupy a second place in the mind beside the species, but is that in which knowledge is completed, i.e. that in which the species is fully thought. Thomas points out that in this the word resembles the light in which a colour becomes visible.
>
> (Gadamer 1975: 386)

Without light, there is no colour and, similarly, without the illumination of language there is no world for humans. Like the colours humans see because of light, the kind of world there is for them exists because they have a language. Language creates the spectrum of possible worldly experiences for humans. Although interesting and erudite, the form of Gadamer's argument is unfortunate here since his emphasis on the Word and on language as an apparently independent entity has understandably led to the accusation that he hypostatises language into a metaphysical entity (e.g. Pleasants 1999; Harrington 2001). Language seems, on this account, to be a transcendental entity which creates the world for humans. Gadamer does seem to be guilty of a form of idealism, as Habermas and many other critics have argued. Although understandable, this reading does not reflect Gadamer's intentions.

Despite the implication of some of Gadamer's writing, he does not want to argue that the world which confronts humans is the product of certain *a priori* and ideal conceptual structures. It is notable that Gadamer explicitly rejects this Kantian vision of language at various points in Part III. In his discussion of Humboldt, Gadamer's meaning begins to become clear. He notes that 'the modern philosophy of man' has shown that 'the linguistic constitution of the world is far from meaning that man's relationship to the world is imprisoned within a linguistically schematised habitat' (Gadamer 1975: 402). Gadamer rejects the position which is typically imputed to him. Language is not a prior and independent entity which imposes upon humans and determines what the world is for them. 'Language' plainly means something different to Gadamer than it appears to when he talks about incarnation. The meaning of the term 'language' begins to become clear in the course of the discussion. Thus, he argues that 'language maintains a kind of independent life over and against the individual member of a linguistic community and introduces him, as he grows into it, to a particular attitude and relationship to the world as well' (Gadamer 1975: 401). Language is more than the individual not because it has a transcendental existence but because it refers to the community of which any individual is part. As humans, individuals are socialised into this community and learn its culture. This culture defines appropriate relations between humans and the attitude which its members take towards the natural world. The practices which they perform in the world are a product of this shared culture. Crucially, this culture is primary. Humans have to share these understandings in order that they can interact with each other and with the world. In an extremely close echo of Wittgenstein's famous claim that humans agree in a form of life, Gadamer claims that 'in a real community of language, on the other hand, we do not first decide to agree, but are already in agreement' (Gadamer 1975: 405). This does not mean that humans robotically consent to what everyone else in their group claims; nor does it mean that language determines what everyone thinks so that all automatically find themselves in agreement. It means, rather, that in order for there to be a community – in which disagreements can in fact occur – there has to be fundamental agreement; group members must be oriented in the first instance to shared understandings and collective interests. Without those, there is no group. The concept of language begins to take on a much more concrete and sociological appearance in the light of this commentary. It is not separate from human social life but implicit within it. Indeed, Gadamer's point is ultimately stronger than this.

> All forms of human community of life are forms of linguistic community: even more, they constitute language. For language, in its nature, is the language of conversation, but it acquires its reality only in the process of communicating.
>
> (Gadamer 1975: 404)

Here, Gadamer is at last explicit and any metaphysical vestiges which his concept of language may invoke are dispelled. Language is not prior to human social communities. On the contrary, human communities 'constitute language'. They sustain language through living conversation. Language has be continually invoked and re-created in the interaction between members of a community. They must actively re-affirm their language through continual exchange. It is possible to re-describe this process in alternative terms. Humans sustain the communities of which they are part insofar as they are able to orient themselves mutually to common understandings – expressed in language. These common understandings are not automatic. Humans have to affirm their common understandings in the course of their interactions with each other. They have to recognise their social relations and the shared practices which those relations demand. Language is the medium for this communication and maintenance of shared understandings and, indeed, language itself is sustained in the course of this interaction. Language does not precede and direct social action from above. Communities decide upon how they will use their language and what it actually means. Gadamer's hermeneutics implies no hypostatisation of language, therefore. On the contrary, his concept of language closely echoes Heidegger's notion of Being. This is the horizon in which humans have their existence; it refers to the shared understandings by which humans orient themselves to each other and, therefore, to the natural world itself. The reality in which humans exist simply cannot be comprehended without recognising these understandings for they are the very medium of human life, making it what it is. Gadamer certainly never employed the term but his hermeneutics advocates a social ontology. Language as common culture, as shared understandings, arises in and is sustained in human social relations. It is this culture and these relations which constitute the distinctive nature of human existence.

It is possible to interpret one passage from Supplement II of *Truth and Method* as an application of this social ontology. There, Gadamer considers Habermas' criticisms of his work and tries to defend himself against the charge of idealism. He begins by challenging Habermas' claim that there are aspects of social reality, social institutions and the economy which are independent of human understanding. According to Gadamer, Habermas only argues for an extra-linguistic dimension to social life because Habermas has too narrow a view of 'linguistic understanding', which he limits to 'cultural tradition' (Gadamer 1975: 495). For Gadamer, the cultural tradition embodied in language is not limited to forms of artistic expression. On the contrary, 'now the cultural heritage of a people is pre-eminently the heritage of forms and techniques of working, of forms and techniques of domination, of ideals of liberty, of objectives of order and the like' (Gadamer 1975: 495). When Gadamer refers to linguistically consti-tuted culture, he is referring to the very aspects of social life which Habermas regards as extra-linguistic. Ironically, Gadamer shares the view of Habermas, Wellmer, Ricoeur *et al.* that the economic aspects of society, its technologies and its labour relations, are the central element in modern society. However, for Gadamer, economic activities are cultural phenomena involving social relations conducted on the basis of assumed shared understandings: 'The encounter with domination and dependence involves the development of our political ideas' (Gadamer 1975: 495). For Gadamer, the putatively material, extra-linguistic world of work necessarily depends upon the kinds of 'political ideas' which the humans involved in them employ. The kind of economic or political reality which exist for humans is itself dependent upon the way humans together define these realities. Given different political or economic concepts – given a different 'language' – alternative social relations will appear.[5] Supposedly material activi-ties like labour are hermeneutic phenomena because they necessarily involve shared understandings which make any activity what it is. People adopt relations towards each other on the basis of these understandings. The economy has defi-nite material effects but the economy refers to a specific set of social relations and practices. These are never independent from the way that people collectively understand what they are doing. Gadamer resolutely defends a social ontology. That ontology in no way reduces social reality either to a transcendent language or to individual interpretation. On the contrary, it emphasises human social rela-tions.

Gadamer's defence of the social ontology is radical:

> But the claim of a philosophical hermeneutic extends even further. It makes the claim to universality...Nothing is left out of this speech community: absolutely no experience of the world is excluded. Neither the specialization and increasingly esoteric operations of the modern sciences nor material

labour and its form of organization, nor the political institutions of domination and governance which bind the society together find themselves outside
this universal medium of practical reason (or unreason).

(Gadamer 1990: 277)

This extreme statement explains some of the hostility which Gadamer has
attracted in his critics but his claim that 'there is nothing outside the speech
community' is no naïve assertion of idealism. For Gadamer, hermeneutics is
universal precisely because human existence is always social; consequently,
humans always and everywhere have to understand what their social relations
involve. Social relations do not simply exist independently of human understandings. Consequently, there is no aspect of human existence which transcends
the common understandings embodied in the language of different communities. It is important that Gadamer's argument is understood here for this passage
seems hyperbolic. He is not claiming that political and institutional realities can
be reduced to a matter of individual interpretation. He explicitly opposes such
idealism when he claims that the universality of hermeneutics 'does not mean
nor entail confinement to the world of meaning' (Gadamer 1986: 284). The
social world is not simply a matter of interpretation. On the contrary, he openly
accepts that social reality consists of actual practices which are not simply
linguistic. He recognises that these activities have real effects and involve material resources: 'It would be absurd to assert that all our experience of the world is
nothing other than a linguistic process' (Gadamer 1990: 278). However, although
real social practices exist, people work, exchange goods and fight, none of these
practices exist independently of the way the people involved understand them.
Gadamer emphasises the point:

> That in no way means – Habermas' imputations [of idealism] notwith-
> standing – that the material existence of practical life is determined by the
> linguistic articulation of consciousness; it means simply that there is no
> social reality, with all its concrete compulsions, which does not also exhibit
> itself in a *linguistically articulated consciousness*.
>
> (Gadamer 1986: 287; 1977: 35)

The term 'linguistically articulated consciousness' is potentially confusing here
as it seems to suggest that consciousness is structured by language. It seems
Gadamer has merely returned to idealism. However, when the concept of
language from *Truth and Method* is remembered, this passage suddenly comes into
focus. Linguistically articulated consciousness refers to the way that human
consciousness is already informed and framed by shared cultural pre-suppositions.
The consciousness explicitly expresses itself by reference to the common understandings embodied in language. Linguistically articulated consciousness ultimately
refers to the shared understandings on the basis of which humans conduct themselves. At this point, the meaning of the passage becomes clear. Gadamer fully
accepts that the world is not a matter of mere individual interpretation; social

reality is not 'determined by the linguistic articulation of consciousness'. However, whatever social practices or social relations do exist, they will necessarily involve human understandings; they are expressed consciously in a shared language, communicating a set of shared beliefs and values. These practices and relations are not independent of what the humans involved in them take them to be. Social reality is not simply a matter of interpretation. Nor are the practices that occur under the name of politics and economics merely linguistic. However, on Gadamer's account, whatever the social reality, it does not exist independently of the shared understandings of the members of a community. The term 'language' refers to this inexorably meaningful dimension of human social reality; it refers to the fact that humans have to understand mutually what their relations involve. No social relation of any sort, however apparently material, exists independently of this common understanding of what it actually demands of the parties involved in it.

The Social Ontology: Two Examples

Although Gadamer's hermeneutics is intended to promote a social ontology, his discussions remain philosophical throughout. He never exemplifies his position empirically. Although Gadamer himself would doubtlessly regard such empirical exemplification as superfluous to his philosophical argumentation, in fact it is useful to consider two examples to emphasise the ontological claims which hermeneutics is making. Charles Taylor's well-known article on the significance of interpretation for the social sciences is pertinent here (1995). There, Taylor compares the example of the traditional consensus of a Japanese village and the western notion of economic bargaining (Taylor 1995: 32–33). Westerners take economic bargaining between two rationally self-interested actors as self-evident on this account. Economic transactions involve no shared understandings; it is self-evident what the parties in the exchange should do. This is exactly what Habermas assumes when he claims that forms of instrumental actions which are 'monitored by success' are objective and precede interpretation (Habermas 1988: 73). Yet, Taylor notes, the apparently objective and self-evident western system of market exchange, in fact, assumes shared understandings. Market exchange only seems objective because westerners are so familiar with the understandings on the basis of which exchanges are conducted; rationally self-interested action is presumed. These cultural pre-suppositions are illuminated, however, when they are contrasted with other cultures. For instance, in the context of a traditional Japanese village, 'our idea of bargaining, with the assumption of distinct autonomous parties in willed relationship, has no place' (Taylor 1995: 33). In the Japanese village, individuals are bound by communal responsibilities. In the light of the particular way in which Japanese villagers regard their relations with others, it would be inappropriate to bargain in the way that westerners regard as self-evident:

> The word, or whatever word of their language we translate as bargaining, must have an entirely different gloss, which is marked by the distinction their

vocabulary allows in contrast to those marked by ours. But this different gloss is not just a difference of vocabulary, but also one of social reality.

(Taylor 1995: 33)

It is not simply that these Japanese villagers have a different language than ours and so describe what is the same fundamental activity – economic bargaining – in an alternative language. Rather, economic activity in a Japanese village is incompatible with western market exchange precisely because Japanese villagers understand these economic transactions in a different way. They do not presume to make these exchanges as private individuals but as representatives of their corporate social group, committed to particular traditions. Consequently, Japanese villagers do not act autonomously like western rational actors, personally seeking to maximise their interests. They look to their social relations with their village and with their elders. Their economic practices are real, with manifest material effects, but those practices (and their effects) are dependent on the way the Japanese actually understand themselves. The economic transactions which take place are always mediated by the understandings which these villagers have of themselves and their fellow villagers. These transactions involve a different idea of what is appropriate in exchange. Above all, the Japanese act in economic exchange by reference to their corporate responsibilities. Even the most apparently material activity, like economic production, is a social phenomenon which assumes shared understandings on the part of the participants. Humans have to understand what their activities actually involve. In the case of economic exchange, transactions cannot occur without the humans involved in them recognising what their relationship to each other is. Social relationships are never self-evident but are dependent on they way members of a society understand them. The participants have to understand what their exchanges actually involve. Hermeneutics does not deny social reality. It insists only that no reality can be comprehended without recognising the way social relations are actually understood in a society.

Once it is recognised that hermeneutics is promoting a social ontology not a form of idealism, it begins to be possible to understand even those social practices, which seem resistant to interpretation, in hermeneutic terms. For instance, as noted in Chapter 4, Roy Bhaskar confidently states that 'fighting a war is not just (or even perhaps necessarily) possessing a certain idea of what one is doing' (Bhaskar 1979: 174). For him, war is evidently resistant to a hermeneutic explanation. War seems to demonstrate decisively that society cannot be reduced merely to the idea which people have of it. War has the most manifestly material consequences. People are killed and their property is destroyed, however they interpret it. It would seem intuitively obvious that war defies hermeneutics. Yet, even here, if hermeneutics is understood as a form of social ontology, it remains relevant. It is notable that Peter Winch has insisted that even war is explicable in purely hermeneutic terms. Winch cites the hypothetical example of war between hunger migrants and an indigenous population. He envisages the arrival of starving immigrants to a country with limited natural resources and the consequent struggle for food which must follow this sudden overpopulation. He chooses this type of war because, if there is a human event where no understandings are involved, this would be it. There are no overtly religious or nationalistic reasons for this war; it is merely a struggle over scarce material resources:

> But even here, although the issue is in a sense a purely material one, the form which the struggle takes will still involve internal relations in a sense which will not apply to, say, a fight between two wild animals over a piece of meat...Human war, like all other human activities, is governed by conventions; and where one is dealing with conventions, one is dealing with internal relations.
>
> (Winch 1977: 130–31)

Even if some form of conflict over scarce resources is inevitable (and certain individuals must be eliminated in this Malthusian competition), the war which actually develops in this situation is still a social phenomenon because it is in no way obvious that the competition over resources should take the form of a fight between the hunger migrants and the natives, as two separate social groups. The eventuality of a war between these groups pre-supposes that their members see themselves in a particular way. For there to be a war between these groups, their respective members must recognise themselves as distinct groups, each with their own collective interests. Yet, those collective interests are not given by objective natural factors. There is nothing in the food shortage which demands that these specific human groups form. Humans could respond to the food shortage in an infinite number of ways. The indigenous population may ally as a whole against the hunger migrants. Yet, other alliances might just as easily emerge. For instance, members of the indigenous population could ally with the hunger migrants to form a group which is powerful enough to monopolise the food resources, forcing other natives to starve. Alternatively, a small elite group of hunger migrants might ally against fellow migrants and the natives. The lines of conflict that might follow from the entry of hunger migrants into a populated area are not self-evident. They do not arise directly from the material facts of food shortage. On the contrary, the nature of the conflict is dependent on the way that the members of the indigenous and incoming populations understand themselves and their relations to each other. That understanding will determine the kind of struggle which occurs. The war which follows is real – people will die – but it is not determined solely by the material fact of scarce resources. The particular lines of battle will be determined by the social groups which exist. These groups are not given by material facts but arise as certain particular constellations of individuals come together to form collective bodies. These collective bodies exist insofar as the members recognise their special relations to each other to the exclusion of others. The kinds of groups which form even in a war of survival depend upon the shared understandings of the humans involved. Humans have to recognise with whom they have allied and against whom they are fighting. They have to understand their social obligations to certain individuals to the exclusion of others. No material fact could ever give rise to that sense of obligation. Only in human consciousness and in human understanding does it arise. It is no less real for that.

Usefully, although Winch does not cite any empirical examples, there are some historical examples of the kind of materialistic war which Winch describes. One of the most striking historical examples of a war of starvation is provided by the collapse of the civilisation on Easter Island before the arrival of Europeans. Easter Island was settled by Polynesians, who brought with them a culture which has been extensively recorded. Polynesian society was ruled by warrior chiefs who dominated over a complex status hierarchy protected by extensive *mana* taboos. From about 1000 AD to 1600 AD, this society reached an extraordinary cultural apogee which involved the erection of hundreds of stone statues with distinctive angular faces on extensive temple platforms. The statues seem to have been a statement of the status of the chiefs themselves or various groups in the social hierarchy. At this time, the population of Easter Island was estimated to have been about 7000, but a dramatic transformation then took place (Keegan 1994: 24–27). Although the original reasons for the collapse are unclear, it is apparent that from about 1600 AD the resources of the island could no longer sustain the increasing population, precipitating a period of internecine warfare in which the so-called 'men of the bloodied hands' came to the fore. These war leaders undermined the unified chiefdom, profaning the strict system of taboos which had sustained it since at least 1000 AD. These new war leaders gathered groups around them and fought for the chiefdom which was now symbolised by possession of the egg of a sooty tern. In the course of their struggles, many of the statues were toppled in acts presumably intended to demonstrate the superiority of one warring group over the other. When Europeans first arrived on the Island in 1722 AD, the indigenous population was only 111. Perhaps denoting the catastrophe in more eloquent terms, at one end of the island a group had dug a channel and ditch which separated it from the rest of the island in an attempt to defend itself from the destructive warfare into which this once unified society had descended.

The Easter Island example is instructive for it is an example of the Malthusian struggle over scarce resources which Winch discussed. Yet, even when faced with starvation, the Polynesian society did not collapse into a war of all against all in which mere animal instinct took over. On the contrary, the Malthusian warfare followed the contours of social relations on this island. The members of this society allied themselves with one or other of the 'men with the bloodied hands', which alliances were achieved only through the shared understandings of the participants. Leaders and followers recognised their social relationship and understood what those relationships enjoined. The warfare was between groups which established themselves on the basis of an understanding of their shared interests. Consequently, the extermination which followed was not given purely by material facts. The fact that the island could not sustain its population did not determine the kind of war which subsequently occurred. The war which followed was a social phenomenon. The groups which fought in it existed insofar as members recognised their collective interests. Indeed, even in this war for mere survival the relationships between the groups was still expressed symbolically. The war leaders did not merely struggle for possession of land but for a symbolic object, the sooty tern's egg, which denoted the most powerful group and, therefore, the war leader who had authority to appropriate and distribute the island's scarce resources. War involved undeniably real effects. In the case of Easter Island, a population of 7000 was reduced in the course of about a century to a little less than 2 per cent of its original size. Yet, the form of this warfare, who fought with whom, who was killed and who survived, is not explicable without reference to the understandings of the humans involved. This does not mean that sociologists need to take into account how particular individuals interpreted their deaths or how individuals personally viewed the conflict. These interpretations are more or less irrelevant. Individual private interpretations are not the basis of social life. Individual interpretations, made alone away from social interaction, are irrelevant to social life unless an individual can persuade other group members to accept these interpretations as the *public* basis of everyday action. Hermeneutics is not interested in individual interpretations away from the shared conception of social relations. On the contrary, hermeneutics focuses on the shared meanings on the basis of which social relations are actually conducted. To paraphrase Wittgenstein, hermeneutics is concerned with meaning (which it interprets) not with individual interpretations. Hermeneutics does not reduce war to individual interpretation but it insists that the warring groups sustain themselves as unities only as long as members recognise their social relations to each other. Any combat which follows is dependent upon the existence of these groups, and war therefore involves human understanding. War has to be understood in terms of a social ontology. The reality of war is not denied by hermeneutics but that reality is never independent of the way those involved in it understand their relations to others.

Hermeneutics does not reduce social reality to individual interpretation. It illuminates only the distinctive properties of social reality. Humans always and everywhere act towards each other on the basis of shared meanings even when they are engaged in a brutal struggle for existence. Social relations do not exist independently of human understanding. Humans have to understand what their relations to each other actually demand; humans have to recognise their bond to each other and that bond ultimately relies on their mutual recognition of it. Hermeneutics recognises the peculiar character of social relations, whose existence necessarily depends upon human understanding. Since this is the reality in which humans always live, the special character of social relations demands a particular kind of approach from the social sciences. The social sciences must recognise the meaningfulness of social relations if they are to deserve the name of science at all. Sociology has to recognise that human social relations inevitably involve human understanding and that understanding must feature in any analysis which is conducted. A science which constantly misunderstands its subject matter is unworthy of the name. Hermeneutics currently represents the most elaborated account of the social ontology and, consequently, it can provide the basis for sociological research today. In contemporary social theory, the distinctive and, indeed, remarkable character of social reality has been forgotten. The true social basis of all institutions has been forgotten and, instead of understanding these phenomena by reference to the social relations of which they are comprised, contemporary social theorists given them an independence which they do not deserve. While contemporary social theory is confounded by its ontological dualism, hermeneutics recognises the reality of human existence. It promotes only a social ontology. Just because social relations are not independent of the ideas that humans hold about them, this does not reduce a hermeneutic sociology to mere idealism. On the contrary, the social ontology represents the most realistic account of social reality that there is or could be.

10 Hermeneutics and Individualism

The accusation that hermeneutics is idealist is always closely related to the claim that it is also individualist. According to contemporary social theory, hermeneutics reduces the social world to the individual's interpretation of it. Realists in particular have argued that because hermeneutics fails to recognise structure it necessarily falls into a specious form of voluntarism in which any individual can do what they will. Margaret Archer, for instance, dismissively describes hermeneutics as 'Individualism': 'The Individualist is committed to social atomism, that is to the claim that the important things about people can indeed be identified independently of their social context' (Archer 1995: 35). For Archer, hermeneutics effectively aligns itself with the methodological individualism of rational choice theory. Bhaskar's realism adopts a similar stance towards hermeneutics. He dismisses Weber's interpretive sociology because it reduces everything to the voluntaristic understandings of the individual. Giddens recognises the contribution of hermeneutics but similarly believes that it overemphasises the agency of the individual. By contrast, Giddens has claimed that his structuration theory is an attempt to recover the subject without lapsing into subjectivism. As we have seen in the last chapter, Habermas also eschews hermeneutics on the grounds that it falsely reduces social life to the individual. For him, individual agency always pre-supposes a structural context in which it can operate. According to contemporary social theory, hermeneutics reduces social life to the individual and it therefore has a facile notion of individual agency. On the account provided by hermeneutics, individuals are free to do as they please. They can interpret the world in any way they like and they can therefore act in any way they choose.

It is worth noting that there is a certain ontological alliance between rational choice theory and hermeneutics, as Archer suggests. Archer is correct that both reject notions of objective social structure; for both, society consists of people. It is consequently understandable why contemporary social theorists have conflated hermeneutics with rational choice theory. The difference between hermeneutics and rational choice theory is demonstrable, however. George Homans, the well-known rational choice theorist and critic of Parsons, usefully illuminates this decisive difference. Initially, he seems to espouse an ontology which is compatible with hermeneutics. He asks, 'What do we mean by social structure?' and claims that, when sociologists appeal to the idea of structure, the reality to which they point can in each case be reduced to a collection of individuals. Homans considers the various definitions of structure: 'organisations, institutions, stratification systems, patterns of interaction or a whole which is greater than its parts' (Homans 1987: 13–15). For Homans, all these definitions are simply misperceptions: 'none of the definitions entails any special kind of explanation for the features particular social structures exhibit or why social structures should exist at all' (Homans 1987: 115). Homans demonstrates that the concept of structure in fact refers to nothing more than individuals:

> The effect in question does not in the least require for its explanation a theory that excludes propositions about the values of individuals. Indeed, Blau would have done much better to call his 'structural effect', a 'collective effect': it concerns the influence of a collection of individuals – but if a collection, still individuals – on another individual… The definitions of 'structure' cited so far do not imply anything distinctively structural in either theory or method.
>
> (Homans 1987: 116)

Homans' reduction of structure to collectivities of individuals suggests an ontological affinity between hermeneutics and rational choice theory but the quotation, in fact, simultaneously demonstrates the very significant divide between rational choice theory and hermeneutics. While both agree that society consists only of humans, rational choice theory has a very different concept of human capabilities. Homans demonstrates the rational choice position with typical lucidity. For him, the individual is the absolute basis of all social life. Ultimately, for Homans, society consists of individuals and individuals always and everywhere act on the basis of rational self-interest:

> I think that accepting the view that the fundamental proposition of the social sciences are the same, and that the propositions are psychological, would be a great advantage to all the these sciences.
>
> (Homans 1967: 73)

For Homans, shared understandings are irrelevant to human interaction whose true basis is the rational pursuit of self-interest, which is programmed universally into the human psyche. For him, social life can be explained by reference to the individual alone. The individual has certain psychological propensities which direct action in logical and inevitable directions. The social relations between humans have no special significance for Homans and he rejects the importance of shared understandings in co-ordinating individual action. Although he believes that individuals act rationally, he regards choice as an 'illusion' (Homans 1967: 103). According to him, humans are biologically programmed to seek certain rewards and will do so in all circumstances: 'I speak of illusion because I myself believe that what each of us does is absolutely determined' (Homans 1967: 104). According to Homans, social order is achieved because each individual is biologically programmed to seek the same ends. Consequently, their purely individualistic calculations are co-ordinated by the external fact of heredity. In promoting a purely psychological explanation of human behaviour, Homans impales himself upon one of the horns of Parsons' utilitarian dilemma. Parsons stressed the objectionableness of this biological solution to the problem of order because it undermined the utilitarian premise of autonomy. Homans renounced the autonomy of rational individuals in order to explain predictable social behaviour. It is at precisely this point that hermeneutics divides itself decisively from rational choice theory. Despite the imputations of various critics, hermeneutics does not suggest that social life can be understood by reference to the individual alone, even though, with rational choice theory, it rejects the idea that society has an existence which is in any way separable from its members. Rather, hermeneutics focuses on social relations conducted on the basis of shared understandings. Although common, it is a serious error to conflate the social ontology of hermeneutics with the genuinely individualist ontology of rational choice theory. For one, there is only the individual; for the other, society must be understood by reference to the social relations between humans.

Although Gadamer has not explicitly engaged with utilitarian or rational choice theory, his hermeneutics is in fact partially inspired by a rejection of exactly the kind of individualising represented by Homans. One of Gadamer's central, though often unspecified, targets throughout *Truth and Method* (1975) is rationalist individualism. In the first part of the work, he rejects the notion of pure artistic genius and the idea that the artwork is interpreted by single individuals alone. Gadamer specifically rejects Kant's critique of judgement, which claimed that 'beauty in nature or art has the same *a priori* principle, which lies entirely within subjectivity' (Gadamer 1975: 51). Although Kant tried to elucidate the universal principles which underlay the sublime, his philosophy accorded with and promoted the wider current of thought at the time. It prioritised personal genius. Gadamer notes that 'by the nineteenth century, the concept of genius was elevated to become a universal concept of value and – together with the idea of the creative – achieved a true apotheosis' (Gadamer 1975: 55). Against the 'aesthetic myth of freely creative imaginative', Gadamer promotes a rigorously social explanation:

> The choice of material and the formation of it still does not proceed from the free discretion of the artist and is not the mere expression of his inner life. Rather does the artist address people whose minds are prepared and chooses what he expects will have an effect on them. He himself stands in the same tradition as the public that he is aiming at and which he gathers around him. In this sense it is true that he does not need to know explicitly as an individual, a thinking consciousness, what he is doing and what his work says....There remains a continuity of meaning which links the work of art with the world of real existence and from which even the alienated consciousness of a cultured society never quite detaches itself.
>
> (Gadamer 1975: 118)

Artists draw on public symbols to communicate messages which an audience is capable of understanding. They draw on traditions which they share with the community for whom their work is directed. Their success lies precisely in the effectiveness of the way in which they draw upon these symbols or traditions to mobilise and change the communities of which they are part. Certainly, great artists are able to utilise symbols in new and suggestive ways but they do not operate in a culture vacuum, producing work which has meaning to the artist alone. Individual artists do not produce artworks in isolation. Artists always work within one tradition or another, embedded in social networks which are crucial to the kinds of work they are able to produce. Their work emerges out of a particular cultural context, from which it takes its cues. Beethoven's genius, for instance, lay in recognising the line of development suggested by Mozart and the classical form and re-working this tradition in a new direction. His virtuosity itself was a social product of this interaction with the preceding classical tradition and his relationship with culturally important social groups, especially in Vienna. Similarly the public response to any particular artwork is always a product of the communities of which any individual is part. The meanings which are read into an artwork arise on the wider cultural horizon. The viewer in front of a Van Gogh stands only nominally alone. The reception of a masterpiece is a product of the social groups of which the viewer is part and which have trained that viewer to respond in particular ways. Consequently, the apparently private emotions which an artwork inspires pre-suppose a wider social group. The agency of the artist and the response of the spectator do not arise out of some pristine personal sensibilities but are derived from the communities of which both are part; artists always exist in a 'continuity of meaning' which links them inexorably to their public. Both artist and public draw upon recognised shared understandings which invest the work of art with significance.

Gadamer notes that this 'continuity of meaning' never stays the same. The understandings which a particular piece of artwork expresses at a particular moment change and, as they do so, the meaning of the artwork alters:

> Works of architecture do not stand motionless on the shore of the stream of history, but are borne along by it. Even if historically-minded ages seek to reconstruct the architecture of an earlier age, they cannot try to turn back the wheel of history.
>
> (Gadamer 1975: 139)

The temporality of artwork emphasises Gadamer's argument. If artworks were the product of private individual genius, then there would be no reason why sensitive connoisseurs in the future could understand these works as the artist intended. A meeting of individual minds should be possible through the artwork. The individual artist and individual viewer would transcend history. However, because each piece of art is a social product drawing on the meanings by which particular historical communities understand themselves, art does not remain pristine. Each artwork is re-invested with a new significance in a new cultural context. The artwork is not an individual but a social phenomenon which has to draw on public meanings in order to have any significance for the community in which it arises. The artwork only ever has life within the wider context of a social community which understands it. Ultimately, the artist's personal genius assumes a social community. This does not deny the artist's virtuosity but it locates that virtuosity within a social context which makes it possible.

Although he is unaware of it, Gadamer's account of social agency illuminates an extremely close affinity between hermeneutics and the interactionist tradition. Although the interactionist and hermeneutic traditions are often regarded as very different, at root Gadamer reveals that they ultimately share similar theoretical premises. It is true that hermeneutics has tended to engage itself in philosophical discussions on the implications of hermeneutics for the social sciences, while interactionism has focused on the empirical study of particular human social interactions. Nevertheless, this differing orientation should not conceal that both traditions concur on certain basic premises. Both operate on the premise that humans act towards each other on the basis of shared understandings and both illuminate the significance of this premise for the social sciences. In the case of Goffman's ethnography of everyday life in America, for instance, the 'rules' of conduct which he illuminates, the avoidance strategies, denial of incidences, the by-plays and body-glosses, work only because the people involved in these encounters are already aware of shared cultural understandings in which their chosen strategies already have a particular meaning:

> Throughout the history of Western civilisation there has been a continuity in official moral ideology establishing the personal attributes that proper males and females should manifest during face-to-face dealings with others…If we examine what it is one participant is ready to see that other participants might read into a situation and what it is that will cause him to provide ritual remedies to of various sorts (followed by relief for these efforts), then we find ourselves directed back again to the core moral traditions of Western culture.
>
> (Goffman 1971: 184)

Underlying each interaction lies a shared form of life, which constitutes the bedrock of each particular encounter. The gestures of each participant in an interaction ritual pre-suppose and draw upon this cultural background, which gives each particular gesture its significance. Consequently, in different cultures, gestures will be invested with different significance and the form of interactions will be very different. Goffman emphasises this cross-cultural diversity on a number of occasions:

> Among the American middle-class, for example, little effort is made to keep the elbow inviolate whereas orifice areas are of concern. And, of course, across different cultures, the body will be differently segmented ritually.
>
> (Goffman 1971: 38)

From the fact that greetings are found among many higher primates, as well as any number of preliterate societies and all civilised ones, it would be easy to conclude that something like access rituals are universally found in societies. But, of course, universals are exactly what good ethnography brings into doubt.

(Goffman 1971: 93)

Goffman notes that, in contrast to western society, in an Arab village 'women do not greet men on village paths and men do not greet women' (Goffman 1971: 93). As Goffman himself emphasises, everyday interaction involves certain shared understandings. These understandings determine how certain actions will be viewed. It gives certain actions a determinate significance, denoting the relationship between people in this situation. Goffman traces the way that those shared understandings of gentlemanly conduct give rise to regular strategies whereby people maintain themselves as western gentlemen or ladies in the course of their encounters. Humans are extremely sensitive to the implications of actions in the light of this shared cultural background. Actions have very specific meanings which point directly to their status. Although it is not usually so described, Goffman's interactionism is a form of hermeneutics. It examines the way that different actions become meaningful in the light of this shared cultural horizon. Indeed, Goffman is able to interpret specific gestures and strategies in the light of his recognition of a western cultural horizon, in which the notion of the gentleman is central.[1] In this way, interactionism recognises that shared understandings are the basis of all social relations; humans have to understand what their interactions imply for their status and the status of others. Hermeneutics and interactionism accept the same pre-supposition. Human social life is distinctively constituted through the shared understandings of its participants. They must recognise their social relations and understand what activities they involve. This gives rise to a shared account of agency in hermeneutics and interactionism. It is evident in Gadamer's work when he discusses artistic genius. There, an individualistic account of agency in which creativity arises from the isolated virtuoso is replaced by a sociological explanation of agency. For Gadamer, artistic genius arises in specific social contexts and is sustained by cultural communities as a whole. Supposedly individual geniuses have to draw on public meanings which they did not personally invent to express themselves. By extension, all human agency is a social product arising in the matrix of social relations. Gadamer's hermeneutic account of agency is important because it replaces individualism with a genuinely sociological explanation of agency. However, because it seems to refer only to the case of artistic agency it has been overlooked. In order to illuminate the profundity of his hermeneutic account of agency, it is necessary to elucidate it by reference to literature which is much more widely known and which explicitly encompasses a much wider range of human activity. It is necessary to consider the interactionist literature and particularly the work of Erving Goffman. There, Gadamer's theory of agency finds elaboration and empirical exemplification.

Hermeneutics and Human Agency

In *The Elementary Forms* (1976), Durkheim discusses the concept of the soul. Echoing the rest of the analysis, Durkheim insists that the concept of a soul is not a primitive illusion. On the contrary, the soul refers to something tangible and real. The soul has a powerful effect on the humans who believe in it. It stimulates them to act in very particular ways and is viewed as the most important part of their personality. Yet, it is, according to Durkheim, incorrect to see the soul as an individualistic entity. Australian aborigines believe that the soul of each tribal member is derived from the totem of the tribe: 'the soul is nothing other than the totemic principle incarnate in each individual' (Durkheim 1976: 248). The totem is fragmented and parts of it internalised by individuals. Although the identity of any aborigine is dependent upon their soul, the soul is not an individualistic product. On the contrary, the soul derives from the totem, which is established only by the group interacting ecstatically. This produces a heightened collective consciousness among the members of the group of their commitment to each other. They become viscerally aware of their social relations and commit themselves to each other. The soul derives from this social creation of the totem. The soul of each individual, although apparently the most personal possession, is, therefore, instilled in them by other group members. The kinds of practices which their soul demands of them are not those which they have privately imagined for themselves. On the contrary, they are those practices which tribespeople mutually impress on each other in moments of ritualistic effervescence. The totem represents the social relations between the members of the group, and the soul, derived from the totem as a fragment of it, represents the individual's relation to other members of the group. The soul is sacred to each individual precisely because it is the product of these social rituals. The soul is sacred because it is a social object recognised by others. It represents the recognition which the individual receives from others and, therefore, it symbolises the individual's very social existence. The soul represents not any internal essence but rather individuals' external relations to others, obliging them to act in ways consistent with those relations even when they are away from the group. The apparently transcendent call of the soul reflects only the obligations which humans' social relations put upon them. Although it is rarely recognised, Durkheim's discussion of the soul involves a quite radical sociology of human agency. Against individualistic accounts, the agency of any human actor is, in fact, the product of the social relations in which an individual is positioned. Agency is not properly a property of the individual but emerges rather from the social relations in which individuals are embedded. Human agency is a function of the kinds of social relations in which they exist. In different relations, humans have different agency. Durkheim's account of human agency provides a genuine sociology of the individual. It is not the autonomous agency of rational choice theory for on the Durkheimian account the essential point is that in social relations, humans mutually invest each other with powers. They would not have these powers if they were genuinely independent in the manner which Homans believes. Although the language is different, Durkheim's discussion of the soul parallels Gadamer's critique of the concept of genius. For both, human agency arises in the context of social relations and is sustained by humans together. Outside society, the individual has no meaningful agency.[2]

It is interesting that Erving Goffman recognised the sociological significance of Durkheim's chapter on the soul. Indeed, this chapter from the *Elementary Forms* has inspired his interactionist approach:

> There [in Durkheim's chapter on the soul] he suggests that the individual's personality can be seen as one apportionment of the collective *mana* and that (as he implies in later chapters) the rites performed to the representations of the social collectivity will sometimes be performed by the individual himself. In this paper, I want to explore some of the senses in which a person in our urban secular world is allotted a kind of sacredness that is displayed and confirmed by symbolic acts.
>
> (Goffman 1967: 47)

Goffman's interactionism effectively illustrates the sociological implications of Durkheim's discussion of the soul to demonstrate the fallacy of individualism.[3] As Goffman himself acknowledges, it is difficult not to think in terms of a unified self which directs social action:

> It is hardly possible to talk about the anchoring of doings in a world without seeming to support the notion that a person's acts are in part an expression and outcome of his perduring self and that this self will be present behind the particular roles he plays at any moment.
>
> (Goffman 1974: 293)

However, although it is very difficult in our culture to discuss human agency without implying the notion of a subject, Goffman himself does not think that human agency can be understood in individualist terms. Goffman argues that this putatively original self is not so much the master of any social situation as a necessary result of it: 'A sense of person can be generated locally' (Goffman 1974: 298).[4] In a social encounter, prior individual selves do not determine the interaction. On the contrary, the agency of each individual in any particular interaction is created mutually (Goffman 1971). In the course of the interaction, the participants mutually adopt a particular kind of role in response to the attitude adopted by the other. Each encounter ritualistically brackets itself from the rest of the social world and the actors in it are locked into an internal dynamic with its own logic (Goffman 1971: 73). Each tries to maintain the other's face, sustaining the line which they seem to be taking: 'the person tends to conduct himself during an encounter so as to maintain both his own face and the face of the other participants' (Goffman 1967: 11). In many encounters status markers suggest what positions should be taken by each participant but, even in these cases, the way a person can act in each encounter is always dependent on the other. Both utilise a prior notion of what is expected of a role to adopt certain appropriate forms of conduct. Thus, Goffman describes how a chief surgeon sustains the good will and efficiency of his surgical team by adopting a dignified attitude throughout. By not pressing his rightful claims of authority too far by threatening sanctions jokingly, he is able to demand from his helpers the agency which the situation demands; they are willing to be deferential and to work well for him (Goffman 1961: 122–23). The surgeon, in turn, is able to be dignified insofar as his team is deferential and competent. The agency of the surgeon and of his team are mutually sustained. In the encounter, humans mutually sustain each other's faces; together they facilitate the agency of the other. In different encounters, humans ultimately have different kinds of agency: 'the individual is allowed and required to be one thing in one setting and another thing in a different setting' (Goffman 1961: 151). Individual agency is a mutual product of the interaction.

Goffman recognises that it is difficult to dispense with a notion of the self entirely. It is difficult not to believe that, between all the various roles which humans fulfil, there is not some unified, personal essence which finds expression in each role. It seems self-evident that in the back-regions away from all roles, in those moments of quiet solitude when humans prepare a face to meet a face, there is not some identifiable private entity. Humans can find a self from behind all the multiple roles they play. Goffman refutes even this:

> But that is no reason to think that all these gleanings about himself that an individual makes available, all these pointing from his current situation to the way he is in his other occasions, have anything very much in common.
>
> (Goffman 1974: 299)

Humans might think of themselves as unified but there is no empirical evidence to support this claim. When considered more closely, it is clear that the self, gleaned together in the backstage area, is itself always a social product. In the backstage, humans attempt to develop a self but they do not invent this self privately. The repertoires and powers which they attempt to develop are learnt from others. Ultimately, the supposedly private self is only another public product which arises as an effect of interaction. When individuals prepare themselves for a social encounter by examining themselves in a mirror, they are not consulting some pristine individual essence which instructs them how they should look. On the contrary, individuals attempt to take on an appearance which fits the social role which they wish to adopt. Looking in the mirror, apparently away from all social contact, individuals, in fact, draw upon social understandings and their social relations. All the time in the background, their social contacts are looking over their shoulder effectively instructing them how they should look; and how, subsequently, they should behave. In other 'private' spaces exactly the same social rituals are occurring, each individual accompanied in their imagination by members of their social group. The most apparently private and intimate essence is in fact a public product. In a different culture, where social relations are conducted in different ways on the basis of alternative understandings, the kind of self the members of a society impute to themselves will be different: 'the culture itself [prescribes] what sort of entity we must believe ourselves to be' (Goffman 1974: 573–74). For Goffman, the reality of the self is perpetually misunderstood. Social theorists fail to recognise that in all times and places human agency is the product of social relations. Humans have agency in the light of the social context. The self refers to the powers an individual can have in a specific set of social relations. Even when supposedly stepping out of their formal role and becoming 'personal', humans are still acting in accordance with the shared understandings of what constitutes appropriate conduct. Their personal self is still a product of their social relations. Like Durkheim, Goffman believes that human agency, down to the apparently most personal ideas of the self, does not rise up from within but is an emanation of collective representations produced in intense moments of interaction. The self is a social product.[5] The self is only assumed to be an independent and stable entity because in contemporary western society most humans live in relatively stable social environments which continually support the concept of a coherent self. Their social relations are regular enough to affirm the individual as a stable agent.

While Goffman rejects the notion of an autonomous self, he does not deny that the idea of the self plays an important part in the interaction. On the contrary, the concept of the self is crucial to the interaction ritual. It is employed to indicate the relationship which participants should take to each other. In each social encounter, individuals will impute to each other a selfhood behind the role which allows each to perform their role effectively. The self is actually a necessary part of the role which any individual performs. It provides the role with authenticity, inspiring trust in those with whom any individual interacts: 'What is important is the sense he provides them through his dealings with them of what sort of person he is behind the role he is in' (Goffman 1974: 298). The self begins, on Goffman's account, to take on a quite distinctive appearance. The self is no longer a private haven but a public space, imputed to anyone who would be a social agent. The putatively autonomous self is in fact as much a social product of the social encounter as the role.

Goffman's interactionism provides empirical and theoretical support for a hermeneutic account of agency but evidence for this account of the self is available elsewhere in the sociological literature. Perhaps the most notorious example of the sociology of agency is Stanley Milgram's experiments on obedience (Milgram 1974). The purpose of Milgram's experiments was to try and reveal how individuals could become involved in apparently inhumane acts of cruelty. Milgram wanted to illuminate how the Holocaust was possible. To this end, he developed an ingenious set of experiments which were intended to test how individuals responded to authority. In the experiments, the subjects were asked to submit others to electric shocks by a white-coated expert. In most of the tests, the experimenter who ordered the subject to administer these shocks explained that the cries of the victim were to be ignored as the shocks caused no lasting damage. Of course, the victim himself was, in fact, also part of the experiment and was merely pretending with impressive realism to be suffering from these electric shocks. In the course of the experiments, Milgram altered the conditions so that sometimes the subject could see the victim or at other times another 'civilian' instead of a white-coated experimenter gave the order for the shocks to be administered. In these cases, the rate of obedience fell but overwhelmingly the experiments demonstrated a human susceptibility to authority which Milgram found disturbing. For the most part, people did simply follow orders. From his experiments Milgram concluded that the only protection which humans had against their natural deference to authority was individual conscience. The ego provides a natural inhibitory mechanism which if sufficiently strong will prevent individuals from obeying the dictats of authority. The problem is that this is a weak defence against the oppressive powers of authority and it is all too easy for individuals to submerge their personal autonomy into authority structures:

> Each individual possesses a conscience which to a greater or lesser degree serves to restrain the unimpeded flow of impulses destructive to others. But when he merges his person into an organisation structure, a new creature replaces autonomous man, unhindered by the limitations of individual morality, freed of human inhibition mindful only of the sanctions of authority.
>
> (Milgram 1974: 205)

Milgram's analysis of his experiments presumed a dualistic social ontology. Abstract and distant authority pressed down upon isolated individuals who could only resist authority if they had sufficient internal moral resources.[6] According to Milgram, the individual is confronted by the objective structures of authority. In this way, Milgram's work echoes the dualistic ontology of contemporary social theory. Like contemporary social theory, he envisages the individual confronted by independent institutional structures which impel the individual into certain courses of action.

The genius of Milgram's experiments cannot be doubted. It took extraordinary imagination to develop these elaborate hoaxes and the experiments do indeed illuminate human agency brilliantly. Yet, ironically, they do not demonstrate the account of human agency which Milgram believes they do. Milgram assumes that those who refused to administer the shocks in the experiment responded to their individual conscience. They had sufficient moral strength to resist authority. Although Milgram does not discuss all of the experiments in detail, his description of those individuals who did refuse suggests that another reading might be possible. In each case, the refusers were of high social status, working professionally in institutions not dissimilar to the university in which Milgram was running his experiment. Milgram describes a professor, an engineer and a medical technician who all refuse to participate in the experiment (Milgram 1974: 64, 102). Milgram ignored the information which he provided about their social background and simply praised their moral courage; they had a strong enough conscience to be prepared to deny the expert. Yet, it seems highly likely that these individuals denied the experimenter not out of any essential humanity; they were not driven by individual conscience. It seems likely that they were able to refuse because their social status allowed them to interact differently with the experimenter than other participants. The experimenter did not awe them with technical superiority, borne of unfamiliarity and ignorance. He was of similar or indeed inferior status to these subjects and his commands carried no particular symbolic weight. In effect, the interaction ritual of the experiment was a different phenomenon for these high-status professional individuals than it was for the lower-status individuals who were also involved. The high-status individuals would have been familiar with circumstances in which an apparent expert could be wrong without a catastrophic loss of face for either party. Their refusal may not have demonstrated the power of essential human conscience. It was more likely that they were able to act differently in the experiment than other subjects because they were members of different social groups. It is notable that the most obedient individuals were those in social groups of low status; they were manual workers, low-grade bureaucrats and housewives (Milgram 1974: 62–63, 96, 97–100, 106). The groups of which these people were part seemed at least a factor in the kind of agency which they could display in interaction with an expert.

Milgram provides further evidence of the social origins of conscience in his culminating discussions in the book. There he tries to demonstrate the wider salience of the experiments by suggesting that not only the Holocaust but the American outrages in Vietnam, and particularly at My Lai, were the product of humanity's unfortunate obedience to authority (Milgram 1974: 202). Milgram examines the transcript from the inquest into My Lai to demonstrate the nine elements of obedience uncovered by the experiments.[7] Milgram's nine points emphasise the way that those implicated in outrages displaced responsibility away from themselves by drawing a distinction between their duty and their personal feelings (Milgram 1974: 203). They suppressed their conscience and simply followed orders. In describing the motivations of the American soldiers at My Lai in this way, Milgram plainly employed the dualistic ontology which is assumed throughout the study: abstract authority imposed upon the individual. In this case, individual soldiers suppressed their individual humanity in the face of an abstract authority. Yet, the transcript from which he draws this analysis of obedience does not support his dualistic vision of private conscience versus monolithic authority. This is revealed with uncomfortable clarity in one of the answers that an interviewed soldier gave to the inquiry:

> Why did I do it? Because I felt like I was ordered to do it, and it seemed like that, at the time I felt like I was doing the right thing, because like I say, I lost buddies. I lost a damn good buddy, Bobby Wilson, and it was on my conscience. So after I done it, I felt good, but later on that day, it was getting to me.
>
> (Milgram 1974: 202)

Milgram fails to discuss this statement but it is highly significant because the soldier employs conscience in the exactly opposite way to Milgram. His conscience did not stop him from committing the atrocities, as Milgram would have us believe. On the contrary, he was driven to kill women and children at the behest of his conscience. He killed them to avenge the death of a close friend and this rendered the killings entirely proper in his eyes. The soldier's statement demonstrates that conscience is not a universal or essential property of human agents. It does not unfailing defend humans from authority. The example suggests that conscience is a product of the groups of which an individual is a part. It is a personal *mana* derived from the collective, invested with intense symbolic and emotional power. This soldier was closely integrated into a platoon unified by the most intense experiences of combat. In the situation which confronted this soldier at My Lai, his conscience demanded these unfortunate actions from him. He did not submit himself to an abstract authority but willingly acted in a way which was consistent with the interests of his group. The authority was not abstract. It was a product of the intense social relations of the platoon of which he was part and to which he actively contributed. His friend, Bobby Wilson, not the Army's code of discipline, was the symbol of this group and the authority which drove him to these terrible acts. Away from the group, in a different social circumstance, he may indeed have questioned his actions at My Lai but this does not denote the existence of an essential, fundamental conscience which always resists authority. It merely affirms the fact that in different social groups different consciences and therefore different agencies are possible. It is not inconceivable that the prick of conscience of which the soldier speaks in fact only occurred to him as the inquest was held and when he was forced to consider what he had done in the light of a very different social group, which no longer approved of his activities. Certainly, there are numerous examples of war criminals (such as Goering as Nuremburg) who are never troubled by the putatively universal conscience which Milgram invokes. So firmly attached do they remain to their original social group that they are convinced of the rectitude of their actions even in the light of the new social circumstances which confront them. They reject the conscience which this new authority is trying to instil in them.

The social ontology promoted by hermeneutics and interactionism has important and direct implications for the issue of power. Agency and power are closely related concepts since both are defined by the ability to do things (Barnes 1988: 58). However, although agency and power have an instrumental meaning, the hermeneutic sociology of agency reveals that power cannot be understood in a simplistic utilitarian way. Since social relations are conducted on the basis of shared meanings, power cannot operate in a causal way. Individuals do not wield power alone. For power to operate in society, for individuals to perform certain acts and to influence others, their acts must be understood by those others. These others have to react in appropriate ways in order for power to function. Closely echoing Foucault's later position, Barry Barnes uses the term 'discretion', which usefully denotes the distinctive operation of social power (Barnes 1988: 58). Power does not simply emanate from a powerful person independently of anyone else. Discretion necessarily implies the acceptance and understanding of others. Other people defer discretion on any particular individual. Consequently, the exercise of discretion – of power – is dependent on the social relations between members of this society, relations which are decisively constituted by the way participants understand them. When these people prioritise different social relations – when they understand their relations to the powerful differently – the once powerful can lose their discretion. They are stripped of their power because their discretion is no longer recognised by those people who once acted upon it. Barnes gives the example of the Iranian revolution, in which the Shah lost his power as a result of a shifting in the way Iranians understood discretion (Barnes 1988: 62). The Shah himself was the same person and, indeed, even after the revolution he was very rich and formally held his title. However, Iranians no longer recognised their social relationship with him. The power which he seemed to hold was in fact conferred on him by the social relations in which he existed. When these wider social relations underwent dramatic transformation, he lost his power.

Barnes' point about the social origin of power can be illuminated by examining the authority of the President of the United States of America. Immediately after the terrorist attacks of 11 September, President Bush was rushed to Air Force One, which remained airborne until the security agencies were certain that the threat was over. President Bush's confinement to Air Force One followed standard procedure in the face of a national threat, the first priority of which is the protection of the President. This is sociologically interesting. In an emergency, the President's authority is only of minimal importance. In the case of September 11, he did not initiate defensive action such as the scrambling of airforce jets or the immediate grounding of all civilian flights. These decisions were made autonomously at much lower levels. The preservation of the President was not essential because he personally determined America's response to the attacks. However, this does not mean that the preservation of the President was irrational. On one level, the death of the President in this national emergency would have been a blow to American morale and a huge triumph for Al-Qaeda. This was doubtless an important factor in defending the President. Yet, there seem to be other important considerations. Even though the President did not personally authorise all the actions that were carried out in his name in this national emergency, his existence was crucial to the way that the various security agencies operated. They operated in recognition of the chain of command, at the summit of which was the President. The President did not monocratically direct operations but he was an important symbol of the relations between different government agencies. They acted in relation to each other in conscious and mutual recognition of the President. Although the President did not give direct orders to these agencies, they were able to work effectively because each recognised the sphere of the others' activities, symbolised by their mutual recognition of the President. The President is a totem, representing the relations between the key institutions of the American state. The President is always the primary security objective because, although his death would not rob America of its decision-making institutions, it would unsettle relations down the administrative chain as different security institutions would be unsure of their relations to each other. Without a common reference point, a totem, uncertainty and interference between institutions might develop. The protection of Bush on September 11 demonstrates the social basis of power. It does not emanate from a single point. Rather, each point, like the Presidency itself, is in fact a product of the relations between different groups and institutions in other parts of the administration. The power of the Presidency is conferred on it by these institutions in their interrelations with each other.[8]

Free to Do Otherwise

The accusation that hermeneutics is individualistic is ironic, for those theorists who are most vocal in making this complaint are those who descend most quickly into exactly the individualism of which they accuse hermeneutics. Archer demonstrates this individualism at its most extreme (Archer 1995). Against Durkheim's claim that identity is given to the individual by society, Archer insists that the certain elements of the self are prior to and separate from society: 'I will use three arguments to rebut the contrary view that our humanity itself is a social gift, in order to maintain that sense of the self, which has been shown to be essential to social life, cannot be derived from life in society' (Archer 1995: 285). She appeals to the fact that each individual is located in a discrete body which ensures their individuality (Archer 1995: 286) but, much more importantly and interestingly, she argues (following Kant) that at a certain point humans must have an autonomous self in order to become social beings:

> Human beings are born into an undifferentiated world such that the primary task has to be the differentiation of objects, meaning that the distinguishing of *social* objects cannot be a predicate but only a derivative of a general human capacity to make distinctions – including, it was maintained, the crucial one between myself and the rest of the world.
>
> (Archer 1995: 286)

The self is autonomous and prior to social interaction because the self has to be able to distinguish itself from its environment. That ability to distinguish cannot be derived externally because the ability to distinguish itself from the rest of the world is crucial to there being a world with which the self can interact in the first place. Thus, Archer explicitly returns to the philosophical traditions of the seventeenth and eighteenth century and, in particular, to the philosophies of Locke and Kant (Archer 1995: 289) by positing a notion of an individual subject who exists before social interaction and who makes society possible:

> Already, in having argued that a sense of self is *a priori* to recognizably social action and to the personal recognition of social responsibilities, a gap has been introduced between self and society.
>
> (Archer 1995: 289–90)

In addition to defining 'personal identity in a neo-Lockean and Kantian manner, as the body plus sufficient continuity of consciousness' (Archer 1995: 289), Archer tries to widen this gap between the self and society by arguing that humans have non-social experience of the natural world (Archer 1995: 290–91). She argues that humans have to eat and this putatively unmediated and directly biological encounter with nature 'from our first day' produces dispositions in them which frame their social experience: 'cumulative experiences of our environment will foster propensities, capacities and aversions which sift the social practices we later seek or shun' (Archer 1995: 291). Archer explicitly argues that there are some aspects of the individual which are independent of any social influence. Indeed, on her description, social life presumes partially autonomous individuals. Given her belief in the existence of objective social structure, it is logical that she should similarly argue for the autonomy of the individual. It is only by preserving this sacred haven that she can avoid total structural determinism. Yet, although the internal logic of her ontology demands an independent individual, her description of the individual is ironic. Although she speciously complains that hermeneutics separates humans from the social context, she and not hermeneutics is explicitly committed to individualism. For her, there just are aspects of individuality which are independent of the social context (see also Archer 2000).

Archer's individualism may be blunt but it is not idiosyncratic. Giddens and Bhaskar have adopted a position which is extremely close to Archer's. Thus, both insist that 'the individual could have acted otherwise' (Giddens 1976: 75; Bhaskar 1979: 114). For all their discussions of the existence of objective structures, Giddens and Bhaskar preserve a private haven within each individual which allows the theoretical possibility of free action at any moment. It is essential that they preserve this haven if they are to avoid the derogation of human actors. Yet, the belief in private human agency is supported neither by argument nor by empirical evidence. Giddens and Bhaskar merely assume that the lone individual is free to act independently of structure, unaware that this assumption leads to the dilemma which Parsons described. If individuals are free, then they could always do otherwise and it would be impossible to explain their adherence to routines which reproduce social order. In this case, the only way to explain regular social action is to deny individuals freedom; they are at some level determined by structure so that they do not act independently and randomly. Committed to a dualistic ontology, Giddens and Bhaskar oscillate between voluntarism and objectivism. They simply equivocate, asserting that sometimes individuals are free and sometimes they are not. In the end, human agency and regular social interaction remain mysterious to contemporary social theory. However, once a social ontology is adopted, human agency can begin to be understood. Humans certainly have extraordinary capacities but those capacities cannot be comprehended independently of the social relations in which they exist. Humans are neither free from nor determined by social structures. Their agency is a product of the social relations in which they find themselves and to which they contribute. Humans mutually sustain each other's agency; they demand from each other certain regular types of conduct by which each maintains their own and others' faces. This does not deny human agency. Humans must actively contribute to their social relations with others; these relations would not exist were they were not actively maintained. Yet, it is important here not to think that social relations are created by initially independent individuals with their own personal agency. Humans never contribute to their social relationships as autonomous individuals. Even at the first encounter, the individual contribution to these relations is already contoured by shared understandings of acceptable action learned from others. The agency which humans certainly possess is ultimately dependent on others, whose agency is similarly dependent on them. Agency is a dialectical phenomenon in which humans actively contribute in ways learned from others to the very social relations which make them what they are. This endows human agency with enormous flexibility, for while an individual is not free to do otherwise, together humans can develop new forms of agency. Individuals cannot randomly decide on new courses of action for these actions would not be understood and would not therefore have the effects which the individual desired. In this case, individual agency would be ineffective or even disastrous. However, in the course of social interaction, humans can together develop new forms of agency. Humans can agree to understand themselves in different ways and learn to invest new actions with significance. Individuals are not free but humans are not determined by an external reality. Humans mutually sustain the agency which all possess. The social relations in which humans are embedded provide the basis of all human agency, including the agency to develop new forms of practice. Hermeneutics does not imply individualism. On the contrary, it operates with a social ontology which always understands human agency as a social product.

11 Hermeneutics and Critique[1]

Habermas' Critique of Hermeneutics

For Habermas, Gadamer's hermeneutics prevents all serious critique because it reduces human existence to a linguistic reality. Consequently, Gadamer's hermeneutics leads necessarily into an uncritical vindication of the status quo. If human interpretation constitutes the reality which confronts them then social reality is a matter of interpretation. Sociologists have no right to go beyond individual interpretations. In this case, it would be possible for definitions to be created which were exploitative but which concealed that exploitation by defining social relations in an egalitarian fashion. The language which is used to describe political relations may illuminate them in a way which is favourable to the powerful while concealing the true reality of these relations. Political superiors, to whom individuals defer, may define their relationships to their subordinates in ways which are in their interests. Hermeneutics has no way of challenging the appeals which the superior makes to tradition, for as long as this appeal is believed in this society, it is the basis of social relations there. Hermeneutics cannot go beyond these relationship-constituting understandings and cannot, therefore, penetrate ideological distortion: 'This "hermeneutic" consciousness of translation difficulties proves to be inadequate when applied to systematically distorted communication' (Habermas 1970: 205). For Habermas, hermeneutics could criticise no political order, no matter how oppressive, because it reduces society merely to the understandings which its members have of it. The members of a society could easily agree upon the meaning of certain social arrangements without recognising the tyranny which these definitions obscured:

> Language is *also* a medium of domination and power. It serves to legitimate the relations of organised force. Insofar as the legitimations do not articulate the power relationship whose institutionalisation they make possible, insofar as that relationship is merely manifested in the legitimation, language is also ideological.
>
> (Habermas 1988: 172)

For Habermas, hermeneutics condemns itself to critical failure; it cannot penetrate these legitimating uses of language. By apparently limiting himself to an idealised account of language, Gadamer blinds himself to the possibility of linguistic manipulation and distortion.

For Habermas, social theory must go beyond hermeneutics if it is to be capable of critique. As we have already seen, Habermas believes that social reality is not completely encompassed by hermeneutics. There is more to society than meaningful social relations. Prior to any interpretations which individuals make about reality exist brute economic and political facts. These constrain any interpretation which individuals can make and they therefore provide the initial grounds for critique. Whatever interpretations an elite or subordinate group may put upon their position, there exists a material social order against which these interpretations are corrigible. These meanings can be corroborated against the objective social system in order that any deliberate distortions by dominant groups can be highlighted. In arguing in this way, Habermas' critical position closely echoes Bhaskar's critical realism, which similarly seeks to expose false consciousness by corroborating individual interpretation against actual social reality (Bhaskar 1979: 80–81). Habermas' ontological dualism forms the basis of his critical method. Interpretations are compared with the prior material structure of a society. When the interpretations misrepresent this reality, they can be rejected as mystifications.

Yet, Habermas aims for a more profound critique than this. For Habermas, the very act of speech itself involves certain transcendental criteria. The purpose of his theory of communicative action and, later, his discourse ethics is to penetrate specific speech acts in order to illuminate the conditions of their production. In this way, the validity of the speech act can be ascertained on its own grounds. Since the hermeneutic process of understanding speech acts operates only at the level of the verbalisations themselves, Habermas proposes a method which precedes hermeneutics and which, unlike hermeneutics, is able to penetrate 'systematically distorted communication':

> The more important occurrences of the patterns of systematically distorted communication are those which appear in speech which is not conspicuously pathological. This is what we encounter in the case of pseudo-communication, where participants do not recognise any communicative disturbance. Pseudo-communication produces a system of reciprocal misunderstandings which due to the false assumption of consensus, are not recognised as such.
>
> (Habermas 1970: 205–06)

Habermas believes that his critical theory alone can illuminate distorted communication. Any true consensus pre-supposes certain conditions, the absence of which denotes a false consensus and, therefore, ultimately no consensus at all. A false consensus occurs when coercion is concealed beneath the ideological veneer of language. Using the model of psychoanalysis, in which patients are cured insofar as they are helped to recognise the repressions which bring them into contradiction with themselves, Habermas attempts to illuminate false consensus. Habermas advocates a return to the original 'scene', where the ideal forms of communication can be identified and where the distortions to the system of communication under analysis can be identified. 'Depth hermeneutics', based on scenic understanding, postulates three basic conditions for adequate agreement. A true consensus is necessarily founded on truth, rightness and truthfulness. The propositional content of a consensus must be factually true, it must accord with the norms of intersubjective relations and it must be an honest expression of the subjects' beliefs and intentions (Habermas 1979: 58). A consensus must be adequate on objective, intersubjective and subjective levels. The establishment of the criterion of truth does not require a 'scenic' understanding. It does not require a reversion to an original scene which provides an internal standard by which the consensus can be judged. This criterion can be tested by the examination of extra-communicative realities which pre-suppose any consensus which is formed. Statements are compared with objective social reality. If they do not match that reality, then they can be declared false. However, the analysis of criterion of intersubjective rightness requires a deeper analysis of the very structure of the consensus. For Habermas, the standard of rightness is analytically implicit within the very concept of a consensus. A consensus, by definition, involves a voluntary agreement which can be reached rationally only if principles are established to which all could willingly consent. It would be impossible for individuals to create a consensus which explicitly disadvantaged some of the participants. To create a consensus on this basis would be to 'deviate from the recognised system of linguistic rules', whose underlying principle is universality. Rules must be able to be applied universally or they are not rules; the analytical definition of a rule is its universal applicability. In the 'original scene', the necessary conditions of a real consensus are demonstrated and this original scene provides a critical counterfactual against which the criteria of intersubjective rightness in any particular community can be compared. The original scene will expose pathological consensus, which contradictorily involves consequences which cannot be universally accepted. In this way, the intersubjective standard of rightness can be tested. Once a false consensus is demonstrated by reversion to the original scene, the criterion of truthfulness, of personal and subjective honesty, is also tested because the rigidity and repetitiousness of the participants demonstrates that they ultimately recognise the incoherence of their position. They cannot be honest because that would undermine the consensus to which they have committed themselves. The specific understandings on the basis of which a consensus emerges pre-suppose certain transcendental linguistic conditions. Habermas, therefore, ultimately advocates two critical methods. The first establishes the objective truth by corroborating interpretations against objective reality. The second tests the validity of intersubjective rightness by a return to an original scene in which the universal criteria of rightness are identifiable.

While hermeneutics concerns itself only with the speech acts themselves, Habermas' 'depth hermeneutics', drawing on the model of psychoanalysis, reveals the transcendental conditions of any possible consensus. They illuminate the prior conditions by which humans in any culture can reach a consensus. Consequently, it can provide a rigorous critique of any particular consensus, for it can show that the shared understandings to which the members of a society agree may involve inegalitarian implications which are actually concealed by this meaningful consensus. Above all, depth hermeneutics can penetrate the forces of tradition and authority, demonstrating that, while a consensus might be accepted simply because it is part of a tradition, it may be pathological. For Habermas, Gadamer's philosophical hermeneutics would be incapable of rejecting an oppressive tradition because it always operates from within a tradition. It allows itself no externalities nor any transcendental conditions by which to reject and criticise a tradition.[2]

Critical Hermeneutics

Habermas claims that hermeneutics is incapable of critique because it reduces social reality to the mere interpretation of it. The way in which humans define their relations determines the reality of that society and the interpreter has no external reality against which to corroborate these interpretations. Yet, in proposing his critical method, Habermas misrepresents hermeneutics very seriously. Hermeneutics never reduced society merely to individual interpretations. Social reality is never a matter of opinion for hermeneutics. Hermeneutics never denies itself access to a wider social reality; it simply insists that the wider social reality consists of social relations, not of objective social structure. A hermeneutic sociology follows Habermas' first critical procedure for it can compare the potentially interested interpretations which certain groups might make at one point in a society against a wider social reality. The claims of elite groups can be compared with the wider context of social relations which persist in any society. In this connection, it might be possible to argue that Marx's critique of political economy was a hermeneutic critique because it undermined political economic theory by comparing it with the reality of the factory system. Hermeneutics does not deny itself access to a social reality which is independent of the interpretations of interested parties. However, although hermeneutics certainly recognises the existence of a wider society against which any interpretation can be corroborated, a hermeneutic critique proceeds somewhat differently to Habermas' critical method. Since the social reality consists of social relations and these relations necessarily involve the understanding of those engaged in them, hermeneutics has to recognise how these people actually conceive their social relations. Hermeneutics must recognise the shared understandings on the basis of which the members of any society interact. It is impossible to give an account of a social order without referring to how the locals actually understand their actions. In order to mount any criticism of a social order, then, consideration must be given to the definitions which members of a particular social group put on themselves. The understanding of what it is to do a thing in a particular culture has to take a primary position. Humans have to understand what their social relations actually involve and demand. Whether social scientists like it or not, they have to reach an understanding of the way people actually define themselves. Consequently, sustainable and effective criticism has to emerge from an understanding of a culture. To impose an interpretation of another culture upon it, against the understandings of the members of that society, is to produce a false account of that society and a necessarily irrelevant form of criticism. Hermeneutics does not limit itself to the way certain groups might conveniently understand their relations to others. It situates the particular understandings of certain groups with the wider social whole. Hermeneutics examines the social relations as a whole in any particular society but in referring to these social relations human understandings have to be considered. Gadamer's point is that these understandings cannot be ignored by the critic for they make those social relations what they are. Critique of a political order requires the sociologist to understand the shared understandings on the basis of which humans in any society interact. It is those understandings which determine what constitutes legitimate action in any society. The political hierarchy cannot be analysed and it cannot, therefore, be criticised without a consideration of the ideas which define it.

The lengthy debate about Zande witchcraft following Peter Winch's famous article (Winch 1964; Wilson 1970; Hollis and Lukes 1982) provides a good illustration of the indispensability of hermeneutics to critique.[3] The debate about Zande witchcraft originated in Evans-Pritchard's famous ethnography of Zande magic, in which he discussed the role of witchcraft and, in particular, the poison oracle (Evans-Pritchard 1937). Among the Azande, witchcraft is believed to be a substance in the bodies of witches which can be transmitted by blood. As Evans-Pritchard demonstrates, witchcraft is an idiom of everyday life among the Azande which is 'ubiquitous': 'it plays a part in every activity of Zande life' (Evans-Pritchard 1937: 63). The Azande typically employ witchcraft to explain any unfortunate incident. Evans-Pritchard emphasises that the Azande recognise empirical causality but they invoke witchcraft to underpin the empirical realm metaphysically. Thus, Evans-Pritchard cites the example of a granary collapsing onto someone as a result of the work of termites. The Zande fully recognise the physical processes which led to the accident but they invoke witchcraft to explain why this granary collapsed at the particular moment when someone was underneath it (Evans-Pritchard 1937: 69). Intimately related to their belief in witchcraft, the Azande are fascinated by the poison oracle, which is a central ritual in Zande life. The poison oracle can be used to predict the future or to ask advice about alternative courses of action but one of its main functions is to determine whether and by whom someone is bewitched. The poison oracle operates by feeding a fowl a small amount of poison, '*benge*'. Certain questions are then asked of the oracle which will be answered by the manner of the fowl's death. The way in which any fowl dies confirms or allays the suspicions of witchcraft which are brought before the oracle. Although all Azande are fascinated by the poison oracle, access to it is strictly controlled. The oracles are controlled by the princes, while fowls and '*benge*' are expensive. Since the oracle is costly it is the 'province of married men' (Evans-Pritchard 1937: 283): 'Poor men who do not possess poison or fowls but who are compelled for one reason or other to consult the oracle will persuade a kinsman, blood-brother, relative-in-law or prince's deputy to consult it on their behalf' (Evans-Pritchard 1937: 283). Not only is access to the oracle restricted on economic grounds but the kinds of witchcraft accusation which can be made are subject to political control. In particular, the king, nobility and even influential commoners (Evans-Pritchard 1937: 104) are never the subject of witchcraft accusations. Indeed, even to suggest that witchcraft played any role in the actions of the king would be perilous:

> It would be treason to say that a man put to death on the orders of his king for an offence against his authority was killed by witchcraft. If a man were to consult the oracles to discover the witch responsible for the death of a relative who had been put to death at the orders of his king he would run the risk of being put to death himself.
>
> (Evans-Pritchard 1937: 75)

To suggest witchcraft in this case would be to undermine the authority of the king and it is consequently outlawed. While political superiors cannot be accused of witchcraft, equals or inferiors are the target of constant witchcraft suspicions. In particular, these accusations arise out of personal enmity between people of similar status who come into frequent social contact and conflict with each other. Significantly, if an accusation of witchcraft is corroborated by the oracle, the witch may be confronted by the plaintiff. In this case, the witch will frequently declare no knowledge of having bewitched the plaintiff but will not usually reject the ruling of the oracle (Evans-Pritchard 1937: 95). He must have inadvertently cursed his rival and now 'wishes him health and happiness' (Evans-Pritchard 1937: 95). The poison oracle identifies the witch but also provides processes by which accusations lead to reconciliation:

> Apart from the fact that good behaviour on both sides is habitual...other factors assist in eliminating friction: the employment of intermediaries between the parties which obviates the necessity of their meeting during the whole affair; the great authority of the poison oracle, for it is useless to protest against its declarations, the social standing of the prince's deputy, for an insult to his messenger is an insult to the prince himself...It is, moreover, to the interest of both parties that they do not become estranged. They have to live together as neighbours.
>
> (Evans-Pritchard 1937: 96–97)

Even the poorest members of Zande society receive some benefits from the poison oracle for it provides them with an outlet for their grievances against their neighbours and a means of reconciliation between them.

Evans-Pritchard is able to illuminate Zande life because he explains the role which witchcraft beliefs play in this society. Without understanding the role of witchcraft and the poison oracle, the behaviour of the Zande is mysterious:

> Usually I have found the Azande courteous and reliable according to English standards but sometimes their behaviour was unintelligible till their mystical notions were taken into account.
>
> (Evans-Pritchard 1937: 265)

It is not insignificant that Evans-Pritchard himself had to suspend his disbelief in witchcraft while he was carrying out his fieldwork among the Azande. Indeed, he was able to establish himself as an important social actor because he was wealthy enough to buy both fowls and '*benge*'. It is simply impossible to explain or even to exist in Zande society without recognising witchcraft. Anthropologists may well dismiss the existence of witchcraft in our own society, as Evans-Pritchard does – 'witches, as the Azande conceive them, cannot exist' (Evans-Pritchard 1937: 63) but any account of the Azande must recognise their beliefs in witchcraft. The way the Azande understand witchcraft is central to the social relations between them. As Evans-Pritchard emphasises, the belief in witchcraft permeates every activity, so that when studying the Azande, any scepticism about witches is simply pointless. Their political relations become incomprehensible.

The Zande witchcraft study demonstrates the necessity of hermeneutic understanding. A society cannot be understood without taking into account the way its members actually understand themselves. The example of Zande witchcraft demonstrates that it is essential to recognise the distinctive under-standings which form the basis of other people's cultures. Yet, the necessity of understanding the other does not mean the end of critique. On the contrary, decisive critique is possible only insofar as sociologists understand the other and are aware of the significance with which they invest their social practices. Following Evans-Pritchard's work, there has been extensive discussion about what light the Zande witchcraft beliefs throw on rationality and western science. The focus of concern here is not how Zande witchcraft beliefs are actually mobilised by the Zande in their relations with each other. Rather the question is why, given their manifest absurdity, do the Zande persist with their irrational views? The debate has focused ultimately on the difference between scientific versus primitive ways of thinking. This debate has been interesting but it has not advanced the understanding of the Azande at all. Criticising the Azande for not being scientific when they consult oracles is not ultimately an analysis; it reveals nothing about this other culture. Nor does it not constitute a critique of this society. It is merely an *a priori* rejection of it.

By contrast, by understanding the role which witchcraft plays in Zande society, it is possible not merely to comprehend this society but also to offer a critique which is relevant to it. The case of Zande witchcraft demonstrates the way in which hermeneutics is capable of critique. Evans-Pritchard reveals that access to the oracle is controlled by political elites: the king, the nobles and, at a lower level, influential and wealthy male commoners. The elite's monopoly of this ritual sustains their social position in Zande society because the possession of an oracle denotes status. It is also an important source of political influence since, as the oracle's statements are always true, the actions which the oracle suggests to those who are granted access to it are *ipso facto* legitimate. Consequently, Zande elites can confer legitimacy on others, with obvious political benefits to themselves. Evans-Pritchard himself experienced the way in which witchcraft was invoked to express political relations. On his departure from the Azande at the end of his fieldwork, Prince Gangura came to Evans-Pritchard's leaving feast. Strangely, the prince arrived unannounced and left in the middle of the night, explaining that this would put witches and sorcerers off his track (Evans-Pritchard 1937: 265–66). Although the prince certainly believed in the existence of witches and sorcerers, his odd arrival and departure can be explained more prosaically. Gangura wanted to come to the feast because Evans-Pritchard was an important colonial visitor to the tribe with close connections to the British authorities, but the prince also felt that to accept an invitation to Evans-Pritchard's leaving feast would be politically demeaning. It would put him on the level of merely a wealthy commoner. Consequently, Gangura's unexpected arrival and departure allowed him to demonstrate his relationship with Evans-Pritchard and, by extension, the colonial authorities without dishonouring himself in the eyes of his subordinates and peers; they would not know that he had in fact attended this feast. The witches and sorcerers which the prince might have attracted to his person symbolise the social dishonour which he might have incurred had he publicly announced his appearance. This is very important for it illuminates the nature of political relations in this society. Among the Azande, social status is threatened when one's reputation is impugned. When members of the Zande are dishonoured, they are socially disadvantaged in their dealings with others; they are actually cursed. Public dishonour is conceived as – and indeed is – a curse. The Zande open themselves to witchcraft curses at precisely the moment when their status is under threat. Zande witchcraft is not irrational but accurately represents status in Zande society. It is the idiom in which social relations in this society are conducted. Witchcraft symbolises the social hierarchy in Zande society and witchcraft curses reflect the shifting contours of social status. Princes are dominant in this order and they monopolise not only the poison oracle but are protected from witchcraft accusations. The Zande political hierarchy, which would remain otherwise mysterious, is illuminated when the significance of witchcraft in this society is understood. This interpretation of witchcraft makes a critique of this society possible because it illuminates the gradient of political inequalities. This critique operates only by means of local understandings. Hermeneutics is not uncritical. It emphasises that the definitions which social actors put upon themselves have to be recognised since these definitions determine what social relations actually are in any culture. Political relations do not exist independently of the way the participants understand them. Against Habermas, hermeneutics does not deny itself access to a social reality which is independent of individual interpretation. It seeks to comprehend social activities by situating them in the grand matrix of social relations. The shared understandings of the members of a society have to feature in any critical account, for these understandings make those relations – however exploitative they might be – what they are. The Zande cannot be understood nor can their political order be criticised independently of their beliefs about witchcraft. Hermeneutics is not uncritical, despite Habermas' imputations.

Habermas' critical theory operates very differently from the hermeneutic method described by reference to the Zande. Habermas' critical theory is able to penetrate layers of mystification by identifying the transcendental conditions of consensus; these conditions provide objective standards of critique.[4] In order to attain these independent standards of critique, Habermas advocates a return to the original scene. The return to the original scene is crucial for it provides a universal grounding for critique. Habermas proposes that these putatively universal principles should be applied to the societies which he wants to criticise. When a society fails to conform to his idealised principles, Habermas declares that a false consensus has been produced. This consensus is sustained only because the members of this community are suffering from false consciousness; they do not recognise their own exploitation. They fail to see that the putatively universal principles to which they have consented necessarily involve unegalitarian social effects. In a false consensus, humans unwittingly submit to their subordination. For Habermas, his critical theory serves the purpose of enlightening the mystified about their true situation. It provides a counterfactual against which pathological social realities can be judged.

Yet, it is not at all clear that this application of supposedly universal principles provides a better critical method than hermeneutics. In particular, it is extremely dubious whether the concept of a false consensus has any analytical value at all. What appears at first glance as 'false consciousness' or as a false consensus is often understandable once the social reality is understood more fully. Once the social relations have been interpreted adequately, apparently mystified conduct becomes comprehensible. Thus, Zande witchcraft beliefs seem at first sight utterly irrational and mystified. Only on full hermeneutic immersion into this culture do these beliefs become understandable and at that point their political relevance becomes clear. The social reality is not obscured by these beliefs; rather the political relations between members of the Zande are lucidly expressed through the idiom of witchcraft beliefs. In his discussion of Weberian sociology, Collins has illuminated the weakness of the concept of false consciousness and it is useful to consider his arguments in relations to Habermas' critical theory. According to Collins, Marxists assume that modern society is characterised by a binary class structure in which the interests of the working class are absolutely opposed to those of the capitalist class. In order to explain the persistence of capitalist society and the absence of any significant revolutionary threat, Marxists have to invoke a theory of false consciousness which suggests that the workers do not recognise their true interests. They are mystified by capitalist ideology so that they do not see their common interests with fellow workers. In fact, as Collins demonstrates, Marxist descriptions of capitalist society are false. Capitalist society is not characterised by a binary class system but by a complex hierarchy of competing status groups. In this hierarchy there are no automatic communal interests between a supposedly unified working class for the working class is not ultimately a unitary entity. It is itself divided into competing and divided status groups, occupying particular niches, which monopolise particular opportunities. Workers do not ally with one another not because they are mystified by capitalism into pursuing deluded interests, but because there are actually no significant shared interests between these groups:

> It is rational for workers in a particular branch of industry to defend their self-interest against workers in other branches, or for union members to defend their interests against non-union workers...Workers in a particular industry may have stronger economic interests in common with their bosses than with workers in rival industries.

> (Collins 1990: 127)

The point is further illustrated by the Paris uprising in 1968. In the initial stages of these protests, labour unions allied themselves with radical student groups. However, this alliance soon dissolved when the students demanded access to the factories, which they intended to destroy in a frenzy of revolutionary zeal. The students thought they would thereby be liberating the workers from their oppression at the hands of capitalist exploiters. In the event, the workers barricaded the factories against the students, explicitly on the grounds that they did not want the factories to be destroyed. Their livelihood depended upon the machinery at which they worked. The workers were not protesting about capitalism *per se* but simply demanding an improvement in their relative position in this social order; they wanted better wages and conditions. The workers shared fundamental interests with the capitalists, even though they were completely aware of the fact that the factory owners earned more money than them. They accepted this situation because they at least achieved a reasonable standard of living in this society. The students meanwhile could happily threaten to destroy the factories since it was highly unlikely that their livelihood would ever depend upon the existence of these institutions in any direct way. The workers of 1968 were not in any way mystified. They saw their interests with absolute clarity and acted decisively upon them, shutting the students out. The consensus on the basis of which they worked was unequal and, yet, some of their interests were delivered under it. Hermeneutics is able to understand unequal consensus. By contrast, Habermas' discourse ethics formally rules that any consensus in which formal equality is not achieved is false. In the history of humanity, social consensus has in almost every instance involved social inequality but the consensus holds because the members of these societies recognise that some of their interests are guaranteed under even apparently exploitative agreements. Operating with an idealised notion of consensus, Habermas imposes what he thinks should be the interests of various groups onto what these groups actually consider to be their interests. Habermas ignores local understandings in favour of his own abstract principles.

Yet, this appeal to abstract universals does not produce a more critical account of social reality; it simply ensures that the social reality is persistently misrepresented and misunderstood.

Ironically, Habermas himself sees the shortcomings of this approach. At other points in his critical theory, Habermas rejects exactly this imposition of cultural standards. Habermas ultimately accepts the hermeneutic point that since social relations do not exist independently of the understandings which humans put on them, social theorists must always seek to interpret these understandings. For instance, his discourse ethics emphasises that the standard of intersubjective rightness has to be considered (1990: 58). The way that people in a particular culture understand themselves avowedly forms an essential part of his critical theory. Moreover, he recognises that the standards of rightness are necessarily culturally specific: 'norms are dependent upon the continual re-establishment of legitimately ordered interpersonal relations' (Habermas 1990: 61). There are no universal criteria of rightness. The concept of what is right is itself dependent on particular shared understandings. When humans operate on the basis of different understandings, when they are engaged in different social practices and embedded in different social relations, their concept of rightness changes. Throughout his work Habermas accepts this hermeneutic point that human society cannot be understood without a consideration of the shared understandings which the members of that society act upon. There is, on this account, no such thing as absolute right. What is right depends on what people in a particular culture given certain understandings mutually take to be right. Rightfulness is dependent on agreement; it does not precede it. Ultimately, Habermas' critical theory accepts the hermeneutic process. Yet, having emphasised the intersubjective basis of rightness, Habermas' discourse ethics reneges on this interpretive claim. The rightful in another society is compared with the ideal counterfactual derived from his discourse ethics, and in every case the local notion of rightfulness is dismissed in favour of Habermas' abstractions. If any local account of rightfulness implies a consensus in which the principle of formal equality is not upheld, then this intersubjective agreement is false, even if the people in this society continue to conduct themselves on the basis of it. Habermas denies what he consistently emphasises. He pays lip-service to intersubjective understandings only to prefer his own abstract principles. Whatever the shared understandings in a particular society, Habermas' supposedly universal principles take precedence. Yet, his supposedly objective critical theory does not in the end produce superior critiques. It merely asserts what should take place in any particular society irrespective of what the members of that society take to be appropriate action.

Hermeneutics and Tradition

One of the most important concepts in Gadamer's hermeneutics is the idea of 'fore-understanding', often translated, with unfortunate implications, as 'prejudice'. Gadamer insists that all human existence pre-supposes certain shared cultural presumptions. Humans are necessarily part of a tradition by which they understand themselves. In emphasising these traditional fore-understandings, Gadamer seems merely to canonise them, and the obscurity of his argument suggests exactly the kinds of reading which Habermas makes. Yet, it is notable that Gadamer has emphasised in the strongest terms that hermeneutics does not vindicate tradition uncritically:

> The notion that, in the education process, tradition as such should be and remain the sole ground for the assessment of prejudices – a view that Habermas attributes to me – flies directly in the face of my thesis that authority rests on knowledge and understanding…Tradition is no proof of validity.
>
> (Gadamer 1986: 286)

Gadamer reiterates the point: 'It is an undue imputation, though, to suppose that I thought that there is no such thing as a loss of authority and emancipatory critique' (Gadamer 1986: 285). Gadamer is explicit: hermeneutics does not unthinkingly affirm tradition. There is a clear contradiction between Gadamer's account of hermeneutics and Habermas' criticisms of it. It is necessary to examine Gadamer more closely to consider whether his hermeneutics is critical or whether Habermas is, indeed, correct and hermeneutics involves only the vindication of tradition. Gadamer's discussion of fore-understandings in Part II of *Truth and Method* (1975), where he considers the interpretation of historical texts, is central to this issue. There, he argues that, although humans live in a particular form of life with its own 'fore-understandings', they are not inexorably trapped within them. They can comprehend other forms of life because all human cultures are similarly based on shared meanings. Humans can understand others because all modes of being are meaningful, but they must interpret the other from within their own horizon of meaning. For Gadamer, the act of interpretation involves the existence of two cultural horizons: the historian's own horizon and the past horizon which the historian wishes to understand. This other horizon must, in fact, be understood within the fore-understandings of the present cultural horizon. The fore-understandings of the present horizon provide the initial critical standards by which the past is understood. The present horizon is the hermeneutic whole in which the past, as an element of the whole, is situated. However, although the horizon of the other must be interpreted in the light of the fore-understandings of the present horizon, this does not mean that humans simply impose our meanings on the other. While the other horizon must be understood in terms the present horizon, the latter is not static. The present horizon is forced to reconsider its fore-understandings as it encounters new horizons. New horizons challenge established understandings when they cannot be fully comprehended within the existing hermeneutic whole. The process of interpretation demands the re-negotiation of contemporary understandings. The new horizon must be incorporated into the horizon of the present so that this part coheres with the hermeneutic whole. The horizon in which humans live will be transformed by its encounter with others. Through the encounter with others, there is a 'fusion of historical' horizons when an alternative consciousness is incorporated into the present mode of being to produce a new self-consciousness (Gadamer 1975: 273). Gadamer describes the fusion of historical horizons as 'effective historical consciousness' (Gadamer 1975: 273), which is characterised by a proper awareness of our own historic specificity. At this moment humans have reached a high level of self-consciousness and they recognise the specific meaning of their own mode of being. As Gadamer himself insists, his hermeneutic emphasis on tradition in no way suggests an adherence to an ossified tradition. On the contrary, in his view only those traditions which constantly challenge their fore-understandings by seeking to understand others are valid. His point is only that the interpretive process must necessarily start from a shared tradition. Fore-understandings provide the ground of initial inter-pretation but they do not set limits on the development of understanding.

In Part III, as discussed in Chapter 9, the full significance of historical hermeneutics and the fusion of horizons is demonstrated. The fusion of horizons does not merely occur when scholars consider the historical record. It is a universal process in human social existence. Humans live in linguistic communi-ties which constitute the world for them. The shared understandings embodied in language do not describe a world which already exists but actually bring a world into being. In order for social groups to persist they will have to re-create the common traditions on the basis of which they act in the world and interact with each other. As Gadamer emphasises, communities sustain their language through conversation; language 'acquires its reality only in the process of communicating' (Gadamer 1975: 404). Linguistic communities have to re-affirm what they mean by certain words. By extension, human communities must actively affirm the shared understandings on the basis of which they interact with each other; tradi-tions have to be periodically restated. His argument here closely echoes Durkheim's discussion of ritual. They have to re-state their common traditions so that all the members of the community understand what they imply; how they should interact with each other and the world. At this point of re-statement there is always a potential fusion of horizons. Shared understandings have to be re-considered in the light of present circumstances. In re-evoking tradition, transformation is eminently possible. Authoritarian cultures may limit this fusion of horizons. They may dogmatically re-assert one account of tradition but this re-assertion is always potentially open to challenge. The present horizon can never be definitively closed down, and in forthcoming re-statements the dogmatic inter-pretation of tradition can be demonstrated to be narrow and limited. A wider fusion of horizons in which alternative interpretations of the group's past are considered can undermine ossified re-iterations of tradition:

> The fusion of recollective and anticipatory moments of understanding in a fore-concept gives the latter critical force. Their formation would necessarily entail an explicit revision of what a tradition's past and future has been understood as being. Such concepts can therefore serve as *possible* checks against the distortion of a tradition by ideological influences.
>
> (Davey 1985: 128)

It is possible to re-consider Gadamer's comments about authority and tradition in the light of these discussions (Gadamer 1975: 248). Gadamer does not vindicate authority absolutely. On the contrary, he explicitly opposes proper authority to 'blind obedience' (Gadamer 1975: 248). The authority invested in tradition does not operate automatically. Traditions have to be periodically re-stated by the group so that all its members understand what practices it actually enjoins. At this point, new evidence, new interpretations and new understandings can be considered and against this developing horizon the tradition must fuse itself. Valid authority will be the product of this new fusion of tradition incorporating these new understandings most coherently. Legitimate authority must constantly re-consider itself in the light of group understandings and social conditions in which group members currently live. Tyranny, by contrast, simply re-affirms a narrow interpretation of itself; group understandings are considered only in relation to a narrow account of the group's past and its present circumstances. For Gadamer, tyranny does not escape from the fusion of horizon; it merely limits the potential of this fusion. It is a dogmatic re-iteration rather than an open re-interpretation of itself in the past and the present. For Gadamer, the fusion of horizons is a necessary process because the common traditions of a group have to be re-stated. Each re-statement provides an opportunity for self-criticism and transformation. Simply because the shared understandings embodied in a tradition are the starting point of any investigation, this does not mean that humans are inexorably trapped within this initial horizon. Precisely because human existence is founded on conscious understanding, it is capable of immanent self-transformation. Indeed, each re-statement of tradition will necessarily involve some transformation of common understandings.

The development of sociology illustrates this process of immanent development. From its origins in the nineteenth century up to the 1960s, sociology was a discipline which focused overwhelmingly on men and on male activities, often unwittingly taking these specifically male activities to denote the total social reality. Sociology replicated the assumptions of the culture in which it was conducted. From the 1960s, feminists began to illuminate the often unseen masculinist bias in sociology, promoting new forms of research specifically designed to rectify this lacuna. The feminist intervention, reflecting a wider transformation of cultural pre-suppositions, has illuminated the fore-understandings of sociology. Yet, it has not done so by reference to universal standards outside all cultural communities, as Habermas' critical theory demands. The feminist critique has risen up immanently within the discipline through recognising the empirical reality of social life. This reality was implicit in every sociological account; they all recognised the existence of women and their activities in society but women were almost invariably subordinated to men and their activities. Hermeneutics never vindicated tradition absolutely. On the contrary, hermeneutics illustrates only the processes by which tradition must be periodically re-established if it is to exist at all. The kinds of critique in which any social scientist can engage are necessarily derived, according to Gadamer, from the traditions of which they are part. Critique does not operate by transcending all cultural pre-suppositions. Critique must start from the fore-understandings in any culture but these fore-understanding are not dogmatic – even in the case of the masculine presumptions of sociology. Fore-understandings are always open to immanent transformation as they are considered in the light of new experience, just as tradition itself undergoes necessary self-transformation.

Habermas believes that he has overcome the cultural particularism of hermeneutics to create universal criteria of critique. It is notable that nowhere in Habermas' discussions of critical theory, from *Knowledge and Human Interests* (1971), through the universal pragmatic and the theory of communicative action up to the discourse ethics, does he provide a single empirical example of his method at work. He never actually applies his critical theory to the analysis of particular cases to demonstrate how his discourse ethics, in fact, provides a superior account of social relations than native accounts. There is no empirical elaboration of how critical theory would actually operate in the face of other cultures. The absence of any empirical exemplification is extremely significant for it demonstrates the reality of Habermas' critical theory. In his abstract discussions, Habermas never attempts a fusion of horizons with cultures. He therefore never challenges his own pre-suppositions. Rather he merely dogmatically asserts the universality of his own abstract principles. He remains within his own idealised horizon. Nevertheless, he is confident that the principles which discourse ethics elucidates are not culturally specific. Habermas insists that his discourse ethics is not merely the abstracted 'reflection of the prejudices of adult, white, well-educated, Western males of today' (Habermas 1990: 197). Thus, for instance, discourse ethics proposes a principle of universality; no principle can be accepted as the basis of a consensus which is not generalisable (Habermas 1990: 65). Discourse ethics proposes a principle of formal political equality. The examples of working-class disunity and the 1968 uprising demonstrated that, in fact, there are frequent historical examples of consensus which were considered reasonable by the participants but which also knowingly involved inequality. It is also significant that the principle of formal political equality is central to modern western political traditions. It constitutes a central concept in the liberal political tradition and finds elaborate expression in the works of political philosophers from Locke onwards. Historically, the principle of formal political equality became particularly important in the nineteenth century, where it was specifically employed to justify the activities of the emergent industrial bourgeoisie. Formal political equality involved a separation of political and economic spheres. Before the state all were equal, but in economic exchange the market was decisive and inequality was the rule. As Marx famously noted, formal political equality before the state actually facilitated gross economic exploitation of the working class because the relations between capital and labour were not a matter of political negotiation. Habermas' notion of consensus is not a universal principle but on the contrary a historically and culturally specific one. It is an abstract formulation of the relationship between citizens and state in modern western societies. Similarly, Habermas also gives the example of humans rights: 'Human rights obviously embody generalizable interests…And yet nobody would argue that these rights, which represent the moral substance of our legal system, are irrelevant from the ethics Sittlich Keit of modern life' (Habermas 1990: 205). Habermas believes that the concept of human rights is self-evidently universal and they can be appealed to critically. Certain cultural practices can be rejected on the basis of them. Yet, human rights pre-suppose certain understandings of the relations between state and citizens which persist in western democracies. They are certainly not universal historically and are, in fact, not universal even in the contemporary era. Typically, human rights are appealed to and acted upon by powerful western states against weak ones, normally located in the Third World. The concept of human rights is comprehensible only within a particular set of political relations between various states. Offending states must be weak enough so that western powers can intervene in their local affairs on the basis of human rights, and western states must feel that their interests are furthered by such intervention. When the United States intervened in Somalia in the early 1990s, human rights were invoked but, in fact, the initiative for this intervention arose because the new President, Bill Clinton, was pressurised by African states who pointed up the hypocrisy of the supposedly liberally president. While he intervened in wars involving white Europeans, he seemed unwilling to relieve the plight of black Africans. The disastrous Somalian intervention was an attempt to demonstrate America's commitment to Africa, thereby sustaining good political relations with African states. In the light of the United States' experiences in Somalia, African states will have to develop even more persuasive political strategies to encourage future American intervention on the basis of putatively universal human rights. Human rights are applied in reference to specific political considerations. It is notable that Third World nations do not try to intervene in the internal affairs of European nations or the United States by appealing to human rights. The political context would make such an appeal to rights absurd. Human rights are not universal but are an expression of the political relations between states in the late twentieth and early twenty-first centuries. In fact, Habermas fully recognises that the application of rights finally undermines any appeal to universality. He notes, for instance, that 'in this abstract formulation, they can be applied without qualification only to standard situations' (Habermas 1995a: 13). The notion of a standard situation is extremely unclear and historically human rights tend to have been applied in situations which it would be difficult to call typical. The appeal to human rights normally involves sensitive political negotiation between various states. Against Habermas' assertions, it seems more likely that the cases when human rights will be applied without qualification are very limited. At the point of qualification, culturally and historically specific understandings and local interests will come to the fore, determining in each case what human rights actually are. At this point, it is simply meaningless to describe human rights as universal. Nevertheless, Habermas continues to insist that he has identified genuinely universal principles.

Habermas' discourse ethics is ultimately a form of idealised liberalism. Habermas' putatively universal principles are only abstracted versions of culturally specific ones. He raises his own culturally specific standards of rightness to the level of a universal. Although he is unaware of it, Habermas does not actually avoid the hermeneutic process in his critical theory. He must being from specific cultural pre-suppositions and, in fact, Habermas recognises this. In discussing the theory of communicative action, Habermas claims that 'communicative actors are always moving within the horizon of their lifeworld; they cannot step outside it' (Habermas 1987b: 126). Human existence is social and shared understandings are consequently essential to it; the partners in interaction must understand what their actions imply and what their relations involve. However, in his discourse ethics, Habermas presumes that while all humans necessarily operate within one lifeworld or another he somehow avoids this social predicament merely by *fiat*; he asserts that he is able to transcend culture. Yet, on Habermas' own account, social theorists, as humans, must themselves be 'always moving within their lifeworld'. Despite his claims to universality, Habermas demonstrates that he must draw upon the cultural pre-suppositions of the western tradition in which he operates; he can never step out of his own lifeworld. His method still operates by situating other cultures within the horizon of his own. In this, Habermas does not avoid the hermeneutic process. However, Habermas' interpretive circle is drastically foreshortened so that he merely imposes his initial cultural pre-suppositions onto the society under analysis. Habermas does not try to interpret the understandings of other cultures in any serious way; he merely dismisses them as false consciousness before he even considers them because they do not accord with his own fore-understandings. At the same time, he merely affirms his own principles as universal. The result is only an impoverished form of hermeneutics which demands that other horizons fit the rigid fore-understandings of Habermas' own horizon. Ironically, Habermas' critical theory vindicates authority and tradition, unwittingly inflating important principles of western society into universals. He ossifies his own lifeworld while ignoring the distinctive cultures of other social communities. Hermeneutics, by contrast, emphasises its cultural origins but is not limited by them.

Hermeneutics is not uncritical. It rejects only shallow and assertive critique which fails to consider local understandings, that make social relations what they are. It is only in this way that those social relations can be understood and that a valid critique can be made of them. If critical theorists dismiss Azande witchcraft beliefs as irrational and focus on the question of how this irrationality persists, then they miss the political role which these beliefs play. A proper critique of Azande society is avoided in place of a barely disguised celebration of western scientific superiority. Hermeneutics, by contrast, fulfils the tasks of Habermas' critical theory. It recognises a social reality against which claims can be corroborated. However, hermeneutics refuses to give social reality an existence independent of local understandings. In order to criticise a society, it is necessary to understand on what basis the members of it interact with each other. However, although local understandings are central to any critical account, hermeneutics also recognises that social scientists must begin from their own cultural fore-understandings. However, simply because hermeneutic critique must begin with native fore-understandings, this does not mean that the sociologist is trapped by them. Hermeneutics does not simply vindicate the traditions in which the critic operates. On the contrary, in the course of critique, which proceeds only through the long and spiralling hermeneutic circle, the interpreter's own cultural assumptions are disclosed. These assumptions form the initial standards of critique but hermeneutics facilitates the immanent development of more coherent and sustainable pre-suppositions. Certainly, hermeneutics insists that no perspective is final. The fusion of horizons is eternal as the present horizon constantly considers its own fore-understandings in the light of new experiences. However, hermeneutics offers a way by which critical understanding can develop, immersing itself in the other and transforming its own standards of judgement at the same time. Critical standards are always open to transformation. The lifeworld in which the critical theorists always move is itself capable of movement. In the act of interpretation, the critical standards of the interpreter are not merely imposed on the other – they are not assumed to be universal – but undergo transformation in order to be able to encompass other understandings in a coherent whole. Against the imputations of Habermas, hermeneutics is not uncritical but the criticism it proposes proceeds along a circular path. That hermeneutic path not only leads to a critical understanding of the society which is being analysed but produces critical self-awareness. The hermeneutic circle leads to a fusion of horizons where the cultural standards which initially inform critique are themselves transformed.

12 Beyond Structure and Agency

Hamlet

> What piece of work is a man, how noble in reason, how infinite in faculties, in form and moving how express and admirable, in action how like an angel, in apprehension, how like a god: the beauty of the world, the paragon of the animals – and, yet, to me what is this quintessence of dust? Man delights not me, nor woman neither.
>
> (*Hamlet* Act II, Scene II)

In one of his most lyrical soliloquies, Hamlet illuminates his tragic predicament. For him, humans are debased and, aware of his own mortal inadequacies, Hamlet rejects the world and disdains humanity. Thus, Hamlet cannot avenge his father's death by challenging his usurping uncle because action would further sully his already corrupt existence. Although violent action is demanded, he remains impotent. His predicament is specifically tragic because he is informed of his uncle's treachery by his father's ghost. His very mode of enlightenment paralyses him by confirming the existence of God and a hellish afterlife to him. As his father tells him: 'To tell the secrets of my prison-house, I could a tale unfold whose lightest word would harrow up they soul, freeze the young blood' (Shakespeare 1982: 216). In place of effective action in the real world, Hamlet simply pretends to go mad; he puts on 'antic disposition' (Shakespeare 1982: 226). He represses his own love for Ophelia even though 'forty thousand brothers could not with all their quantity of love make up my sum' (Shakespeare 1982: 391–92); this intimate social contact and its possible progeny would be defiling. With his faked insanity he drives Ophelia away, significantly recommending the world-rejecting life of a convent to her: 'Get thee to a nunnery'. Hamlet's feigned madness is appropriate because his eternal dissatisfaction with the world and his fellow humans is insane. The total rejection of the world which Hamlet attempts is impossible. He has to act in the world. Yet, because his actions are only half-willed, they are more disastrous than those carried out deliberately by human beings whom Hamlet regards as corrupted. Thus, he kills the idiotic but innocent Polonius by accident:

Queen. O me what hast thou done?
Hamlet. Nay, I know not. Is it the King?

(Shakespeare 1982: 320)

However, while he would have been able to kill the king unintentionally, he baulks at the real opportunity he is presented with when he passes the king praying in the chapel soon after *The Mousetrap* in the climax of Act III.

And am I then reveng'd,
To take him in the purging of his soul,
When he is fit and season'd for his passage?
No.

(Shakespeare 1982: 317)

Worse still, later in the play he sends Rosencrantz and Guildenstern deliberately to their deaths in England, for which callous act he excuses himself with ease:

Why, man they did make to love to this employment.
They are not near my conscience, their defeat
Does by their own insinuation grow.

(Shakespeare 1982: 397)

It is significant that at this point, where Hamlet has acted most deliberately in the play to ensure his own friends' deaths, he dismisses the call of his conscience, when it should have prevented Rosencrantz and Guildenstern's condemnation. His justifications for his act are self-serving. The two servants acted throughout out of love for Hamlet, whom they were trying to assist, and out of natural obedience for a sovereign of whose true character they were unaware. As a human, Hamlet must necessarily interact with others; he must act in the world. However, his transcendentally oriented conscience obliterates other humans and, consequently, his acts are inappropriate. They are individualistic and idiosyncratic. The tragedy of Hamlet is that his natural heroism, emphasised at the start of the play with the description of his contribution to the defeat of the older Fortinbras, is hobbled by his metaphysical enlightenment. He knows the soiling reality of the world and cannot therefore act in it.

The young Fortinbras constitutes an important contrast to Hamlet, for while he starts the play without a father or a kingdom, and in a plainly subordinate position to the soldierly Hamlet, he inherits both Scandanavia and Denmark by the end of the piece. Unlike Hamlet, he is not fettered by a conscientious concern with the metaphysical. He is concerned only with the human social world. The difference between the active Fortinbras and the impotent Hamlet is economically demonstrated in Act IV, Scene IV, when Hamlet meets Fortinbras as the latter leads his army to Poland. Hamlet recognises that, while he has every reason to act against his uncle, Fortinbras willingly risks everything 'for an eggshell' (Shakespeare 1982: 346). In contrast to Hamlet, Fortinbras is completely integrated into his social world and the highest value for him is recognition from his peers and subordinates, honour:

While to my shame I see
The imminent death of twenty thousand men,
That, for a fantasy and trick of fame,
Go to their graves like beds, fight for a plot
Whereon the numbers cannot try the cause

(Shakespeare 1982: 346)

While Fortinbras prioritises his honour and every act is the deliberate and bold pursuit of status, Hamlet not only rejects all recognition from others, but cannot even understand the reality of honour. His miscomprehension of honour as a form of social recognition is demonstrated in his most famous soliloquy:

To be, or not to be, that is the question:
Whether 'tis nobler in the mind to suffer
The slings and arrows of outrageous fortune,
Or to take arms against a sea of troubles
And by opposing end them.

(Shakespeare 1982: 277–78)

Although he acknowledges honour ('nobility'), he falsely internalises and individualises an irreducibly social value. Nobility is not a property of the mind, for nobility is imputed to individuals on the basis of their actions and assumed by individuals on the basis of the reactions of others to them. Honour is an irreducibly social phenomenon which necessarily assumes the existence of others. His decision of whether to act or not is already decided negatively from the outset; he has already eliminated other people from his world with and against whom he can act. Instead, Hamlet lives an isolated existence where he faces God and the afterlife alone. In this barren world, denuded of social interaction, Hamlet, as an isolated individual, is impotent.

The obsequies over Hamlet's death emphasise the dichotomy in the play between metaphysical delusions and human action. Hamlet is effectively buried twice, once as a tragically impotent hero and a second time as a true soldier. Thus Horatio's peroration affirms the existence of the very afterlife which crippled Hamlet, 'Good night, sweet prince, And flights of Angels sing thee to thy rest' (Shakespeare 1982: 416). Fortinbras' farewell strikes a different note, emphasising human reality not the metaphysical:

Let four captains
Bear Hamlet like a soldier to the stage,
For he was likely, had be been put on,
To have prov'd most royal; and for his passage,
The soldier's music and the rite of war
Speak loudly for him.

(Shakespeare 1982: 418)

Had Hamlet not been put upon by metaphysical concerns – had he not tragically learned of his predicament from his father's ghost and been deflected from social reality, he would have been a hero. He would have acted effectively in the real world through his interactions with other human beings.

The Hamlets of Sociology

Contemporary social theory assumes a dualistic ontology of structure and agency; the individual is confronted by an objective social reality. Certainly contemporary social theory argues that individuals contribute to the creation of this objective reality but it also insists that this reality can never be reduced merely to human social relations. In an unwitting echo of Parsons' middle and later period, contemporary social theorists across the entire political spectrum, from Giddens, Habermas and Bhaskar to Bourdieu and Foucault, try to explain how the individual reproduces this prior social structure. The lone individual confronts an imposing and distant structure. The dualistic ontology is now hegemonic and in this resides the irony and even the tragedy of sociology today, and these structures are maintained by a conceptual structure which directs individual action. A discipline whose primary discovery was the power of human social relations now disdains this living process in favour of static models which depict a deadened structure imposing upon the individual. Although irony escapes them, contemporary social theorists are academic Hamlets ignoring human social relations. They prefer to live in a world in which isolated individuals are confronted by a distant autonomous being, structure. For them, mere human social relations are inadequate. For these theorists, society cannot be explained merely by reference to the great flow of interactions between innumerable humans. Society has a structure which precedes and imposes upon the individual.

Hermeneutics, by contrast, recognises only social relations conducted on the basis of shared understandings. Given its disdain for social relations, it is logical that contemporary social theory should reject hermeneutics. Misunderstanding the implications of the social ontology, hermeneutics is imputed to be idealist, individualist and uncritical. Because hermeneutics insists that social reality cannot be explained without taking shared understandings into account, hermeneutics is accused of reducing society to the opinion which any individual has of it; whatever an individual believes to be reality is reality. Consequently, individuals are free to do whatever they want and no criticism of them is possible. Since these understandings define what that reality actually is, they can never be criticised, for they can never be inadequate to the social reality. On each of these counts, these theorists are wrong. Hermeneutics does not deny the often brutal reality of social action. It insists only that social relations cannot be comprehended without taking into account the common understandings on the basis of which humans interact with each other. The acts which humans perform and the effects which they have necessarily involve understanding. Humans have to understand what their acts *mean*. The act is not independent of the meaning which is imputed to it. This does not reduce social reality to individual opinion but it does insist that social reality cannot be comprehended independently of the collective beliefs about what it is. The misperception of hermeneutics seems to arise partly from a misunderstanding of the concept of interpretation. Due to its historical origins in textual exegesis, hermeneutics has always emphasised interpretation. Contemporary social theorists have consequently assumed that when applying hermeneutics to the social sciences this approach similarly prioritizes the way humans interpret their situation. The word 'interpretation' is misleading here. It implies a high level of reflexive activity on the part of the individual. It suggests that individuals personally interpret the situations in which they find themselves. The active process of individual interpretation is not denied by hermeneutics but, as far as hermeneutics is concerned, it is minimally a subordinate phenomenon in human social life. Social relations do not primarily involve individual interpretation of what they are about (normally made after the fact anyway) but shared understandings which are necessarily drawn upon by the participants. For hermeneutics, these shared understandings are central to social life for they define what that life will be. Social scientists interpret these understandings in order to comprehend the significance of social actions in particular contexts; in the course of social interaction, humans do not actually interpret these understandings. They act by reference to them. Their acts have the effect that they do give a shared body of understanding about what an action means in any particular culture. Hermeneutics is concerned with shared meanings, not individual interpretations. A hermeneutic sociology does not imply a focus on the personal interpretations of social actors. Hermeneutics interprets social relations in the light of the shared understandings on the basis of which people interact in any culture. It does not claim that social interaction is the product of individual interpretation.

Since social reality is constituted by the way social actors mutually define it, agency is not the property of the individual. Agency arises in the social relations between humans. An act only has the impact which it does when others recognise what it is intended to do. Even the most apparently powerful social agents have discretion conferred on them by others. Finally, since all human interaction is conducted on the basis of shared understandings, criticism can proceed only when the significance of these understandings is recognised. It is impossible to criticise a social relation without first understanding it because it is impossible to know what a human act actually is without some account of what the actor intended by it. The sociologist must understand the significance of certain practices in a particular culture, for this significance determines what they are. It is impossible to describe social relations without reference to these understandings and it is consequently impossible to criticise a particular society without engaging in some form of interpretation. Even to reject a social practice, the social scientist has to recognise what those people involved in it think they are doing. Hermeneutics never denied itself access to a social reality against which the claims of interested groups might be corroborated. However, it does understand this social reality in distinctive terms. Similarly, critique follows a hermeneutic spiral, unavoidably attending to the way local actors understand what they are doing which is initially judged from within a particular but not rigid cultural horizon. In the course of its analysis, hermeneutics transforms its own pre-suppositions and, in this way, comes to a better understanding of the society under study and of itself.

Despite its disdain for hermeneutics, contemporary social theory is, in fact, an immanent form of the social ontology. In every case, the institutional concept of structure is reducible to social networks, each involving active social relations between humans. States, corporations, classes and the economic system are all ultimately complex matrices of social relations between humans. These institutions are real but the relations which make up an institution are never independent of the understandings which people have of them. A social relation always involves a conceptual element but it no less real for all that. On the contrary, it is the conceptual element which renders it so binding. Humans mutually recognise the fact that they are obligated to each other. This recognition appears elusory and yet it is an utterly concrete power which binds humans together and sustains even the most apparently objective institution. Similarly, when Foucault, Bourdieu and Giddens invoke the idea of a conceptual structure which directs individual action, they are ultimately forced to admit that in every case the final tribunal of action is not the rule followed by the individual but the group. As members of groups, linked together in social relationships, humans together agree how they should conduct themselves. Humans look to each other to decide on how to go on and they hold each other mutually to that decision. The rule itself is silent. The social ontology promoted by hermeneutics is implicit in the work of every contemporary social theorist because society cannot be explained without reference to the social relations between humans. Social reality consists of social relations. These theorists all ultimately recognise social reality but they dare not speak its name.

Hermeneutics overcomes the contemporary social theory by replacing a dualistic ontology of structure and agency with a social one. For hermeneutics, social relations are the social reality. This is the premise of hermeneutic theory. As such, hermeneutics is not complex; indeed, it is obvious but its implications are profound. As Homans noted: 'I must freely acknowledge that everything I have said seems to me obvious. But why cannot we take the obvious seriously?' (Homans 1987: 15). Homans eventually slipped into individualism and finally biologism. Nevertheless, his advocacy of the obvious was important. By constantly returning to the obvious, sociologists avoid the false reification and abstraction which dualistic theories inevitably encounter. Hermeneutics offers a genuine grounding for contemporary social theory and above all else it demands a resolutely empirical programme of research. It demands from sociology not merely private contemplation about what social reality must be like but detailed empirical investigation of social reality in all its rich diversity. Hermeneutics insists that sociologists can analyse a social practice only by understanding it and such understanding is only possible once they have immersed themselves in the meaningful reality which they wish to investigate. Hermeneutics offers a fruitful path for sociological research into the new century. In the light of the profound transformations which the world is currently undergoing, as a new political and economic order is being developed which encompasses the entire globe in ever more tightly knit networks of interdependence, it is very important that hermeneutics and its emphasis on real empirical research are heeded. Unfortunately, contemporary sociology, especially in Europe, is dominated by dualism. Instead of attending to empirical detail, many contemporary sociologists prefer to promote abstract and formal models based on what social reality should be like; they blindly impose the dualistic model of structure and agency on the stream of social interaction. Indeed, ontological dualism has become more radical and the two sides of this dualism, structure and the individual, have increasingly fallen apart and remain almost beyond reconciliation. In sociology today, sterile objectivism or facile individualism has overtaken any genuinely sociological research. The reality of human social relations is effaced either by an abstract consideration of the social system or by a celebration of the putatively autonomous individual.

The Sociology of Life Itself

Classical sociology was concerned with illuminating and criticising European modernity. Marx, Weber and Durkheim all prioritised human social relations in order to account for the extraordinary development of modernity. Although Hegel's interests were philosophical, he was similarly concerned with the actuality of human social relations. Indeed, his decisive philosophical intervention was to demonstrate, against Kant, the centrality of social relations to human existence. Human history in all its bloody reality came before abstract philosophical speculation. Indeed, philosophy itself was a historical product, the intellectual manifestation of *Geist*. A 'hermeneutic' strand is detectable in all their writings, although Hegel, Marx, Weber and Durkheim never used such a term. They were all committed to a social ontology at certain points in their work. Indeed, the most powerful and enduring parts of their work were precisely where they promoted this social ontology. Hegel brilliantly recognised the dynamic properties of social interaction in his master–slave dialectic. Marx laid out a genuinely social ontology in *The Theses on Feuerbach* (1978) and employed this theory in his *Eighteenth Brumaire* (1977c) and in the last part of the first volume of *Capital* (1977b). Weber described a hermeneutic theory in his discussion of status groups which was empirically exemplified in his analysis of the Junkers and China. Durkheim's social ontology begins to emerge most clearly from *Suicide* (1952) and is exemplified in his brilliant analysis of primitive religion. There the potency of human social relations is described with brilliant force.

Contemporary sociology should draw on classical sociology; it should resurrect this collective memory in order to sustain itself. The discipline can be re-invigorated through a creative fusion with the past. Giddens is correct that 'any appropriation we make from nineteenth-century social thought has to be a thoroughly critical one'; these texts have to be re-interpreted in the light of the current context to elucidate their significance and an attempt has been made here with such an end in mind. Yet, he is wrong when he claims that 'these ideas must be radically overhauled today' (Giddens 1988: 1). This re-appropriation of classical sociology does not require nearly as thoroughgoing a reformation of the writings of Marx, Weber and Durkheim as Giddens advocates. Some of the passages in these classical texts are examples of sociological analysis at its most powerful. Sociologists today are concerned with different empirical matters, and the society which they are analysing has changed very significantly, but the best writings of Marx, Weber and Durkheim can never be superseded in the manner which Giddens suggests. They employ a social ontology in a manner which can be followed almost exactly today. In each case, contemporary social practices must be understood as the historical products of social relations between humans. Sociologists should examine the way that social relations and the understandings on which they are based are undergoing immanent transformation as humans locked in social relations, in groups and in institutions, demand changes from each other. Sociologists should trace the new webs of social relations which now encompass the entire globe. One of the most important lessons which classical sociology teaches is that sociology cannot proceed in advance of the empirical material to hand. The social ontology demands empirical research. Analysis follows immersion into the actuality of empirical reality rather than the assertive application of assumed categories to a shallow understanding of actuality. Classical sociology cannot instruct exactly which social phenomenon are the most important in contemporary society – sociologists must decide that for themselves – but it demands that, as sociologists, they open themselves to social phenomena. Sociologists need to immerse themselves in the visceral reality of social life. Sociologists need to find our own *foci* of empirical interest which illuminate contemporary society, in the way that Marx discovered the factory, Weber the Junkers and Durkheim religion. Once sociologists have oriented themselves in the first instance to reality – and not to their immediate understanding of what reality must be – the theoretical framework outlined in the most important works of classical sociology provides the grounding for the analysis of that particular social practice. While ontological dualism is obsolete, classical sociology provides a rich resource for a social ontology. Of course, contemporary social theorists implicitly recognise all this. In the margins of their work, the social ontology is powerfully re-stated. Society is a complex web of social relations between people out of which arise even the largest and most powerful institutions. Society is hopelessly misrepresented by the mechanics of structure and agency. Society should not be seen as a structure but as an ever shifting sea of social relations, sustained through an endless current of exchange and counter-exchange, each one involving active human consciousness.

As Hegel completed *The Phenomenology of Spirit* to the accompaniment of the bloody reality of European history outside his very study, he described the early nineteenth century as a 'birth-time'. He correctly recognised the dramatic forces of social transformation which were coursing through Europe at the time. It is clear that, nearly, two hundred years after the *Phenomenology* was written, Europe is now once again in another 'birth-time'. The revolution which Europe is currently undergoing may, at the moment, be less bloody than the post-Revolutionary world which Hegel knew but the transformation of the social order may be even more profound. The increasing dominance of multinational corporations and the financial markets has produced very significant transformations in the kinds of social solidarities which are currently developing. The unified nation-state is being subverted by these global economic forces, which are promoting transformations at the regional, national and supranational levels. One of the central features of the new global economy is the development of new forms of communication which facilitate a thickening of transnational social and economic ties. The nation-state is being re-shaped by mass immigration into all western European countries. This is minimally demanding a new concept of nationhood and is producing increasing social antagonism at the local level between immigrant and indigenous groups. The international order which crystallised in the eighteenth century and was ratified after the eventual defeat of Napoleon in 1815 is currently unravelling. While it will certainly remain a critical institution for the foreseeable future, the nation-state is no longer always the primary unit of mobilisation and identification. New forms of solidarity and new political institutions are emerging whose form is still only obscure.

In order to study these extraordinary historical transformations, it is useful to follow the lead of classical sociology and to employ the social ontology to analyse specific empirical developments. The best perspective on current changes is likely to be given by carrying out hermeneutic research into particular areas of contemporary social life. Generalising upon abstractions only confirms the prejudices of the theorists and does not contribute to an understanding of reality. In order to illuminate present transformations, any empirical area of investigation is equally valid here as long as it is studied in its full social and historical context. It would be possible to study political developments at the level of the European Commission or the state, business and economic transformations, the rise of new social movements, educational changes, scientific advances, the media, new forms of art or even sport. All these areas would illuminate the processes of historical change. Yet, there is one area of human activity whose centrality to the present era has become increasingly apparent in the last decade: warfare. While the apocalyptical prospect of the Cold War has receded, the threat of violent conflict at any point in the globe has increased. In the light of the new threat of terrorism and the development of a unilateral and interventionist United States foreign policy, civilians are now confronted with the threat of immediate and random violence at almost any location. Consequently, warfare may provide a particularly apposite focus of study today as its threat is diffused throughout the world. In Europe, warfare has become an increasingly important topic of political concern and there have been extensive discussions about the possibility of a unified European foreign policy to counter the new threats which confront nation-states today. Some European states have begun to consider the desirability of a European military capability in the light of this new strategic context. The terrorist attack on 11 September 2001 and the subsequent Afghan and Iraqi wars have only emphasised the importance of this strategic issue. The question of war is a central issue in contemporary society and, consequently, it should be a crucial area for sociological research. As an analytical focus, warfare has some particular heuristic advantages. Since military action is one of the most sensitive areas of state policy, the development of military capability will reveal the inter-relations between nation-states and illuminate the possible re-negotiation of national sovereignty with particular clarity. An analysis of military capability may provide an empirical illustration of the actual processes of historical trans-formation in the way that the factory illuminated historic processes in the middle of the nineteenth century for Marx. In specific reference to Europe, the possible development of a joint military capability may provide a useful focus for the development of the European Union. It may illuminate the political reality of Europe today with particular clarity.

Sociology cannot understand the development of European defence collabo-ration, the development of new military strategies or new forms of terrorism by reference to structure and agency. The dualistic ontology cannot explain the fluid and dynamic processes of transformation which are currently occurring.[1] European military developments, for instance, will not be the product of struc-ture, nor of individuals singly reproducing or transforming institutional structure. All the institutions which might be termed 'structure' by dualistic sociologists are in every instance reducible to networks of social relations in particular locations in Europe. The development of military capability involves powerful institutions but, in every case, these consist of co-ordinated social relations between humans and have to be understood in terms of these social networks. National governments are complex networks of politicians and bureaucrats, mutually influencing each other. These networks are themselves related to others, the media, corporations, pressure groups, and to the differentiated mass of citizens. Similarly, the Commission, NATO and the various national militaries also finally consist only of a complex series of social networks and interrelated social groups. When Tony Blair announced Britain's commitment to the European Defence and Security Policy in St Malo in 1998, he was not reproducing or transforming structure. He was announcing the development of new institutional relationships between Britain and France, which would form the basis of any coherent defence policy. Certainly, there were institutional pressures which drove Blair towards this alliance at that time, but these pressures were themselves traceable to certain strategically situated groups and networks. A European defence capability will emerge insofar as these groups in various European countries develop social rela-tions of sufficient strength that new social alliances develop at political and military levels which are oriented to new collective norms. At the political level, the governments of member states, assisted by the Commission, will have to develop sufficiently similar interests that they can pool their sovereignty in the sphere of defence if any European force is conceivable.

Yet, European defence capability cannot be studied merely at the political level. The reality of any defence capability will rely on the actual armed forces themselves. At the military level, national forces will need to develop similar professional cultures so that they can work alongside each other. These new pan-European forces will emerge only if there is sufficient interaction between military professionals that they are able to develop shared understandings which genuinely enjoin collective action from them. The officer corps in each country is critical here since it determines how forces are employed strategically and operationally. Since the end of the Cold War, the British officer corps has consciously developed new forms of 'doctrine' in recognition of the changing strategic context which confronts the British armed forces. This doctrine has emphasised the need for flexibility and co-operation because deployments in the new era are most likely to take an expeditionary or interventionist form (Joint Warfare Publication 2001). The officer corps has attempted to develop a command culture which will meet the demands of these kinds of deployments. By contrast, the German officer corps has responded quite differently to the current strategic situation. Faced with a different political and historical context, German officers have displayed only limited interest in British doctrine and methods (Sarotte 2001: 18). They regard international intervention as politically dangerous and protect universal conscription as a means of tying the military to civil society. The prospects of a common European military culture arising out of close social ties between the military elites of member states is extremely unlikely. Yet, whether a common culture emerges or does not, a dualistic ontology is obsolete in understanding current developments. Neither developments at the level of the state nor the transformation of the officer corps in Europe can be explicated and understood by reference to structure and agency. In every case, the sociologist encounters only social networks which mutually agree upon certain forms of action. Whatever form the European defence policy takes, it will involve the social relations between groups in various locations in Europe. This complex interaction will be conducted on the basis of shared meanings and from it new social groups may arise. The development of a European defence policy cannot be usefully understood as structures which are reproduced by the agent. They consist of networks of social relations which flow dynamically over time as the humans in them develop new relationships and affirm old ones with each other. Such a hermeneutic account of European defence policy does not reduce this social reality to individual opinion; nor does it suggest that individuals in this emergent reality can do as they please. The individuals who are part of these institutions are bound into mutually sustaining social relations which constitute what these institutions are and what they can do. A dualistic ontology ossifies the mercurial stream of social relations. It is analytically ineffective because it has no understanding of what social reality actually is.

It is the role of sociology to illuminate emergent social forms. As Hegel famously noted 'the owl of Minerva flies only at dusk'. It is difficult to recognise the historical significance of certain social transformations as they are occurring; only later does their true importance appear. Hegel may have been right, but perhaps by observing empirical reality from a hermeneutic perspective sociology can gain a pre-emptive vision of the 'birth-time' in which we are now living.

Sociology may be able to provide an early glimpse of the new dawn but it will not do so by flying into a cloud of theoretical abstractions premised on ontological dualism. Sociology may be capable of providing a foresight, if it proceeds on a sound theoretical basis and orients itself in the first instance to empirical realities. If sociology commits itself to the social ontology given by hermeneutics and looks to the way various forms of life actually operate before it assumes how they must in fact work, then sociology may be able to illuminate the present. Above all, sociology must overcome the indifference towards what humans actually do which predominates in social theory today. Against contemporary social theory's disdain for human life, sociologists must cultivate a fascination for human social relations in all their rich diversity. This fascination demands the closest observation of the details of human social practice. The world in which sociologists live is human and, consequently, for all its brutalities and inanities, this is the world which they must explain. To efface this world in favour of abstractions and reifications is not to produce a better world or a better account of the real world; it is to do nothing. Indeed, it is to do worse than nothing, for this analytical inactivity is only a misdirected and pointless form of activity. Inactive sociology will not have the disastrous effects of Hamlet's disdain for human existence but it will minimise the relevance of the discipline. The discipline will continue to train students for employment but it will not illuminate to them the distinctive reality of this social order – or human existence more generally. Simultaneously, it will perpetuate an ever more insular professional status group whose members bore rather than inspire one another. As such, sociology will be a desiccated occupation. Marx, Weber and Durkheim were evidently entranced by the strange reality of human society and their best writings effuse a sense of wonder at that reality. Unfortunately, most contemporary sociologists prefer to disdain the vibrant reality of social relations in favour of the marble simplicities of ontological dualism. Life delights them not. It is important now to turn back to life.

Notes

1 Structure and Agency

1 Although William Sewell is concerned that Giddens' concept of structure is objectivist, he ultimately affirms Giddens' ontological position. Employing the concept of structure in the conceptual sense, he proposes ways in which it can be rendered more flexible and open to individual transformation, but the dualistic ontology of structuration theory endures: 'Agents are empowered by structures, both by the knowledge of cultural schemas that enables them to mobilize resources and by the access to resources that enables them to enact schemas' (Sewell 1992: 27).

2 See Chapters 3 and 4 for a longer discussion of the dualism of these contemporary social theories.

3 In his Wittgensteinian critique of 'critical social theory', Nigel Pleasants has described this hegemony as a 'new consensus' in contemporary social theory, which he similarly believes consists of ontological realism but also epistemological relativism (1999: 5).

4 Interestingly Luhmann cannot sustain his objectivism and in his writing he has to appeal to the concept of trust. He has to admit that, at certain points, social order is explicable only when the consciously shared understandings of humans are taken into account. Humans trust each other when they recognise that others are committed to the same values and ends.

5 In the fields of gender and race, the same dualism is detectable and, in both, there has been a shift from a focus on structure (e.g Rex 1983, 1986; Rex and Moore 1967) to the individual (Kristeva 1993; Jackson 1999; Lash and Featherstone 2001; Nederveen Pietersee 2001; Gilroy 2001). Michael Banton's work is interesting here because, despite its flawed attempt to provide a rational choice account of racial discrimination, it in fact operates with a genuine social ontology (Banton 1983).

6 For a longer discussion of Baudrillard, see King 1998a, 1998b.

7 Touraine's work on new social movements and his critique of 'classical' accounts of class affirm that the political ontology of modern society does not consist of individuals confronting an objective economic reality but of groups of individuals coalescing to monopolise and indeed create opportunities for themselves (Touraine 1971, 1981). However, Touraine himself is guilty of descending into exactly the kind of dualism which he rejects in the works of others. The individual subject becomes the focus of attention and is contrasted with the institutional reality of modern society. He ultimately adopts a position similar to the later Giddens, Hall, Lash and Urry (Touraine 1988, 1995).

8 Elias is mistaken in thinking that modern manners replaced merely natural behaviours. Medieval conventions were as socially developed as modern ones; they were simply different.

9 Michel Foucault, of course, has made an important contribution to the analysis of this dual process of state and individual formation. It is the fundamental theme of his

entire *oeuvre* and he traces the dual rise of the 'subject' and new state bureaucracies through an examination of mental institutions, medical practice, knowledge and sexuality, but he captures this dual movement most strikingly (and perhaps most successfully) in his work on prisons, *Discipline and Punish*.

10 See Alasdair MacIntyre's work for further discussion of the rise of the modern individual (MacIntyre 1986; also Taylor 1989).

2 The Relevance of Parsons

1 Although Joas has suggested that Parsons' convergence thesis is contrived and unconvincing – Simmel is omitted because he does not fit the thesis (Joas 1996: 20) – Parsons was, in fact, correct about the close affinity between the positions adopted by Weber and Durkheim.

2 There are other passages in *The Structure of Social Action* when the initial references to the concept of social structure, as opposed to social relations, appear (e.g. Parsons 1966a: 39).

3 This shift in focus from action to the social system is highlighted by the fact that this stage in Parsons' career is often termed his 'structural-functionalist' period (Parsons 1952: 19; P. Hamilton 1983: 19). It is easy to see why the works written in this period have been interpreted as objectivist, since Parsons' writing is bleakly abstract in these works. Rocher maintains that this middle period is better characterised as 'systemic' rather than structural-functionalist (Rocher 1974: 155).

4 It is interesting to compare this description of roles and their function with one which Parsons gives earlier in the work: 'Since a social system is a system of processes of interaction between actors, it is a structure of relations between actors involved in the interactive process which is essentially the structure of the social system' (Parsons 1952: 25). This account of roles is consistent with his voluntary theory of action. Individuals mutually sustain their social roles by adherence to certain common values to which they publicly commit themselves. Unfortunately, Parsons resorts to a dualistic account of the social system thereafter.

5 In a somewhat contrived manner, Parsons tried to argue that the AGIL model was directly compatible with the pattern variables. In fact, the only obvious parallel between the two besides their formalism was that they both operated with four categories.

6 As Alexander rightly argues, Parsons' formalism becomes bizarrely arbitrary at various moments in his middle and third period (e.g. Alexander 1983: 157–58, 174, 182, 230).

7 As Joas has noted, 'Gouldner's polemic was part of a wider reaction against Parsons which has ensured the continued misreading of him today' (Joas 1996: 7–8).

8 In a recent publication, Barry Barnes (2000) has argued on similar lines to those forwarded here that there is a close connection between Talcott Parsons and Anthony Giddens. Zygmunt Bauman has also noted that Giddens skirts 'dangerously close to Parsons' (Bauman 1989: 42) because he wants to incorporate 'both voluntary and knowledgeable actors and the system' and therefore returns to 'the dual concern which triggered Parsons' work in *The Structure of Social Action*' (Bauman 1989: 42). Similarly, Mestrovic argues that, like Parsons, Giddens is still overwhelmingly concerned with the (modernist) problem of order (Mestrovic 1998: 3). However, although Bauman and Mestrovic point to the Parsonianism of Giddens' structuration theory, they do not develop this connection. Bauman promotes a hermeneutic social theory, while Mestrovic mounts a broader political and cultural polemic against Giddens.

9 It is possible that Parsons' notion of latency implicitly recognised the curious status of this kind of everyday, taken-for-granted knowledge.

10 Some critics, such as Archer (1982), have argued that structuration theory involves an unsustainable confusion of analytical (and ontological) levels.

11 When Giddens employs the term 'structures' in the plural, he refers to the institutional realities of the social system and not to the virtual rules and resources of 'structure' (in the singular).

3 Structure, Habitus, Discourse

1 Bourdieu has written on a wide range of subjects, which include social theory (1977a, 1990a), ethnography (1977a, 1979), education (1977b, 1988b, 1996a, 1996b), culture and class and consumption (1984). A small cottage industry has grown up around the various fields in which Bourdieu has worked; for instance, concerning his analysis of culture, see Fowler (1996, 1997); or for his examination of education, see Archer (1983) and Gorder (1980).
2 Commentators have also defined the habitus in this way (e.g. Garnham 1986: 425; Jenkins 1993: 81; Schatzki 1987: 133).
3 Bourdieu claims that there is a direct linkage of taste to economic conditions, which Schatzki rightly criticises as a category error (1987: 131–32).
4 See Evens (1999: 15–16).
5 As David Bloor has emphasised, there is an inevitable uncertainty about the future application of any rules. He calls this indeterminacy 'rule finitism' (Bloor 1983, 1997). Rules do not have an infinite realm of application. They apply only to a limited array of cases and, even then, the next application is uncertain.
6 For the rule-individualist argument to be sustainable, certain internal mental processes would have to be identifiable which independently prescribed individual action in each case. The mental process ensures that different individuals always take a rule the same way independently of each other. For Wittgenstein, such mental processes independently directing rule-following are simply not identifiable; and Wittgenstein repeatedly employs the examples of mathematics, the use of colour words and pain to illustrate the point. He employs these examples because they seem to support an internalist and mentalist account of rule-following most strongly but in each case the supposedly decisive internal processes determine nothing (see Kripke 1982). Public social agreement is the basis of rule-following.
7 David Bloor has argued that Winch's discussion of legal reasoning returns to exactly the kind of rationalist and individualist account of rule-following which Wittgenstein rejected (Bloor 1983: 170–81). In fact, a Wittgensteinian account of rule-following is recoverable from Winch.
8 The existence of these two contradictory strands within Bourdieu's writing explain the notably mixed reception of his work by commentators. On the one hand, the critics who have focused on the notion of the habitus have argued that this concept slips back into exactly the kind of objectivism Bourdieu refutes (e.g. Evens 1999; Schatzki 1987, 1997; Bouveresse 1995; Brubaker 1985; Jenkins 1982, 1993; DiMaggio 1979; Garnham and Williams 1980; Lamont and Lareau 1988; de Certeau 1988). On the other hand, certain other commentators highlighting those 'practical' passages of Bourdieu's work maintain that he has gone a long way towards overcoming the dualism of structure and agency, presenting a genuine advance in social theory (e.g. Wacquant 1987; Harker 1984; Taylor 1993; Dreyfus and Rabinow 1993).
9 In fact this passage slips towards the very objectivism to which the notion of 'fuzziness' is opposed.

4 The Reality of Realism

1 At this point, Bhaskar's transformational model of social action becomes almost indistinguishable from structuration theory and Bhaskar deliberately points up this connection (Bhaskar 1979: 45).

2   The very different philosophical styles and resources upon which Bhaskar and
    Habermas have respectively drawn have obscured any underlying similarity between
    their social philosophies. Nevertheless, both are concerned with social emancipation
    and the development of a critical theory and both have been influenced by Adorno, if
    only negatively in the case of Habermas.

3   Habermas demonstrates the close connection between those contemporary theorists
    like Giddens, Foucault and Bourdieu who focus on structure as a system of rules and
    those realists like Bhaskar who use the term 'structure' to refer to institutional reali-
    ties. Habermas demands a universal ethics which is culturally specific and, as with the
    original ideal speech situation, he asserts that two basic conditions attend upon
    discourse ethics. Firstly, the principles agreed in the course of discourse are universal
    (U), and secondly they are agreed in discourse (D) (Habermas 1990: 65). Individuals
    will put themselves in each others' shoes (Habermas 1995a: 49). In this way, the ethics
    will be universal because in discourse when people agree intersubjectively they must
    rationally accept only those principles which can be accepted by all. Although
    Habermas seems to emphasise social processes by which groups establish shared
    meanings for themselves, discourse ethics eventually denies this interactive dimension.
    There is no real debate or negotiation here. The principles underlying discourse are
    universal and can be rejected only if an individual reneges on a consensus itself. As
    with Giddens, Bourdieu and Foucault, Habermas postulates the existence of certain
    independent rules which prescribe only one possible outcome, thereby ensuring the
    reproduction of the system. There is no genuine interaction on Habermas' discourse
    model, just as there was none in the various descriptions of structure, habitus and
    discourse. Discourse ethics finally imposes upon the individual, limiting action to one
    possible and putatively rational course. In this way, Habermas demonstrates the close
    consensus in contemporary social theory.

5   Hegel and the Concept of *Geist*

1   In the *Philosophy of Right*, Hegel proposed that the dialectical development of human
    consciousness overcame not only philosophical dualisms but also the political divide
    between citizens and state. Absolute Spirit appeared in the political actuality of the
    post-Napoleonic Prussian state. The Prussian state embodied in actuality the
    moments of universality, particularity and individuality in a final adequate form.

2   The immanence of *Geist* is expressed at other points in Hegel's writing (e.g. Hegel
    1977: 184), where he rejects psychological models of cognition which regard indi-
    vidual cognition as a mirror which merely represents the external world.

3   Kaufman has discussed the meaning of *Geist*, noting that the word also means
    'breath' and 'wind' and is etymologically related to 'yeast' and 'geyser'. The word
    refers to a moving force, the essence of life (Kaufmann 1966: 269).

6   From Praxis to Historical Materialism

1   Gramsci satirised the reductionism of Feuerbach's premise that 'man is what he eats'
    (Gramsci 1971: 354): 'If this assertation were true, then the determining force or
    matrix of history would be the kitchen and revolutions would coincide with radical
    changes in the diet of the masses' (Gramsci 1971: 354).

2   Alasdair MacIntyre has similarly argued that Marx was unfortunately unable to apply
    the insights from the *Theses of Feuerbach* to the rest of his work (MacIntyre 1998).

3   The sentences which precede the famous phrase about hand-mills affirm Marx's
    ontological dualism. Significantly, Marx argues that 'social relations are closely bound
    up with productive forces'. Against the *Theses*, productive forces consisting decisively
    of technologies stand apart from social relations.

4 Production is similarly prior in *Grundrisse* (Marx 1973: 50). The same ontological dualism is evident in his discussions about class (Marx 1977a: 53).

7 Status Groups and the Protestant Ethic

1 Although Randall Collins has claimed (1986) that Weber's *General Economic History* illuminates the minor position of the Protestant Ethic thesis in Weber's corpus, that work in fact concludes with an important discussion of Protestantism. The Protestant Ethic thesis is still given a decisive role in explaining the rise of capitalism.

2 Oakes, for instance, cites the interesting empirical example of the medieval entrepreneur, Godric of Norfolk; in a fit of remorse at the wealth which he had accumulated, Godric gave all his property to the Church and became a hermit (Oakes 1988: 85). This example, however, does not seem to show that there were no rational merchants in the medieval period; Godric was certainly rational as an entrepreneur. It seems to illustrate rather that in this period the Church was politically and culturally dominant. The rational practices of businessmen were not always given the legitimacy that they would receive later, driving some of them, like Godric, to extreme actions.

3 According to Hugh Trevor-Roper (1967), the Reformation precipitated an authoritarian reaction by the Catholic Church in an attempt to defend itself. This reaction obstructed the activities of entrepreneurs in Italy and Spain, in particular, and consequently from the end of the sixteenth century there was a migration of entrepreneurial talent from southern to northern Europe. Many of these southern entrepreneurs became Protestants as they moved north, for similar reasons presumably as the Protestant converts whom Weber saw in America. Trevor-Roper emphasises not the theological details of Protestantism and certainly no intrinsic psychological logic which drove individual entrepreneurs (he notes that successful Protestants were as keen to display their wealth as any of the Medicis or Fuggers), but the broadly Erasmian culture of Holland and England in particular, where reforming sects were accepted tolerantly.

4 In fact, Weber rejected the notion that *The Protestant Ethic* involved a purely psychological mechanism in which an autonomous idea compelled the individual to act in particular ways: 'He [Fischer] even accuses me of an "idealist interpretation of history", deriving capitalism from Luther. I emphatically rejected any such "foolish" thesis' (Chalcraft and Harrington 2001: 32). Against Rachfahl's accusation of idealism, Weber adopted a similar line: 'Yet, my critic offers not the slightest evidence for his audacious assumption that I was undertaking an idealist interpretation of history' (Chalcraft and Harrington 2001: 45). Weber also claimed that he had argued that Protestantism was only one factor in the rise of capitalism: 'I portray them only as one constitutive element among others of this "spirit"' (Chalcraft and Harrington 2001: 71). Yet, elsewhere, he decisively retracts that claim and once again re-affirms his idealism:

> It is simply untrue when Rachfahl claims out of the blue that the 'vocational ethic' known to 'ascetic' Protestantism (in my sense) prevailed in the Middle Ages as well. The point is that 'ascetic' Protestantism has created for capitalism a corresponding 'soul', the soul of a 'man with a calling' who *does not need* the same means of feeling at one with his actions as the man of the Middle Ages.

> (Chalcraft and Harrington 2001: 73)

For all his qualifications, Weber holds an unmodified position.

5 Weber's ideal types are also an example of his idealism. With the ideal types, he commits himself to a formal analytical Kantianism, but the ideal types are not merely

analytical. At various points, there is a heavy suggestion that the ideas embodied in them direct individual action in particular historical eras.

8 Society and Ritual

1   While Durkheim dismisses imitation as a psychological cause of suicide, he recognises that there are cases of suicide by contagion when large numbers of individuals in a social group commit suicide together in the face of certain threats. Unlike imitation, contagion proves Durkheim's point: the cause of suicide is not to be sought in individual psychology but rather in certain social factors: 'The conclusion is forced that they all depend on a more general state which all more or less faithfully reflect...We must investigate this state without wasting time on its distant repercussions in the consciousness of individuals' (Durkheim 1952: 149).

2   This is an example of Durkheim arguing somewhat tendentiously by elimination (Lukes 1973: 32). Although it might be unlikely, it is not impossible that there might be random factors which impel individuals in each case to commit suicide though these unrelated factors occur with the same annual frequency across the population, giving rise to a stable suicide rate.

3   Durkheim's suggestion that social facts should be treated at things has provoked consistent misunderstanding. However, at least at one level, this aphorism should be read only as a methodological injunction. Sociologists should try to adopt a dispassionate relationship to their subject of study, attempting to rid their analysis of obviously ideological or moralising elements. As Durkheim notes, 'Good and evil do not exist for science' (Durkheim 1966: 47). Sociologists should not study suicide or crime from the perspective that these activities are wrong but rather with a view to discovering how it is that certain suicide or crime rates persist in any particular society.

4   In the secondary literature, some critics have argued that there was a break in Durkheim's work after 1895, when ideas became more important than social forces (Lukes 1973; Alexander 1982; Parsons 1966a). Others have against this break (Giddens 1972, 1992; Nisbet 1967; K. Thompson 1982). On my reading, there is no absolute break in his work, for social interaction is present in *The Division of Labour* and in all his earlier works.

5   This passage should not be read as implying that away from the group humans return to some primordial individual existence. This particular group consciousness fades as social relations to other humans become more important. Humans are effectively embedded in other social relations, themselves sacred, which may begin to take precedence.

6   Parsons (1966a) rightly recognised a convergence between these two theorists. He rightly noted that Durkheim's study of ritual exemplified the voluntary theory of action but he wrongly suggested that the outlines of this same theory could be seen in Weber's notion of charisma. In fact, his interpretation of Weber's description of charisma was contrived and forced. Parsons failed to note the passages in which Weber explicitly and obviously committed himself to the voluntary theory: his empirical and theoretical work on status groups.

9 Hermeneutics and Idealism

1   Richard Rorty adopts a similar ontological position to hermeneutics (1997: 5) and has been similarly criticised for his putative idealism.

2   Mueller-Vollmer claims that Dilthey was wrong about Schleiermacher's intuitionism (Mueller-Vollmer 1986: 8).

3   It is a curious fact that, despite Heidegger's practical orientation and his recognition that the *Dasein* could develop only by 'being-in-the-world', he failed to recognise that modern technology was also a form of meaningful existence. Heidegger rejected modern technology as inauthentic (Heidegger 1996b). Yet, the development and use of technology has always pre-supposed certain shared ways of being-in-the-world.

4   Heidegger's famous discussion of Van Gogh's *Peasant's Shoes* repeats the point. This painting did not represent these shoes objectively but illuminated the place which this idea of peasant life had in contemporary European culture (Heidegger 1996a).

5   Searle has recently made the same argument with typical elegance (Searle 1995: 33).

10 Hermeneutics and Individualism

1   Similarly, although Barnes describes himself as an interactionist, his belief that social relations are constituted by the knowledge of the participants in them aligns him closely with Gadamer. Barnes notes that the knowledge which constitutes society is self-referring; the very knowledge or belief in some aspect of social reality brings that into existence: 'Our beliefs constitute the context which makes them what they are' (Barnes 1988: 49).

2   The sociology of agency reveals that the philosophical paradoxes of compatibilism and incompatibilism, of freedom and determinism are the product of a misconception. Humans are conceived of as being free or determined only insofar as they are viewed as isolated individuals.

3   In some cases Goffman seems to commit himself to reductive individualism. Goffman's individualism emerges most strongly in *The Presentation of Self in Everyday Life*, where the concept of the 'backstage' implies a unified individual identity behind each encounter (Goffman 1984: 114–15). Goffman is not alone in this interactionist tradition in seeming to promote an individualist account of social interaction. In his famous analysis of Agnes, the transvestite male, Garfinkel adopts a similar position. Agnes was born male but, always convinced of his femininity, he gradually transformed himself into a woman, reflexively adopting contemporary forms of feminine dress and behaviour. For Garfinkel, Agnes constitutes a usefully extreme example of a universal phenomenon – the reflexive creation of a social identity (Garfinkel 1967). The Agnes case implies that humans can reflexively always do otherwise. Individuals can create and transform themselves.

4   The work of Howard Becker (1971) confirms Goffman's argument about the social basis of individual agency.

5   Following Durkheim and Goffman, Randall Collins has illustrated the social production of the self through a sociology of philosophy (Collins 2000). He has shown that intellectual production has never been the result of private and personal genius but always emerges within a particular social milieu.

6   Milgram uses the phrase 'agentic state' to describe the subordination of the individual to authority. Barnes has noted the irony of this term since the phrase neatly captures the reality of human agency which Milgram misunderstands (Barnes 2000: 58–60). Human agency is a social product depending on other people. Humans necessarily act as agents for others.

7   Milgram's nine points were: 1. People are dominated by an administrative not moral outlook. 2. A distinction between personal feelings and duty is drawn. 3. Individual values are derived from the institution. 4. Euphemisms guard against the moral implications of the act. 5. Responsibility shifts upwards. 6. Actions are justified by a set of constructive purposes. 7. It is bad form to object to events. 8. There are psychological adjustments to ease the strain of immoral orders. 9. Career aspirations and technical routines dominate (Milgram 1974: 204–05).

8   Interestingly, Barnes argues that the attribution of freedom to an individual involves precisely the opposite. To impute freedom to others is to demand that they act

according to group understandings and in line with group interests. To be called a free actor is to be denied the possibility of any personal agency whatsoever.

11 Hermeneutics and Critique

1   Although hermeneutics and interactionism share fundamental presumptions, both promoting a social ontology, it is on the issue of critique that hermeneutics demonstrates itself to be a wide-ranging theory. As this chapter is intended to show, hermeneutics has explicitly developed a critical 'method' which follows from the social ontology, while this critique is only implicit in interactionism. Consequently, at this point hermeneutics encompasses interactionism, and it is for this reason that a hermeneutic rather than an interactionist sociology is promoted in this book, even though the close connection between the two traditions is recognised throughout.

2   Habermas is not alone in forwarding this line of argument against Gadamer. It has become commonplace to accuse his philosophical hermeneutics of being uncritical (Warnke 1987: 136–37; Skinner 1985: 37; Wellmer 1974: 46–50; J. Wolff 1975a: 816; 1975b: 123; Eagleton 1983: 73). Foucault also rejects hermeneutics because it is putatively uncritical. In his archaeologies, Foucault wants to circumvent interpretation entirely, for interpretations necessarily imply the creation of knowledge and therefore power. Foucault's archaeology does not want to implicate itself with power in any way and consequently he believes that his archaeological method merely presents discourses objectively as the monuments which they are (Foucault 1972: 138–39). His analysis of discourses is in fact an interpretation. Foucault is simply deluded to deny that a hermeneutic process lies at the heart of his entire work.

3   I am indebted here to Nigel Pleasants' interesting discussion of Winch's article on the Zande and its philosophical implications (Pleasants 2000).

4   Habermas' critical theory attempts to reconcile Hegel and Kant. He accepts Hegel's critique of Kant's categorical imperative that any morality is inseparable from a particular ethical life but insists, nevertheless, that, while there is a diversity of ethical lives, certain universals are detectable in line with Kant's transcendental critique (Habermas 1995a: 1–13). In effect, with his discourse ethics he wants to retain the form and force of Kant's categorical imperative while attending to Hegel's concern with the actuality of life.

12 Beyond Structure and Agency

1   See Archer (1979) or Mouzelis (1995) for an attempt to perform sociological analysis by reference to a dualistic ontology.

Bibliography

Adorno, T. (1973) *The Jargon of Authencity*, trans. K. Tarnowski and F. Will, London: Routledge and Kegan Paul.

——(1990) *Negative Dialectics*, trans. E. Ashton, London: Routledge.

Albrow, M. (1970) *Bureaucracy*, London: Macmillan.

Alexander, J. (1982) *Theoretical Logic in Sociology, Volume 1: positivism, presuppositions and current controversies*, London: Routledge and Kegan Paul.

——(1983) *Theoretical Logic in Sociology, Volume 3: the classical attempt at theoretical synthesis: Max Weber*, London: Routledge and Kegan Paul.

——(1984) *Theoretical Logic in Sociology, Volume 4: the modern reconstruction of classical thought: Talcott Parsons*, London: Routledge and Kegan Paul.

——(1996) 'Critical Reflections on *Reflexive Modernization*', *Theory, Culture and Society*, 13(4): 133–38.

Alexander, J. and Giesen, B. (1987) 'Introduction: From Reduction to Linkage: the long view of the micro-macro debate', in Alexander, J. Giesen, B. Munch, R. and Smelser, N. (eds) (1987) *The Micro–Macro Link*, London: University of California.

Alexander, J. Giesen, B. Munch, R. and Smelser, N. (eds) (1987) *The Micro–Macro Link*, London: University of California.

Anderson, P. (1993) *Lineages of the Absolutist State*, London: New Left Books.

Andrevski, S. (1984) *Max Weber's Insights and Errors*, London: Routledge and Kegan Paul.

Archer, M. (1979) *Social Origins of Educational Systems*, London: Sage.

——(1982) 'Morphogenesis versus Structuration: on combining structure and action', *British Journal of Sociology*, 33(4): 456–83.

——(1983) 'Process Without System', *Archives européennes de sociologie*, 24(1): 196–221.

——(1988) *Culture and Agency: the place of culture in social theory*, Cambridge: Cambridge University Press.

——(1995) *Realist Social Theory: the morphogenetic approach*, Cambridge: Cambridge University Press.

——(1996) 'Social Integration and System Integration: developing the distinction', *Sociology*, 30(4): 679–99.

——(2000) *Being Human: the problems of agency*, Cambridge: Cambridge University Press.

Aron, R. (1965) *Main Currents in Social Theory, Volume 1*, trans. R. Howard and H. Weaver, London: Weidenfeld and Nicolson.

Avineri, S. (1968) *The Social and Political Thought of Karl Marx*, Cambridge: Cambridge University Press.

Baert, P. (1998) *Social Theory in the Twentieth Century*, Cambridge: Polity.

Baker, G. and Hacker, P. (1988) *Wittgenstein: Rules, Grammar and Necessity, Volume 2: an analytical commentary on the Philosophical Investigations*, Oxford: Blackwell.

Banton, M. (1983) *Racial and Ethnic Competition*, Cambridge: Cambridge University Press.

Barnes, B. (1988) *The Nature of Power*, Cambridge: Polity.

——(1995) *The Elements of Social Theory*, London: University College London.

——(2000) *Understanding Agency*, London: Sage.

Baudrillard, J. (1975) *The Mirror of Production*, trans. M. Poster, St Louis: Telos.

——(1981) *For the Critique of the Political Economy of the Sign*, trans. C. Lewin, St Louis: Telos.

——(1990a) *Fatal Strategies*, New York: Semiotext(e).

——(1990b) *Simulacra and Simulation*, trans. S. Glaser, Ann Arbor: University of Michigan Press.

Bauman, Z. (1973) *Culture as Praxis*, London: Routledge and Kegan Paul.

——(1978) *Hermeneutics and Social Science*, London: Hutchinson.

——(1987) *Legislators and Interpreters*, Cambridge: Polity.

——(1989) 'Hermeneutics and Modern Social Theory', in Held, D. and Thompson, J. (eds) *Social Theory of Modern Societies: Anthony Giddens and his Critics*, Cambridge: Cambridge University Press.

Becker, H. (1971) *Sociological Work: method and substance*, London: Allen Lane.

Beloff, M. (1954) *The Age of Absolutism: 1660–1815*, London: Hutchinson.

Bendix, R. (1960) *Max Weber: an intellectual portrait*, London: Heinemann.

Bendix, R. and Roth, G. (1971) *Scholarship and Partisanship: essays on Max Weber*, London: University of California Press.

Benton, T. (1977) *Philosophical Foundations of the Three Sociologies*, London: Routledge and Kegan Paul.

Bernstein, R. (1972) *Praxis and Action*, London: Gerald Duckworth.

——(1985) *Habermas and Modernity*, Cambridge: Polity.

Bhaskar, R. (1978) *A Realist Theory of Science*, Sussex: Harvester.

——(1979) *The Possibility of Naturalism*, Sussex: Harvester.

——(1986) *Scientific Realism and Human Emancipation*, London: Verso.

——(1991) *Philosophy and the Idea of Freedom*, Oxford: Blackwell.

——(1993) *Dialectic: The Pulse of Freedom*, London: Verso.

Bidet, J. (1979) 'Questions to Pierre Bourdieu', *Critique of Anthropology*, 13–14 (Summer): 203–8.

Blau, P. (1964) *Exchange and Power in Social Life*, London: Wiley.

Bleicher, J. (1980) *Contemporary Hermeneutics*, London: Routledge and Kegan Paul.

Bloor, D. (1983) *Wittgenstein: a social theory of knowledge*, London: Macmillan.

——(1997) *Wittgenstein, Rules and Institutions*, London: Routledge.

Blumer, H. (1969) *Symbolic Interactionism*, Englewood Cliffs, New Jersey: Prentice Hall.

Bourdieu, P. (1977a) *Outline of a Theory of Practice*, trans. R. Nice, Cambridge: Cambridge University Press.

——(1977b) *Reproduction in Education, Society and Culture*, trans. R. Nice, London: Sage.

——(1979) *Algeria 1960*, trans. R. Nice, Cambridge: Cambridge University Press.

——(1984) *Distinction: a social critique of the judgement of taste*, trans. R. Nice, London: Routledge and Kegan Paul.

——(1988a) *The Political Ontology of Martin Heidegger*, trans. P. Collier, Cambridge: Polity.

——(1988b) 'Vive la Crise! For heterodoxy in social science', *Theory and Society*, 17(5): 773–87.

——(1990a) *The Logic of Practices*, trans. R. Nice, Cambridge: Polity.

——(1990b) *In Other Words*, trans. M. Adamson, Cambridge: Polity.

——(1996a) *Homo Academicus*, trans. P. Collier, Cambridge: Polity.

——(1996b) *The State Nobility*, trans. L. Clough, Cambridge: Polity.

Bourdieu, P. and Wacquant, L. (1992) *An Invitation to Reflexive Sociology*, London: University of Chicago Press.

Bouveresse, J. (1995) 'Rules, Dispositions and Habitus', *Critique*, 51: 579–80: 573–94.

Brodbeck, M. (ed.) (1968) *Readings in the Philosophy of the Social Sciences*, London: Macmillan.

Brubaker, R. (1985) 'Rethinking Classical Sociology: the sociological vision of Pierre Bourdieu', *Theory and Society*, 14(6): 745–75.

——(1993) 'Social Theory as Habitus', in Calhoun, C. LiPuma, E. and Postone, M. (eds) *Bourdieu: critical perspectives*, Cambridge: Polity.

Bryant, C. and Jary, D. (eds) (1991) *Giddens' Theory of Structuration*, London: Routledge.

Bubner, R. (1975) 'Theory and Practice in the Light of the Hermeneutic–Criticist Controversy', *Cultural Hermeneutics*, 2(4): 337–52.

Buckley, W. (1968) 'Society as a Complex Adaptive System', in Buckley, W. (ed.) *Modern Systems Research for the Behavioural Scientist*, Chicago: Aldine Publishing.

Burger, T. (1976) *Max Weber's Theory of Concept Formation*. Durham, North Carolina: Duke University Press.

——'Talcott Parsons, the Problem of Order in Society, and the Program of an Analytical Sociology', *American Journal of Sociology*, 83(2): 320–99.

Calhoun, C. LiPuma, E. and Postone, M. (eds) (1993) *Bourdieu: critical perspectives*, Cambridge: Polity.

Callinicos, A. (1985) 'Anthony Giddens: a contemporary critique', *Theory and Society*, Vol. 14(5) 133–66.

——(1987) *Making History: agency, structure and social change*, Cambridge: Polity.

Carver, T. (1982) *Marx's Social Theory*, Oxford: Oxford University Press.

Chalcraft, D. and Harrington, A. (2001) *The Protestant Ethic Debate: Max Weber's replies to his critics, 1907–10*, trans. A. Harrington and M. Shields, Liverpool: Liverpool University Press.

Cicourel, A. (1981) 'Notes on the Integration of Micro- and Macro-levels of Analysis', in Knorr-Cetina, K. and Cicourel, A. (eds) *Advances in Social Theory and Methodology: towards an integration of micro- and macro-Sociology*, London: Routledge.

Cixous, H. (1994) 'The Newly Born Woman', in Sellers, S. (ed) *The Hélène Cixous Reader*, London: Routledge.

Clark, J, Modgil, C and Modgil, J. (eds.) (1990) *Anthony Gidden: consensus and controversy*, London: Falmer Press.

Cohen, G. (1988) *Karl Marx's Theory of History: a defence*, Oxford: Clarendon.

Cohen, I. (1990) 'Structuration Theory and Social Order: five issues in brief', in Clark, J. Modgil, C. and Modgil, J. (eds) *Anthony Giddens: Consensus and Controversy*, London: Falmer Press.

Collingwood, R. (1992) *The Idea of History*, Oxford: Oxford University Press.

Collins, R. (1979) *The Credential Society*, London: Academic Press.

——(1981a) 'Micro-translation as a Theory-building Strategy', in Knorr-Cetina, K and Cicourel, A. (eds.) *Advances in Social Theory and Methodology: towards an integration of micro- and macro-Sociology*, London: Routledge.

——(1981b) 'On the Microfoundations of Macrosociology', *American Journal of Sociology*, 86(5): 984–1014.

——(1986) *Max Weber: a skeleton key*, London: Sage.

——(1989) 'Review of Homo Academicus', *American Journal of Sociology*, 95(2): 460–63.

——(1990) *Weberian Sociological Theory*, Cambridge: Cambridge University Press.

——(2000) *The Sociology of Philosophies*, London: Belknap Press.

Comte, A. (1974) *The Essential Comte*, London: Croom Helm.

Corrigan, P. and Sayer, D. (1991) *The Great Arch*, Oxford: Blackwell.

Coser, L. (1960) 'Durkheim's Conservativism and its Implications for his Sociological Theory', in Wolff, K. (ed.) *Emile Durkheim: 1858–1917*, Columbus, Ohio: Ohio State Press.

Craib, I. (1992) *Anthony Giddens*, London: Routledge.

Dahrendorf, R. (1968) 'Out of Utopia: towards a reorientation of sociological analysis', *Essays in the Theory of Society*, Stanford, California: Stanford University Press.

Davey, N. (1985) 'Habermas' Contribution to Hermeneutical Theory', *Journal of the British Society for Phenomenology*, 16(2): 109–31.

de Beauvoir, S. (1998) *The Second Sex*, trans. H. Parshey, London: Pan.

de Certeau, M. (1988) *The Practice of Everyday Life*, trans. S. Rendall, London: University of California.

de Tocqueville, A. (1955) *The Old Regime and the French Revolution*, New York: Doubleday.

Dilthey, W. (1976) *Selected Writings*, Rickman, H. (ed.), Cambridge: Cambridge University Press.

Di Maggio, P. (1979) 'Review Essay: on Pierre Bourdieu', *American Journal of Sociology*, 84(6): 1460–74.

Douglas, J. (1973) *The Social Meaning of Suicide*, Princeton, New Jersey: Princeton University Press.

Dreyfus, H. and Rabinow, P. (1982) *Michel Foucault*, Brighton, Sussex: Harvester.

——(1993) 'Can There Be a Science of Existential Structure and Social Meaning?', in Calhoun, C. LiPuma, E. and Postone, M. (eds) *Bourdieu: Critical Perspectives*, Cambridge: Polity.

Durkheim, E. (1952) *Suicide*, trans. J. Spalding and G. Simpson, London: Routledge and Kegan Paul.

——(1956) *Education and Sociology*, Glencoe, Illinois: Free Press.

——(1957) *Professional Ethics and Civic Morals*, London: Routledge and Kegan Paul.

——(1959) *Socialism and Saint Simon*, London: Routledge and Kegan Paul.

——(1963) *Incest*, trans. E. Sagarin, New York: Lyle Stewart Inc.

——(1964) *The Division of Labour in Society*, trans. G. Simpson, London: Collier Macmillan.

——(1965a) *Sociology and Philosophy*, trans. D. Pocock, London: Cohen and West.

——(1965b) *Montesquieu and Rousseau*, trans. R. Manheim, Ann Arbor, Michigan: University of Michigan.

——(1966) *The Rules of Sociological Method*, trans. S. Solavay and J. Mueller, London: Collier Macmillan.

——(1973) *Moral Education*, trans. by E. Wilson and H. Schnurer, London: Collier Macmillan.

——(1976) *The Elementary Forms of the Religious Life*, trans. J. Ward Swain, London: George Allen and Unwin.

——(1977) *The Evolution of Educational Thought*, trans. P. Collins, London: Routledge and Kegan Paul.

——(1978) *On Institutional Analysis*, trans. M. Traugott, London: University of Chicago Press.

——(1986) *On Politics and the State*, trans. W. Halls, Cambridge: Polity.

Eagleton. T. (1983) *Literary Theory*, Oxford: Blackwell.

Elias, N. (1978) *What is Sociology?*, London: Hutchinson.

——(1987) *The Civilising Process,. Volume. 1: the history of manners*, Oxford: Blackwell.

——(1982) *The Civilising Process,. Volume 2: state formation and civilisation*, Oxford: Blackwell.

Engels, F. (1977) 'Preface to Capital', in Tucker, R. (ed.) *The Marx–Engels Reader*, New York: Norton.

Evans-Pritchard, E. (1937) *Witchcraft, Oracles and Magic among the Azande*, Oxford: Clarendon.

Evens, T. (1999) 'Bourdieu and the Logic of Practice: is all giving Indian-giving or is "Generalized Materialism" not enough?', *Sociological Theory*, 17(1): 3–31.

Fanon, F. (1968) *The Wretched of the Earth*, trans. C. Farrington, New York: Grove Weiden-feld.

Findlay, J. (1970) *Hegel: a re-examination*, London: George Allen and Unwin.

Finlayson, J. (2000) 'Modernity and Morality in Habermas' Discourse Ethics', *Inquiry*, 43: 319–40.

Foucault, M. (1972) *The Archaeology of Knowledge*, trans. A. Sheridan, London: Tavistock.

——(1974a) *The Order of Things*, London: Tavistock.

——(1974b) *The Birth of the Clinic*, trans. A. Sheridan-Smith, London: Tavistock.

——(1977a) 'Nietzsche, Genealogy, History', *Language, Counter-Memory, Practice*, trans. D. Bouchard and S. Simon, Oxford: Blackwell.

——(1977b) *Madness and Civilisation*, trans. R. Howard, London: Tavistock.

——(1982a) 'Afterword: The Subject and Power', trans. L. Sawyer, in Dreyfus, H. and Rabinow, P., *Michel Foucault*, Brighton, Sussex: Harvester.

——(1982b) *I, Pierre Rivière, Having Slaughtered My Mother, My Sister, and My Brother: a case of parricide in the 19th century*, trans. F. Jellinek, Nebraska: University of Nebraska.

——(1986) *The Uses of Pleasure: the History of Sexuality, Volume 2*, trans. R. Hurley, Harmondsworth: Viking.

——(1990a) *The History of Sexuality, Volume. 1*, trans. R. Hurley, Harmondsworth: Penguin.

——(1990b) *The Care of the Self: the history of sexuality, Volume 3* , trans. R. Hurley, Harmondsworth: Penguin.

——(1995) *Discipline and Punish*, trans. A. Sheridan, New York: Vintage.

Fowler, B. (1996) 'An Introduction to Pierre Bourdieu's "Understanding"', *Theory, Culture and Society*, 13(2): 1–16.

——(1997) *Pierre Bourdieu and Cultural Theory*, London: Sage.

Fuller, S. (1995) 'Review Essay: is there life for sociological theory after the sociology of scientific knowledge?', *Sociology*, 29(1): 159–66.

Gadamer, H.-G. (1975) *Truth and Method*, trans. W. Glen-Doepel, London: Sheed and Ward.

——(1977) 'On the Scope and Function of Hermeneutical Reflection', in *Philosophical Hermeneutics*, London: University of California Press.

——(1986) 'Rhetoric, Hermeneutics and the Critique of Ideology', in Mueller-Vollmer, K. (ed.) *The Hermeneutic Reader*, Oxford: Blackwell.

——(1990) 'Reply to My Critics', trans. J. Thompson, in Ormiston, G. and Schrift, A. (eds) *The Hermeneutic Tradition: from Ast to Ricoeur*, Albany, New York: State University of New York Press.

Garfinkel, H. (1967) *Studies in Ethnomethodology*, London: Prentice-Hall.

Garnham, N. (1986) 'Extended Review: Bourdieu's *Distinction*', *Sociological Review*, 34(2): 423–33.

Garnham, N. and Williams, R. (1980) 'Pierre Bourdieu and the Sociology of Culture: an introduction', *Media, Culture and Society*, 2(3): 209–23.

Gartmann, D. (1991) 'Culture as Class Symbolization or Mass Reification? A critique of Bourdieu's Distinction', *American Journal of Sociology*, 97(2): 421–47.

Gellner, E. (1968) 'Holism versus Individualism', in Brodbeck, M. (ed.) *Readings in the Philosophy of the Social Sciences*, London: Macmillan.

Gelven, M. (1970) *A Commentary on Heidegger's Being and Time*, London: Harper.

Gerth, H. and Wright Mills, C. (eds) (1991) *From Max Weber*, London: Routledge.

Giddens, A. (1972) 'Four Myths in the History of Social Thought', *Economy and Society*, 1(4): 357–86.

——(1976) *New Rules of Sociological Method*, London: Hutchinson.

——(1977a) *The Class Structure of Advanced Societies*, London: Hutchinson.

——(1977b) 'Functionalism: après la lutte', in *Studies in Social and Political Theory*, London: Hutchinson.

——(1979) *Central Problems in Social Theory*, London: Macmillan.

——(1981) *A Contemporary Critique of Historical Materialism, Volume 1: power, property and the state*, Cambridge: Polity

——(1982) *Profiles and Critiques*, London: Macmillan.

——(1985) *A Contemporary Critique of Historical Materialism, Volume 2: the nation-state and violence*, Cambridge: Polity.

——(1988) *Central Problems in Social Theory*, London: Macmillan.

——(1991) *The Consequences of Modernity*, Cambridge: Polity.

——(1992) *Capitalism and Modern Social Theory*, Cambridge: Cambridge University Press.

——(1993) *The Transformation of Intimacy*, Cambridge: Polity.

——(1994) 'Living in a Post-Traditional Society', in Beck, U. Giddens, A. and Lash, S. *Reflexive Modernisation*, Cambridge: Polity.

——(1995a) *The Constitution of Society*, Cambridge: Polity.

——(1995b) *Modernity and Self-Identity*, Cambridge: Polity.

——(1995c) *Beyond Left and Right*, Cambridge: Polity.

——(1998) *The Third Way*, Cambridge: Polity.

Giesen, B. (1997) 'Review Essay: old wine in new bottles', *American Journal of Sociology*, 103(2): 461–63.

Gilroy, P. (2001) *Between Camps*, Harmondsworth: Penguin.

Gimenez, M. (1999) 'For Structure: a critique of ontological individualism', *Alethia*, 2(2): 19–25.

Goffman, E. (1961) *Encounters: two studies in the sociology of interaction*, New York: Bobbs Merrill.

——(1966) *Behaviour in Public Places*, London: Free Press, Macmillan.

——(1967) *Interaction Ritual*, New York: Pantheon Book.

——(1969) *Where the Action Is*, London: Allen Lane, Penguin.

——(1970) *Strategic Interaction*, Oxford: Blackwell.

——(1971) *Relations in Public*, London: Allen Lane, Penguin.

——(1974) *Frame Analysis*, Harmondsworth: Penguin.

——(1984) *The Presentation of the Self in Everyday Life*, Harmondsworth: Penguin.

Gorder, K. (1980) 'Understanding School Knowledge: a critical appraisal of Basil Bernstein and Pierre Bourdieu', *Educational Theory*, 30(4): 335–46.

Gould, C. (1978) *Marx's Social Ontology*, Cambridge, Massachussett's Institute of Technology.

Gouldner, A. (1971) *The Coming Crisis in Western Sociology*, London: Heinemann.

Gramsci, A. (1971) *Selections from the Prison Notebooks*, London: Lawrence and Wishart.

Habermas, J. (1970) 'On Systematically Distorted Communication', *Inquiry*, 13: 205–18.

——(1971) *Knowledge and Human Interests*, trans. J. Shapiro, London: Beacon Press.

——(1974) *Theory and Practice*, trans. J. Viertel, London: Heinemann.

——(1976) *Legitimation Crisis*, trans. T. McCarthy, London: Heinemann.

——(1977) 'A Review of Gadamer's Truth and Method', in Dallmayr, F. and McCarthy, T. (eds) *Understanding and Social Inquiry*, London: University of Notre Dame Press.

——(1979) *Communication and the Evolution of Society*, trans. T. McCarthy, London: Heinemann.

——(1986) 'On Hermeneutics' Claim to Universality', in Mueller-Vollmer, K. (ed.) *The Hermeneutic Reader*, Oxford: Blackwell.

——(1987a) *The Philosophical Discourse of Modernity*, trans. F. Lawrence, Cambridge: Polity.

——(1987b) *The Theory of Communicative Action, Volume. 2: Lifeworld and system: a critique of functionalist reason*, trans. T. McCarthy, Cambridge: Polity.

——(1988) *On the Logic of the Social Sciences*, trans. S. Weber Nicholsen and J. Stark, Oxford: Polity.

——(1990) *Moral Consciousness and Communicative Action*, trans. C. Lenhardt and S. Weber Nicholsen, Cambridge: Polity.

——(1991) *The Theory of Communicative Action, Volume. 1: reason and the rationalization of society*, trans. T. McCarthy, Cambridge: Polity.

——(1993) 'Work and Weltanschauung: the Heidegger controversy from a German perspective' in Dreyfus, H. and Hall, H. (eds) *Heidegger: a critical reader*, Oxford: Blackwell.

——(1995a) *Justification and Application*, trans. C. Cronin, Cambridge: Polity.

——(1995b) *Postmetaphysical Thinking*, trans. W. Hohengarten, Cambridge: Polity.

——(1996) *The Structural Transformation of the Public Sphere*, trans. T. Burger with F. Lawrence, Cambridge: Polity.

Hall, S. (1990) 'The Meaning of New Times', in Hall, S. and Jacques, M. (eds) *New Times: the changing face of politics in the 1990s*, London: Lawrence and Wishart.

Hall, S. and Jefferson, T. (1976) *Resistance through Rituals*, London: Harper-Collins.

Hall, S. Critcher, C, Jefferson, T. Clarke, J. and Roberts, B. (1978) *Policing the Crisis: mugging, the state and law and order*, London: Macmillan.

Hamilton, A. (2000) 'Max Weber's Protestant Ethic and the Spirit of Capitalism', in Turner, S. (ed.) *The Cambridge Companion to Weber*, Cambridge: Cambridge University Press.

Hamilton, P. (1983) *Talcott Parsons*, London and Chichester, Sussex: Tavistock and Ellis Horwood.

Harker, R. (1984) 'On Reproduction, Habitus and Education', *British Journal of Sociology of Education*, 5(2): 117–27.

Harré, R. (1979) *Social Being: a theory for social psychology*, Oxford: Blackwell.

Harré, R. and Secord, P. (1976) *The Explanation of Social Behaviour*, Oxford: Blackwell.

Harrington, A. (2001) *Hermeneutic Dialogue: a critique of Gadamer and Habermas*, London: Routledge.

Harrington, A. and Chalcraft, D. (eds) (2001) *The Protestant Ethic Debate: Max Weber's replies to his critics, 1907–1910*, trans. A. Harrington and M. Shields, Liverpool: Liverpool University Press.

Hegel, G. (1894) *The Philosophy of Mind*, trans. W. Wallace, Oxford: Clarendon.

——(1953) *Reason in History*, trans. R. Hartman, Indiannapolis: Bobbs-Merrill.

——(1956) *The Philosophy of History*, trans. J. Sibree, New York: Dover.

——(1967a) *The Phenomenology of Mind*, trans. J. Baillie, London: Harper Torchbooks.

——(1967b) *The Philosophy of Right*, trans. T. Knox, New York: Oxford University Press.

——(1977) *The Phenomenology of Mind*, trans. A. Miller, Oxford: Oxford University Press.

Heidegger, M. (1967) *Being and Time*, trans. J. Macquarrie and E. Robinson, Oxford: Blackwell.

——(1996a) 'The Origin of the Work of Art', in Heidegger, M., *Basic Writings*, trans. and ed. D. Krell, London: Routledge.

——(1996b) 'The Question Concerning Technology', in Heidegger, M., *Basic Writings*, trans. and ed. D. Krell, London: Routledge.

——(1996c) 'Letter on Humanism in Heidegger, M., *Basic Writings*, trans. and ed. D. Krell, London: Harper Row.

——(1996d) 'Being Dwelling Thinking', in Heidegger, M., *Basic Writings*, trans. and ed. D. Krell, London: Harper Row.

Hekman, S. (1986) *Hermeneutics and the Sociology of Knowledge*, Oxford: Polity.

Held, D. and Thompson, J. (eds) (1989) *Social Theory of Modern Societies: Anthony Giddens and his critics*, Cambridge: Cambridge University Press.

Hennis, W. (ed.) (1988) *Max Weber: essays in reconstruction*, trans. K. Tribe, London: Allen and Unwin.

Heydebrand, W. (1972) 'The System of Modern Societies', *Contemporary Sociology*, 1: 387–95.

Hill, C. (1961) 'Protestantism and the Rise of Capitalism', in Fischer F. (ed.) *Essays in the Economic and Social History of Tudor and Stuart England*, Cambridge: Cambridge University Press.

Hirst, P. (1982) 'The Social Theory of Anthony Giddens: a new syncretism?', *Theory, Culture and Society*, 1(2): 78–82.

Hodges, H. (1944) *Wilhelm Dilthey*, London: Kegan Paul.

Hollis, M. and Lukes, S. (eds) (1982) *Rationality and Relativism*, Oxford: Blackwell

Homans, G. (1967) *The Nature of Social Science*, New York: Harbinger Books, Harcourt, Brace and World Inc.

——(1987) *Certainties and Doubts: Collected Papers 1962–1985*, New Brunswick, New Jersey: Transactions Books.

Hook, S. (1936) *From Hegel to Marx*, London: Victor Gollancz.

hooks, b. (1981) *Ain't I a Woman*, London: Pluto.

How, A. (1980) 'Dialogue as Productive Limitation in Social Theory: the Habermas–Gadamer Debate', *Journal of the British Society for Phenomenology*, 11(2): 131–43.

——(1985) 'A Case of Creative Misreading: Habermas' Evaluation of Gadamer's Hermeneutics', *Journal of the British Society for Phenomenology*, 16(2): 132–44.

——(1995) *The Habermas–Gadamer Debate and the Nature of the Social: Back to Bedrock*, Aldershot: Avebury.

Howard, M. (2000) *War in European History*, Oxford: Oxford University Press.

Husserl, E. (1931) *Ideas: general introduction to pure phenomenology*, trans. W. Boyce Gibson, London: George Allen and Lane.

——(1970) *The Crisis of European Sciences and Transcendental Phenomenology*, Evanston, Illinois: Northwestern University Press.

Inwood, M. (ed.) (1985) *Hegel*, Oxford: Oxford University Press.

Jackson, S. (1999) *Heterosexuality in Question*, London: Sage.

Jenkins, R. (1982) 'Pierre Bourdieu and the Reproduction of Determinism', *Sociology*, 16(2): 270–81.

——(1993) *Pierre Bourdieu*, London: Routledge.

Joas, H. (1996) *The Creativity of Action*, trans. J. Gaines and P. Keast, Oxford: Polity.

Joint Warfare Publication (2001) *British Defence Doctrine*, Shrivenham: Joint Doctrine and Concepts Centre.

Kalberg, S. (1994) *Max Weber's Comparative-Historical Sociology*, Cambridge: Polity.

Kant, I. (1992) *A Critique of Pure Reason*, trans. N. Kemp, Oxford: Clarendon.

Kaufman, W. (1966) *Hegel: reinterpretation, texts and commentary*, London: Weidenfeld and Nicolson.

Keat, R. and Urry, J. (1982) *Social Theory as Science*, London: Routledge and Kegan Paul.

Keegan, J. (1994) *A History of Warfare*, London: Pimlico.

Kennedy, P. (1999) *The Rise and Fall of the Great Powers*, London: Fontana.

King, A. (1998a) 'A Critique of Baudrillard's Hyperreality: towards a sociology of post-modernism', *Philosophy and Social Criticism*, 24(4): 47–66.

——(1998b) 'Baudrillard's Nihilism and the End of Theory', *Telos*, 112 (Summer): 89–106.

——(1999a) 'Against Structure: a critique of morphogenetic social theory', *Sociological Review*, 47(2): 199–227.

——(1999b) 'The Impossibility of Naturalism: the antinomies of Bhaskar's realism', *Journal for the Theory of Social Behaviour*, 29(3): 267–88.

——(2000a) 'The Accidental Derogation of the Lay Actor: a critique of Gidden's concept of structure', *Philosophy of the Social Sciences*, 30(3): 326–83.

——(2000b) 'Thinking with Bourdieu against Bourdieu: a practical critique of the habitus', *Sociological Theory*, 18(3): 417–33.

Kitching, G. (1988) *Karl Marx and the Philosophy of Praxis*, London: Routledge.

Knorr-Cetina, K. and Cicourel, A. (eds) (1981) *Advances in Social Theory and Methodology: towards an integration of micro- and macro-sociology*, London: Routledge.

Kojeve, A. (1969) *An Introduction to the Reading of Hegel*, New York: Basic Books.

Kolakowski, L. (1978) *Main Currents of Marxism*, Oxford: Clarendon.

Kripke, S. (1982) *Wittgenstein on Rules and Private Language: an elementary exposition*, Oxford: Blackwell.

Kristeva, J. (1993) 'Women's Time', in Moi, T. (ed.) *The Kristeva Reader*, Oxford: Blackwell.

Lamont, M. (1989) 'Slipping the World Back in: Bourdieu on Heidegger', *Contemporary Sociology*, 18(5): 781–83.

Lamont, M. and Lareau, A. (1988) 'Cultural Capital: allusion, gaps and glissandos in recent theoretical developments', *Sociological Theory*, 6(2) Fall: 153–68.

Lash, S. and Featherstone, M. (2001) 'Recognition and Differences: politics, identity, multiculture', *Theory, Culture and Society*, 18(2): 1–20.

Lash, S and Urry, J. (1987) *The End of Organised Capitalism*, Cambridge: Polity.

——(1994) *Economies of Signs and Space*, London: Sage.

Layder, D. (1981) *Structure, Interaction and Social Theory*, London: Routledge and Kegan Paul.

Lehmann, H. and Roth, G. (1993) *Weber's Protestant Ethic*, Cambridge: Cambridge University Press.

Lockwood, D. (1964) 'Social Integration and System Integration', in Zollschan, G. and Hirsch, W. (eds) *Explorations in Social Change*, London: Routledge.

——(1967) 'Some Remarks on *The Social System*', in Demerath, N. and Peterson, R., *System, Change and Conflict*, New York: Free Press.

Luhmann, N. (1989) *Ecological Communication*, trans. J. Bednarz, Cambridge: Polity.

——(1995) *Social Systems*, trans. J. Bednarz with D. Baecker, Stanford: Stanford University Press.

——(1997) 'The Limits of Steering', *Theory, Culture and Society*, 14(1): 41–57.

Lukes. S. (1973) *Emile Durkheim: his life and works*, London: Penguin, Allen Lane.
MacIntyre, A. (1972) *Hegel: a collection of critical essays*, London: University of Notre Dame Press.
——(1986) *After Virtue*, London: Duckworth.
——(1998) 'The Theses on Feuerbach: a road not taken', in Knight, K. (ed.) *The MacIntyre Reader*, Cambridge: Polity.
McCarthy, T. (1984) *The Critical Theory of Jurgen Habermas*, Cambridge: Polity.
McCarthy, T. and Hoy, D. (1994) *Critical Theory*, Oxford: Blackwell.
McNay, L. (1992) *Foucault and Feminism*, Cambridge: Polity.
Mannheim, K. (1976) *Ideology and Utopia*, London: Routledge and Kegan Paul.
Marcuse, H. (1968) *Reason and Revolution: Hegel and the rise of social theory*, London: Routledge and Kegan Paul.
Marshall, G. (1982) *In Search of the Spirit of Capitalism*, London: Hutchinson.
Marx, K. (1970) *Economic and Philosophic Manuscripts of 1844*, trans. M. Milligan, London: Lawrence and Wishart.
——(1971) *A Contribution to the Critique of Political Economy*, London: Lawrence and Wishart.
——(1973) *The Grundrisse*, trans. D. McLellan, St Albans: Paladin.
——(1977a) *The German Ideology*, trans. S. Ryazanskaya, London: Lawrence and Wishart.
——(1977b) *Capital, Volume 1*, trans. S. Moore and E. Aveling, Moscow: Progress Publishers.
——(1977c) *The Eighteenth Brumaire of Louis Bonaparte*, in Marx, K. and Engels, F., *Selected Works*, London: Lawrence and Wishart.
——(1977d) *The Civil War in France*, Peking: Foreign Language Press.
——(1978) 'The Theses on Feuerbach', in Tucker, R. (ed.) *The Marx–Engels Reader*, New York: Norton.
——(1984) *The Poverty of Philosophy*, Moscow: Progress Publishers.
——(1990) *Economic and Philosophical Manuscripts*, in McLellan, D. (ed) *Karl Marx: selected writings*, Oxford: Oxford University Press.
——(1992) 'Critique of Hegel's Doctrine of the State', in *Karl Marx: early writings*, trans. R. Livingstone and G. Benton, Harmondsworth: Penguin.
——(1996) 'Critique of the Gotha Programme', in Carver, T. (ed. and trans.) *Marx's Later Political Writings*, Cambridge: Cambridge University Press.
McGinn, C. (1984) *Wittgenstein on Meaning: an interpretation and evaluation*, Oxford: Blackwell.
Merquior, J. (1985) *Foucault*, London: Fontana.
Mestrovic, S. (1998) *Anthony Giddens: the last modernist*, London: Routledge.
Milgram, S. (1974) *Obedience to Authority*, London: Pinter and Martin.
Misgeld, D. (1977a) 'Discourse and Conversation: the theory of communicative competence and Hermeneutics in the light of the debate between Habermas and Gadamer', *Cultural Hermeneutics*, 4(4): 321–44.
——(1977b). 'Critical Theory and Hermeneutics: the debate between Habermas and Gadamer', in O'Neill, J. (ed.) *On Critical Theory*, London: Heinemann.
——(1979) 'On Gadamer's Hermeneutics', *Philosophy of Social Science*, 9(2): 221–39.
Mouzelis, N. (1995) *Sociological Theory: what went wrong? Diagnosis and remedies*, London: Routledge.
Mueller-Vollmer, K. (1986) *The Hermeneutics Reader*, Oxford: Blackwell.
Nederveen Pietersee, J. (2001)'Hybridity, So What?: the anti-hybridity backlash and the riddles of recognition', *Theory, Culture and Society*, 18(2–3): 219–46.
Nisbet, R. (1967) *The Sociological Tradition*, London: Heinemann.
Norman, R. (1981) *Hegel's Phenomenology*, Brighton, Sussex: Harvester.

Oakes, G. (1988) 'Farewell to the Protestant Ethic?', *Telos* 78: 81–94.

——(1989). 'Four Questions Concerning the Protestant Ethic', *Telos*, 81: 77–86.

Outhwaite, W. (1985) 'Hans-Georg Gadamer', in Skinner, Q. (ed.) *The Return of Grand Theory in the Human Sciences*, Cambridge: Cambridge University Press.

——(1987) *New Philosophies of Social Science*, London: Macmillan.

Palmer, R. (1977), *Hermeneutics: interpretation theory in Schleiermacher, Dilthey, Heidegger and Gadamer*, Evanston, Illinois: Northwestern University Press.

Parsons, T. (1952) *The Social System*, London: Tavistock.

——(1966a) *The Structure of Social Action*, New York: Free Press.

——(1966b) *Societies: Evolutionary and Comparative Perspectives*, Englewood Cliffs, New Jersey: Prentice-Hall.

Parsons, T. Bales, R. and Shils, E. (1953) *Working Papers in the Theory of Action*, New York. Free Press.

Parsons, T. and Bales, R. (1955) *Family, Socialization and Interaction Process*, Glencoe, Illinois: Free Press.

Parsons, T. and Smelser, N. (1956) *Economy and Society*, London: Routledge and Kegan Paul.

Pellicani, L. (1988) 'Weber and the Myth of Calvinism', *Telos*, 75: 57–85.

——(1989) 'Reply to Guy Oakes', *Telos*, 81: 63–76.

——(1994) *The Genesis of Capitalism and the Origins of Modernity*, trans. J. Colbert, New York: Telos.

Philp, M. (1985) 'Michel Foucault', in Skinner, Q. (ed.) *The Return of Grand Theory in the Human Sciences*, Cambridge: Cambridge University Press.

Piccone, P. (1998) 'Re-Thinking Protestantism, Capitalism and a Few Other Things', *Telos*, 78 (Winter): 95–108.

Pleasants, N. (1997) 'Free to Act Otherwise? A Wittgensteinian deconstruction of the concept of agency in contemporary social and political theory', *History of the Human Sciences*, 10(4): 1–28.

——(1999) *Wittgenstein and the Idea of a Critical Social Theory*, London: Routledge.

——(2000) 'Winch and Wittgenstein on Understanding Ourselves Critically: descriptive not metaphysical', *Enquiry*, 43(3): 289–317.

Polt, R. (1999) *Heidegger: an introduction*, London: University College Press.

Popper, K. (1976) *The Open Society and Its Enemies, Volume II: the high tide of prophecy: Hegel, Marx and the aftermath*, London: Routledge.

Porpora, D. (1993) 'Cultural Rules and Material Relations', *Sociological Theory*, 11(2): 212–29.

Poster, M. (1984) *Foucault, Marxism and History*, Cambridge: Polity.

Postone, M. LiPuma, E. and Calhoun, C. (1993) 'Introduction: Bourdieu and social theory', in Calhoun, C. LiPuma, E. and Postone, M. (eds) *Bourdieu: critical perspectives*, Cambridge: Polity.

Racevskis, K. (1983) *Foucault and the Subversion of Intellect*, London: Cornell University Press.

Rex, J. (1983) *Colonial Immigrants in a British City: a class analysis*, London: Routledge and Kegan Paul.

——(1986) *Race and Ethnicity*, Milton Keynes: Open University Press.

Rex, J. and Moore, R. (1967) *Race, Community and Conflict: a study of Sparkbrook*, London: Oxford University Press.

Ricoeur, P. (1973) 'Ethics and Culture: Habermas and Gadamer in dialogue', *Philosophy Today*, (Summer) 153–65.

——'The Model of the Text', in Dallmayr, F. and McCarthy, T. (eds.) *Understanding Social Inquiry*, London: University of Notre Dame Press.

——(1990) 'Hermeneutics and the Critique of Ideology', in Ormiston, G. and Schrift, A. *The Hermeneutic Tradition: from Ast to Ricoeur*, Albany, New York: State University of New York Press.

Robbins, D. (1991) *The Work of Pierre Bourdieu*, Milton Keynes: Open University Press.

Rocher, G. (1974) *Talcott Parsons and American Sociology*, London: Nehon.

Rorty, R. (1993a) 'Heidegger, Contingency and Pragmatism', in Dreyfus, H. and Hall, H. (eds) *Heidegger: a critical reader*, Oxford: Blackwell.

——(1993b) 'Wittgenstein, Heidegger and the Reification of Language', in Guignon, G. (ed.) *The Cambridge Companion to Heidegger*, Cambridge: Cambridge University Press.

——(1997) *Contingency, Irony and Solidarity*, Cambridge: Cambridge University Press.

Rubinstein, D. (1981) *Marx and Wittgenstein: social praxis and social explanation*, London: Routledge and Kegan Paul.

Runciman, W. (1972) *A Critique of Max Weber's Philosophy of Social Science*, Cambridge: Cambridge University Press.

Russell, B. (1961) *The History of Western Philosophy*, London: Allen and Unwin.

Samuelson, K. (1957) *Religion and Economic Action*, London: Heinemann.

Sarotte, M. (2001) 'German Military Reform and European Security', *Adelphi Paper* 340, New York: Oxford University Press.

Savage, M. Barlow, J. Dickens, P. and Fielding, T. (1992) *Property, Bureaucracy and Culture: middle class formation in contemporary Britain*, London: Routledge.

Sayer, A. (1992) *Method in Social Science*, London: Routledge.

Sayer, D. (1987) *The Violence of Abstraction*, Oxford: Blackwell.

Schatzki, T. (1987) 'Overdue Analysis of Bourdieu's Theory of Practice', *Inquiry*, 30(1–2): 113–35.

——(1997) 'Practices and Actions: a Wittgensteinian critique of Bourdieu and Giddens', *Philosophy of the Social Sciences*, 27(3): 283–308.

Schleiermacher, F. (1986) 'Foundations: general theory and art of interpretation', in Mueller-Vollmer, K. (ed.) *The Hermeneutics Reader*, Oxford: Blackwell.

Scott, A. (1997) 'Modernity's Machine Metaphor', *British Journal of Sociology*, 48(4): 561–75.

Searle, J. (1995) *The Construction of Social Reality*, Harmondsworth: Penguin.

Sewell, W. H. (1992) 'A Theory of Structure: duality, agency, and transformation', *American Journal of Sociology*, 98(1): 1–29.

Shakespeare, W. (1982) *Hamlet*, Oxford: Arden.

Sheridan, A. (1980) *Michel Foucault: the will to truth*, London: Tavistock.

Shotter, J. (1992) 'Is Bhaskar's Critical Realism Only a Theoretical Realism?', *History of the Human Sciences*, 5(3): 157–73.

Skinner, Q. (ed.) (1985) *The Return of Grand Theory in the Human Sciences*, Cambridge: Cambridge University Press.

Smart, B. (1983) *Foucault, Marxism and Critique*, London: Routledge and Kegan Paul.

——(1985) *Michel Foucault*, Chichester, Sussex and London: Ellis Horwood and Tavistock.

Soll, I. (1985) 'Charles Taylor's *Hegel*', in Inwood, M. (ed.) *Hegel*, Oxford: Oxford University Press.

Solomon, R. (1972) 'Hegel's Concept of "Geist"', in MacIntyre, A. (ed.) *Hegel: a collection of critical essays*, London: University of Notre Dame Press.

Steiner, G. (1978) *Heidegger*, Sussex: Harvester Press.

Stinchcombe, A. (1990) 'Milieu and Structure Updated: a critique of the theory of structuration', in Clark, J. Modgil, C. and Modgil, J. (eds.) (1990) *Anthony Gidden: consensus and controversy*, London: Falmer Press.

Stones, R. (1996) *Sociological Reasoning: towards a post-modern sociology*, London: Macmillan.

Suchting, W. (1992) 'Reflections upon Roy Bhaskar's "Critical Realism"', *Radical Philosophy*, 61, (Summer) 23–31.

Sulkunen, P. (1982) 'Society Made Visible: on the cultural sociology of Pierre Bourdieu', *Acta Sociologica*, 25(2): 102–15.

Swartz, D. (1977) 'Pierre Bourdieu: the cultural transmission of social inequality', *Harvard Educational Review*, 47(4): 545–55.

Tarde, G. (1969) *On Communication and Social Influence: selected papers*, London: University of Chicago Press.

Taylor, C. (1972) 'The Opening Arguments of the Phenomenology', in MacIntyre, A. (ed.) *Hegel: a collection of critical essays*, London: University of Notre Dame Press.

——(1975) *Hegel*, Cambridge: Cambridge University Press.

——(1979) *Hegel and Modern Society*, Cambridge: Cambridge University Press.

——(1984) 'Foucault on Freedom and Truth', *Political Theory*, 12(2): 152–83.

——(1989) *Sources of the Self*, Cambridge: Cambridge University Press.

——(1993) 'To Follow a Rule…', in Calhoun, C. LiPuma, E. and Postone, M. (eds). *Bourdieu: critical perspectives*, Cambridge: Polity.

——(1995) 'Interpretation and the Sciences of Man', in Taylor, C., *Philosophy and the Human Sciences: philosophical papers 2*, Cambridge: Cambridge University Press.

Thompson, J. (1981) *Critical Hermeneutics*, Cambridge: Cambridge University Press.

——(1989) 'The Theory of Structuration', in Held, D. and Thompson, J. (eds) *Social Theory of Modern Societies: Anthony Giddens and his critics*, Cambridge: Cambridge University Press.

Thompson, K. (1982) *Emile Durkheim*, Chichester: Ellis Howard and Tavistock.

Tilly, C. (ed.) (1975) *The Formation of National States in Western Europe*, Princeton, New Jersey: Princeton University Press.

Touraine, A. (1971) *The Post-Industrial Society*, New York: Random House.

——(1981) *The Voice and the Eye*, Cambridge: Cambridge University Press.

——(1988) *The Return of the Actor*, Minneapolis: University of Minnesota Press.

——(1995) *Critique of Modernity*, trans. D. Macey. Oxford: Blackwell.

Trevor-Roper, H. (1967) 'Religion, the Reformation and Social Change', *Religion, the Reformation and Social Change*, London: Macmillan.

Turner, S. (1994) *The Social Theory of Practices*, Cambridge: Polity.

——(ed.) (2000) *The Cambridge Companion to Weber*, Cambridge: Cambridge University Press.

Urry, J. (1982) 'Duality of Structure: some critical issues', *Theory, Culture and Society*, 1(2): 100–6.

Van Creveld, M. (1999) *The Rise and Decline of the State*, Cambridge: Cambridge University Press.

Varela, C. and Harré, R. (1993) 'Conflicting Varieties of Realism: causal powers and the problems of social structure', *Journal for the Theory of Social Behaviour*, 26(3): 313–25.

Wacquant, L. (1987) 'Symbolic Violence and the Making of the French Agriculturalist: an enquiry into Pierre Bourdieu's sociology', *Australian and New Zealand Journal of Sociology*, 23(1): 65–88.

Warnke, G. (1987) *Gadamer: hermeneutics, tradition and reason*, Oxford: Polity.

Weber, M. (1947) *The Theory of Social and Economic Organisation*, trans. T. Parsons, Glencoe, Illinois: Free Press.

——(1949) ' Objectivity in Social Science and Social Policy', in *The Methodology of the Social Sciences*, trans. E. Shils and H. Finch, New York: Free Press.

——(1952) *Ancient Judaism*, trans. D. Martindale and H. Gerth, Glencoe, Illinois: Free Press.

——(1958a) *The Protestant Ethic and the Spirit of Capitalism*, trans. T. Parsons, New York: Charles Scribner's Sons.

——(1958b) *The City*, trans. by D. Martindale and G. Neuwirth, New York: Free Press.

——(1958c) *The Religion of India*, trans. by D. Martindale and H. Gerth, Glencoe, Illinois: Free Press.

——(1961) *General Economic History*, trans. F. Knight, Glencoe, Illinois: Free Press.

——(1964) *The Religion of China*, trans. H. Gerth, London: Collier Macmillan.

——(1965) *The Sociology of Religion*, London: Methuen.

——(1976) *The Agrarian Sociology of Ancient Civilisation*, London: New Left Books.

——(1978) *Economy and Society*, trans. E. Fischoff, London: University of California Press.

——(1991a) 'The Social Psychology of World Religions', in Gerth, H. and Wright Mills, C., *From Max Weber*, London: Routledge.

——(1991b) 'Capitalism and Rural Society in Germany', in Gerth, H. and Wright Mills, C., *From Max Weber*, London: Routledge.

——(1991c) 'The Protestant Sects and the Spirit of Capitalism', in Gerth, H. and Wright Mills, C., *From Max Weber*, London: Routledge.

Wellmer, A. (1974) *Critical Theory of Society*, New York: Seabury Press.

Wilson, B. (ed.) (1970) *Rationality*, Oxford: Polity.

Williams, E. (1970) *Europe of the Ancien Regime*, London: Pimlico.

Winch, P. (1964) 'Understanding a Primitive Society', *American Philosophical Quarterly*, 1(4): 307–24.

——(1977) *The Idea of a Social Science and Its Relation to Philosophy*, London: Routledge and Kegan Paul.

——(1990) 'Preface to the Second Edition', *The Idea of a Social Science and its Relation to Philosophy*, London: Routledge and Kegan Paul.

Wittgenstein, L. (1964) *Remarks on the Foundations of Mathematics*, trans. G. Anscombe, Oxford: Blackwell.

——(1974) *Tractatus Logico-Philosophicus*, trans. D. Pears and B. McGuiness, London: Routledge and Kegan Paul.

——(1976) *Philosophical Investigations*, trans. G. Anscombe, Oxford: Blackwell.

——(1989) *The Blue and Brown Books*, Oxford: Blackwell.

Wolff, J. (1975a) 'Hermeneutics and the Critique of Ideology', *Sociological Review*, 23(4): 811–28.

——(1975b) *Hermeneutic Philosophy and the Sociology of Art*, London: Routledge and Kegan Paul.

Wolff, K. (ed.) (1960) *Emile Durkheim: 1858–1917*, Columbus, Ohio: Ohio State Press.

Wrong, D. (1964) 'The Oversocialized Conception of Man in Modern Sociology', in Coser, L. and Rosenberg, B. (eds) *Sociological Theory: a book of reading*, London: Macmillan.

Zollschan, G. and Hirsch, W. (eds) (1964) *Explorations in Social Change*, London: Routledge.

Index

aboriginal tribes 152-5, 198; in Australia 157, 198; religion 153
Absolute Geist 94, 97
Absolute Mind 90, 170
absorption of role norms 28
action frame of reference 23
Adorno, Theodor 172
Africa 102, 224
after social theory 84-5
agency and structure 3-19, 197
AGIL schema 27
agricultural revolution 112-13
Alexander, J. 6, 25
alienation 75, 120
altruistic suicide 150
amor fati 41
anomic suicide 150
anthropology 60
archaeology 43, 47
Archer, Margaret 5, 192-3, 206-7
art 180, 194-5
Australia 157, 198
authority 202-3, 222
autonomy 10-11, 15, 21-2, 27; and discourse 64; of self 206; utilitarian premise of 194
autopoiesis 9-10
avoidance strategy 196
awe 154
Azande people 213-17

Bales, Robert 27
Baudrillard, Jean 12
Bauman, Zygmunt 135
Beethoven, Ludwig van 195
Being and Time 171-8
being-in-the-world 179
Beloff, Max 16
benefices 136

benge 213-17
Bentham, Jeremy 46, 48
beyond dualism 18-19
beyond structure and agency 227-38; Hamlet 227-30; Hamlets of sociology 230-33; sociology of life itself 233-8
Bhaskar, Roy 5, 68-72, 165, 187; and hermeneutics 165; and individualism 207; and Marx 85; realism 68-72, 192, 210, see also hermeneutics
binary schematism 10
birth-time 235, 237
Blau, Peter 6
bodily motions 14
body-gloss 196
Bonaparte, Louis 110-113
Borges, Jorge 44-5
Bourdieu, Pierre 7, 39-67, 172, 230; 'practical theory' 59-62
bourgeoisie 134-5
by-play 196

Callinicos, Alex 7-8
Calvin, John 130-31
Calvinism 131, 134, 158
cannibalism 102
Capital 107, 110-114, 118, 120
capitalism 4, 133, 218
chatter 172
child sexuality 43
China 122, 128-9, 136-7; literati 128-9, 137
'Chinese Encyclopaedia' 44-5
clanspeople 154-5
class 62, 77-8, 124; responses 78
Class Structure of Advanced Societies 39
classical sociology 87-162; from praxis to historical materialism 107-121; Hegel and the concept of Geist 89-106;

lessons from 158-61; society and ritual 140-62; status groups and the Protestant ethic 122-39
codes 9, 45-6, 79-80; code possession 9; purposive-rational 80
Cold War 235-6
collective interests 123-5
collective representations 143-4, 147, 150-58
collective understanding 23
commodity fetishism 117-18, 120
communication 8
Comte, Auguste 3, 89, 169; Comtean positivism 140
concept of Geist 89-106, 158
conceptual definition of structure 7
conditioning of animals 59
conduct 57, 196, 208
confluent love 11
Confucianism 128-9
consciousness 35, 58, 90-95, 101, 155; appeals to language 101; collective 153, see also practical consciousness
Contemporary Critique of Historical Materialism 39
contemporary ontological dualism 40
contemporary social theory 1-86; reality of realism 68-86; relevance of Parsons 20-38; structure and agency 3-19; structure, habitus, discourse 39-67
continuity of meaning 195
conventions 55
corporate responsibility 187
corruption 144
critical hermeneutics 212-19
critique of Geist 94-7
critique and hermeneutics 209-226; critical hermeneutics 212-19; Habermas' critique of Gadamer 209-212; hermeneutics and tradition 219-26
Critique of Pure Reason 92
cross-border migration 19
crowds 141
cult of the individual 17
culture 27-8, 55, 57, 60, 184
currents 141, 144, 158

Dasein 172-8
de Beauvoir, Simone 90
De Tocqueville, Alexis 15-16
de-coding 35
death 174
deity 95

denial of incidences 196
depth hermeneutics 211-12
derogation 7
Descartes, René 175-8
determinism 49-52
deus ex machina 144
devaluation of humanity 180
deviance 29-30
dialectic transformation 9
Dilthey, Wilhelm 123, 169-72, 175; concept of life 123, 169, 171; parallel with Hegel 170
Discipline and Punish 46-7, 63-6
discourse, structure, habitus 39-67
discretion 204-5
discursive consciousness 32
disdain 227, 238
Distinction 41
distortion 210
division of labour 148-50
Division of Labour 90, 148
doing otherwise 206-8
dualism 18-19, 140; Durkheimian 140-44; ontological 25-31
durable disposition 42
Durkheim, Émile 3-5, 16-17, 22-5, 140-62, 198-9; classic texts of 85; death of 140; dualism 139-44, 157; social ontology 144-7
dynamic power of human intercourse 5

Easter Island 189-90
economic bargaining 187
Economic and Philosophical Manuscripts 110
economic transactions 186
Economy and Society 122-4, 138
ecstasy 154
ecstatical unity 174
education 141
effective historical consciousness 221
effervescence 154-6
ego 28
egoistic suicide 150
Eighteenth Brumaire 110-111, 120, 233
Elementary Forms 151-3, 156-7, 198-9
11 September 205-6, 236
Elias, Norbert 14-15
elite groups 212
Enclosure movement 111
Enlightenment 168
equipment 175
esteem 24

ethnography of America 196
Europe 13-19, 43, 46, 129, 234-5;
    modernity 43, 46, 129, 132, 157
evolutionary theory 22
existence as existentiell 172
existential hermeneutics 160
exploitation 75, 118
extra-communicative reality 211

false consensus 211, 217
false gods 67
feminism 90
Feuerbach, Ludwig 107-9, 113-14; critique
    of religion 107; Marx's Theses on 110
field 41
food shortages 188
force majeur 144-6
fore-havings 176
fore-understanding 219-23
forms of life 55, 57
Foucault, Michel 7, 39-67, 72, 135, 204;
    death of 42; and Nietzsche and Weber
    85; power 62-6
Frankfurt School 90, 135
free labour 112-13
free sexuality 49
freedom 17, 38, 46, 207-8
freedom to do otherwise 206-8
French Revolution 15, 105
Freud, Sigmund 28-9, 32
Freudianism 28-9, 36
from praxis to historical materialism 107-
    121; historical materialism 113-19;
    praxis 107-113; the two Marxs 119-21
Fuggers 130, 132
functional differentiation 9
functionalism 20
fuzziness 62

Gadamer, Hans-Georg 160, 165-91, 194-
    7, 209-212; contemporary
    hermeneutics 181, 183, 194; notion
    that language is ostentive 181
Garfinkel, Harold 33, 59, 160
Geist 89-106, 233; Absolute 94; critique of
    94-7; definition 91; as deity 95;
    difficulties with translation 104; re-
    thinking 97-106
genealogy 47-8
genius 194-7
German Historical School 169
German Ideology 114-15, 167
gibberish 34

Giddens, Anthony 7, 10-13, 20, 25-7, 30-
    67; and individualism 207; and Parsons
    85; practical consciousness 58-9;
    structuration theory 31-8, 192
'Giddens lite' 10
God 95, 130-31, 149, 155; Word of 181-2
Godwin, William 22
Goffman, Erving 33, 59, 160, 196-201
governmentality 52
Gramsci, Antonio 12, 90
grey on grey 138
group membership 124
guilt 29; Freudian 29

Habermas, Jürgen 6-7, 20-21, 72-6, 192;
    and classical sociology 85; critique of
    Gadamer 165-7, 209-212; realism 72-6
habits 59
habitus, discourse, structure 39-67
Hall, Stuart 12
Hamlet 227-33; disdain 227, 238; and
    sociology 230-33
happiness 24
Hegel and the concept of Geist 89-106;
    concept of Geist 90-94, 158; critique of
    Geist 94-7; origins of social ontology
    89-90; parallel with Dilthey 170; re-
    thinking the Geist 97-106
Hegel, Georg 72, 89-106, 159; concept of
    Geist 89-106, 158
hegemony 38, 158
Heidegger, Martin 72-3, 160, 171-7, 180;
    existential hermeneutics 160; relevance
    of 181-2
heredity 194
hermeneutics 70, 160-61, 163-238; beyond
    structure and agency 227-38; critical
    212-19; and critique 209-226; and
    human agency 198-206; and idealism
    165-91; and individualism 192-208;
    origins of 168-86; and tradition 219-26;
    as universal method of comprehension
    168; and war 190, see also Heidegger,
    Martin
historical materialism 113-19
History of Sexuality 43, 47, 65
Hobbes, Thomas 21
Holocaust 201-3
Homans, George 192-4, 232-3; critic of
    Parsons 192; illusion 193-4
horizons 220-21, 225
human agency 20, 38, 50, 198-206
human rights 223-4

humanity 4-5
Humboldt, Karl 182
hunger migrants 188
Husserl, Edmund 72-4, 171
hyperreality 12
hypostasis 151, 182

id 28
Idea of a Social Science 58
idealisation 167
idealism 24-6, 167, 177, 182, 187
idealism and hermeneutics 165-91;
    Habermas' critique of Gadamer 165-7,
    209-212; origins of hermeneutics 168-
    86; two examples of social ontology
    186-91
ideology 13
idle talk 172
illusion 46, 56, 193-4
imitation 143
inauthentic existence 172, 174
incarnation 181
individual agency 200
individual interpretation 24
individualism 15-16, 108, 192, 207; free to
    do otherwise 206-8; and hermeneutics
    192-208; hermeneutics and human
    agency 198-206, see also Archer,
    Margaret
insurrection 65
interaction 148, 196
interactionism 197
interchange model 27
internalisation 28, 36
internationalization 20
interpenetration 9
interpretation 56
interpretive sociology 122-39, 160, 217
interpretivism 167
interpsychology 142, 144
intersubjective constitution 8
intersubjectivity 9
intransitive existence 69
Iranian revolution 205
irrationality 66
isolation 15, 195

Japan 186-7
Joas, H. 21, 23
Judaeo-Christian morality 47
Junkers 126-7, 234

Kabyle people 41, 61
Kant, Immanuel 23, 90-92, 169, 172;
    beauty in nature 194; definition of
    personal identity 207; philosophical
    tradition of 206; vision of language 182
knowledge 45-7, 72-3
Knowledge and Human Instincts 74
Knowledge and Human Interests 167, 223

labour power 117-18, 126-7
language-use 52, 101, 166-7, 173, 178-86;
    and consciousness 101
langue 34-5, 44
Lash, Scott 11
latency 27
Legitimation Crisis 83
lessons of classical sociology 158-61
Lévi-Strauss, Claude 40, 43, 61, 85
Leviathan 14, 21, 25, 30
Leviathan 21
life 4, 17, 123, 132, 233-8; forms of 55, 57,
    see also Dilthey, Wilhelm
lifestyle 123-6, 129
lifeworld 74-6, 82-3, 225
linguistic constitution of human existence
    179
linguistic manipulation 210
linguistic turn 160
linguistically articulated consciousness 185-
    6
literati 128-9, 137, see also China
Locke, John 21, 169, 206; definition of
    personal identity 207; philosophical
    tradition of 206
love of destiny 41
Luhmann, Niklas 8-13, 20
Luther, Martin 130

madness 43, 46; understanding of 46
Madness and Civilisation 46
mal-integrated persons 29
Malthus, Thomas 21-2, 188-9
Malthusian competition 188
Mammon 132
mana 204
mana taboos 189
manners 14-15
Mannheim, Karl 13
market exchange 186
Marshall, Alfred 22
Marx, Karl 4-5, 22, 72, 107-8, 115-21;
    classic texts of 85, 114; critique of
    Hegel 94-5, 97; and realism 158; the

two Marxs 119-21; Weber's opposition to 122
Marxism 217-18
mass immigration 235
master-slave dialectic 90, 98-103, 105, 158, 233
material reward 24
materialism 107-121
mathematics 54
meaning 56
Medicis 130, 132
mental categories 23
metaphysical entities 69-70
Milgram, Stanley 201-4
Mill, John Stuart 169
mirage 84
misperception 193, 231
modernity 10, 43, 46, 135
Modernity and Self-Identity 11
Moral Education 146
moral obligation 23, 146
morphogenetic social theory 5
mortality 174
motivation 28-9
Mouzelis, Nicos 6
Mozart, Wolfgang 195
mutual reactions 148
My Lai 203-4

nachbilden 171
nacherleben 171
nausea 41
Nazism 172
need 20
neo-functionalism 20
New Rules of Sociological Method 165
Nietzsche, Friedrich 45-8, 72, 85, 178
nihilism 73
nine elements of obedience 203
noble savages 144
noblesse de robe 63, 129
nominalism-realism 25
normality 43
nothingness 173
nullity 173

objectivism 40, 171
obligation 152
ontological dualism 6-8, 25-31, 37-40, 65-6, 109; contemporary 40; and Weber 129-30
ontological hiatus 5
ontological security 36-7

oppressiveness 40
order 22, 24, 31
Order of Thing 44
organism 50
origins of hermeneutics 168-86
origins of social ontology 89-90

Outline 59, 62
paedophilia 43
panopticon 46, 48
Pareto, Vilfredo 22
Paris uprising 218
parochial solitude 79
parole 35
Parsons, Talcott 9, 20-38, 83, 140, 160; middle and later period 230; ontological dualism 25-31; social ontology 21-5; utilitarian dilemma 194, 207
pattern variables 27
pattern-maintenance 27-8
pessimism 135, 137
Phenomenology of Mind 91, 94, 97, 102-5, 234-5; difficulties with translation 104; structure 100-101
Philosophical Discourse of Modernity 72-4, 82
Philosophical Investigations 52-3
philosophy 90-92
Philosophy of History 102
plastic sexuality 10-11
poetry 179
poison oracle 213-17
Popper, Karl 13, 118
possession/non-possession of codes 9
post-Fordist society 11-12, 83
post-modern realism 6
Poverty of Philosophy 114
power 46, 62-6, 127, 204; and agency 204; practical consciousness and practice 66-7
practical consciousness 58-9, 66-7; practice and power 66-7
practical philosophy 167
'practical theory' 59-62
practice 66-7; practical consciousness and power 66-7
praxis 107-121; theory of 113
prejudice 219, 223
present-at-hand 175
Protestant ethic 122-39; critique of 132-8
Protestant Ethic and the Spirit of Capitalism 122, 130, 133-8

Protestant sects in America 134
Protestantism 111, 130, 150
Prussia 97, 126-7
psychoanalysis 32, 210-212
psychological idealism 177
psychological well-being 37
psychopathic acts 46
punishment 24
purposive-rational acts 75, 80; codes 80

radical perspectivism 45
randomness 30-31, 45, 50
rational choice 192
re-thinking Geist 97-106
realism 68-86, 177; after social theory 84-
    5; of Bhaskar 68-72, 210; of Habermas
    72-6; social ontology of 76-84
reality of realism 68-86; after social theory
    84-5; Bhaskar's realism 68-72;
    Habermas' realism 72-6; social
    ontology of realism 76-84
rebellion 29-30
Reformation 111-12, 132, 135
relevance of Parsons 20-38; Giddens'
    structuration theory 31-8; Parsons'
    ontological dualism 25-31; Parsons'
    social ontology 21-5
religion 107, 138-40, 151-3; aboriginal
    153; Feuerbach's critique of 107; origin
    of 151; sociology of 138-9
Religion of China 122, 129
repression 28
resonance 9
revenge 65, 227
revolution of the subject 12
Ricouer, Paul 167
rise of the state 13-18
ritual and society 140-62
role-fulfilment 32, 35
role-individualism 77
Rousseau, Jean Jacques 144-5
rule-determinism 50-52
rule-following 51-2, 54-5, 57-8, 136, 160;
    co-ordinated 55; rules of 76
rule-individualism 49-58, 62
rules 39-40, 50, 54, 61
Rules of Sociological Method 141-4
Russell, Bertrand 52

sacredness 3-4, 24
sanctions 24
Sartre, Jean-Paul 40, 85, 179
Saussure, Horace 34-5, 43, 178

Schleiermacher, Friedrich 168-9;
    development of hermeneutics 168
Second Sex 90
self as a social product 201
self-awareness 3
self-consciousness 93-6, 98-9, 103, 173-6
self-entrapment 74
self-equilibrating mechanism 27
self-esteem 24
self-fulfilment 24
self-identity 10
self-immolation 143-4, 150-51
self-interest 193
sense of the game 60
sense of humour 3
service of impersonal social usefulness 131
sexual molestation 49
sexuality 10-11, 43-4, 49; child 43; in
    classical societies 43; plastic 10-11
ship of fools 46
sib 128-9
sich hineinversetzen 171
sick role 29-30
significance of individual 11
slots 69, 76
social action 4
social currents 141, 144, 158
social interaction 24
social mobilisation 119
social ontology 21-5, 144-7, 186-91;
    origins of 89-90; of realism 76-84; two
    examples in hermeneutics 186-91
social order 22, 24, 31, 40
social reality 3-4, 12-13, 39
social relations 3, 58
social rules 35, see also rules
Social System 26-7
social theory 3-13; after 84-5;
    contemporary 1-86, 159, 165, 191
society and ritual 140-62; collective
    representations 150-58; Durkheimian
    dualism 140-44; Durkheim's social
    ontology 144-7; lessons of classical
    sociology 158-61; the substratum 147-
    50
sociology 89; definition and origins 89;
    development of 222-3; of life 233-8; of
    religion 138-9
sociology of agency 201
Sociology of Religion 122, 138
Socrates 45, 91
solidarity 156
soteriology 133

soul 198
spatiality 176
stability 30
status groups and the Protestant ethic 122-39; critique of the Protestant ethic 132-8; Protestant ethic 130-31; sociology of religion 138-9; status groups 122-30
status honour 123-9, 132-4
Stones, R. 6
stratification model 32
stratified ontology 70-71
stretching 7, 31-2
structural-functionalism 9, 36-7
structuration theory 7-8, 31-8, 49-50
structure 39-40, 192
structure and agency 3-19, 227-38; beyond dualism 18-19; rise of the state 13-18; social theory 3-13
structure, habitus, discourse 39-67; Bourdieu's 'practical theory' 59-62; discourse 42-9; Foucault's power 62-6; Giddens' practical consciousness 58-9; the habitus 40-42; practical consciousness, practice, power 66-7; rule-individualism 49-58; structure 39-40
Structure of Social Action 20-22, 25-6, 33, 37
structuring structure 41
Stuart Restoration 112
subculture 29-30
subject-object dualism 40, 93-4, 96-7
subjectivism 24, 32, 40
subjectivity 194
subordination 64
substratum 141, 147-51, 157; mutual reactions 148
subversiveness 63
Suicide 143-5, 147-8, 150-52, 233
suicide act 142-3, 147, 150-51; types of 150
suicidogenetic currents 143, 150-52
super-ordination 64
superego 28
susceptibility to authority 202-3; nine elements of 203
symbols 44, 151, 157, 195
systemic reproduction 39

taboos 189
tacit knowledge 33
Tarde, Gabriel 142-5, 148
Taylor, Charles 186

television 12
tension management 27
Theory of Communicative Action 73-5, 82
theory of imitation 143
theory of voluntary action 22, 24-5, 29, 140
Theses on Feuerbach 110, 114-20, 130, 158, 233
Third Way 39
Thompson, John 8
time-space presence 34
totem 154-5, 159, 198; President Bush as 205-6
touched by divinity 46
towards a hermeneutic sociology 163-238; beyond structure and agency 227-38; hermeneutics and critique 209-226; hermeneutics and idealism 165-91; hermeneutics and individualism 192-208
Tractatus 52
trades unions 119, 125
tradition 219-26
transcendence 177
transformational model of society 5, 71-2, 81
Truth and Method 181, 184-5, 194, 220
two Marxs 119-21
tyranny 16, 49, 52, 102, 209

understanding of madness 46
unequal consensus 218
Urry, John 11
utilitarian dilemma 22, 24, 194
utilitarianism 21, 23-5, 149, 169
utopia 13

values 26-8
Van Gogh, Vincent 180, 195
verbalisation 210
verstehende sociology 75
vindication of status quo 209
violence 15
virtuosity 60-61, 195-7
volition 95, 143-4
voluntarism 24
voluntary action 22, 24-5, 29, 140

Wacquant, Loic 51
war 187-90
war criminals 204
Warring Kingdoms 128

Weber, Max 4-5, 22-5, 43, 85, 122-39;
    classic texts of 85; death of 140;
    interpretive sociology 122-39, 192, 217;
    opposition to Marxism 122, 138
well-being 37
Weltanschauung 122
Winch, Peter 187-9, 213
Wittgenstein, Ludwig 52-6, 58, 62, 183;
    notion that language is ostentive 181;
    relevance of 76, 160
Word of God 181-2
word-usage 53
work 175
worldhood of the world 176
Zande witchcraft 213-17